Sharing Good News

SHARING GOOD NEWS

Handbook on Evangelism in Europe

Edited by Gerrit Noort, Kyriaki Avtzi
and Stefan Paas

World Council of Churches Publications

SHARING GOOD NEWS
Handbook on Evangelism in Europe
Edited by Gerrit Noort, Kyriaki Avtzi, and and Stefan Paas

WCC Publications is the book publishing programme of the World Council of Churches. Founded in 1948, the WCC promotes Christian unity in faith, witness and service for a just and peaceful world. A global fellowship, the WCC brings together 345 Protestant, Orthodox, Anglican and other churches representing more than 550 million Christians in 110 countries and works cooperatively with the Roman Catholic Church.

Opinions expressed in WCC Publications are those of the authors.

Scripture quotations are from the New Revised Standard Version Bible, © copyright 1989 by the Division of Christian Education of the National Council of the Churches of Christ in the USA. Used by permission.

Cover design: Adele Robey, Phoenix Graphics
Book design and typesetting: Michelle Cook / 4 Seasons Book Design
ISBN: 978-2-8254-1687-7

World Council of Churches
150 route de Ferney, P.O. Box 2100
1211 Geneva 2, Switzerland
http://publications.oikoumene.org

CONTENTS

Kwabena Asamoah-Gyadu

Rev. Prof. J. Kwabena Asamoah-Gyadu, PhD, is an ordained minister of the Methodist Church Ghana. He is currently the Baëta-Grau Professor of Contemporary African Christianity and Pentecostal/Charismatic theology at the Trinity Theological Seminary in Legon (Ghana). He has researched and written extensively on Christianity in Africa and Pentecostalism, including African immigrant churches in both Europe and North America.

Kyriaki Avtzi

Ms Kyriaki Avtzi has studied theology in Greece, the United Kingdom, the United States of America, and Switzerland. She holds a bachelor's degree in theology from the Theological Faculty of the Aristotle University of Thessaloniki, Greece, and a master's degree from the Graduate Theological Union in Berkeley, California, USA. She is currently completing her doctorate at the University of Geneva, in collaboration with the Institute of Postgraduate Studies on Orthodox Theology at the Orthodox Centre of the Ecumenical Patriarchate in Geneva. In 2009 she was appointed as the executive secretary for mission in Europe for the Conference of European Churches (Geneva). Since 2011 she has held the position of programme executive for evangelism at the World Council of Churches. In that capacity she facilitated the production of this handbook.

Debbie den Boer

Ms Debbie den Boer holds a bachelor's degree in theology and a master's degree in missional communities from the Theologische Universiteit Kampen (Netherlands). She is starting a PhD trajectory around the initiation of young people in the Christian faith and community. She writes in the fields of mission and youth work. She is a member of the Dutch Reformed Churches in the Netherlands. She made a significant contribution to the production of this book by assisting the editors and editing the footnotes of this book.

Francis Brienen

Ms Francis Brienen is Deputy General Secretary of the United Reformed Church in the United Kingdom, with special responsibility for mission. She is from the Netherlands and has lived and worked in the United Kingdom for 25 years. Prior to working for the United Reformed Church she was on the staff of the Council for World Mission, where she was responsible for education in mission, various youth in mission programmes, and the programme on the community of women and men in mission. She is the editor of various worship and prayer books and has published articles reflecting on contemporary missiological issues.

Darko Djogo

The Very Reverend Darko Djogo PhD is an archpriest in the Serbian Orthodox Church. Due to the war he had to move from Sarajevo to Pale. From 2002 to 2006 he attended what was then known as the St Basil of Ostrog Orthodox Theological Academy (today Theological Faculty). From 2006 to 2008 he pursued his master of theology degree at St Basil of Ostrog Orthodox Theological Faculty. In 2010 he defended his PhD thesis on the christological eschatology of Rudolf Bultmann and Jürgen Moltmann. In 2007 he joined the faculty of the St Basil of Ostrog Theological Faculty. He participated in many philosophical-theological and interreligious conferences. At this moment he also serves as manager of the programme of cooperation with Andrei Saguna Orthodox Theological Faculty (Sibiu, Romania).

Vladimir Fedorov

Rev. Prof. Dr Vladimir Fedorov is an archpriest of the Russian Orthodox Church (Moscow Patriarchate). In 1970 he graduated from the Leningrad State University (mathematical faculty) and in 1977 he graduated from the Leningrad Orthodox Theological Academy. He holds PhDs in theology and philosophy. He teaches at the Russian Christian Academy for Humanities in St Petersburg and is the director of the Orthodox Institute for Missiology and Ecumenism. During the last ten years he also has taught psychology of religion at the St Petersburg State University. He has published more than 130 articles in ten languages, including many on missiological and ecumenical issues.

Rebecca A. Giselbrecht

Dr Rebecca A. Giselbrecht received her PhD from Fuller Theological Seminary in mission history and theology. She is currently doing post-doctorate study in practical theology at the University of Zurich and was named director of the Center for the Academic Study of Christian Spirituality at the University of Zurich in 2015. Her habilitation focusses on practices of piety, character, and virtue development in the Protestant tradition. She edited and translated the volume *Sacrality and Materiality: Locating Intersections* (Vandenhoeck & Ruprecht, 2015).

Brother John of Taizé

Born in Philadelphia, Pennsylvania, USA, Brother John entered the Taizé Community in France in 1974. In Taizé, among other occupations, he helps the young and not-so-young visitors enter into the world of the Bible. He spends part of his time in the United States and Italy to lead meetings and prayers with young adults. He has written some ten books, translated into several languages, on biblical topics. The most recent is *Friends in Christ: Paths to a New Understanding of Church* (Orbis, 2012).

Knud Jørgensen

Knud Jørgensen received his MTh from the University of Copenhagen, and his PhD, in missiology, from Fuller Theological Seminary. A journalist and a theologian, he served with Radio Voice of the Gospel, Addis Ababa (Ethiopia), the Lutheran World Federation (Geneva), the International Mass Media Institute (Kristiansand, Norway), the Go out Centre (Hurdal, Norway), Norwegian Church Aid, the Mekane Yesus Seminary (Addis Ababa), and the mission foundation Areopagos. He was dean of Tao Fong Shan (Hong Kong) until 2010. He is an adjunct professor at the MF Norwegian School of Theology and at the Lutheran Theological Seminary in Hong Kong. He has published several books and articles on journalism, communication, leadership, and mission. He is one of the editors of the Regnum Edinburgh Centenary Series.

Dimitra Koukoura

Prof. Dr Dimitra Koukoura teaches homiletics at the School of Theology of Aristotle University of Thessaloniki (AUTh) in Greece. She was the first woman to be elected at the AUTh in the early 1990s. She studied classics and theology at AUTh. At the Sorbonne and the Catholic Institute of Paris she studied linguistics, social linguistics, and Byzantine history. She has published four books on homiletics and rhetorics, a book on the role of women in the Orthodox Church, and an introduction to the study of theology. She has also published various articles on re-evangelism and the transmission of the gospel in today's world. She has been involved in the ecumenical movement since the 1980s in various capacities, representing the Ecumenical Patriarchate (member of the Commission Churches in Dialogue of the Conference of European Churches; member of the Standing and Plenary Commission of Faith and Order of WCC). Now she is an acting member of the central committee of WCC, of the facilitators group of Global Christian Forum (GCF), and of the academic board of Elijah Interfaith Institute.

Wonsuk Ma

Rev. Dr Wonsuk Ma is a Korean Assemblies of God minister who presently serves as executive director of Oxford Centre for Mission Studies, Oxford, United Kingdom. Previously, he and his wife, Julie, served as missionaries in the Philippines for 27 years, where they were involved in theological education, evangelism, church planting, leadership training, research, and writing. His latest book (co-written with his wife) is *Mission in the Spirit: Towards Pentecostal/Charismatic Missiology* (Regnum Books International, 2010).

Gerrit Noort

Rev. Dr Gerrit Noort is an ordained minister of the Protestant Church in the Netherlands and serves as director of the Netherlands Mission Council. He received his doctorate at Utrecht University. From 1986 till 2010 he worked for the department of mission and world service of the Protestant Church in the Netherlands in different capacities. From 1991 to 1995 he lived in Indonesia, where he was a lecturer at the theological academy of the Church of Central Sulawesi. Gerrit Noort is involved in training for mission and evangelism and is a lecturer of missiology at Theologische Universiteit Kampen (Netherlands). He regularly publishes on mission and missiology.

Dawit Olika Terfassa

Mr Dawit Olika Terfassa has a BTh from Mekane Yesus Theological Seminary (Ethiopia) and a master of philosophy in theology from Norwegian School of Theology (MF). He is a member of the Ethiopian Christian diaspora community and is involved in its teaching and preaching. He is currently a doctoral student at the Norwegian School of Theology in Oslo, working on a project that analyzes the growth of his home church, the Ethiopian Evangelical Church Mekane Yesus (EECMY). He has been administrator and evangelist of a congregation, instructor, dean of study, coordinator for theological education by extension (TEE), and principal at Nekemte Christian Education College (NCEC) within the EECMY in Ethiopia. He has published a number of articles on reverse mission and on migration and theological education.

Donna Orsuto

Prof. Dr Donna Orsuto is a professor of spirituality at the Pontifical Gregorian University in Rome. Originally from the United States, she also lectures and leads retreats worldwide. She has written two books and numerous articles in the area of spirituality. Active in ecumenical and interreligious dialogue, Dr Orsuto serves as a member of the Commission for Ecumenism and Dialogue of the Diocese of Rome. She is also the director of the Lay Centre at Foyer Unitas in Rome (www.laycentre.org).

Stefan Paas

Prof. Dr Stefan Paas is professor of missiology and intercultural theology at Vrije Universiteit Amsterdam, and professor of missiology at Theologische Universiteit Kampen (the Netherlands). Previously, he has worked as a teacher, a mission consultant, evangelist, and church planter. He writes extensively in the fields of mission, evangelism, apologetics, biblical studies, and political theology. Dr Paas is married with three children, and he is a member of the Christian Reformed Church in the Netherlands.

Martin Reppenhagen

Dean Dr Martin Reppenhagen studied theology in Wuppertal, Tübingen, Pune/India, and Heidelberg. He received his doctorate in theology on a study about missional church in the United States of America. His research interests are missional church, evangelism, and missiology. In 1994–95 he was a guest lecturer at Union Biblical Seminary Pune/India. From 1996 to 2004 he ministered as a parish and youth district pastor. In the years 2004 to 2014 he was a research fellow and an associated director of the Research Institute for Evangelism and Church Development of Greifswald University (Germany). Since 2014 he has been dean in the Protestant Church of Baden (Germany). Dr Reppenhagen is married with three children.

FOREWORD

"The church is called to renew its methods of evangelism to communicate the good news with persuasion, inspiration, and conviction." So states *Together towards Life: Mission and Evangelism in Changing Landscapes,*[1] the new ecumenical mission affirmation of the World Council of Churches (WCC) (§109).

Evangelism and Christian education are interrelated in vision and vocation for the renewal of mission and evangelism. A holistic approach to the latter entails both theological education and training in evangelism, both in theory and praxis. At the same time, the radically changing denominational and religious landscape in Europe—and globally—presents the churches with the challenging opportunity to renew the expressions of their witness, in search of new ways of making the message of the gospel relevant within secular, multicultural, and multireligious contexts.

In response to the changed concepts of mission work in relation to evangelism, the WCC's Commission on World Mission and Evangelism (CWME), through the evangelism project, launched a process of regional consultations addressing the place of evangelism in theological education and missiological formation in all continents. The process for the region of Europe included two consultations followed by two drafting meetings, all aimed toward the completion and eventual publication of the present book by WCC Publications. A great number of esteemed academics and mission practitioners from across Europe and, in some cases, from the global constituency contributed throughout the process to the successful development of this book.

---

1. Jooseop Keum, ed., *Together towards Life: Mission and Evangelism in Changing Landscapes* (Geneva: WCC Publications, 2013).

It is therefore with great joy that CWME and WCC welcome this much-anticipated theological study on evangelism in Europe. Our hope and aspiration are that through the illustrated contextualized, fresh approaches to evangelism, this book will prove to be an important tool for theological faculties of academic institutions across Europe, as well as for churches and mission agencies offering programmes on missiological formation.

I would like to thank sincerely the members of the editorial group, who have accompanied the entire endeavour with tireless commitment and great work: Ms Francis Brienen, Prof. Dr Donna Orsuto, Rev. Dr Wonsuk Ma, Rev. Dr Martin Reppenhagen, Mr Dawit Olika Terfassa, and the three editors, Rev. Dr Gerrit Noort, Prof. Dr Stefan Paas, and Ms Kyriaki Avtzi. An additional word of thanks is due to Ms Debbie den Boer for her editorial support in the final stages of the process.

Let me also express my gratitude to CWME and in particular to its director, Rev. Dr Jooseop Keum, as well as to the Associate General Secretary for Mission and Unity of the WCC, Rev. Dr Hielke Wolters, for their ongoing support and encouragement of the work for evangelism.

Metropolitan Dr Geevarghese Mor Coorilos
Moderator, Commission on World Mission and Evangelism
World Council of Churches

Gerrit Noort and Stefan Paas

Evangelism in Human Life

If "evangelism" means the sharing of good news, human life is evangelistic to the core. As soon as human beings feel that they have discovered something new, interesting, and good to have, or when they feel responsible for the misery of others, they start sharing. Our cultures are rife with this type of benevolent bonding. People write blogs, tweets, and articles; they welcome strangers and refugees; they go into politics to put things right; they travel to other countries to build schools and drill wells. We love to share information and wisdom; we love to communicate "good news." Large companies trust this fundamental instinct when they unembarrassedly talk about "evangelism marketing" and the power of "testimonials." This is what it means to be social beings. It is what it means to be capable of enthusism, pity, and responsibility.

The writers of the New Testament knew the expression "to evangelize" before they became Christians. They knew it from their Greek translation of the First Testament, for example in Isaiah 52:7, where it reads: "How beautiful upon the mountains are the feet of the messenger who announces peace, who brings good news." They also knew it from its use in secular realms, for example in announcements of royal births or great victories. Was there a better word to denote the most wonderful news that they had heard of, the news that God had done something unique and world changing in Jesus' life, death, and resurrection? So they wrote about the *euangelion*, the "gospel" of Jesus Christ, and they "evangelized" throughout the cities of the Roman Empire.

As simple and logical as this seems, the concept of "evangelism" is not that straightforward and self-evident anymore, at least not for Christians in the West. Here Christianity's honeymoon is long past. The sharing of the good news has been compromised by a history of colonialism outside Europe, and a history of Christendom within Europe. In our cultural imagination, the gospel of Jesus Christ has become almost inextricably linked with memories of cultural superiority, authoritarianism, and obscurantism. Many Christians have become shy; they may still have enough faith for themselves, but they feel embarrassed about any attempt to persuade others. There is too much historical baggage, too much insecurity about the claims of faith in a rational age.

In some ways this credibility crisis of Christianity is connected to a wider lack of trust among Western cultures. The West is not so certain of itself anymore. It has lost its guiding narratives, and what is left are fragments at best. Populists and nationalists, shouting empty promises, pop up everywhere. New nations rise to power; new narratives fuel the imaginations of the world's masses. Increasingly, Christians find themselves marginalized in societies that feel decentred themselves. Western nations have become extremely pluralistic and deeply insecure. We all know that the world that used to be will not return, but we do not know how our future will be. The only thing we know is that we possess most of the world's wealth, and we are scared to lose it. Fear, rather than confidence, begins to penetrate the secularized nations of the West.

And yet, this may be the time in which Christians can rediscover what it means to bring good news as people who are "foolish and weak." This may be the time to learn all over again what "witnessing" means: not to talk from a position of power, but from a position of a weakness that is joyfully embraced. After all, even if we accept that many mistakes have been made and that many more will be made, there is an inescapable evangelistic logic within Christianity. It can be summarized as follows:

- if we are emotionally affected—even if tempered by doubts—by Jesus, his story, and his kingdom, it makes no sense to look down out of principle on people who recommend this experience to others and want to share their enthusiasm with them;

- if we are rationally convinced—even if only hesitantly—that unique truth and wisdom can be found in Jesus and his story, it makes no sense to reject out of principle attempts to persuade others of this;

- if we are volitionally committed—even if with some reserve—to practical consequences that can be drawn out of Jesus and his story, it makes no sense to criticize out of principle those who think that human lives would be enriched by following Jesus.

Even if this may sound far too minimalistic for many Christians, it is the very least we can say about the importance of evangelism. It is not only rooted in our basic social instincts; it is also part of the fundamental structure of Christianity itself. We cannot *not* evangelize; therefore, we'd better learn to do it well.

Recent Developments

Historically, evangelistic mission was something that European missionaries did outside of Europe. The European continent itself was considered fully evangelized. Even today this seems the case—that is, if we may believe the *Atlas of Global Christianity*, published in 2009 and inspired by the centenary of Edinburgh 1910. Measuring evangelism "by assessing whether individuals have had an adequate opportunity to hear the gospel and to respond to it, whether they respond positively or negatively," Europe's evangelized population in 1910 was 97.5 percent. In Finland, Slovenia, Malta, and Spain even 100 percent of the population had been evangelized. In 2010 the percentage of the evangelized in Europe was still quite high, at 96.2 percent. Romania, with 99.7 percent, is now the most evangelized country in the world. Thus, even though the percentage of the Christian population in Europe is declining, the percentage of the so-called evangelized seems quite stable. The *Atlas* then goes on to divide the world into "unevangelized, Non-Christian" (world A; fewer than 50 percent evangelized), "evangelized, Non-Christian" (world B; at least 50 percent evangelized, but fewer than 60 percent Christian), and "Christian" (world C; more than 60 percent Christian) countries. While world A and B countries are mainly in northern Africa and Asia, the whole of the American continent, most of the sub-Saharan countries, and Europe (with minor exceptions) belong to world C. Thus, Europe, according to these recent statistics, still remains predominantly Christian and almost completely evangelized.[1]

Although one may question the theological value or explanatory power of such statistics,[2] they help to understand why many European theologians and pastors have not prioritized evangelism in Europe. They consider preaching, pastoral care, and diaconal ministry more urgent than proclaiming the good news to non-Christians. During most of European history evangelism was left to marginal Christian groups of a pietistic or revivalist nature. There were exceptions here and there, but, altogether, David J. Bosch's comment about European theology seems justified: "[A]s Europe became Christianised and Christianity became the established religion in the Roman Empire and beyond, theology lost its missionary dimension."[3]

Only recently has this begun to change. Several developments have contributed to the renewed attention for evangelism in European churches and among European theologians. One important influence has been, of course, the challenge of secularization. As of the beginning of the 20th century the reality of de-Christianization dawned upon the theological imagination. Rather than seeing evangelism as the revitalization of lapsed Christians, church leaders became increasingly aware that Europe was transforming into a genuine mission field. Some even started speaking of a new paganism in Europe. One of those was Lesslie Newbigin, focussing on England: "If God is driven out, the gods come trooping in. England is a pagan society and the development of a truly missionary encounter with this very tough form of paganism is the greatest intellectual and practical task facing the Church."[4] Currently, all over Europe churches are rediscovering their missionary heritage, and exciting new initiatives are being deployed.

Globalization has also contributed to this new awareness. After the colonial period, Christians from other parts of the world have increasingly found

---

1. Todd M. Johnson and Kenneth R. Ross, eds., *Atlas of Global Christianity* (Edinburgh: Edinburgh University Press, 2009), 308–313.
2. Siga Arles, "World Religion Database: Realities and Concerns," *International Bulletin of Missionary Research* 34, no. 1 (2010): 20: "disease of *numberitis*."
3. David J. Bosch, *Transforming Mission: Paradigm Shifts in Theology of Mission* (Maryknoll, NY: Orbis, 1991), 489.
4. Lesslie Newbigin, *Unfinished Agenda: An Updated Autobiography*, 2d ed. (Edinburgh: St. Andrews Press, 1993), 236. Prominently within the WCC: W. A. Visser 't Hooft, "Evangelism among Europe's Neo-Pagans," *International Review of Mission* 66, no. 264 (October 1977): 349–60.

new homes in European nations. This has not only led to the revitalization of a Christian presence in many European cities, it has also brought new and rather unfamiliar forms of Christianity to the European imagination. The jury is still out on deciding to what extent African and Asian Christians will be able to re-evangelize Europe, but it is clear that Christians from the South and the East are quite unembarrassed about the importance of evangelism. Malawian theologian Harvey C. Kwiyani speaks in this context about the "evangelisthood of all believers,"[5] and this seems to express the lived theology of immigrant Christian communities quite well. Both an increasing intercultural theological awareness and the presence of new vital Christian communities have reframed the theological discussion about mission and evangelism.

Finally, there have been substantial developments within the ecumenical movement as well. While older oppositions between ecumenicals who were into social action and Evangelicals who were into evangelism may have been exaggerated, there is an extent to which the ecumenical movement shared the embarrassment about evangelism that was so typical of Western churches. This is no longer the case. Report after report has been issued, all highlighting the importance and urgency of evangelism as the very heart of Christian mission. The fact that the Orthodox and many Pentecostals have joined the ecumenical movement has certainly played a role in this reinvigoration of evangelism, alongside the developments sketched above. These ecumenical reports have been flanked by similar developments in the Roman Catholic Church, where a number of popes have emphasized the necessity of a "re-evangelization" of Europe, culminating in Pope Francis's inspiring apostolic exhortation *Evangelii Gaudium* ("The Joy of the Gospel," 2013). In short, evangelism is back at centre stage.

This Handbook

This book testifies to the renewed interest in evangelism within the ecumenical movement. Its origin lies in an initiative taken by the Commission on World Mission and Evangelism (CWME) of the World Council of Churches (WCC). In 2012 it launched a series of regional consultations on the place of evangelism in theological education and missiological formation. The principal objective

---

5. Harvey C. Kwiyani, *Sent Forth: African Missionary Work in the West* (Maryknoll, NY: Orbis, 2014), 58–60.

of this process was to evaluate and enhance training programmes for evangelism by fostering ecumenical cooperation among faculties and networks. The first consultation, in the European region, was held in Bossey (Switzerland), 28–31 October 2012. The consultation brought together about 30 participants from 16 countries across Europe, representing churches, ecumenical and educational institutions, as well as mission bodies.

Amongst the main issues addressed during the consultation was the importance of relating Christian witness to the changing landscape of Europe by developing contextual evangelistic approaches. Focussing on the significance of having practical involvement in the ministry of evangelism at the heart of theological education, participants acknowledged that churches "are in need of a missiological agenda for theology rather than just a theological agenda for mission." The participants of the consultation affirmed that a freshly reimagined, renewed understanding and a new commitment to evangelism are needed. As the consultation observed a lack of resources for teaching evangelism, it recommended to the WCC the "development of an ecumenical handbook for teaching evangelism in Europe, which addresses the challenges and best practices."[6] The present study is a direct result of this recommendation.

The book is meant as a textbook to be used in formal and informal theological education. It can also be used by practitioners as a quick introduction into many issues, as it contains an almost exhaustive overview of everything that is important in the field of evangelism. The book is divided into four parts. The first part, after an introductory chapter on the meaning and use of evangelism, describes the history of evangelism in Europe and the challenges that currently face those who want to evangelize this continent. Part 2 presents different theological approaches to the subject, seen from Roman Catholic, Orthodox, Protestant, Pentecostal, and immigrant perspectives. The third part provides a number of case studies from all over Europe. This part alone makes it worthwhile to read this book and reflect on it. This part also contains a number of theological reflections on the case studies, pertaining to conversion, methodology, ecclesiology, and spirituality. The fourth part concludes the book with a chapter on education and on a common understanding of evangelism.

Composing this handbook has been an ecumenical project in itself. Its contributors, both women and men, represent a wide number of WCC

---

6. Kyriaki Avtzi, Anne Marie Kool, Mikhail Goundiaev, and Gerrit Noort, "Report WCC-Consultation on Evangelism in Theological Education and Missional Formation in Europe, 28–31 October 2012, Bossey, Switzerland" (Geneva: WCC, 2013), 11 (unpublished report).

member churches, as well as CWME-affiliated bodies. All the major confessional traditions of Christianity are represented, insofar as they play a role in Europe. This includes writers from migrant churches and Pentecostal authors. The editors have also tried to achieve a balanced representation of the immense variety of the European continent, even if this is virtually impossible. Therefore, the book contains contributions from the far West (United Kingdom) to the far East (Russia), and from the far South (Italy) to the far North (Sweden). It describes and reflects on ancient monastic forms of evangelism and on modern, Internet-based forms. Thus, the book offers its readers the most complete overview of current evangelism in Europe that is possible. We are quite confident that there is no study available on this subject at this moment that is more exhaustive and more ecumenical. But of course, this is for its users to decide.

PART ONE

Evangelism and Its Context in Europe

CHAPTER 1

Martin Reppenhagen

Evangelism: Scope, Limits, and Definitions

1.1 Rethinking Evangelism

Evangelism is deeply rooted in the gospel. Deriving from the Greek verb *euangelizein*, which is frequently used in the New Testament to describe the preaching of the gospel, evangelism means simply telling or offering the good news of the gospel. In that sense evangelism is an undertaking with a good content that brings joy to those hearing the message. In most of the Bible translations, however, *euangelizein* is not translated as "to evangelize," but as "to preach (the gospel)." Traditionally, this was then equated with pulpit preaching, making *euangelizein* an inner-church activity while relating "evangelism" to specific (often somewhat less important) events for those outside the church. This traditional view, however, has begun to change in recent Christian discourse. Today, many leading theologians say that a church without evangelism is a contradiction in itself. Evangelism may be called the "church's beating heart." And deficiencies in evangelism would definitely lead "to serious heart failure."[1]

1. Eberhard Jüngel, "Referat zur Einführung in das Schwerpunktthema; Synode der EKD 1999 in Leipzig," in Kirchenamt der Evanglische Kirche Deutschland, ed., *Reden von Gott in der Welt. Der missionarische Auftrag der Kirche an der Schwelle zum 3. Jahrtausend* (Hannover: EKD, 2001), 15.

As crucial as the word *evangelize* seems to be in the ministry of Jesus and the apostles, however, its definition remains contested. There are those who have a broad understanding of evangelism, including witness, proclamation, Christian presence in the world, and even social work. Others may focus on the verbal aspect of evangelism, while others equate evangelism with a specific type of doing evangelism. Some may insist that the time for evangelism in Europe is over and today's evangelism is just proselytizing Christians of other churches. Others just feel unprepared to share their faith or don't feel the need to do so in a postmodern and pluralistic society. Many outside the church and even a few inside the church may equate evangelism with intolerance and may opt for banning evangelism.

During the last decades a rethinking of evangelism in Europe has occurred, amounting to what may even be called a renaissance of evangelism in Europe. There is a new interest in evangelism in Europe, because "for those who experience Christ as the ground of their being" it seems self-evident "that they have to share this ground of their being with others," as Walter Hollenweger wrote in his influential book *Evangelism Today: Good News or Bone of Contention?* back in the 1970s. Thus, evangelism becomes a crucial part of the life of the church. Although theological reflection may not necessarily produce evangelists, there is a deep need for the Christian "to give an account of the process of sharing to himself, to his fellow Christians and to non-Christians."[2]

By these words we have already introduced the theme of evangelism. In the remainder of this chapter I first describe important biblical material pertaining to evangelism. The Bible is and should be the ground of our reflection on a subject as important as this. Second, I summarize some recent theological developments in the theology of evangelism.

1.2 Evangelism in the Bible

1.2.1 Methodological complexity

Traditionally, any theological reflection on evangelism would start with the biblical texts, after which it would proceed to a systematic theory of evangelism. The relation between scripture and today's evangelism, however, seems to be more complex than was often assumed. Even the scriptural basis seems to be rather complex and varied, making it difficult to speak of one single biblical

---

2. Walter J. Hollenweger, *Evangelism Today: Good News or Bone of Contention?* (Belfast: Christian Journals, 1976), 5.

4

foundation. The plural "foundations" seems to be more appropriate.[3] While reflecting on missiology, David J. Bosch speaks of "models of mission" or "paradigm shifts" instead of "biblical foundations." In his major work he focusses on the complexity and diversity of missionary concepts in the biblical texts and in Christian history.[4] There just isn't one single "developed theory of evangelism" of early Christianity that we can take as a foundation for our practice, William J. Abraham writes. Even "the picture of the early Christians marching out to evangelize the Roman Empire in order to fulfil the Great Commission is a myth."[5]

Pointing out these complexities is not a theological capitulation but, rather, a realization that seeking "biblical precedents or literal biblical mandates" for all modern evangelistic activities is an anachronistic approach. The Bible is not a book full of recipes for our modern practice. Thus, it may be more appropriate to speak of a biblical "grounding" and "orientation" of evangelism, while trying to take the multiple choir of voices in the Bible seriously.[6]

In my reflections on evangelism in the Bible, I start with a brief word study before going on to further considerations from the Bible. This discussion is definitely selective and limited in scope but nevertheless basic for today's understanding of evangelism.

1.2.2 Brief word study of euangelizo (ευαγγελιζω)

The word *euangelizo* (ευαγγελιζω—"to evangelize") is found 54 times in the New Testament, and its basic meaning may be rendered as "to proclaim/bring a good report."[7] Besides the nontechnical sense with varying objects, *euangelizo* has become a technical term for proclaiming the message of Christ, designating

---

3. Donald Senior and Carroll Stuhlmueller, *The Biblical Foundations of Mission* (Maryknoll, NY: Orbis, 1983).

4. David J. Bosch, *Transforming Mission: Paradigm Shifts in Theology of Mission* (Maryknoll, NY: Orbis, 1991), 15. Others, like Heinrich Balz, start with today's mission and end up with a biblical verification; cf. Balz, *Der Anfang des Glaubens: Theologie der Mission und der jungen Kirchen* (Neuendettelsau: Erlanger Verlag für Mission und Ökumene, 2010), 18ff.

5. William J. Abraham, "A Theology of Evangelism: The Heart of the Matter," in Paul W. Chilcote and Laceye C. Warner, eds., *The Study of Evangelism: Exploring a Missional Practice of the Church* (Grand Rapids: Eerdmans, 2008), 19.

6. Marc R. Spindler, "The Biblical Grounding and Orientation of Mission," in Frans Verstraelen et al., eds., *Missiology: An Ecumenical Introduction—Texts and Contexts of Global Christianity* (Grand Rapids: Eerdmans, 1995), 125. A still quite helpful study and modern classic is Michael Green, *Evangelism in the Early Church* (Grand Rapids: Eerdmans, 1970). Five biblical models of evangelism have been elaborated in Frances S. Adeney, *Graceful Evangelism: Christian Witness in a Complex World* (Grand Rapids: Baker Academic, 2010), 14–26.

7. Georg Strecker, "ευαγγελιζω," in Horst Balz and Gerhard Schneider, eds., *Exegetical Dictionary of the New Testament*, vol. 2 (Grand Rapids: Eerdmans, 1991), 69–70.

"the salvific meaning of the Christ-event." In this context the term is used for preaching that aims at repentance and faith. Christological in content, *euangelizo* focusses on conversion and baptism.[8] In some cases the term is used absolutely without object, usually translated as "to proclaim the gospel."[9]

For Paul, "ευαγγελιζο refers to the total task of the apostle in proclamation," without distinguishing between a missionary or inner-church situation. Examples of missionary proclamation are, for instance, Romans 15:20; 1 Corinthians 1:17; 9:16-23; and Galatians 4:13. Especially the aorist tense of the verb refers to the first proclamation of the gospel (1 Cor. 15:1-2; 2 Cor. 11:7). Although this missionary situation is the primary focus for *euangelizo*, Paul uses the term for his proclamation to Christians as well (Rom. 1:15; Gal. 1:16, 23). For both—Christians and non-Christians alike—the desired outcome of proclaiming the gospel is a response of faith.

In three passages (Acts 21:8; Eph. 4:11; 2 Tim. 4:5), the term *euangelistes* ("evangelist") is used as a reference to the ministry of a proclaimer serving "the church through the proclamation of the gospel. A clearly demarcated church office is not apparent." This "evangelist" was not just an inner-church ministry, however, as a closer look at Philip shows. As one of the deacons (Acts 6:5), he evangelized in Samaria, on the way with the Ethiopian minister, and at Azotus (Acts 8:5, 26-39, 40). While travelling he spread the gospel of Christ, people came to faith in Christ, and they were baptized. It is quite difficult to see an established office of distinct evangelists in the early church, although Ephesians 4:11 writes: "The gifts he gave were that some would be apostles, some prophets, some evangelists [*euangelistas*], some pastors and teachers." It is possible this should be read dimensionally, as a reference to a role which could be taken up by all representatives of the church and even by all Christians.

1.2.3 Old Testament background

With reference to the Old Testament, *euangelizo* "can be rendered *announce (eschatological) salvation*." The Hebrew word for "proclaim" (*BSR*) in essence involves the bringing of good news.[10] In Isaiah 61:1, *BSR* is even used in an absolute way, meaning "good news of deliverance." Thus, it is part of thanksgiving and praise.[11] Especially in Isaiah 52:7 (and Nah. 2:1) the messenger is

---

8. Acts 8:12; 8:35-36; 11:20-21; 14:15, 21.
9. Luke 9:6; Acts 14:7; 1 Cor. 1:17.
10. Stephen T. Hague, "bsr," in Willem A. VanGemeren, ed., *New International Dictionary of Old Testament Theology and Exegesis*, vol. 1 (Carlisle, UK: Paternoster, 1996), 775–77.
11. Ps. 40:10; Ps. 96:2; Is. 60:6.

"bearer of good news . . . , the good news of God's salvation . . . leading to a climax: peace, good, salvation—your God reigns. . . . It entails a condition where all things are in their proper relation to each other, with nothing left hanging, incomplete, or unfulfilled . . .; it entails a condition of freedom from every bondage, but particularly the bondage resultant from sin. . . ."[12]

The good news of salvation is then related to or results from God's kingship, not only over Israel but over the entire world. God reigns and therefore salvation is at hand. Hence, there seems to be a tension between God as being king in the here and now, and God as becoming king in the eschatological future. This future, however, is at hand right now. The "being-king" of Yahweh "is being proclaimed as 'becoming-king', because Yaweh's kingship of the world is not a condition but an event that is now in the process of commencing (cf. Is. 52:7-10)."[13] The anointed Servant/Messiah in the Servant Songs in the book of Isaiah proclaims the good news "to the oppressed, to bind up the brokenhearted, to proclaim liberty to the captives, and release to the prisoners; to proclaim the year of the Lord's favour, and the day of vengeance of our God; to comfort all who mourn" (Is. 61:1-2). "Here the Servant/Messiah himself is the one who brings the good news of God's triumph. Because he has done what no one else could do (Is. 53:4-5,10-12; 59:15b-21; 61:1-6), he is not only the preacher of the good news—he *is* the good news, able to give (61:3) what he announces." In that sense his word accomplishes that of which it speaks. Proclaiming deliverance is bringing deliverance in face of misery and hardship.

The addressees of this message of salvation are the poor: "Those who are broken by life that they have no more heart to try; those who are bound up in their various addictions that liberty and release are a cruel mirage; those who think that they will never again experience the favour of the Lord, or see his just vengeance meted out against those who have misused them; those who think that their lives hold nothing more than ashes, sackcloth, and the fainting heaviness of despair."[14] In Matthew 11:5 (Luke 4:18; 7:22), Jesus cites from Isaiah 61, characterizing his work with the work of the anointed, which is again closely linked to the proclamation of God's kingship (Luke 4:43).

---

12. John N. Oswalt, *The Book of Isaiah, Chapters 40–66*, The New International Commentary on the Old Testament (Grand Rapids: Eerdmans, 1998), 368.
13. Bernd Janowksi, cited in Philip J. Nel, "mlk," in Willem A. VanGemeren, ed., *New International Dictionary of Old Testament Theology and Exegesis*, vol. 2 (Carlisle, UK: Paternoster, 1996), 956–65.
14. Oswalt, *Book of Isaiah*, 564ff.

1.2.4 Other vocabulary

Quite close to *euangelizo* is *kerusso* (κηρυσσω), which actually means "to proclaim something in public." "κηρυσσω ανδ κηρυγμα [*kerygma*— 'proclamation'] are relevant in the beginnings of the Christian mission in connection with corresponding expressions (e.g., *euangelizo*)."[15] It seems that both terms more or less have the same meaning.[15] Thus, Luke speaks of Jesus' proclamation of the kingdom of God as "to proclaim [*euangelizesthai*] the kingdom of God" (Luke 4:43), while Matthew renders it as "to announce [*kerussein*] the gospel [*euangelion*] of the kingdom" (Matt. 4:23). In Matthew 4:17 it is said: "From that time Jesus began to proclaim: 'Repent, for the kingdom of heaven has come near.'" The content of Jesus' public proclamation is the kingdom of God and the call for repentance to God. This proclamation aims at an answer from those who listen to the message. The kingdom of God is present in Jesus' person and ministry (Mark 1:14-15), while still having a future dimension (Matt. 15:1-13; Mark 9:1; 14:25). It is there already, and it is yet to come.

In the book of Acts Christ is at the centre of *kerusso*. Here, the term clearly has a missionary connotation, characterizing the flow of the gospel beyond Jerusalem. Jesus, the proclaimer of the kingdom of God, has become the proclaimed Christ. "There is little doubt that this eschatological tone of Jesus' kingdom ministry had enormous impact on the early church, including its motivation for mission."[16] For Paul, *kerusso* marks the preaching of the gospel; it is "the explication of the faith that has been made possible through the proclamation."[17]

1.2.5 Conclusion

On the basis of this limited word study one may summarize that evangelism is the proclamation of the good news of salvation brought in the person and work of Jesus Christ. Evangelism is the gospel, the *euangelion* (euaggelion), at work.

1.3 Further Biblical-Theological Reflections on Evangelism

A fully developed theological vision for evangelism today cannot be derived merely from word study.[18] Further considerations and observations are needed.

---

15. Otto Merk, "κηρυσσω," in Balz and Schneider, *Exegetical Dictionary*, 2:288–92.
16. Senior and Stuhlmueller, *Biblical Foundations*, 156.
17. Rom. 10:8, 14ff; 1 Cor. 1:21; 1 Cor. 15:11, 14.
18. Abraham, "Theology of Evangelism," 20.

In this section I look into Jesus' ministry, some practices of evangelism in the early church, and the apostolic ministry of Paul.

1.3.1 Proclaiming the good news of the kingdom (Jesus' ministry)

According to the Synoptic Gospels, Jesus' proclamation can be summarized as follows: "proclaiming the good news of the kingdom of God" (Matt. 4:23; cf. Luke 4:43). And since "the kingdom of God has come near," this announcement is followed by an appeal of repentance: "repent, and believe in the good news" (Mark 1:15). The nearness of God's reign is, according to Jesus, "good news," a message of salvation for humankind. And while announcing the kingdom of God in words, it is Jesus in person who brings the benefits of this future kingdom. "But if it is by the finger of God that I cast out the demons, then the kingdom of God has come to you" (Luke 11:20).

Linking his message to the Isaianic passages discussed above, Jesus identifies his gospel as good news for the poor. Jesus brings deliverance for the oppressed. Asked by John the Baptist whether he is the expected one, Jesus answers with reference to Isaiah 61:1: "The blind receive their sight, the lame walk, the lepers are cleansed, the deaf hear, the dead are raised, and the poor have good news brought to them" (Matt. 11:5). And in Luke 4:18 Jesus reads from this prophetic text in the synagogue of Nazareth, adding: "Today this scripture has been fulfilled in your hearing" (Luke 4:21). These references are in congruence with Jesus' saying in the Beatitudes: "Blessed are the poor in spirit, for theirs is the kingdom of heaven" (Matt. 5:3).

Many have discussed whether the poor who are mentioned here must be considered as poor in material or, rather, in spiritual ways. This dilemma, however, seems to be false to begin with. The poor are not blessed *because* they are poor; neither can the promise of the kingdom of heaven be reduced to a strictly spiritual understanding. Thus, Jesus' proclamation is closely linked to healing the sick and liberating the demon possessed. His gospel is a full gospel, forgiving sins, casting out demons, and addressing injustice (see ch. 8.2.4, below).

Another important observation from the ministry of Jesus for our understanding of evangelism is how Jesus encountered people, especially the marginalized and needy. Several encounters with lepers, blind men, tax collectors, and other marginalized people, are narrated in the gospels. As a man, he even dared to be in contact with women. Thus, he was accused: "The Son of Man came eating and drinking, and they say, 'Look, a glutton and a drunkard, a friend of tax collectors and sinners!'" (Matt. 11:19; cf. Luke 7:34).

If the kingdom of God is at the centre of Jesus' proclamation, then Christ himself became the centre of the gospel proclamation after Easter. This proclamation of Christ as the saviour was combined with charitable activities. Adolf von Harnack points out ten different types of these activities by the early church, such as giving of alms, supporting widows and orphans as well as sick people, caring for prisoners and poor people, burying the dead, and being hospitable. The Christian church had a good reputation because of its charitable deeds within its fold and for others.[19] And this is not the least reason for the expansion of the church in the first centuries throughout the Roman Empire. Any (re-)consideration of evangelism needs to keep that in mind. This inner linkage between Christian proclamation and Christian conduct cannot be overestimated.

1.3.2 The expansion of the early church

The dynamic spread of the Christian message and the planting of churches in the neighbouring countries of the Mediterranean Sea during the first and its succeeding centuries is mostly a story of success. Beginning in Jerusalem, later in Antioch and Rome, and in almost every major city of the Roman Empire, Christian churches were started. Some of these churches were planted by intensive missionary outreach, like the one by the apostle Paul and his team workers. The Acts of the Apostles and Paul's epistles testify to the success of this enterprise. The majority of churches, however, were not planted by strategic evangelistic outreach. Although we do not know much about actual numbers of missionaries, we may assume that "professional" travelling pioneer evangelists like Paul were a minority of those who spread the gospel. As a fulltime missionary Paul made it his "ambition to proclaim the good news, not where Christ has already been named" (Rom. 15:20).[20]

Without belittling Paul's efforts in mobile evangelistic outreach, the spreading of the gospel and the planting of churches took shape predominantly in the Holy Spirit moving "ordinary" people, bringing them to faith and enabling them to be witnesses of Christ in their families and networks (cf. ch. 8.2.2, below). According to Luke's testimony in the book of Acts this movement started in Jerusalem at Pentecost with "devout Jews from every nation under heaven" welcoming Peter's message and being baptized (Acts 2:5, 41). Most

---

19. Adolf von Harnack, *Die Mission und Ausbreitung des Christentums in den ersten drei Jahrhunderten* (Leipzig: J. C. Hinrichs, 1902), 105–148.
20. For a thorough and exhaustive study of the early Christian mission see Eckhard J. Schnabel, *Urchristliche Mission* (Wuppertal: R. Brockhaus Verlag, 2002).

likely quite a few of these Jews went back to their home countries in the diaspora and spread the gospel of Christ they had received. Others spread the gospel by moving from one place to another, such as Prisca and Aquila, who were associated with Paul's evangelistic work and active in evangelism in Corinth, Ephesus, and Rome (see ch. 8.2.2, below). These day-by-day contacts with family members, neighbours, colleagues, clients, and tradesmen were evangelistic opportunities for Christian witness. Within and through this networking the gospel connected with people.[21] Evangelistic outreach in this early period may thus be seen as a spontaneous outflow of Christian faith and community rather than organized or strategically planned evangelism.[22]

The house church of about 30 to 50 people from different social backgrounds became the early Christian centre of evangelism or mission for the local context, establishing itself as a third party between Jewish synagogue and Greek culture club, or between the circle of the family and the polis. These house churches acted like open systems in bridging and bonding. Closely linked in worship, Christian teaching, and bread breaking, they were in contact with other churches. As a sisterly and brotherly community living a life *coram Deo* and having a new ethos, they were attractive for outsiders. In these communities, stories of Christ and his gospel were told and the early Christians were keen to share this message with others.[23] Being a witness of Christ, individually or in community, may describe this Christian existence quite well (Acts 1:8; John 13:35; 1 Pet. 2:12).

The local Christian community became the major agency for mission and evangelism.[24] Wolfgang Reinbold, in his study on mission in the early church, points to worship gathering with its important evangelistic sensitivity (1 Cor. 14:23-25). In this way, he asserts, the church grows.[25] Most important here is the basic evangelistic or missionary orientation of the gathered community in worship.[26]

---

21. Udo Schnelle, "Die Attraktivität der frühchristlichen Gemeinden: Ein Modell für die Zukunft?," in Michael Domsgen and Dirk Evers, eds., *Herausforderung Konfessionslosigkeit. Theologie im säkularen Kontext* (Leipzig: Evangelische Verlagsanstalt, 2014), 73–92.

22. Wolf-Henning Ollrog, *Paulus und seine Mitarbeiter: Untersuchungen zu Theorie und Praxis der paulinischen Mission* (Neukirchen-Vluyn: Neukirchener Verlag, 1979), 130. See also von Harnack, *Mission und Ausbreitung*, 266ff.

23. Wolfgang Reinbold, *Propaganda und Mission im ältesten Christentum: eine Untersuchung zu den Modalitäten der Ausbreitung der frühen Kirche* (Göttingen: Vandenhoeck & Ruprecht, 2000), 283, 346.

24. Ibid., 202.

25. Ibid., 195ff.

26. Jürgen Becker, Paulus. *Der Apostel der Völker* (Tübingen: Mohr Siebeck, 1998), 270.

Against this background, it may strike us as rather odd that the apostle Paul rarely commands the early Christians to evangelize. "It is . . . a striking fact that in all his letters to the churches Paul never urges on them the duty of evangelism. He can rebuke, remind and exhort his readers about faithfulness to Christ in many matters. But he is never found exhorting them to be active in evangelism."[27] Beyond the Pauline missionary enterprise and some other strategic missionary enterprises, the overall expansion of the early Christian church did not happen by planned action. There are, however, some hints in the Pauline letters where Paul expected support of the Christian communities not only through their sending money or co-workers, but through their evangelistic action and outreach as well imitation of his example.[28] While Paul went from place to place to plant churches (Rom. 15:20), the local church was evangelistically active in its context (1 Thess. 1:6-8). And although the biblical basis isn't quite extensive, it may be true that other important cities like Jerusalem and later Antioch saw it as their responsibility to send out missionaries or evangelists to other territories.[29]

1.3.3 Some observations of Pauline practice

Throughout his letters Paul emphasizes the fact of being commissioned by the risen Lord to proclaim the gospel: "I became its servant according to God's commission that was given to me for you, to make the word of God fully known" (Col. 1:25). Thus, Paul saw "his evangelism as a priestly duty to the nations, significantly adding that he specially made it his ambition to exercise his gospel ministry 'where Christ was not known' (Rom. 15:16-22; notice his quotation of the Servant passage from Is. 52:15, which speaks of the knowledge of the Servant among the nations)."[30] For this very reason he travelled throughout the northern territories of the Mediterranean Sea using the synagogues in the Jewish diaspora and the fresh new Christian communities in different houses

---

27. Lesslie Newbigin, *Mission in Christ's Way: Bible Studies* (Geneva: WCC Publications, 1987), 4.

28. Peter T. O'Brien, *Gospel and Mission in the Writings of Paul: An Exegetical and Theological Analysis* (Grand Rapids: Baker, 1993), 126ff.; Robert L. Plummer, *Paul's Understanding of the Church's Mission: Did the Apostle Paul Expect the Early Christian Communities to Evangelize?* (Milton Keynes, UK: Paternoster, 2006), 143ff. For an overview of the different positions, see Plummer, *Paul's Understanding.*

29. For Jerusalem, see Rudolf Pesch, *Evangelisch-Katholischer Kommentar zum Neuen Testament: Die Apostelgeschichte, Volume 2: Apg 13-28* (Zürich: Benziger, 1986), 19; David G. Peterson, *The Acts of the Apostles*, The Pillar New Testament Commentary (Grand Rapids: Eerdmans, 2009), 375ff. For wandering evangelists, see Green, *Evangelism*, 167ff.

30. Christopher J. H. Wright, *The Mission of God: Unlocking the Bible's Grand Narrative* (Downers Grove, IL: IVP Academic, 2006), 124.

as mission bases for his evangelistic outreach. Right from the very beginning of his mission journeys this happened through teamwork. Around 40 persons are mentioned in the so-called proto-Pauline letters as being involved in the extensive work of being sent by churches, as team workers and even as independent missionaries. Although called Paul's "co-workers," Paul himself saw them and him as both commissioned by God: "For we are God's servants, working together" (1 Cor. 3:9).[31]

With this motivation,[32] Paul concentrated on mission to certain strategic cities. In these major cities and towns in different regions Paul evangelized through direct proclamation, in debates, in personal or public dialogical conversations, in house gatherings, or in synagogues. Even miracles belonged to his evangelistic ministry (see ch. 8.2.2, below).[33] Although focussed on his mission "to the ends of the world" (Rom. 15:28: Spain), he kept contact with and nurtured the new churches by writing and visiting. Taking Paul as an evangelistic model, one has to concur that proclaiming the gospel by extensive travelling and sometimes remaining at a distinct place for a certain time, planting churches and nurturing them, are all duties of an evangelist.

Although Paul addressed different audiences in different, distinct ways, one may nevertheless conclude that "the convictions forged in Paul's own inaugural experience—that Jesus was the Christ and that God was now offering salvation to all through the death and resurrection of his son—formed the basic platform of his mission message."[34]

Paul's missionary or evangelistic self-understanding may be best summarized with the words of 2 Corinthians 4:7-15, starting with "But we have this treasure in clay jars. . . ." Three main themes important for evangelism can be seen in these verses: "power in the midst of weakness" (vv. 7-9); "life in the midst of death" (vv. 10-12); and "faith leading to speech" (vv. 13-14). Weak and limited human beings are entrusted with the gospel as a salvation-bringing

---

31. See also Edward Earle Ellis, "Coworkers, Paul and his," in Gerald F. Hawthorne, Ralph P. Martin, and Daniel G. Reid, eds., *Dictionary of Paul and His Letters* (Downers Grove, IL: InterVarsity, 1993): "In Acts and the Pauline letters some one hundred individuals, under a score of titles and activities, are associated with the apostle at one time or another during his ministry" (183).

32. Michael Green points to three motivations; see Green, *Evangelism*, 236–55.

33. Senior and Stuhlmueller, *Biblical Foundations*, 332–39. The Acts of the Apostles contain a number of narrated occasions when evangelists like Philip or apostles like Peter and Paul addressed Jews and Greeks with the gospel. Just compare the encounter with Lydia (Acts 16) with the philosophical debate on the Aeropagus (Acts 17). Or compare the evangelistic proclamation to different audiences. There are similarities but significant differences. E.g., see the three examples of evangelistic engagement with pagan worshippers in Acts in Lystra (Acts 14:8-20), Athens (Acts 17:16-34), and Ephesus (Acts 19:23-41).

34. Ibid., 187.

message for the very reason that it is by God's might and power but not by human possibilities. It is based on the truth of the word and the power of the Spirit. But although the good news is told and displayed by "perishable earthenware," and this testimony may be called "defective testimony," by the work of the Spirit and by the grace of God it comes up effectual.[35]

1.4 Current Theological Understandings of Evangelism

1.4.1 Experiences and definitions

For many today within or outside the church, evangelism or evangelizing is closely associated with Billy Graham–types of evangelism that have their roots in the 18th-century Methodist revival meetings. The first evangelistic gathering in Europe in that sense may well be the open-air meeting of miners in Bristol in 1739, who were addressed by the revivalist George Whitefield. These gatherings spread all over Britain and later all over Europe. North American evangelists like Charles Finney and Dwight L. Moody followed this tradition in the 19th century, running evangelistic campaigns in Europe. Billy Graham continued this tradition in the 20th century, making it into a worldwide campaign. Until the 1960s or even 1970s this specific "rallying" method of evangelism was so successful that evangelism became identified with a single evangelist leading tent meetings or evangelistic campaigns in stadiums or halls, accompanied by a choir and fellow Christians giving a testimony. For quite a few churches and congregations, to be "evangelistic" meant, and perhaps still means, to have a tent set up once a year or to run evangelistic campaigns with a preacher called an "evangelist." Although this specific method for evangelism usually doesn't attract thousands of people for a single event like it did in the past, especially in the more secularized parts of Europe, it is still considered and practiced as a possible way for evangelism in quite a few churches.

Perhaps because this practice has been so dominant for a long time, "evangelism" has become a polluted term, associated with rudeness and intolerance, for many Europeans. It seems that "the very word 'evangelism' sets many people's teeth on edge."[36] Many (older) people describe negative experiences they have had with evangelism, of evangelists have shouting at them to convert

35. Lesslie Newbigin, *The Light Has Come: An Exposition of the Fourth Gospel* (Grand Rapids: Eerdmans, 1982), 20.
36. John Finney, *Emerging Evangelism* (London: Darton, Longman & Todd, 2004), 7.

and to lift their hands. Some point to proselytism (cf. chs. 8.1.3 and 8.2.4, below) or to efforts in just growing or maintaining one's own church by evangelism. Recent publications on evangelism by the World Council of Churches or local and national church bodies usually take up these issues and distance themselves from negative habits and practices. Dealing with evangelism, then, also means the "work of binding up the wounds of our fathers and mothers in evangelism."[37]

With all that in mind one should be hesitant to define "evangelism" in too narrow a way, by limiting it to a specific form or method. And despite the popular but narrow understanding of evangelism just described, the term and other related ones have become widely used since the 1970s. Indeed, it has become quite common for Roman Catholics to talk about "evangelization," while Protestants mainly use "evangelism." Although these terms overlap in their use, "evangelism" may refer to "(a) the activities involved in spreading the gospel . . . and (b) the theological reflection on these activities," whereas "evangelization" may be used to refer to "(a) the process of spreading the gospel or (b) the extent to which it has been spread. . . ."[38] Thus, the latter term is close to "Christianization" or even "civilization." Others, including non-Catholics, prefer "evangelization" for practical reasons, partly because so many Catholics use it and partly because the term *evangelism* is too much associated with specific methods.[39] Another possible distinction defines "evangelism" as the sharing of the good news by Christians on a day-to-day basis and "evangelization" as referring to more organized and planned forums, like special meetings or campaigns. Altogether, the variety of use is rather bewildering. Therefore, in the following, the word *evangelism* is mainly used in line with WCC usage of the term.

Regardless of which term is preferred, very different definitions and interpretations can be behind them. Sometimes these differences cause misunderstandings, even more so because different understandings are often connected with the same term. Therefore, it is helpful to keep several definitions in mind that have been in use and are obviously still used. Evangelism has been defined:

---

37. Abraham, "Theology of Evangelism," 22.
38. David J. Bosch, "Evangelism, Evangelization," in Karl Müller et al., eds., *Dictionary of Mission: Theology, History, Perspectives* (Maryknoll, NY: Orbis, 1997), 151.
39. Finney, *Emerging Evangelism*, 8. See also Darrell L. Guder, *Be My Witnesses: The Church's Mission, Message, and Messengers* (Grand Rapids: Eerdmans, 1985), 133ff.

a. "according to *method* and *style*. It is then primarily understood as public preaching of a revivalist nature to large . . . audiences by specially gifted (often itinerant) 'evangelists'";

b. "in terms of results: evangelism is communicating the gospel effectively; it is producing converts";

c. "in terms of its 'objects' . . . distinguished from mission." While mission refers to people not yet being Christians, evangelism refers to the calling back or re-Christianization of already-baptized people.

While these definitions are a first and rough guide for understanding (traditional views of) evangelism in its different aspects, they are still in danger of reducing evangelism to questions of method, results, or objects.[40] As such, "evangelism" runs the risk of becoming the pragmatic, methodological branch of mission. Therefore, on the way toward a definition of evangelism, the relationship between mission and evangelism has to be considered.

1.4.2 Mission and evangelism

Mission and evangelism seem to be partners or even twins, because they are often used in combination. Thus, the 2013 WCC affirmation *Together towards Life* speaks of "mission and evangelism in changing landscapes." The same can be said of the 1982 document *Mission and Evangelism: An Ecumenical Affirmation,* and the WCC commission dealing with these issues is called "Commission on World Mission and Evangelism" (CWME).

This opens up the question *how* they are related to each other and what makes them different. To begin with, we have to admit that in many ways both terms were and are used interchangeably. Evangelicals even tend to say, "Historically the mission of the church is evangelism alone."[41] Thus, in many ways "mission," "evangelism," and then especially "witness" are more or less describing the same thing.

In many 20th-century documents, however, a tension can be observed between these words. Especially in times when "mission" and "evangelism" were seen as suspect terms, "witness" became a substitute in many WCC and national church publications. In recent Roman Catholic publications, on the other hand, one finds tendencies to replace "mission" with "evangelization." "Interestingly,

---

40. Bosch, "Evangelism, Evangelization," 151ff.
41. Arthur P. Johnston, *The Battle for World Evangelism* (Wheaton, IL: Tyndale House, 1978), 18.

perhaps as a reflection of the rather strong aversion to the word 'mission' that had emerged in the churches and in theology and (ironically!) missiology, the pope uses the word 'evangelization.' However, the meaning of the terms is the same, and we believe that they can be used interchangeably," write Roman Catholic missiologists Stephen Bevans and Roger Schroeder.[42] *Evangelii Nuntiandi* is quite a good example of that, understanding "evangelization" as a kind of umbrella term referring to the whole church being sent into the world, while the term *mission* is rarely used. While *Ad Gentes* focusses on the missionary nature of the church having a broad understanding of mission, *Evangelii Nuntiandi* widens the understanding of evangelization as the church's "deepest identity," because "any partial and fragmentary definition which attempts to render the reality of evangelization in all its richness, complexity and dynamism does so only at the risk of impoverishing it and even of distorting it."[43]

Beyond the Roman Catholic Church, similar attempts have been made to develop a very broad understanding of "evangelism," including deeds of justice, peace, and human development, while omitting the term *mission*, which is so often associated with Western imperialism and colonialism. Despite these tendencies both terms—*mission* and *evangelism*—are still in use and are even going through a kind of renaissance. Churches in Europe speak more openly of "mission" and "evangelization," meaning "evangelism." This happens often interchangeably. In some contexts "mission" is preferred, in others "evangelism." Here and there it seems to depend on which of the two terms is regarded the more polluted one. Keeping that in mind, it seems nevertheless quite helpful to differentiate between the meanings of both words. Thus, it has become customary to take "mission" as an umbrella term describing God's sending of the church or a church in mission, being sent. "Mission," then, includes the church's social involvement, prophetic ministry, interchurch aid, development aid, caring responsibility, and evangelism. All these dimensions are part of the one mission, but no single one of them can be exclusively equated with the church's mission. They are all related to and depend on each other.[44] Thus, "evangelisation is mission, but mission is not merely evangelisation."[45]

42. Stephen B. Bevans and Roger P. Schroeder, *Prophetic Dialogue: Reflections on Christian Mission Today* (Maryknoll, NY: Orbis, 2011), 144.
43. Pope Paul VI, "Apostolic Exhortation: *Evangelii Nuntiandi*," 8 December 1975, *Acta Apostolicae Sedis* 68 (1976), par. 17.
44. For a helpful discussion on this, see David J. Bosch, "In Search of a New Evangelical Understanding," in Bruce J. Nicholls, ed., *In Word and Deed: Evangelism and Social Responsibility* (Exeter, UK: Paternoster, 1985), 81ff.
45. Jürgen Moltmann, *The Church in the Power of the Spirit: A Contribution to Messianic Ecclesiology*, trans. Margaret Kohl (London: SCM Press, 1977 / Minneapolis: Fortress Press, 1993 [1975]), 10.

Therefore, mission and evangelism are linked together, but they are not the same "in such way that *mission* is understood as the total task God has set the church for the salvation of the world or as the church's ministry of stepping out of itself, into the wider world, in this process crossing geographical, social, political, ethnic, cultural, religious, ideological, and other frontiers or barriers. Evangelism, in contrast, may then be regarded as one of several dimensions of the wider mission of the church, indeed the core, heart, or center of mission."[46] Although some may dispute whether evangelism is the "center of mission" and therefore somehow ultimate, there seems to be an increasing consensus to distinguish between "mission" and "evangelism" in such a way.

This distinction is also found in the WCC documents from 1982 and 2013, on mission and evangelism. Mission then is "the life-giving mission of the Triune God," which is coined as *missio Dei*,[47] and evangelism is "to bear witness to the vision of abundant life for all in the new heaven and earth."[48] Here, evangelism is an essential part of God's mission in the world and a specific responsibility of the church. Starting with the focus on a missionary God, because "mission begins in the heart of the Triune God," the church as a "community of hope" is sent into the world.[49] And while discovering "more deeply its identity as a missionary community, its outward-looking character finds expression in evangelism."[50] Here *Together towards Life* follows quite obviously the understanding of *Mission and Evangelism: An Ecumenical Affirmation* and of *The Cape Town Commitment* of 2010, which states: "Our engagement in mission, then, is pointless and fruitless without the presence, guidance and power of the Holy Spirit. This is true of mission in all its dimensions: evangelism, bearing witness to the truth, discipling, peace-making, social engagement, ethical transformation, caring for creation, overcoming evil powers, casting out demonic spirits, healing the sick, suffering and enduring under persecution."[51]

Mission, then, is seen as the mission of God (*missio Dei*), which springs up from the very heart of God for the benefit of God's creation. In that sense mission flows from God's very own nature and follows the logic of God's love

46. Bosch, "Evangelism, Evangelization," 152.
47. Tormod Engelsviken, "*Missio Dei*: The Understanding and Misunderstanding of a Theological Concept in European Churches and Missiology," *International Review of Mission* 92, no. 367 (October 2003): 481–97; John G. Flett, *The Witness of God: The Trinity, Missio Dei, Karl Barth, and the Nature of Christian Community* (Grand Rapids: Eerdmans, 2010).
48. World Council of Churches, *Together towards Life: Mission and Evangelism in Changing Landscapes* (Geneva: WCC Publications, 2013), par. 1.
49. Ibid., par. 2.
50. Ibid., par. 79.
51. The Lausanne Movement, *The Cape Town Commitment* (Cape Town, 2010), 12.

for the world. The church is then part of this mission flowing from God. "The missionary God who sent the Son to the world calls all God's people (John 10:21), and empowers them to be a community of hope."[52] In that sense the church is part of God's sending to the world. "The church . . . came into being for the sake of mission."[53] Mission describes, therefore, God's sending the Son and the Son's sending the church to the world. The crucial part of this "being sent" is evangelism.

While the different aspects of evangelism will be explored later in this book, the following definition by South African missiologist David J. Bosch may serve as a good working definition:

> that dimension and activity of the church's mission which, by word and deed and in the light of particular conditions and a particular context, offers every person and community, everywhere, a valid opportunity to be directly challenged to a radical reorientation of their lives, a reorientation which involves such things as deliverance from slavery to the world and its powers; embracing Christ as Savior and Lord; becoming a living member of his community, the church; being enlisted into his service of reconciliation, peace, and justice on earth; and being committed to God's purpose of placing all things under the rule of Christ.[54]

---

52. WCC, *Together towards Life*, par. 2.
53. Ibid., par. 57.
54. Bosch, *Transforming Mission*, 420.

CHAPTER 2

Stefan Paas

Evangelistic Mission in Europe: Seven Historical Models

2.1 Europe as a "Mission Field"

In 1963 the WCC Department on World Mission and Evangelism adopted the slogan "mission in six continents."[1] This sentence, according to Emilio Castro, attempted to express "the fact that the day is over when countries could be divided into 'Christian' and 'pagan' areas."[2] Moreover, by the 1980s we could observe on different frontiers a renewed attention for evangelism as the heart of Christian mission. In 1982 the World Council of Churches published the report *Mission and Evangelism: An Ecumenical Affirmation*, in which a new appreciation for evangelism was combined with WCC's traditional strong emphasis on social justice. The recent report *Together towards Life: Mission and Evangelism in Changing Landscapes* (2013) continues this approach, while the influence of the Pentecostal movement and Eastern Orthodoxy can be noted

1. Ronald K. Orchard, ed., *Witness in Six Continents: Records of the Meeting of the Commission on World Mission and Evangelism of the World Council of Churches held in Mexico City, December 8th to 19th, 1963* (London: Edinburgh House Press, 1964).
2. Emilio Castro, *Freedom in Mission: The Perspective of the Kingdom of God: An Ecumenical Inquiry* (Geneva: WCC Publications, 1985), 161.

as new elements.[3] In the Evangelical movement a more or less opposite shift has taken place: in several manifestos we find a growing emphasis on holistic or integral mission (social justice, ecology) alongside evangelicalism's traditionally strong focus on evangelism.[4]

Looking at Europe, the contextual aspect immediately comes into view. Prominent European politicians, especially from the Christian Democratic side of the spectrum, now and then refer to the Christian "soul" of Europe. Theologians and other thinkers point to the increasing "speechlessness" with regard to religiosity in general and Christianity in particular. The pluralization of European nations leads to questions of a missiological nature, just like the migration of non-Western Christians to this continent. Recent developments in the Roman Catholic Church are also interesting. Post–Vatican II documents such as *Ad Gentes* (1965), *Evangelii Nuntiandi* (1975), *Redemptoris Missio* (1990), and *Evangelii Gaudium* (2013) have accelerated theological reflection on mission and evangelism among Catholics. Moreover, since the early 1990s several popes have focussed emphatically on what has been called the "re-evangelization of Europe."

This general awareness of Europe as a field of mission, in combination with a renewed attention for evangelism as the heart of mission, was not a sudden breakthrough caused by the end of colonialism and the atrocities of the Second World War. To a large extent it was the formal acceptance of grassroots insights that had been present for a long time among missionary practitioners. In fact, throughout history many Europeans have been quite prepared to admit that Europe was not very "Christian" at all. Thus, it has always been necessary to "make explicit and unambiguous the centrality of the incarnation, suffering, and resurrection of Jesus Christ."[5] In this chapter I will present seven different paradigms or models of evangelism that have been used in Europe, and that—to some extent—still influence our approaches of evangelism today. These models are: (1) peaceful propagation, (2) Christianization as civilization, (3) reform, (4) revival, (5) the worldview approach, (6) humanization, and (7) power evangelism.

---

3. For a comparison and analysis of both documents, see Jan A. B. Jongeneel, "'Mission and Evangelism' (1982) and 'Together towards Life'" (2013)," *Exchange* 43 (2014): 273–90.
4. For a survey of this development, see C. René Padilla, "Integral Mission and Its Historical Development," in Tim Chester, ed., *Justice, Mercy, and Humility* (Paternoster, UK: Carlisle, 2003). See also C. René Padilla, *Mission between the Times: Essays on the Kingdom* (Grand Rapids: Eerdmans, 1985).
5. World Council of Churches, *Together towards Life: Mission and Evangelism in Changing Landscapes* (Geneva: WCC Publications, 2013), 29.

2.2 Peaceful Propagation

Christianity entered Europe as a minority movement. In the book of Acts we find narratives of the apostle Paul preaching in cities in Greece and Macedonia in the middle part of the 1st century CE (cf. chs. 1.3.3, above, and 8.2.2, below). Most likely, however, he was not the first Christian to evangelize there. Probably, soon after the events in Jerusalem that formed the beginning of the Christian movement, Christianity travelled along trade routes, carried by unknown witnesses who may have proclaimed the gospel as far as Spain. Paul's own apostolic ministry ended in Rome, Italy, where he probably suffered martyrdom. Also, the New Testament contains letters, mainly by Paul, to Christians and churches in Europe, demonstrating that there was a vital Christian presence in many cities in the 50s and 60s CE.[6]

In this first stage Christianity was usually looked at as a Jewish sect, and as such it was tolerated. Its status was never secured, however, and discrimination to the extent of outright persecution was part and parcel of the Christian experience almost from its hour of birth. Becoming a Christian, therefore, implied determination and conviction.[7] Probably, the number of Christians in the Western Roman Empire remained quite small until the 4th century, when the measures of the emperors Constantine and Theodosius made it attractive (if not profitable) to become a Christian. Meanwhile, however, Christianity gradually increased its numbers. Around 400 CE it possibly comprised around 10 percent of the population in the Roman Empire, with its main concentrations in the Greek-speaking East and in the cities.[8]

Christianity's growth in these first centuries can be explained by (but not reduced to) a fruitful combination of lifestyle and witness.[9] First, Christians emphasized marital fidelity both by men and women, while they allowed their women to marry rather late compared to Roman standards. This made it attractive for women to become Christians. Second, while Roman society endorsed abortion (causing the death of many women) and infanticide (especially of

6. One of the most complete surveys of early Christian mission is Eckhard J. Schnabel, *Urchristliche Mission* (Wuppertal: R. Brockhaus Verlag, 2002), trans. as *Early Christian Mission* (Downers Grove, IL: InterVarsity, 2004).
7. Stephen Neill, *A History of Christian Missions*, 3d ed. (London: Penguin Books, 1990), 35–39.
8. For a rough estimation of the number of Christians preceding the conversion of Constantine, cf. Rodney Stark, *The Rise of Christianity: How the Obscure, Marginal Jesus Movement Became the Dominant Religious Force in the Western World in a Few Centuries* (San Francisco: HarperCollins, 1997), 4–13. For the concentration of early Christians in the cities, cf. Wayne A. Meeks, *The First Urban Christians: The Social World of the Apostle Paul* (New Haven: Yale University Press, 1983).
9. Stark, *Rise of Christianity*.

girls), Christians opposed these practices vehemently. This meant not only that Christians gradually outbirthed their pagan neighbours; it also meant that Christian communities usually contained more women than men. As Roman society, by its misogynic practices, had a surplus of men, it seems that pagan men often married Christian women. Apparently, this created opportunities for evangelism, as, for example, the first letter of Peter demonstrates (1 Pet. 3:1-7). Third, Christians gained a good reputation by their conduct in public life, especially in trading and during times of epidemic diseases. Often, Christians remained when others fled, looking after the sick and burying the dead.

In this way Christianity came to Europe, in particular to the southern parts. Some scholars think that this peaceful propagation of Christianity—in contrast with its more violent spread in the North—can explain Christianity's character as a deeply embedded folk religion in, for example, Italy and Greece, as opposed to Christianity's position in northwestern Europe.

2.3 Christianization as Civilization

In 312 CE the emperor Constantine converted to Christianity after Christ appeared to him in a dream predicting his victory in a battle with his rival. Subsequently, he issued an Edict of Toleration (313 CE), thus effectively ending Christianity's status as a suspect minority movement. One of his successors, Theodosius, made Christianity the official religion of the Roman Empire (380 and 392 CE). These measures introduced an entirely new dynamic for Christianity. Not only had it become a respected religion almost overnight; it also had assumed the role of the ruling religion, with effective powers to legislate against other religions. In less than 50 years the number of Christians grew from 10 to more than 50 percent of the population. From now on Christian bishops were to be the representatives of the state religion, whereas persons with political ambitions could only pursue their dreams by becoming Christians. Thus, toward the end of the Western Roman Empire it had become the "normal" thing to be a Christian; it was good for your social status and your career.

The collapse of the Western Empire (usually dated 476 CE) made an end to the political structures of the classic Roman world, but not to Roman civilization as such. In the absence of a wide-stretching political government, the church by and large became the inheritor of this civilization. In large areas, churches and (increasingly) monasteries were the only effective providers of culture, reading, law, and art. Several Germanic tribes who fought over the political inheritance of Rome had converted to Christianity already in the end-stage of the Empire. Logically, Christianity, being the prime cultural survivor of the awe-invoking civilization of Rome, was to become the religious and cultural heart of these new European kingdoms. In the next centuries this Christian-Roman-Germanic civilization was spread, particularly by Frankish kings like Clovis and Charlemagne, into northwestern Europe.[10] Their actual missionary force consisted of "a stream of inspired ascetics," of whom a considerable number came from the recently Christianized island of Ireland.[11] Historian Peter Brown characterizes this mission as a "*mission civilisatrice*," meaning that the Christianity that these missionaries brought was always an inseparable mixture of Roman law and traditions, on the one hand, and Christian faith, on the other.[12]

It is hard to tell to what extent the conversion of these northern tribes was deep-seated. Christian mission was part of the political process of extending the Frankish Christian empire, and thus functioned in a societal order that was maintained with force. While in these tribal societies people would normally follow the religion of their king, this did not mean that they had a profound understanding of or even a great deal of sympathy for this religion. Also, historical research shows that these Christianized tribes usually kept pre-Christian habits and beliefs close at hand. In short, their Christianity seems to have been syncretistic, to say the least.[13] An exception to this rule were the monasteries that developed as centres of Christian learning and practice in these days.[14] Also, some missionaries developed early methods of contextualization, as, for example, Gregory the Great's letter to the British bishop Augustine (596 CE) demonstrates, and by the translation of the gospels in the Saxonian language (around 830 CE), presenting Christ as a feudal lord and his disciples as knights (*Heliand*).

According to Stephen Neill, the baptism of the Lithuanian king Jagiello (15 February 1386) "marks the end of European paganism as an organized

10. Cf. Neill, *History of Christian Missions*, 39–96.

11. Andrew F. Walls, "The Translation Principle in Christian History," in *The Missionary Movement in Christian History: Studies in the Transmission of Faith*, 8th ed. (Maryknoll, NY: Orbis, 2004), 37.

12. Peter Brown, *The Rise of Western Christendom: Triumph and Diversity, A.D. 200–1000* (Oxford: Blackwell, 2003).

13. Cf. Anton Wessels, *Europe: Was It Ever Really Christian? The Interaction between Gospel and Culture* (London: SCM Press, 1994); Alan Kreider, *The Change of Conversion and the Origins of Christendom* (Harrisburg, PA: Trinity Press International, 1999).

14. David J. Bosch, *Transforming Mission: Paradigm Shifts in Theology of Mission* (Maryknoll, NY: Orbis, 1991), 230–36.

body."[15] From now on Europe was a Christian continent, that is, all Europeans—apart from some clearly defined outsider bodies—were considered Christians by baptism, laws were purported to be based on Christian principles, and church and state worked closely together. Moreover, Europe became increasingly covered by a dense network of cathedrals, churches, monasteries, and schools, all contributing to the further spread of Christian beliefs and values, and to a strong symbolic presence of Christianity in every nook and cranny of the continent.

2.4 Reform

In the late medieval period there was increasing discontent among committed Christians about the lack of Christian depth in the majority of the Europeans, including many clergymen. Much of this protest was rooted in the monasteries, with their attachment to the *vita perfecta* (perfect life) and *conversio* (conversion), but many educated laypeople and church leaders supported it. Time and again programmes were launched to raise the level of education of the clergy. By preaching, instruction, obligatory confession and church attendance, liturgical innovation, and a more effective church organization, attempts were made to "convert Christians" (Peter Nissen).

The various Protestant Reformations in the 16th century can be considered as examples of this type of Reform Christianity, which aimed for the conversion of Christians. If we accept that this urge to bring Christianized peoples to a more committed Christianity is a form of mission, this may also help us to reframe the discussion about the reformers' sense of "mission."[16] In earlier studies it was often stated that the Protestant reformers did not believe in mission. Much depends, however, on the definition of the word. Since the Roman Catholic nations Portugal and Spain were in direct contact with unbaptized peoples in South America, the idea of worldwide evangelization could take root much earlier among Roman Catholics, something that Catholic theologians did not hesitate to hold against their Protestant opponents. In this respect the 16th-century Protestant reformers generally had a more limited horizon,

---

15. Neill, *History of Christian Missions*, 96.
16. Cf. Paul Wetter, *Der Missionsgedanke bei Martin Luther* (Bonn: Verlag für Kultur und Wissenschaft, 1996); Thomas Schirrmacher, ed., *Martin Bucer als Vorreiter der evangelischen Mission* (Bonn: Verlag für Kultur und Wissenschaft, 2006); Thomas Schirrmacher, ed., *Calvin and World Mission: Essays* (Bonn: Verlag für Kultur und Wissenschaft, 2009).

sometimes affecting their concept of mission. It seems wise not to focus too much, however, on the presence of words like "mission" in the works of the (Catholic and Protestant) reformers of the 16th century. The massive move to "Reform Christianity" in early modern Europe, with its attempts to convert whole populations to a serious and personal type of Christianity, should be considered as a prefiguration of the missionary movement that started in the late 18th century. To a great extent, in its totalizing approach ("the ends of the earth") and its emphasis on personal Christianity, this missionary movement was all about repeating the reform experience within European Christianity during the previous centuries. So, instead of attempting to "read back" the missionary movement of the 18th and 19th centuries into the Reformation age ("Did the Reformers share 'our' sense of mission?"), we might do better to "read forward" the ethos of this Age of Reform in the younger movement (see below).

Thus, in the aftermath of the Reformation, Europe was divided between Roman Catholic and Protestant spheres of influence. For more than a century these different traditions targeted territories controlled by their opponents, treating these areas in practice as mission fields. For example, in the first part of the 16th century a number of small Protestant communities had originated in France. They met in private homes for prayer, singing, and Bible reading. Sometimes these amorphous groups were called "planted churches" (*églises plantées*), which in this context means something like "preliminary church" or "church-to-be."[17] Between 1555 and 1562 the Reformed city of Geneva sent out ordained pastors to these groups, on their own request, in order to render them into full churches (*églises dressées*). When the first war of religion ended this period of mission, approximately forty Reformed churches had been formed all over France.[18] These early Protestant missions in Europe, whatever we may think of their theological legitimacy, were just as dangerous and demanding as any mission overseas. The same goes for Roman Catholic missions to territories ruled by Protestants. In 1622 Pope Gregory XV founded the *Sacra Congregatio de Propaganda Fide* (Sacred Congregation for the Propagation of the Faith), with the explicit goal not only to reorganize foreign missions, but also to re-establish ecclesiastical structures in territories that had been lost to the Reformation. In fact, this made every Protestant nation a mission field.

---

17. Cf. Peter Wilcox, "Eglises plantées and églises dressées in the Historiography of Early French Protestantism," *The Journal of Ecclesiastical History* 44, no. 4 (1993): 689–95.
18. Andrew Buckler, *Jean Calvin et la mission de l'Eglise* (Lyon: Olivétan, 2008), 137–52.

Catholic evangelists travelled as far as Sweden and Norway to establish the Catholic faith.

Nevertheless, all this was done within the framework of Christendom (see ch. 3.2.1, below, for an explanation of "Christendom"). Protestants and Catholics agreed on the concept of one religion within one nation, even if at the time it could not be decided yet which religion a country would accept (as in France). The Augsburg Treaty of 1555 transferred the transnational Christendom system to a national level: people had to accept the religion of their rulers or move to an area where their own religion was practiced (*cuius regio eius religio*). In a system like this, "evangelism," to use the anachronism, was meant to "normalize" the religious situation within a certain territory. In other words, its function was to bring as many people as possible into the church of the realm, and thus establish a truly Christian state. Other churches were persecuted (as in France and Germany), or at least severely restricted in their attempts to "evangelize" (as in Holland and England).

Within the early Reformation tradition, only the "radical" wing of the Reformation could think without limitations of Europe as a true mission field. The Anabaptists rejected the assumptions of territorial Christianity (such as infant baptism), and believed that the Great Commission applied to all believers at all times. They also criticized the magisterial reformers' (especially Luther's) emphasis on justification by faith alone, since they believed that this resulted in a separation of justification and ethics, and thus in a superficial, nominal religion. In this way they preserved—at least for a while—a mobile Christianity, consisting of committed disciples, as in the early church (a "believers' church"). Today's critics of "Christendom" find much of their inspiration in this left wing of the Protestant Reformation.

2.5 Revival

Already in the 17th century, Jesuit workers who evangelized nominal Catholics in the French countryside considered their own work as "mission" in every meaning of the word. Their experience in the North American mission field had taught them that there was not so much difference between Breton farmers and Native Americans. "On both sides of the Atlantic, Jesuits shared the same apostolic ideals and the same ideas of the mission; they had a similar attitude towards the people they sought to convert, used similar methods of persuasion, and expected similar results."[19]

More or less the same was true in Protestant areas. The limited success of the Reformation in converting the baptized masses of Europe caused a growing discomfort within circles of committed Christians in the 17th and 18th centuries. In Germany, the Pietist movement broke with the formal Christianity of Lutheran orthodoxy. They aimed at a true conversion of individuals, and the formation of small groups of believers within the national church (*Volkskirche*). They redefined mission as an enterprise of ordinary Christians, rather than (colonial) governments and church hierarchies. Also, they relativized "national" or "territorial" Christendom. Instead, they promoted the fellowship of believers, transcending national or confessional borders. The emphasis on a deep-felt, individual experience of conversion, connecting the newborn Christian with brothers and sisters in different nations and denominations, was also typical for the 18th- and early-19th-century revivals in England and America. These movements were characterized by a modern, "democratic" tendency, empowering "ordinary" Christians to band together in "societies" and commit themselves to mission, evangelism, and service. Moreover, in line with the growing emphasis on empirical truth in modern times, they advocated an "experiential" Christianity—a religion of the heart. To be a Christian one must have experienced a "heart strangely warmed" (John Wesley), a personal encounter with the saving Lord Jesus. This experience would normally result in a holy life of discipline and abstinence, which subsequently would lead to a restoration of society. Christianity was thus seen as a major force of social and personal discipline, both by churches and secular authorities, and therefore essential in the creation of civilized societies.

Revivalist preachers—or "evangelists" as they were often called—typically addressed their nominally Christian audiences without much regard for church membership, baptism, or a formal knowledge of the Bible. In this context the term "baptized pagan" was used by many a revivalist in order to shock his audience into repentance. Since the Middle Ages the word *pagan* or *heathen* had been used to denote peoples living outside the borders of Christendom. The word had roughly the same meaning and contained the same implications as the Greek word translated as "barbarian." It referred to people distinct in skin colour and language, and with an inferior level of civilization. If these

---

19. Dominique Deslandres, "*Exemplo aeque ut verbo*: The French Jesuits' Missionary World," in John W. O'Malley et al., eds., *The Jesuits: Cultures, Sciences, and the Arts, 1540–1773* (Toronto: University of Toronto Press, 1999), 267.

people became Christians, their descent was not erased by baptism. A converted Native American, an African slave, or an Indian Christian was usually called a "baptized pagan." But now "baptized pagan" could be used within the confines of Christendom as an equivalent of "nominal Christian," and many 19th-century preachers and evangelists used it as such.

This kind of rhetoric shows that, regardless of all theoretical distinctions between "foreign missions" and "home missions" that have been drawn later, both types of mission were organized along the same lines, out of the same motives, and more than once by the same people, right from their beginnings. For example, Johann Hinrich Wichern, who established the German *Innere Mission* (domestic mission), stated in 1857 that his mission was the "continuation or resumption" (*Fortsetzung oder Wiederaufnahme*) of the earlier mission work in Europe "to conquer the Judaism and paganism that was still unbroken or had regained its strength." In his opinion, mission to the pagan world (*Heidenmission*) and *Innere Mission* were "two aspects of the same service."[20] On the other hand, the "revivalist" part of this mission shows that it was based on the assumption of an at least superficially Christianized population. After all, "revival" assumes that there is something that can be "re-vived."

2.6 The Worldview Approach

Although the World Missionary Conference of Edinburgh in 1910 was still cherishing a rather unproblematic territorial understanding of Christendom that should be expanded to the ends of the earth, a completely different chord was struck at the Jerusalem gathering of 1928. The American missiologist Rufus Jones contributed a paper to the conference, with the significant title "Secular Civilization and the Christian Task." He made it clear that the time of "Christian nations" was over, if it had ever existed at all: "We go to Jerusalem then, not as members of a Christian nation to convert other nations which are not Christian, but as Christians within a nation far too largely non-Christian, who face within their own borders the competition of a rival movement as powerful, as dangerous, as insidious as any of the great historic religions."[21]

---

20. Quote in H. J. Margull, "Über die Einheit von Weltmission und Volksmission," in *Zeugnis und Dialog: Ausgewählte Schriften* (Hamburg: Missionsakademie an der Universität Hamburg, 1992), 49–50.
21. Rufus M. Jones, "Secular Civilization and the Christian Task," in International Missionary Council, *The Christian Life and Message in Relation to Non-Christian Systems of Thought and Life, Report of The Jerusalem Meeting of the International Missionary Council, March 24th–April 8th, 1928* (London: International Missionary Council, 1928), 273.

With the benefit of hindsight we may say that here, for almost the first time in an "official" document by a leading Christian body, an awareness can be found of the Western world as a mission field and of the church as intrinsically missionary. Even more interesting, perhaps, was Jones's introduction of the "rival movement" of "secular culture." This terminology was consciously modeled after the way non-Western religions, like Hinduism or Islam, had been described in the Edinburgh conference of 1910. In other words, Jones suggested that Christianity within the borders of its historic heartland had found a formidable adversary, an alternative "religion," as it were. It was yet another way to say that Europe had become a mission field as any other part of the world where Christianity had to struggle with other religions and philosophies, every bit as resistant as the great world religions. Even within the West it was no longer self-evident to be a Christian, either nominally or seriously.

We might say, therefore, that Jerusalem 1928 saw the birth of a new, "ideological" paradigm of mission in Europe. Around the Second World War this would be expanded further by adding "neo-paganism" as another competitor of Christianity, one that had been suppressed by formal Christianity for a long time, but would now reappear at the surface of society. In 1938 the Dutch missiologist Hendrik Kraemer published his famous book *The Christian Message in a Non-Christian World*, in which he defined Western "relativism" and "secularism" as rebellious ideologies, forgetful of their Christian origins. Especially the rise of nazism ("tribal religion") was a matter of concern. According to Kraemer, nothing demonstrated more clearly "that the Christian Church, religiously speaking, in the West as well as in the East, is standing in a pagan, non-Christian world, and has again to consider the whole world its mission field, not in the rhetorical but in the literal sense of the word."[22]

This opposition of Christianity against other, competing philosophies of life would be the basis for the worldview-driven approach of mission to the West that characterized the postwar contributions of influential Protestant writers like Lesslie Newbigin and David J. Bosch. Alongside the conceptual pairs of "true vs. false Christianity" (in the post-Reformation conflict between Catholics and Protestants) and "serious vs. nominal Christianity" (in the age of revivals) a new pair came into being, that of "Christianity/gospel vs. culture." This rather intellectual approach defined both Christianity and other life views first and foremost as "thought-systems" or "worldviews," that is, more or less

---

22. Hendrik Kraemer, *The Christian Message in a Non-Christian World* (New York: Harper & Brothers, 1938), 16–17.

coherent patterns of ideas concerning the what and why of human life and the world we live in.

This relationship of Christianity with what has been termed "secular culture" or "humanism" remained an important part of discussions in missionary conferences. Thus, by the middle of the 20th century there was a general awareness, at least among leading theologians, that many (Western) Europeans, perhaps even the majority, were not Christians, and that Christianity had to dialogue and compete with other, very strong life views in its own historic heartland. Also, there was a widely shared opinion that the churches were to turn toward mission, to find ways to the hearts and lives of secular people.

2.7 Humanization

For some, this analysis of living in a new "mission field" did not go far enough. These critics, often inspired by the German theologian Dietrich Bonhoeffer, advocated that the whole traditional missionary framework, dividing the nation into Christians and potential Christians had crumbled. Modern humanity had lost a sense of ultimate meaning; humans did not need God anymore to explain the world, to support morality, or to give meaning to life. Influenced by Bonhoeffer's analysis of culture, the Dutch missiologist Johannes Hoekendijk rejected the church-centred idea of mission in the theology of Kraemer and others. The church should not try to draw the world into its fold, but it should follow the agenda set by the world, since this was the place where God realized God's purposes.[23] Others, like the missionary statesman M. M. Thomas, asserted that it is not necessary for people to join the church or to call themselves Christians. Rather, Christian mission should point toward the "humanization" of the world, and invite all people of good will to join this cause.[24]

From this point of departure new, "post-ideological" (or even "post-missionary") perspectives have emerged in our days, rejecting allegedly worn-out oppositions like "Christianity" vs. "secularism," and turning to more inclusive approaches, such as the common search of humanity for wisdom, unity, love, liberation, and redemption. The crucial question in this paradigm, however,

23. Johannes C. Hoekendijk, *The Church Inside Out* (Philadelphia: Westminster, 1966).
24. Cf. M. M. Thomas, "The Meaning of Salvation Today—A Personal Statement," in Roger E. Hedlund, *Roots of the Great Debate in Mission: Mission in Historical and Theological Perspective* (Bangalore: Theological Book Trust, 2002), 269–77.

is the matter of witness to Jesus Christ and his kingdom. Is the kingdom of God closely linked to Jesus Christ as he is revealed in the scriptures, or is it rather a symbol for God's general providence in creation? If it is the first, then the necessity of evangelism as witness to Jesus Christ is underlined. If it is the second, however, it becomes unclear why people should believe in Jesus and follow him in order to be part of the movement of the kingdom. Also, this might mean that the church does not really have its own voice anymore, since, after all, it is the world that sets the agenda.[25] Thus, the question may be asked how this latter perspective relates to the salvific work of Jesus Christ, and how it can maintain a distinct presentation of his kingdom without identifying it with whatever the world considers good and just.

Nevertheless, more moderate versions of this approach have demonstrated how important it is to link evangelism to the cause of the kingdom and the restoration of God's world. To be evangelized means to be invited in this cause, as there is no taking part in Christ without taking part in his mission. Thus, this model draws people away from a single-minded interest in the "benefits" of the gospel, and urges them to consider the "mission" of the gospel (Karl Barth).

2.8 Fighting the Powers

Probably the most influential model of evangelism today is connected with the worldwide, fast-growing movement of "neo-Pentecostalism." There are many similarities with older Pentecostalism, such as speaking in tongues, baptism in the Spirit, healing, and prophecy. We also find a number of specific traits, however, among which a strong emphasis on holistic and material salvation (healing, wealth, fitness, etc.), and on words of power. Furthermore, neo-Pentecostalism is characterized by its fondness of theatrical performances, such as dramatic prayer healings, large worship meetings with all sorts of body movements, so-called Jesus marches, public baptismal events in swimming pools and the like, and travelling apostles with impressive "spiritual careers."

In Europe the movement is represented mostly by African immigrant churches, but also by newcomers like the Australian multinational Hillsong. Clearly, these churches look at Europe as a continent in need of revival. Classic themes recur, such as the pointing out of moral corruption, and the necessity of restoring a Christian culture by a multitude of individual conversions. As

---

25. For an elaborate discussion, see see Stefan Paas, *Church Planting in the Secular West: Learning from the European Experience* (Eerdmans: Grand Rapids 2016), chs. 2 and 4..

regards evangelism, this movement thus stands firmly in the revivalist tradition of the 18th and 19th centuries. However, it adds its own flavour.[26] Crucial in a neo-Pentecostal approach of evangelism/revival is the concept of "power" which must come from above. This in itself is not a new idea for Christians, but neo-Pentecostals claim that this power can be invoked by believers, in particular through common prayer and worship.

Cultural differences determine to a large extent how this basic idea is worked out. In West African migrant churches, for example, the concept of "spiritual warfare" is often found.[27] This is a form of prayer in which—with a loud voice and a variety of body movements—battle is waged against invisible spiritual powers that allegedly keep Europe in their possession. This concept is connected with a dualistic worldview: there are two empires that constantly fight each other over souls and nations. Believers can contribute to this warfare by intense, continuous, common prayer. Evangelism is a "power encounter." If there are no victories in the spiritual domain, people and societies will not be converted.

In a Western neo-Pentecostal church like Hillsong this concept of "power" gets a slightly different shape. Rather than the idea of spiritual warfare, we find an element that is more often brought forward in wealthier environments. This is the idea that God influences the world through the successful lives of believers, people with impact and influence. When people encounter a Christian who is so evidently blessed, they encounter the Holy Spirit. The presence of such Spirit-filled people can eventually change whole societies. The path toward such a national revival leads through the planting of (preferably large) churches which are centres of prayer and worship. The church is, as it were, an energy plant, a "power-house" from which renewing power floods into the country. Consequently, this leads to a missionary approach that is primarily focussed on worship and the formation of churches. Through the church, and especially through massive, enthusiastic praise, God will be "tangible" and "audible" in society. Power from God is "sucked down," so to speak, in a roaring worship service, whereafter this power finds its way into the world through the changed lives of a multitude of believers.

---

26. See esp. Paas, "The Crisis of Mission in Europe: Is There a Way Out?," *Scandinavian Evangelical e-Journal* 3 (2012).

27. Cf. René Holvast, *Spiritual Mapping in the United States and Argentina, 1989–2005: A Geography of Fear* (Leiden: Brill, 2008).

2.9 Concluding Remarks

This historical overview shows that evangelism—presenting Christ in an "explicit and unambiguous" way—has always been part of the experience of European Christians. Depending on social and cultural conditions, however, it has assumed different shapes. The long history of Christendom, with its close connection of Christianity and politics, still looms large in many missionary analyses of Europe. To some extent, many missionary models still seem eager to either assume or restore a Christianized nation. In this sense, the lessons from the earliest stages of the church, in which Christianity was truly a minority religion in the world, may be more relevant than ever. Also, revivalism seems to exert a large influence well into our 21st century. This is no surprise, as this tradition has done so much to shape current understandings of evangelism. Revivalism, however, may be too dependent on the concept of a (nominally) Christian culture, where there is still something to be "re-vived." Increasingly, evangelism in the current European context must be done within a truly missionary framework and in a pioneering spirit.

CHAPTER 3

Stefan Paas

Challenges and Opportunities in Doing Evangelism

3.1 Introduction

Europe is an immensely complex continent, representing an astounding variety of cultures, histories, religions, peoples, and languages. It would be arrogant, to say the least, to even pretend that one contribution could discuss every relevant issue for evangelism from Sweden to Italy, and from Russia to Ireland. In this chapter we will focus on three structural developments that affect the evangelization of Europe, without asserting that these developments equally present themselves in each and every European nation. If we summarize these developments under the (rather unsatisfactory) catchword of "secularization," we must immediately add that they are more clearly visible in the North and the West of Europe than in the South and the East. Also, the process of secularization, while present to some extent in every part of the modern world, runs various historical pathways depending on, for example, the very different ways in which church–state relationships are structured in Europe. All that aside, there is no doubt that these developments are increasingly influential all over

Europe, even if in different degrees. They are here labelled as "post-Christendom," "post-Christianity," and "postmodernity."[1] Together these developments largely define the challenges for evangelism in (large areas of) Europe, and they also show us new opportunities.

3.2 Post-Christendom and the Rise of a Religious Market

3.2.1 *What is post-Christendom?*

"Christendom" is the English translation of the Latin *christianitas*, a term that was used in early sources to denote areas ruled by Christian kings. According to an authoritative study, Christendom can be defined as "a society where there were close ties between the leaders of the church and those in positions of secular power, where the laws purported to be based on Christian principles, and where, apart from certain clearly defined outsider communities, every member of society was assumed to be a Christian."[2] If this is what "Christendom" entails, the word "post-Christendom" (literally: "*after*-Christendom") points to the reality in which Europe increasingly leaves this idea of a Christian society with Christian rulers behind. Social scientists often call this process the "differentiation" of society. Using an image, we could say that many European nations used to be constructed as pyramids, with the church at the top holding everything together. Now they have become pizzas, with many different slices, the church being one of them. "Religion" has become a sector of society rather than its integrative centre.

As societies are complex tapestries, post-Christendom is a process with several dimensions. On a closer look we can see that post-Christendom starts to take place when evangelism is handed over from the secular government, executing its *ius reformandi*, to the church. Historically, for many European Christians the secular government had the responsibility to bring its subjects into the church of the realm, following the principle *cuius regio eius religio* (literally, "whose realm, his religion"), or an equivalent thereof (see ch. 2.4,

---

1. This chapter is largely based on Stefan Paas, "Post-Christian, Post-Christendom, and Post-modern Europe: Towards the Interaction of Missiology and the Social Sciences," *Mission Studies* 28, no. 1 (2011): 3–25; idem, "The Crisis of Mission in Europe: Is There a Way Out?," *Scandinavian Evangelical e-Journal 3* (2012): 16–51; idem, *Vreemdelingen en priesters: Christelijke missie in een postchristelijke omgeving* (Zoetermeer: Boekencentrum, 2015), esp. ch. 2 (39-60).
2. Hugh McLeod, "Introduction," in Hugh McLeod and Werner Ustorf, eds., *The Decline of Christendom in Western Europe, 1750–2000* (Cambridge: Cambridge University Press, 2003), 1.

above, for more on this). In modernity this has changed. Religion has increasingly become a matter of the church rather than the state. Thus, Christianity and citizenship are gradually separated. Yet, in this stage there can still be a privileged church, and the state can still accept a responsibility to protect this church and to legislate against its competitors—Christian or otherwise (typically called "sects" or "foreign religions"). In other words, this first stage of post-Christendom does not mean that all religions have the same rights, or that there is no symbolic power connected with being a member of the church of the realm. It seems that in some European nations—especially in the East and the South—this type of post-Christendom is more or less the routine until today.

The second stage of post-Christendom includes the disestablishment of the church: increasingly, there is no longer one privileged church in every nation. The national church loses its central position; it becomes a movement like any other religious movement. In fact, this means a full acceptance of religious pluralism, including the acceptance of other religions such as Islam. This strict separation between church and state has been the cornerstone of the constitution of the United States. In Europe, many nations still have an established church, like Denmark or England. Often this establishment is symbolic rather than factual, however, meaning that the church and its officials play a visible role in national celebrations and that the ruling dynasty are supposed to be members of the national church.

These two building blocks of post-Christendom (separation of church and state and the acceptance of religious pluralism) can be observed almost everywhere in the modern world, albeit in different ways and degrees. The actual "feel" of a post-Christendom society, however, is influenced to a large extent by other, concurring developments, such as laws regulating church membership or churchgoing or official prayers during government meetings. In constitutional monarchies like the Netherlands or Denmark only the monarch is not free to choose his or her own religion or no religion at all. But the rest of us may do as we please.

Also, "post-Christendom" means the removal of "package deals." In many places in Europe the church was in control of poverty relief (diaconal ministry), education, health care, and the like. This meant, very basically, that it was better for you to listen to a sermon and to be a member of the church. Today, this is still the case in many countries (including the United States), thus moderating the effect of official separation of church and state, and influencing the actual exercise of the freedom of religion. After all, such "package deals" make it difficult not to belong to the dominant church in a certain society (or to any church). Especially in northwestern Europe, however, the welfare state has largely removed these tasks from the church.

To sum this up, "post-Christendom" simply means to have arrived at a stage in a culture where most of these historical bonds between the church and secular power have been separated. In these nations people can lead their private and public lives without any meaningful relationship with the church and its message. Such countries are in many ways "after" Christendom, even if the vestiges of Christendom can be seen everywhere. The most obvious consequence of this process is the rise of religious liberty. In a post-Christendom nation it is possible to be a citizen in full rights, without being a member of the church or even without being religious at all. No longer are there any privileges involved in being a Christian of the right kind (i.e., a member of the national church), or even in being a Christian at all.

3.2.2 Evangelism after Christendom

Post-Christendom has huge consequences for evangelism. In a certain way, we might say, it is post-Christendom that, more than anything else, underlines the need for evangelism in modern societies. In the previous chapter we have seen that modern evangelism (revivalism, worldview evangelism) emerged in 19th- and 20th-century Europe as a response to beginning secularization. It is easy to see why. Post-Christendom takes away extrinsic motivations to be or to become a Christian. It won't help your career, for example, if you go to church. In a post-Christendom society there is no longer an obligation or need to belong to the church (or any other religious organization), apart from an intrinsic motivation. You go to church only if you want to, and as long as you want to.[3] Therefore, churches can no longer expect that people will come anyway. People will not go to church to enhance their social standing, to find a spouse, to receive money, to have an ecstatic experience, or to please their parents. All this can be found outside the church, and usually with fewer strings attached. This means that people must be *persuaded* to become Christians.

---

3. Cf. Grace Davie, *The Sociology of Religion* (London: Sage, 2007): "In Europe as well as America, a new pattern is gradually emerging: that is a shift away from an understanding of religion as a form of obligation and towards an increasing emphasis on consumption or choice. What until moderately recently was simply imposed (with all the negative connotations of this word), or inherited (a rather more positive spin) becomes instead a matter of personal inclination. I go to church (or to another religious organization) because I want to . . . so long as it provides what I want, but I have no obligation either to attend in the first place or to continue if I don't want to" (96).

Today, people will only join the Christian community if they can find something there that cannot be found anywhere else. This is a challenge and an opportunity at the same time. Post-Christendom forces the church to focus on this one question: What is our "unique selling point"? Or, to turn the question around: What is it that people look for if they come to church at all? What is it that they can find nowhere else? Our post-Christendom age must lead us to a passionate commitment to the unique core of our Christian faith. This is the single most important question that we must answer: *What is it that our neighbours can only find in the Christian community and nowhere else?* As simple as the answer may be, it is often not taken seriously enough.

If we have found this "pearl of great value" (Matt. 13:46), it is important to present it in the best way we can. The mystery of faith is encountered through the sacraments, music, community, mission, preaching, good talks, drinking coffee, reading, singing, worshipping, and so forth. In our post-Christendom age all these things must be done with excellence. Here, most churches in Europe still have a long way to go. Behind us are centuries of self-evident cultural Christianity. Hence, the criticism of religious-market theorists such as Rodney Stark.[4] If you have a religious monopoly, and if you are supported by the state, financially and in other ways, it is easy to become lazy—like any monopolist. Whatever you do, no matter how few people you draw, you will get paid. There is no need to mobilize the Christian crowd, since the clergy does not really need their support. And as long as the culture is more or less "Christian," as was the case in Christendom, you do not feel very tempted to win new people for the faith. Somehow you feel that they belong to you anyway. So, the taking away of privileges will force the church to raise the level of its motivation and the quality of its activities.

3.3 Post-Christianity and the Call for a Mature Faith

3.3.1 What does post-Christianity mean?

The most familiar kind of evangelism, as we know it, was developed in the 18th and 19th centuries, during the great revivals in Europe and the United States. Great evangelists, like George Wesley, George Whitefield, Jonathan Edwards, and Dwight Moody were known as "revivalists." Basically, conversion in a revivalist setting means the turn from a "nominal" or "cultural" Christianity

---

4. Such criticism can be found in many publications. See, e.g., Rodney Stark, "Efforts to Christianize Europe, 400–2000," *Journal of Contemporary Religion* 16, no. 1 (2001): 105–123.

toward a committed Christianity, via a personal experience of God's grace for sinners (cf. ch. 2.5, above). Its basic message is (or was): "You know what you should be, but you do not live up to that. Repent and embrace a new life, based on God's love and forgiveness." This was the essentially Methodist framework that has so influenced our thoughts about evangelism. Today, we often meet this framework in another, more therapeutic version that leaves out sin and judgment, and underlines unconditional acceptance instead. There is a lot of evangelism nowadays that presents God as a therapist-at-large who heals our pain, who will always be with us, and who accepts us no matter what we do.

But, regardless of whether we do evangelism in a traditional, moralist way or in a modern, therapeutic way, we assume that someone knows what we mean with words like "God," "Jesus," "the cross," "sin," and "love." We assume that this person more or less knows the biblical story and, moreover, accepts the authority of the Bible. We also assume that this person believes in the integrity of the servants of the gospel. The only thing that needs to be done is to take a "decision for Christ" or to "really believe that God loves you as you are." Classic revivalism of this type assumes that people somehow know what Christianity is all about, and that they accept its standards more or less. They feel guilty because they do not go to church as often as they are supposed to, or because their lives do not meet Christian norms. Or they experience a loss of meaning as a consequence of their distance from the church, and they desire to become part of it even if they do not know how. To be clear, this can still be the case in a post-Christendom society. The United States is an obvious example. There, many people are attracted to Christianity even if they don't have to be. Also, in a number of European countries there are large groups of people who are somehow still oriented toward Christianity, and who can be invited to a more active Christian lifestyle by a rather brief and concentrated evangelistic action.

Where "post-Christianity" has taken its course, however, this is no longer the case. Post-Christianity means that Christianity itself has become quite incredible and unattractive for many people in these nations. A post-Christian society is a society where strong cultural objections exist against Christianity. This may result in atheism, although committed atheists are still a small minority in most European countries. For most people it will lead to a spiritual interest (after all, there must be "something out there"), while keeping their distance from Christianity and the church. They may use certain elements from the Christian tradition (for example, going on a pilgrimage or wanting their wedding ceremony in a church), but they combine them with elements from other traditions (*bricolage* or "patchwork religion"). The Christian story is no longer the ruling story of a post-Christian culture. It is just one of many stories, and it can be used and combined in whatever way we want. And, of course, a post-Christian culture increasingly does not *know* the Christian story, since most people do not have an opportunity to become familiar with it.[5]

So, a post-Christian society by and large means this: there is a small group of committed Christians (people who are Christians because they want to and not because they must), a similarly small group of committed unbelievers (people who find religion ridiculous or dangerous), and a large group in the middle that is pressured from both sides, but in general does not find Christianity all that plausible. Moreover, other institutions have developed, such as the media, the arts, and the education system, that operate on thoroughly secular and libertarian principles and are often very critical toward religion.

It would take too much space here to go into the roots of unbelief in European culture. Part of the story, of course, is the rationality of the modern world. We have created a world that is largely under our technological control; we have developed instruments that help us to explain virtually everything—from thunder to morality. No longer do we feel threatened by dark forces and evil magic; we have isolated ourselves against this by clear thinking. We can be successful in our daily lives without religion. This is what the Canadian philosopher Charles Taylor describes as "the Immanent Frame."[6] Modern life is increasingly a life under human control. Moreover, many people believe that religion—at least strong religion—is dangerous. It stirs up many violent passions. And even if it is more or less peaceful, it still curbs the human enjoyment of earthly pleasures by its rigid norms. It turns us away from the common human good, and thus makes us an enemy of ordinary human desires (friendship, sex, entertainment, work).

As some of the most modern nations of the world are very religious indeed, there is no necessary logic to why so many European nations are so resistant against religion. It is a certain cultural "mood" or, as Taylor would have it, a cultural "spin" that leads so many Europeans to think that "science has disproved God" or that "religion is a danger for society."[7] It is not a well-thought-out,

---

5. Cf. David Martin, "Believing without Belonging: A Commentary on Religion in England," in David Martin, *Christian Language and its Mutations: Essays in Sociological Understanding* (Aldershot, UK: Ashgate, 2002): "There is a blankness appearing in the younger generations which is more a uniform ignorance than a considered reflection" (154).

6. Charles Taylor, *A Secular Age* (Cambridge: Belknap Press/Harvard University Press, 2007), 539–93.

7. Ibid., 548–56.

knock-down argument that insulates many Europeans against Christianity, but a cultural narrative that is made *attractive* rather than convincing. In a post-Christian culture it is attractive to keep your distance from religion, because it is widely believed that this is a sign of maturity and autonomy. To be religious means to be infantile; it means that we are not mature enough to take life as it is. To grow up means that we say goodbye to Santa Claus and God. This is the kind of "spin" that closes the immanent frame for transcendence. Science has not disproved God, and religion is not any more dangerous than a secular worldview. But many people want to believe this, because it resonates with a deep longing in our hearts to be grown-up, brave, and authentic.[8] Religion is for children. This is why parents expect their children to grow out of religious feelings when they grow up. And this is why most adults are not attracted to serious religion, even if they want to experiment with spirituality now and then. Moreover, since there is always an element of immaturity and projection in religious faith, this criticism appeals to many believers, making them insecure and thus eroding their missionary zeal.

3.3.2 Opportunities for evangelism

The opportunity arising from this is twofold. Of course, we need clever arguments and sound theology to refute the criticisms that are brought up against Christianity: criticisms such as "it is impossible to believe in God after the Enlightenment." We need churches that are unembarrassed about difficult questions, churches that are welcoming places for inquirers. We need people who are able to explain Christianity to a crowd that does not know the Bible and does not speak "Christianese." And it seems that post-Christian nations are producing some of the most creative Christian thinkers on the planet.[9] In a global perspective, Europe may be a "laboratory for new forms of faith, new structures of organization and interaction, that can accommodate to a dominant secular environment."[10]

Yet, there may be another, more profound opportunity which is a challenge at the same time. Christians in post-Christian nations must think hard about the question why so many people find such anti-Christian criticisms attractive in the first place. Part of our evangelistic mission in the West must

---

8. Ibid., 559–66.
9. Think of Jacques Ellul (France), Charles Taylor (Canada), Eberhard Jüngel (East Germany), Tomáš Halík (Czech Republic), etc.
10. Philip Jenkins, *God's Continent: Christianity, Islam, and Europe's Religious Crisis* (Oxford: Oxford University Press, 2007), 19.

be to unravel these deep cultural narratives of autonomy and heroism. Our main missionary and educational problem may not be that we don't have any good arguments, but that we don't have a widely appealing vision of what it means to be a religious *adult*. Only if people start to believe that a Christian life is an adventurous life, only fit for the brave, will they be prepared to look at arguments defending it. If we are really followers of Jesus, we are disciples of the most mature man that has ever lived. Christianity is not about good people who get rewarded and the bad being punished. It is not about escaping reality in cozy religious parties, sharing comforting fairy tales. It is about following a man who was ultimately good, who was deeply loved by his Father, and yet was called to suffering and death because he loved his people and he hated the powers that enslaved them. If this is not adventurous and brave, I do not know what is. So, the best apologetic in a post-Christian culture is to have a "provocative church" (Graham Tomlin): a church that means business in following Jesus.[11]

3.4 Postmodernity and the Call to Be Fully Human

3.4.1 A *fuzzy* concept

The third large cultural shift that affects our evangelism is called "postmodernity." The term *postmodern* is rather fuzzy: it is used to explain a wide range of cultural phenomena, like pluralism, consumerism, relativism, hyper-individualism, and the collapse of authority. To simplify the issue: premodernity can be described as an era of "natural knowledge." A premodern farmer just "knew" that the earth was flat, he "knew" that kings were destined to rule over him, he "knew" that the old woman next door was a witch, and he "knew" that his fields needed a blessing in order to have a good harvest. All of this knowledge was mainly unreflective, a result of participating in social practices. It was anchored in ontologies of God and nature. Now, modernity can be characterized as a series of attempts to separate "real" from "false" knowledge, a quest for certainty by the application of human reason. Again, put as simply as possible,

---

11. When young people in the West think that the church is obsolete, then this can only change, says Douglas John Hall, ". . . when the . . . distance between church and world, faith and life, gospel and context is in some real measure overcome, or, speaking positively, only where the church lives unprotectedly in the midst of the world, where faith is a dialogue with life (not only an internal dialogue of the community of faith itself), where the gospel engages and is engaged by context." See Hall, *The Cross in Our Context: Jesus and the Suffering World* (Minneapolis: Fortress Press, 2003), 177.

modernity's prime questions were "Why is this so?" and "Who says?" It was an attempt to find the very foundations of knowledge and belief, foundations that needed no further proof. As a result, the fundamental ontologies started to erode. In the end, nothing seemed as "natural" or self-evident as it was first believed. Nothing is "just the way it is"; it can be analyzed, criticized, abolished, or reorganized on a different basis.

Once this process of deconstruction has begun, however, it cannot be stopped. It does not halt when we have discovered (or invented) scientific progress, human rights, democracy, and secular societies. It is like an acid; it keeps eating away certainties. Thus, it was only a matter of time before modernity started to turn in on itself. The detached, objective "self," the unmoved mover of all quests for certainty, became "de-centred" when its historicity and locality were revealed by the sociology of knowledge and language philosophy. In short, the postmodern condition "pertains to one's awareness of the deconstructibility of all systems of meaning and truth."[12]

Thus, there is no single story that gives meaning to our culture. As a consequence, people encounter different life views every day. Postmodern societies have become incredibly pluralistic. Of course, this makes us aware of the arbitrariness of our own views. Whatever seemed once "natural" appears to be merely one choice among many others. And this raises questions about how we find our convictions in the first place. "Postmodernity" refers to an age where people have become aware of the instability of their own life views (and, consequently, those of others).[13] We may think that we have come to our views by applying the right method, by using our rational faculties, and excluding our prejudice. But in reality we are driven by our biological nature, emotions, deep moral instincts, affections, social environment, and so forth. So, after all, our beliefs are not very rational at all. They are later rationalizations of views that we have adopted in a much more "visceral" way, instinctively, driven by fear, love, or passion.

---

12. Kevin J. Vanhoozer, "Theology and the Condition of Postmodernity: A Report on Knowledge (of God)," in Kevin J. Vanhoozer, ed., *The Cambridge Companion to Postmodern Theology* (Cambridge: Cambridge University Press, 2003), 13.
13. Cf. Anthony C. Thiselton, *Interpreting God and the Postmodern Self: On Meaning, Manipulation and Promise* (Edinburgh: T&T Clark, 1995).

3.4.2 Postmodernity and evangelism

What does this mean for evangelism? Traditionally, evangelism tries to change people by focussing on their convictions. You *believe* that you are good, but *in fact* you are a sinful person. You may believe that God will let you in God's heaven, but if you had read the Bible, you would think otherwise. Or, in a more modern way: you believe that you are a worthless person, but you know that God loves you just as you are. If you only could believe that Jesus died for you, your whole world would change. You would throw away your idols, everything you have put your trust in, and you would embrace your true identity, and so on. This kind of evangelism is not wrong, far from it. But the problem is that it always works from beliefs to life change. In other words, it starts with "worldview," and it assumes that people will change once they have been taught to accept the rational truths about their lives. In this way, a lot of evangelism looks like a spiritual variety of rational emotive therapy (RET): it assumes that our problems (emotional and spiritual) are caused by irrational and illogical beliefs, and that the best way to help people is to contest these beliefs. In other words, conversion happens primarily through addressing the mind. And so we produce books and websites, or we preach, so that people may be changed.

But are we really like that? If there is truth in postmodern insights, we must assume that this is not how conversion usually happens. Faith is not inspired primarily by beliefs, but by emotion and instinct. This may be what the apostle Paul hinted at when he said that faith works through love (Gal. 5:6). The difference between belief and unbelief is not a matter of rational convictions but a matter of different orientations, or "loves" (St Augustine). The Christian faith is not primarily an argument; it is "affection" (Jonathan Edwards). It seems that postmodern insights are not so new after all! All the great theologians of the past knew that our deep decisions for or against Christ (and other decisions as well) are affective and emotional rather than rational.[14] Usually, we develop our rational convictions to explain and justify positions we have taken because they attracted us in the first place.

This explains why a certain argument for or against Christianity will be convincing for person A, but utterly unconvincing for person B. This does not mean that A is more (or less) rational than B, but it is because A deep down *wants* this argument to be true, whereas B does not want it to be true. This is what is meant above with "unmasking" the deep cultural narratives against

---

14. For this "liturgical" approach to Christian formation, see esp. James K. A. Smith, *Desiring the Kingdom: Worship, Worldview, and Cultural Formation* (Grand Rapids: Baker Academic, 2009).

Christianity in our culture. These narratives do not appeal to our *reason* in the first place, but they touch our deepest *longings and desires*. They appeal to the kind of people we want to be.

For evangelism this implies that we need to take humans more seriously. We should not treat them as if they were "brains in vats." Conversion is a process that happens mostly under the waterline of reason. It happens through changes in our affections. How do we fall in love? Not through arguments, that is for sure (even if they play a role in supporting and clarifying our choice). Music, images, the beauty of a building, smells, temperature, good stories, the general atmosphere, the kind of people that are around, their attitude and friendliness are all important for the conversion of newcomers.[15] All these things are not just nice "extras"; they are "sacraments," as it were. These are the ways in which the gospel is embodied in nonrational ways, so that it can touch the whole person rather than just their brain.

Altogether, this means that we must be careful with our worldview-driven, traditional ways of evangelism. What we need is a more holistic approach that does justice to our humanity. Interestingly, exactly this happened in the early church (cf. ch. 8.2.4, below). There, evangelism was usually not a proclamation aimed at a decision "on the spot." Rather, it was a spun-out process that sometimes took several years and that contained Bible study, one-on-one conversations, worship services, certain rituals, teaching Christian disciplines, coaching and spiritual direction, fasting, and so forth.[16] With this ancient practice in the back of his mind, William Abraham defines evangelism as a "set of intentional activities which is governed by the goal of initiating people into the kingdom of God for the first time."[17] In short, we need an approach of evangelism that is holistic (not just rational) and process oriented (people do not come to the faith in one big decision, but in a series of mini-decisions).

Finally, the deep-rooted skepticism of postmodernity is an important issue for evangelism. This works out in two ways. Some churches will offer clear answers and role patterns to religious seekers. These churches are usually strongly family oriented, and they help people to find direction in an extremely fuzzy culture. It is important that there are churches like that, as long as they work with integrity. But many religious seekers, especially those

---

15. Miranda Klaver, *This Is My Desire: A Semiotic Perspective on Conversion in an Evangelical Seeker Church and a Pentecostal Church in the Netherlands* (Amsterdam: Pallas Publications, 2011).

16. See William Harmless, *Augustine and the Catechumenate* (Collegeville, MN: Liturgical, 1995); Stefan Paas, *De werkers van het laatste uur: de inwijding van nieuwkomers in het christelijk geloof en in de christelijke gemeente* (Zoetermeer: Boekencentrum, 2003), esp. 187–203.

17. William J. Abraham, *The Logic of Evangelism* (Grand Rapids: Eerdmans, 1989), 95.

who are young, will not feel at home in churches where there is little place for doubt and criticism. For postmodern people it is very difficult to believe anything with the same innocence as their ancestors. Their commitments will always be somewhat "ironic." So, we need churches that give room for doubt and exploration, churches that hold their people "lightly."[18] Paradoxically, this requires strong convictions and a solid theological framework. If the church has no convictions, it will not offer an environment for doubt. So, it is important to be clear about what you believe, and yet be genuinely understanding toward skepticism with regard to religion. A lot of this will depend on the spiritual maturity of the leaders.

3.5 Conclusion

In summary: What are the conditions for evangelism in Europe today? In this chapter I have discussed three major cultural shifts that make evangelism stranger than it used to be. Out of this, six challenges follow. These challenges are, at the same time, opportunities:

1. *We need to focus on our core business.* What is it that makes us unique? What is the pearl of great value that can be found nowhere else? If we don't know our unique selling point, we have a huge problem.

2. *We must leave behind a monopolist attitude* and be serious about the quality of our programmes and the level of motivation of our members. This will become very urgent, as the state increasingly cuts its ties with the church.

3. *We need good theology and apologetics.* It is important that theology is done in the marketplace, that it goes "public" again.

4. *We need a convincing picture of Christian adulthood.* Christianity must become an adventure again, a challenge for the brave.

5. *Evangelism must be holistic.* We must take seriously that human beings are primarily driven by instincts and affections rather than by reason. Therefore, we need a great variety of approaches, and especially those approaches that target the emotions and affections of people. Here,

---

18. Cf. Alan Jamieson, *A Churchless Faith: Faith Journeys beyond the Churches* (London: SPCK, 2002).

we could learn a lot from shopping malls or sporting events. How do they produce "convincing experiences"? How do they attract people and change them?

6. *Evangelism is a process of discovery*, a quest rather than a momentary decision. Very often, it will take years for someone in Europe to become a Christian. And even then, we must always keep in mind that a Christian has never arrived. As postmodern people we remain confused and skeptical about much of what we believe. For many people in our culture, their conversion is a period or a "phase" they go through (just as unbelief is seldom a completely closed position). As churches we must be flexible enough to understand that and remain in contact with people, even when they lose sight of us for a while. In fact, churches must constantly evangelize those for whom they feel responsible.

All this will require a great deal from our churches. A key point in this chapter is that we have real choices to make. The church is not a passive victim of anonymous trends. The church consists of human beings, who are players in these trends, inspired by their faith in the God of all ages. The church can make choices about its institutional life, its commitments, and its core values, and all this can greatly affect its appeal.[19]

Some young, secular people from the Netherlands perhaps have presented the most important choice to us. Some years ago, the Protestant Church in Amsterdam started a project to find out how it could reconnect with young people in the city. They appointed two people, both in their twenties, to lead this project. They set up some focus groups with secular twenty-somethings in the city. In one of the first meetings they asked their non-Christian peers, "What should the church in this city do to make you interested?" One of them answered, "Well, I'm not that interested in the church, actually. But Jesus, yes, he is pretty cool. You know, the church should do something with Jesus! Yeah, that would help!"

If there is a future for the church in Europe, it must regroup around Jesus. If a community of people sets out to live like Jesus, to cross barriers to the have-nots, to connect "good" and "bad" people, to challenge selfishness and arrogance, it will find out several things. It will find out that it will be alone

---

19. Thus, Linda Woodhead, "From Christendom to Christianity: Beyond Secularisation Theory," in Martin Reppenhagen and Michael Herbst, eds., *Kirche in der Postmoderne* (Neukirchen-Vluyn: Neukirchener Verlag, 2008), 109.

and despised. Following Jesus is the best way to become a stranger again. It will find out that there are "people of peace" in the most unexpected places, welcoming them amidst an unwelcoming society. It will find out that its own love and moral strength is highly insufficient, and thus it will rediscover what it means to be sinful. And it will find out that, deep in the heart of such an idealistic project, there is our dependence on the mystery of the cross. Instead of preaching doctrinal truths about sin and atonement to our nations, we need in a way to start over again. We need to start the project of rediscovering the cause of Jesus, and in this cause we may find Jesus himself as our teacher and saviour. If anything, this will be the way out of the crisis of mission in the West. As always, Jesus is the way and the door to our future.

PART TWO

Evangelism and Theological Perspectives

CHAPTER 4

Martin Reppenhagen

Contemporary Theological Discourse on Evangelism

4.1 Introduction

Trying to give an overview of the contemporary theological discourse on evangelism is quite a bold undertaking. The practice of evangelism "is a complex and multi-layered process"[1] and the different understandings are multifaceted. Although "evangelism" as a concept has been used quite frequently during the last few decades, most of the time it seems to be a topic or practice only in a few niches of a church. Throughout church history, however, these individuals, societies, monastic orders, and mission organizations have kept mission and evangelism alive both inside and outside established churches.

Quite a few decades ago, Dutch missiologist Hendrik Kraemer wrote *The Christian Message in a Non-Christian World*, in which he stated: "There is the obligation to strive for the presentation of the Christian truth in terms and modes of expression that make its challenge intelligible and related to the peculiar quality of reality in which they live." And he continued that this should

---

1. Bryan P. Stone, *Evangelism after Christendom: The Theology and Practice of Christian Witness* (Grand Rapids: Brazos, 2007), 316.

happen "against the background of the universal human problems of aspiration, frustration, misery and sin, because these men and women must be for us in the first place human beings, fellow-men, and not non-Christians."[2] It seems that this obligation is no less important today. In every time and context Christians are called to be witnesses of Jesus Christ, which is the basis for evangelism. Even more, now that a long period of Christian domination in Europe has all but crumbled away, there is a new awareness of the evangelistic responsibility of the church and every Christian.

"We have to teach evangelism," writes German practical theologian Michael Herbst, against the background of a postsocialistic and secularized society with its growing number of de- and unchurched people. "We have to show that evangelism is a permanent dimension of a local church that is open and inviting, that loves to give a warm welcome to seekers, and that longs to give unchurched people as many opportunities as possible to experience the gospel."[3] In many ways Christians are challenged to give reason for their faith. In many contexts the growing challenge is just religious indifference. The religious quest is privatized or even absent in a disenchanted world. How do churches deal with those who are quite happy without faith or even without quest for God? They usually don't have anything against religion; rather, questions of faith and religion are just absent in their life and they don't miss anything.[4] They are "religiously unmusical."[5] This is of important significance, because how does the church communicate a religious message to those who are not asking religious questions? As Dietrich Bonhoeffer asked, "How can Christ become Lord of the religionless as well?"[6] The challenge still remains always to "be ready to make your defense to anyone" (1 Pet. 3:15).

---

2. Hendrik Kraemer, *The Christian Message in a Non-Christian World*, 3d ed. (Grand Rapids: Kregel, 1956), 303.

3. Michael Herbst, "Evangelism in Theological Education," *International Review of Mission* 96, nos. 382–383 (2007): 265ff.

4. Graham Tomlin, *The Provocative Church* (London: SPCK, 2002), 2; see also Hans-Martin Barth, *Konfessionslos glücklich: Auf dem Weg zu einem religionstranszendenten Christsein* (Gütersloh: Gütersloher Verlagshaus, 2013); Eberhard Tiefensee, "Chancen und Grenzen von 'Mission'—im Hinblick auf die konfessionelle Situation in den neuen Bundesländern," in Matthias Bartels and Martin Reppenhagen, eds., *Gemeindepflanzung—ein Modell für die Kirche der Zukunft?* (Neukirchen-Vluyn: Neukirchener Verlag, 2006), 68–85.

5. Max Weber coined that term as a self-description, but he was aware of religion. Today's "religious unmusicals" don't care for religion, thus the term is a description by religious about nonreligious people.

6. Dietrich Bonhoeffer, "Letter 30 April 1944," in Eberhard Bethge, ed., *Dietrich Bonhoeffer: Letters and Papers from Prison* (London: SCM Press, 1981), 92.

In this chapter I will begin with some general comments on the meaning of "evangelism." Then I will present an overview of current theological approaches to evangelism, based on recent documents from different Christian traditions. After a discussion of these views, I will concentrate on the relationship between evangelism and the church, as this relationship is increasingly considered as crucial in contemporary debate.

4.2 Current Perspectives on Evangelism

4.2.1 Dilemmas

To discuss the different aspects and understandings of evangelism one may start with the statement that "evangelism is the outflow of hearts that are filled with the love of God for those who do not yet know him." This sentence defines evangelism as an "outflow of hearts," pointing to the motivation for evangelism by asserting that "the heart of God longs that all people should have access to the knowledge of God's love and of his saving work through Jesus Christ."[7]

In similar tones the Roman Catholic document *Evangelii Nuntiandi* defines evangelism as "the proclamation of salvation in Christ to all who do not believe in him, announcing forgiveness of sins, calling people to repentance and faith and to a new life in the power of the Holy Spirit."[8] Evangelism is here related to the "liberation from everything that oppresses people but which is, above all, liberation from sin and the Evil One, in the joy of knowing God and being known by him."[9]

Speaking of "salvation" or "liberation" leads to the question, What is meant by these terms? Is salvation just an otherworldly bliss or is it, rather, overcoming inner-worldly injustice? Both perspectives can be found. Another issue is the relationship between individual salvation and the restoration of creation. When salvation is presented as a personal gift, how is this related to kingdom concerns of healing the sick and overcoming evil in this world? Yet another question pertains to the relationship between the here and now. When the World Council of Churches' report *Together towards Life* speaks of "abundant life" or "fullness of life" and relates them to liberation of the oppressed, how

---

7. The Lausanne Movement, *The Cape Town Commitment* (Cape Town, 2010), 15, 36.
8. Pope Paul VI, "Apostolic Exhortation: *Evangelii Nuntiandi*," 8 December 1975, *Acta Apostolicae Sedis* 68 (1976): 9.
9. David J. Bosch, "Evangelism, Evangelization," in Karl Müller et al., eds., *Dictionary of Mission: Theology, History, Perspectives* (Maryknoll, NY: Orbis, 1997), 153.

is this related to the eschatological gift from God? A final point of discussion, to mention just these few, is the relationship between salvation through Christ alone, and the saving and restoring work of the Spirit in all creation. Although there have been many attempts to overcome dichotomies, there can still be seen different emphases in the various approaches to evangelism. Here I will briefly present and discuss some different positions.

4.2.2 Evangelism as communication of the gospel

In the discussion around evangelism, the focus is increasingly put on communication. Some even prefer "communication of the gospel" as a substitute for evangelism.[10] The understanding of evangelism as communication can be traced back to Hendrik Kraemer's *Communication of the Christian Faith*.[11] Speaking and listening are core elements of evangelism as communication of the gospel.

Even more, communication requires a *mutual* relationship. Evangelism is never one-sided; evangelists should not try to enforce their opinion. Evangelism is conversation and encounter with the other. Following this understanding, the other cannot only been seen as an object of mission anymore, but as its subject as well. Like the Christian faith, evangelism lives by listening. Thus, preaching the gospel or being a witness of the gospel cannot be done just *for* the other, it is also done *with* the other. German missiologist Theo Sundermeier points to the fact that the church needs the other to be the church and even goes so far as to critically question Bonhoeffer's understanding of a "church for others." Sundermeier votes for a "church *with* others."[12] This opposition may be rather virtual, though. As messenger of the good news, the church is also "church for others," but this only can happen while the church is with others.

Thus, communicating the gospel is a reciprocal undertaking with different asymmetric constellations, keeping in mind that total equality is rarely achieved and most communicative processes have shifting asymmetries. With this focus

---

10. Other substitutes which have been discussed are "witness" or "presence."

11. Hendrik Kraemer, *The Communication of the Christian Faith* (Philadelphia: Westminster, 1956). To speak of "the communication of the gospel" seems to be more appropriate. To distinguish between gospel and faith is important here, because it is the good news of the gospel which is communicated, not the Christian faith as such.

12. Theo Sundermeier, "Begegnung mit dem Fremden. Plädoyer für eine verstehende Missionswissenschaft," in Volker Küster, ed., *Konvivenz und Differenz: Studien zu einer verstehenden Missionswissenschaft* (Erlangen: Verlag der evangelisch-lutherischen Mission, 1995), 81ff.; Theo Sundermeier, *Mission—Geschenk der Freiheit: Bausteine für eine Theologie der Mission* (Frankfurt am Main: Lembeck Verlag, 2005), 38; see also David J. Bosch, *Transforming Mission: Paradigm Shifts in Theology of Mission* (Maryknoll, NY: Orbis, 1991), 375.

on a reciprocal undertaking, evangelizing is a dynamic process and not just an exercise in getting people into church or even making them Christians. Rather, it is expansion and deepening of the sphere of the gospel.[13] Christians "can only witness in humble boldness and bold humility to our understanding of that gospel."[14]

Although this means that role definitions of evangelizer and evangelized are not as clear-cut as was once believed, it does not mean to suspend or refuse any claim of truth for the sake of tolerance or for an open process. There is still a given message to be transmitted, a Christ to be confessed, a gospel to be told. Any truth claim is an invitation to examine that claim in dialogical comprehension.[15] Behind this approach stands the acceptance of the radical perspectivity of any cultural view or reality, but at the same time the desire to retain the possibility of communication between different cultures and worldviews. Thus, "dialogical comprehension" is achieved through a mutual process in listening and speaking.[16] Therefore, the challenge of evangelism is to be part of a symbiotic process, because the truth claim of the gospel demands a dialogical interdependence "to communicate the own position with the medium of the language of the other."[17] The hope or aim combined with this communication of the gospel is new faith, which only God can give.[18]

Sometimes the term *authentic* is added to describe such an understanding of evangelism.[19] "Authentic evangelism is grounded in humility and respect for all, and flourishes in the context of dialogue."[20] With authentic evangelism the church appears as a "church-crossing-frontiers-in-the-form-of-a-servant."[21] For such a "church-crossing-frontiers" individual, believers seem to be of growing importance because "the fate of belief depends much more than before on

13. Henning Wrogemann, "Wer betreibt Inkulturation? Evangelium und Kulturen im Spannungsfeld von Machtkonstellationen, Anerkennung und kritischem Dialog," *Zeitschrift für Mission* 32, no. 3 (2006): 234–52.
14. Bosch, *Transforming Mission*, 420.
15. Christoph Schwöbel, *Gott im Gespräch: Theologische Studien zur Gegenwartsdeutung* (Tübingen: Mohr Siebeck, 2011), 166.
16. Ibid., 7ff.
17. Ibid., 88.
18. Heinrich Balz, *Der Anfang des Glaubens: Theologie der Mission und der jungen Kirchen* (Neuendettelsau: Erlanger Verlag für Mission und Ökumene, 2010), 212.
19. According to Charles Taylor, "authenticity" is the marker of our age. Charles Taylor, *A Secular Age* (Cambridge: Belknap Press/Harvard University Press, 2007), 473ff. However, following Taylor's definition of authenticity, what "authentic evangelism" means is "evangelism with integrity."
20. World Council of Churches, *Together towards Life: Mission and Evangelism in Changing Landscapes* (Geneva: WCC Publications, 2013), 89.
21. David J. Bosch, *Witness to the World: The Christian Mission in Theological Perspective* (Atlanta: John Knox, 1980), 248.

powerful intuitions of individuals radiating out to others."[22] So, in the end, a humble, mutually challenging communication of the gospel requires believers who know themselves as dependent on God and who are without fear of the other.

4.2.3 Evangelism as invitation

To describe evangelism only in terms of "communicating the gospel" or "witness" may lack the emphasis on *invitation* to faith in Christ. As American missiologist Darrell L. Guder writes, "Evangelization is, at its core, communication. It is making the story known. Its intention is not only to tell the good news, but also to invite those who hear to respond and to become part of the witnessing community."[23] The term *invitation* is important for a fuller understanding of evangelism. For some, aiming at a response may be suspect because it is associated with manipulation or with a specific method of invitation, like the altar call in tent meetings. But invitation is an act of freedom, because if the gospel sets people free, evangelism can only be done in a context of freedom. Within such a context the way to invite people is to invite them to freedom.[24] Thus, while "*evangelism does aim at a response*,"[25] everyone may respond to the gospel in a positive, negative, or indifferent way. Any pushing or manipulation contradicts the content of the gospel.

But what, exactly, does this invitation entail? In missiological literature different aspects are mentioned: it is an invitation to repentance, to the gospel, to the kingdom of God, to Jesus Christ, to the church, to the heavenly feast, to abundant life, to the love of God. Regardless of their differences, all these approaches agree that evangelism without invitation is not an option. The Roman Catholic missiologists Stephen Bevans and Roger Schroeder even go so far as to say that "without the practice or intention of introducing others into a relation with God through and in Jesus, the church's missionary activity remains just that—the *church's* activity and not participation in *God's* activity."[26]

---

22. Taylor, *Secular Age*, 531ff. An example for that is John Sentamu, *John Sentamu's Faith Stories: 20 True Stories of Faith Changing Lives Today—Presented by the Archbishop of York, Dr John Sentamu* (London: Darton, Longman and Todd, 2013).

23. Darrell L. Guder, *The Incarnation and the Church's Witness* (Eugene, OR: Wipf & Stock Publishers, 2004), 34.

24. Sundermeier, *Mission*, 20ff.

25. Bosch, *Transforming Mission*, 413.

26. Stephen B. Bevans and Roger P. Schroeder, *Constants in Context: A Theology of Mission for Today* (Maryknoll, NY: Orbis, 2004), 358.

Sometimes the motif of invitation is combined with a claim of urgency. Evangelism is an urgent undertaking and therefore has priority. Others strictly refuse this because they fear that this will become a reason for manipulation and pushing others. Be that as it may, one may consider, with Dietrich Bonhoeffer: "'To-day if ye shall hear his voice, harden not your hearts' (Heb. 4.7). That is evangelical preaching. Is this ruthless speed? Nothing could be more ruthless than to make men think there is still plenty of time to mend their ways. To tell men that the cause is urgent, and that the kingdom of God is at hand is the most charitable and merciful act we can perform, the most joyous news we can bring."[27]

4.2.4 Word and deed in evangelism

Most of today's definitions of evangelism emphasize an integral or holistic understanding of evangelism. Doing so, they try to overcome a sad legacy of keeping word and deed apart,[28] a dichotomy quite often found in modern Western thinking. Evangelism is done "by word and deed, proclamation and presence, explication and example."[29] Likewise, *Together towards Life* states: "Evangelism is sharing the good news both in word and action. . . . if our words are not consistent with our actions, our evangelism is inauthentic. The combination of verbal declaration and visible action bears witness to God's revelation in Jesus Christ and of his purpose."[30] *Together towards Life* goes on to include other aspects to evangelism as well, like "prophetic vocation which involves speaking truth to power."[31]

Other voices, however, stress the verbal character of evangelism, without denying the importance of social action. According to them, evangelism stands "exclusively for an action of verbal communication in which the name of Jesus is central."[32] Evangelism is then "the verbal proclamation of the gospel" as "an activity defined by the intent to witness to Jesus Christ and invite the hearer to believe."[33]

27. Dietrich Bonhoeffer, *The Cost of Discipleship*, rev. ed. (New York: Macmillan, 1963), 233ff.
28. With the term *deed*, social action, healing ministry, political engagement, and caring for justice and the earth can be summed up.
29. Bosch, "Evangelism, Evangelization," 153. See also Pope Francis, *Evangelii Gaudium—The Joy of the Gospel: Apostolic Exhortation on the Proclamation of the Gospel in Today's World* (London: Catholic Truth Society, 2013).
30. WCC, *Together*, 86.
31. Ibid., 91.
32. Lesslie Newbigin, "Cross-currents in Ecumenical and Evangelical Understandings of Mission," *International Bulletin of Missionary Research* 6, no. 4 (October 1982): 149.
33. Michael W. Goheen, *Introducing Christian Mission Today: Scripture, History, and Issues* (Downers Grove, IL: InterVarsity, 2014), 84.

Stating that word and deed somehow belong together is important, but it is not enough. Their relationship must be worked out in order to meet concerns that an evangelism that carries too much weight will become detracted from verbal witness (cf. ch. 8.2.2, below). On the other hand, in evangelistic practice differences between holistic perspectives and "word-alone" perspectives may not be so huge after all. Surely, even those who define evangelism as verbal communication see an indispensable link between evangelistic proclamation and social action.[34] Social or political action are, according to them, not *part* of evangelism but nevertheless closely *linked* to it—distinct, but not separated. "All our mission must therefore reflect the integration of evangelism and committed engagement in the world," which is called "integral mission."[35] David J. Bosch speaks here of a "creative tension" between different dimensions of mission, including the church's social involvement, prophetic ministry, interchurch aid, development, caring responsibility, and evangelism.[36]

4.2.5 Proclamation and social action

The discussion about word and deed in evangelism is connected to another discussion, which has been quite heated in previous decades. This is the debate about the roles of and the relationship between proclamation and social action in Christian mission. Without trying to portray the whole debate, especially between the Lausanne Movement and the World Council of Churches since the 1970s, we briefly describe five models that may be helpful to "map" and understand this discussion.[37]

a. *The diastatic model—evangelism and social action are to be separated.* According to this understanding, any social action may water down the proclamation of the gospel and has to be avoided. Especially in premillennialist traditions this is the case, because the only mission of the church is to save souls from the coming judgment and destruction of the world. Since there is only an eschatological hope, there can be no

---

34. Christopher J. H. Wright, *The Mission of God's People: A Biblical Theology of the Church's Mission* (Grand Rapids: Zondervan, 2010), 28.

35. Lausanne Movement, *Cape Town Commitment*, 20.

36. David J. Bosch, "In Search of a New Evangelical Understanding," in Bruce J. Nicholls, ed., *In Word and Deed: Evangelism and Social Responsibility* (Exeter, UK: Paternoster, 1985), 81ff.

37. I follow here Henning Wrogemann, *Missionstheologien der Gegenwart: Globale Entwicklungen, kontextuelle Profile und ökumenische Herausforderungen* (Gütersloh: Gütersloher Verlagshaus, 2013), 138–41; Erhard Berneburg, *Das Verhältnis von Verkündigung und sozialer Aktion in der evangelikalen Missionstheorie unter besonderer Berücksichtigung der Lausanner Bewegung für Weltevangelisation (1974–1989)* (Wuppertal: R. Brockhaus Verlag, 1997), 107–148.

hope for this world. Doing social action is like oiling the wheels of a car that runs into a ravine.

b. *The preparatorial model—social action makes room for evangelism.* Here social action is a point of contact or a bridge for evangelism. It prepares for evangelism.

c. *The consecutive model—social action as fruit of evangelism.* Here, social action is a result of evangelism, because (new) Christians will start doing good deeds for others. The best way to further social action is to concentrate on verbal evangelism and make as many new Christians as possible.

d. *The complementary model—social action and evangelism as the two foci of mission.* Christian mission has two mandates. Both are distinct from each other, but they are both indispensable parts of mission. Whether evangelism is always a priority here is a matter of debate. This model has been quite strong in the Lausanne Movement.

e. *The model of identification—social action as evangelism.* Here, social action *is* evangelism. Any distinction is refused. This model was quite influential in the postmillennialist social-gospel movement and for the WCC conferences in the 1960s. Salvation and social progress are more or less equated. All eschatology seems only to have an inner-worldly meaning.

Whether we include both word and deed in our understanding of evangelism or whether we emphasize the verbal aspect of evangelism, separating evangelism from social action emaciates the gospel, while equating evangelism with social action dilutes it.[38] The challenge of evangelism may be characterized as follows: "the church and the Christian are to *be* the witness, *do* the witness, and *say* the witness."[39]

4.2.6 Evangelism and discipleship

That evangelism "provokes conversion"[40] seems not to be an issue of great debate. (For a further discussion on evangelism and conversion, see ch. 8.1,

---

38. Bosch, *Witness to the World*, 202, 212.
39. Darrell L. Guder, *Be My Witnesses: The Church's Mission, Message, and Messengers* (Grand Rapids: Eerdmans, 1985), 91.
40. WCC, *Together*, 84.

below.) But what does it mean to be converted? It is remarkable how many traditional theories of evangelism and pastoral care ignored the topic of discipleship, while focussing on church membership or membership care.[41] Even within the Evangelical tradition, somehow the focus was more on counting converts than on nurturing disciples. However, "[b]iblically, the real challenge for the church is to make disciples (i.e., those who are actively and consciously following the way of Jesus), not to make converts (those who take a tentative first step towards Jesus)."[42]

How is evangelism related to discipleship? Does evangelism focus on discipleship—that is, is it a crucial element of "the intentional grounding"? Or is discipleship the second stage after conversion, as a part of subsequent Christian formation? It seems that those referring to conversion as a more sudden experience favour a distinction between evangelism and discipleship,[43] while those who understand conversion as a process are more willing to connect discipleship closely with evangelism. The line between both understandings is difficult to draw, however, because both sides emphasize the importance of discipleship. Both sides would agree that "in short, evangelism is simply the initial formation of genuine disciples of the Lord Jesus Christ."[44] But they differ in their distinct emphasis. In the end, this issue is related to older theological questions about the relationship between grace and law, or justification and sanctification. Interestingly, profound theological debates tend to recur in the context of evangelism.

Although evangelism and discipleship are distinct from each other, they are not separated. Discipleship is not a choice or Christianity 2.0 for church members or converts, but it is a direct consequence of conversion. There is no conversion without discipleship. Receiving the gospel and responding to the grace of God by faith results, therefore, in Christian formation or transformation. Here, Christopher Wright even brings in the notion of good works as a vital part of a Christian life: "The gospel speaks of a salvation that is *by grace* and *unto good works*. Grace comes first and is received by faith. And faith

---

41. Sake Stoppels, *Oefenruimte: Gemeente en parochie als gemeenschap van leerlingen* (Zoetermeer: Boekencentrum, 2013).

42. Richard V. Peace, "Conflicting Understandings of Christian Conversion: A Missiological Challenge," *International Bulletin of Missionary Research* 28, no. 1 (January 2004): 9.

43. Donald McGavran's juxtaposition of discipling and perfecting as two consecutive stages may still have some influence in writings standing in the tradition of the church-growth movement but is not a position held by the Lausanne Movement.

44. William J. Abraham, "A Theology of Evangelism: The Heart of the Matter," in Paul W. Chilcote and Laceye C. Warner, eds., *The Study of Evangelism: Exploring a Missional Practice of the Church* (Grand Rapids: Eerdmans, 2008), 30.

demonstrates its existence through obedience."[45] According to that understanding, evangelism is linked to the invitation to grace, while discipleship is linked to a faithful life as a Christian.

Thus, a distinction between converts and disciples is not possible. The invitation to faith includes the calling "to specific changes, to renounce evidences of the domination of sin in our lives and to accept responsibilities in terms of God's love for our neighbour."[46] Thus, "evangelism aims at conversion which is a call to repent and enter the kingdom; this will mean a turn to God, a commitment to radical and costly obedience, and participation in the community that embodies the kingdom."[47]

All this may raise the impression that discipleship has to do with "ethical transformation" and with the law rather than grace. There seems to be a tendency in recent publications on mission and evangelism to have a specific focus on ethics. But equating discipleship with Christian service for life would limit the scope of discipleship. Neither the Christian faith nor discipleship is based on a list of moral injunctions to be done or to be lived. Discipleship is not just about fixing the world—or about fixing the church, for that matter. Here, it is important to keep in mind that it is not involvement in Christian service which makes people Christians; rather, people are Christians by the grace of God alone. The call to discipleship is an invitation to trust in and to follow Christ. Thus, the notion of discipleship in the gospels was summarized by the apostle Paul as "to believe in Christ." Faith in Christ is the centre or basis of all discipleship. Following that distinction, Christians are called to be disciples of Jesus Christ because the Christian truth "is not just to be 'believed in' as by mere intellectual or mental assent; it is truth to be 'participated in.'"[48]

What does this mean in concrete terms? "To become a disciple is to be incorporated into God's new community through baptism and to side with the poor and the oppressed. To put it differently, it is to love God and our neighbor," David J. Bosch writes in his exposition of Matthew 28:16-20. In making disciples, people should be taught "to observe all that I have commanded

---

45. Ibid., 194.

46. World Council of Churches, *Mission and Evangelism: An Ecumenical Affirmation* (Geneva: WCC Publications, 1982), par. 11.

47. Michael W. Goheen, *"As the Father Has Sent Me, I Am Sending You": J. E. Lesslie Newbigin's Missionary Ecclesiology* (Zoetermeer: Boekencentrum, 2000), 288.

48. Kwame Bediako, *Jesus and the Gospel in Africa: History and Experience* (Maryknoll, NY: Orbis, 2004), 115.

you"—something which Bosch sees specified in the double command of love (Matt. 22:37-38).[49]

Since discipleship can't be just taken for granted, this also raises the question about Christian or spiritual formation. "Spiritual formation is our continuing response to the reality of God's grace shaping us into the likeness of Jesus Christ, through the work of the Holy Spirit, in the community of faith, for the sake of the world." This results, then, in the "active participation in serving God and sharing in God's work in the world,"[50] because God is calling and sending with authority those who trust in God. Writing on so-called fresh expressions of church in the United Kingdom, Michael Moynagh speaks of *maturity* as a goal of formation. "Maturity is movement into God's reign, which is the *telos*, the goal of the church."[51] And *The Cape Town Commitment* of 2010 states: "Biblical mission demands that those who claim Christ's name should be like him, by taking up their cross, denying themselves, and following him in the paths of humility, love, integrity, generosity, and servanthood. To fail in discipleship and disciple-making, is to fail at the most basic level of our mission."[52]

How does formation happen? Apart from instruction and example, *practice* may be the core element. "Discipleship fundamentally entails a set of disciplines, habits, and practices that are undertaken as regular, concrete, daily practices," Walter Brueggemann states, and he points to the four disciplines of the early church, with reference to Acts 2:42. These disciplines "stand exactly between the entry of baptism and the mounting of mission." They are (1) *teaching* (as "instruction into the tradition"); (2) *fellowship* (because "the church is a face-to-face community of people"); (3) *breaking of bread* (as "solidarity in eating"); and (4) *prayer*. To these disciplines Brueggemann adds "the recovery of Sabbath as a day of disengagement from the power of production and consumption" as well as "generosity, compassion, and forgiveness." These latter disciplines are grounded in the former four.[53]

---

49. David J. Bosch, "The Structure of Mission: An Exposition of Matthew 28:16-20," in Chilcote and Warner, eds., *Study of Evangelism*, 82ff. Although there can't be any doubt that the double command of love plays an important role in the teaching of Jesus, one wonders whether the whole gospel of Matthew or at least the teaching segments are meant here.

50. Jeffrey P. Greenman, "Spiritual Formation in Theological Perspective: Classic Issues, Contemporary Challenges," in Jeffrey P. Greenman and George Kalantzis, eds., *Life in the Spirit: Spiritual Formation in Theological Perspective* (Downers Grove, IL: InterVarsity, 2010), 24, 27.

51. Michael Moynagh and Philip Harrold, *Church for Every Context: An Introduction to Theology and Practice* (London: SCM Press, 2012), 330.

52. Lausanne Movement, *Cape Town Commitment*, 48.

53. Walter Brueggemann, "Evangelism and Discipleship: The God Who Calls, the God Who

While Brueggemann speaks of disciplines, Michael Moynagh sees "three implications for Christian formation."[54] First, Christians are present in the world "working distinctively for the welfare of creation" as well as bringing humility and forgiveness to everyday lives. Christians side with the vulnerable and marginalized. Second, discipleship is not an individualistic undertaking, but a communal activity. Christians need community, because "they must be formed by the Christian gathering to which they belong." Third, Christian formation is "connected to the living tradition," which means being part of the wider church, being connected with the worldwide and ecumenical fellowship of churches. "This formation will be a continuing process, undertaken within the gathering-in-life and in the church at large."

It has become clear that discipleship is based on biblical study and eucharistic community having its fruits in bringing the gospel to the world and caring for the needy. In the early church the conduct among the Christians and how they interacted with others was the centre part of their witness. A community of converts is a community of disciples and therefore a community of witnesses. At the same time, it has to be admitted that with a focus on discipleship the masses can't be attracted. It is what Robert Schreiter called an "elitist approach" held in opposition to "popular religion." "It holds up an ideal of Christian commitment and service that invites a deeper realization of the mystery of Christ. Its sense of action presses toward the realization of a genuinely just society."[55] As important as the emphasis on discipleship is, it shouldn't lead to a sectarian approach that makes the church simply a safe haven in a hostile world. This can be the danger of an "elitist approach" without being balanced by a strong missional grounding of the church. Mission, holistic, humble, and passionate mission prevents communities of disciples from becoming arrogant sects. "In its self-understanding Christianity returns to what it originally aspired to be: the leaven in the lump, the salt that has not lost its savour."[56]

Of course, if evangelism and formation for discipleship are so closely linked, this will put evangelism much more into the heart of the church: its preaching, its pastoral care, its instruction, its mutual care, and so on. In other

Sends," in Chilcote and Warner, *Study of Evangelism*, 230ff. According to Bryan Stone, *Evangelism after Christendom*, the marks of the early church were "jubilation, unity, consensus through spiritual discernment, material sharing, inclusive table fellowship, bold proclamation and public defiance of the powers" (106).

54. Moynagh and Harrold, *Church for Every Context*, 345ff.

55. Robert J. Schreiter, *Constructing Local Theologies*, 15th ed. (Maryknoll, NY: Orbis, 2008), 132.

56. David Martin, *On Secularization: Towards a Revised General Theory* (Aldershot, UK: Ashgate, 2005), 119.

words, these developments within the realm of mission and evangelism directly pertain to the church. To this subject we now turn.

4.3 Evangelism and the Church

4.3.1 The rediscovery of mission in the church

For quite a few people, evangelism was or still is a special enterprise of mission-minded Christians standing in the Pietistic or Evangelical tradition; or it is just one element of the churches' work among others, but mostly limited to a niche. This, however, completely changed during the last decades. Thus, Eberhard Jüngel compared mission and evangelism with the "church's beating heart":

> If the church had a beating heart, evangelization and mission would mark the rhythm of its heart and deficits in its missionary activity. Deficiencies would immediately lead to serious irregular heartbeats. . . . Therefore whoever is interested in a healthy circulation of church life must also be interested in mission and evangelization. . . . However, something is not right with the heartbeat of the church if mission and evangelization are not the cause of the whole church.[57]

Here, mission and evangelism are placed at the centre of the church and made into a responsibility of the whole church. The health of the church depends on mission and evangelism. In that sense, the church is a *mission-shaped* or *missional church*. Or, to follow the Second Vatican Council, the church is "missionary by its very nature."[58] Going back in the history of the ecumenical movement, the first study on evangelism done in the 1950s "did not produce a definition nor a method for evangelism. It produced a statement on the church. It was a simple statement: 'The rediscovery of evangelism implies a revolution in the life of the churches'."[59]

---

57. Eberhard Jüngel, "Referat zur Einführung in das Schwerpunktthema; Synode der EKD 1999 in Leipzig," in Kirchenamt der Evanglische Kirche Deutschland, ed., *Reden von Gott in der Welt. Der missionarische Auftrag der Kirche an der Schwelle zum 3. Jahrtausend* (Hannover: EKD, 2001). See also Margaret W. Kohl, "Mission: The Heart of the Church in the New Millennium," *Journal of Asian Mission* 8 (2006): 3–21.
58. Stephen B. Bevans, "Ecclesiology since Vatican II: From a Church with a Mission to a Missionary Church," *Verbum SVD* 46, no. 1 (2005): 27–56.
59. The statement was made by J. C. Hoekendijk as former secretary for evangelism of the World Council of Churches. See Hans Jochen Margull, "Evangelism in Ecumenical Perspectives," *The*

4.3.2 The church as a missional church

Since its first appearance at the end of the 1990s, the term "missional church" has been widely used to understand the church on the basis of the *missio Dei*.[60] The neologism "missional" describes a paradigm shift that is breaking with the traditional understanding of mission as something the church does besides other (often more important) things, and it focusses on mission as the essence of the church. The missional church is a church being sent by God.

> A missional church is a church that is shaped by participating in God's mission, which is to set things right in a broken, sinful world, to redeem it, and to restore it to what God has always intended for the world. Missional churches see themselves not so much sending, as being sent. A missional congregation lets God's mission permeate everything that the congregation does—from worship to witness to training members for discipleship. It bridges the gap between outreach and congregational life, since, in its life together the church is to embody God's mission.[61]

According to this understanding, mission (and evangelism) cannot any longer be just one of the many different duties and services of the church. The church is challenged to rediscover mission or evangelism not as a new duty among others, but as its ecclesiological DNA. Mission "is this living, divine, and human fellowship which actively reaches out, sharing in God's reconciliation of the world and thus with God's own life from all eternity."[62] The worshipping community is the witnessing community, and vice versa.[63] The whole understanding of a missional church is based on the understanding that mission and evangelism are inextricably linked to ecclesiology.

With this understanding, those who advocate a missional church take up what earlier has been called "incarnational mission," and they make it fruitful

---

Ecumenical Review 16, no. 2 (1964): 133. Although the study report failed, the ecclesiological challenge remains.

60. Although the term is older, its usage today can be traced back to Darrell L. Guder, ed., *Missional Church: A Vision for the Sending of the Church in North America* (Grand Rapids: Eerdmans, 1998). See also Martin Reppenhagen, *Auf dem Weg zu einer missionalen Kirche: Die Diskussion um eine "missional church" in den USA* (Neukirchen-Vluyn: Neukirchener Verlag, 2011).

61. Lois Y. Barrett, ed., *Treasure in Clay Jars: Patterns in Missional Faithfulness* (Grand Rapids: Eerdmans, 2004), x.

62. John G. Flett, "*Missio Dei*: A Trinitarian Envisioning of a Non-Trinitarian Theme," *Missiology* 37, no. 1 (2009), 15.

63. Mortimer Arias, "Centripetal Mission, or Evangalization by Hospitality," in Chilcote and Warner, eds., *Study of Evangelism*, 424–35.

for ecclesiology.[64] Especially for Europe or the Western world this understanding of church and mission seeks to overcome what Charles Taylor has called the "excarnation" of faith, that is, "a transfer out of embodied, 'enfleshed' forms of religious life, to those which are more in the head."[65] Missional church advocates' focus on community helps to overcome the danger of modern evangelism becoming merely a religious expression of Western individualism. This type of evangelism can be recognized by its concentration on individual benefits of the gospel (eternal salvation) at the expense of the gospel's mission (to participate in the mission of God).[66] An evangelizing church is a witness of God's reign, which invites people to join the community of the kingdom of God. "Evangelism as aimed at people being brought into the visible community of believers."[67]

4.3.3 Evangelism as essentially ecclesial

As important as the recognition of the missionary nature of the church is the thesis that "mission is essentially ecclesial."[68] To cite Dietrich Bonhoeffer: "The church is God's new will and purpose for humanity."[69] Church and mission are interrelated because without God's mission (*missio Dei*) there is no church and "without church there can be no evangelism or mission."[70] Taking up this understanding, Bryan Stone speaks of an "ecclesial construal of mission."[71] Stone bases this approach on the understanding of salvation as ecclesial, because the shape of salvation "in the world *is* a participation in Christ through worship, shared practices, disciplines, loyalties, and social patterns of his body."[72] As a

64. The term *incarnational* was used to describe mission, e.g., in the documents of the WCC's World Mission Conference in San Antonio and the Lausanne Movement's International Congress on World Evangelization in Manila, both in 1989 and may be traced back to the 1960s when John A. MacKay spoke of an "incarnational principle"; cited in Darrell L. Guder, "Incarnation and the Church's Evangelistic Mission," *International Review of Mission* 83, no. 330 (July 1994): 421ff. For a deeper discussion, see Ross Langmead, *The Word Made Flesh: Towards an Incarnational Missiology* (Dallas: University Press of America, 2004).

65. Taylor, *Secular Age*, 771.

66. Darrell L. Guder, *The Continuing Conversion of the Church* (Grand Rapids: Eerdmans, 2000), 191.

67. Bosch, "Evangelism, Evangelization," 153.

68. Bosch, *Transforming Mission*, 372.

69. Dietrich Bonhoeffer, *Sanctorum Communio: A Theological Study of the Sociology of the Church*, trans. Joachim von Soosten, Reinhard Kraus, and Nancy Lukens, *Dietrich Bonhoeffer Works*, vol. 1, ed. Clifford J. Green (Minneapolis: Fortress Press, 2009), 141.

70. Bosch, *Transforming Mission*, 416.

71. Bryan P. Stone, "The Ecclesiality of Mission in the Context of Empire," in Viggo Mortensen and Andreas Østerlund Nielsen, eds., *Walk Humbly with the Lord: Church and Mission Engaging Plurality* (Grand Rapids: Eerdmans, 2010), 109.

72. Stone, *Evangelism after Christendom*, 15.

consequence of this understanding the church does not just *have* a mission, but *is* mission. "That is why all Christian evangelism is fundamentally rooted in ecclesiology. It can even be said that the church does not really need an evangelistic strategy. The church *is* the evangelistic strategy."[73] The focus here is not on the church as such, but on the local and contextual Christian community. In its specific context the congregation serves as an evangelistic community.[74]

In line with this understanding the Evangelical Lutheran Church of America coined the slogan "After the death of evangelism: The resurrection of an evangelizing church."[75] Evangelism is no longer a programme or part of a church strategy, something the church *does*. Evangelism cannot be equated with specific evangelistic events or campaigns and it cannot be delegated to parachurch societies, but is a responsibility of the whole church.

This, however, shouldn't lead to false oppositions. Even an evangelizing church may need specific events, campaigns, programmes, or even a strategy. The specialized evangelist is not an outdated function. After all, the church has the ministry of the evangelist (Eph. 4:11), and hopefully there will always be many gifted men and women who are active in intentional evangelism. Even an evangelizing church could need the assistance of church organizations ministering on behalf of the church. We may think here of the distinction between "dimension" and "intention" (see ch. 7.1.1, below). An evangelizing church is still in need of locations of evangelistic concentration and persons "who are willing to invest their whole lives to be Christian pioneers outside the frontiers of the churches, wherever in the world it may be,"[76] because without intentional action, the missionary dimension of the church will be lost.[77] Evangelism may deteriorate to an empty phrase without intentional, purposeful dynamics in

---

73. Ibid., 15. See also Lesslie Newbigin, *The Reunion of the Church: A Defence of the South India Scheme* (London: SCM Press, 1948), 10: "a church which is not a mission is not a church."

74. The terms *church*, *congregation*, and *community* have different meanings in different churches. Sometimes they are interchangeable. Usually, the term *church* points to the overall church, while "congregation" means the local church being part of a parochial system. But even that can be different from church to church. Here, the term *congregation* is used to describe the local church, but not necessarily meaning a parish.

75. Richard H. Bliese and Craig van Gelder, eds., *The Evangelizing Church: A Lutheran Contribution* (Minneapolis: Fortress Press, 2005), 113.

76. Hans Raun Iversen, "Incarnation, Congregation and Mission," in Moti Lal Pandit, Helle Meldgaard, and Mike Garde, eds., *Identity in Conflict: Classical Christian Faith and Religio Occulta: Essays in Honour of Prof. Johannes Aagard* (New Delhi: Munshiram Manoharlal Publishers, 1998), 203ff.

77. Lesslie Newbigin, *Die eine Kirche, das eine Evangelium, die eine Welt: Die christliche Mission heute*, 2d ed. (Stuttgart: Evangelischer Missionsverlag, 1961), 40. For the distinction between dimension and intention for the understanding of mission, see also Hans-Werner Gensichen, *Glaube für die Welt: Theologische Aspekte der Mission* (Gütersloh: Gütersloher Verlagshaus, 1971), 80–95.

the church. Taking up Stephen Neill's famous adage about mission, one may say, "If everything is evangelism, nothing is evangelism."[78]

Nevertheless, the church "constitutes both the public invitation and that to which the invitation points."[79] Although the church is not the goal of evangelism, and evangelism first and foremost invites all to the gospel and the kingdom of God, evangelism happens from, with, and for the church, because "what it means 'to believe' in that cross and resurrection requires being made a participant in a community whose existence depends on the miracle of the resurrection."[80] For that reason, the local congregation has been called the "hermeneutic of the gospel"[81] or "a living commentary on the gospel."[82] Good examples of this understanding of ecclesiology are the emphasis on fresh expressions of church in the Church of England and a growing number of other European churches, or the work in small community churches in the Roman Catholic Church.[83]

This focus on the church or the Christian community has its hermeneutical significance, because "the crucial thing is not what happens *in me*, in my consciousness, but what happens *between me and someone else*," as John Zizioulas writes. "The church as the body of Christ points to a mysticism of communion and relationship through which one is so united with the 'other' (God and our fellow man) as to form one indivisible unity through which otherness emerges clearly, and the partners of the relationship are distinct and particular not as individuals but as persons."[84] Knowing God and God's revelation are thus only possible through the venture of a communal existence of faith.[85] This

---

78. "If everything is mission, nothing is mission." See Stephen Neill, *Creative Tension: The Duff Lectures, 1958* (London: Edinburgh House Press, 1959), 81.

79. Stone, *Evangelism after Christendom*, 15.

80. Stanley Hauerwas, "Beyond the Boundaries: The Church Is Mission," in Mortensen and Nielsen, eds., *Walk Humbly with the Lord*, 61.

81. Lesslie Newbigin, *The Gospel in a Pluralist Society* (Grand Rapids: Eerdmans, 1989), 222.

82. Kevin J. Vanhoozer, *The Drama of Doctrine: A Canonical Linguistic Approach to Christian Theology* (Louisville: Westminster John Knox, 2005), 418.

83. Archbishop's Council on Mission and Public Affairs, *Mission-shaped Church: Church Planting and Fresh Expressions of Church in a Changing Context* (London: Church House Publishing, 2004); with quite a few examples from European countries; Ryan K. Bolger, ed., *The Gospel after Christendom: New Voices, New Cultures, New Expressions* (Grand Rapids: Baker Academic, 2012); Christian Hennecke, ed., *Kleine Christliche Gemeinschaften verstehen ein Weg, Kirche mit den Menschen zu sein* (Würzburg: Echter Verlag, 2009).

84. John D. Zizioulas, *Communion and Otherness: Further Studies in Personhood and the Church* (London: T&T Clark, 2006), 306ff.

85. Peter Stuhlmacher, *Biblische Theologie des Neuen Testaments, Band 1: Grundlegung: Von Jesus zu Paulus* (Göttingen: Vandenhoeck & Ruprecht, 1992), 11.

gives the church a central meaning for evangelism. Without church, no evangelism; without evangelism, no church.

Christian worship and evangelism are interlinked—and this not just in terms of gathering and sending. The church's mission and evangelism are based on the eucharist, which "is the primary proclamation of the love Christ showed by his death and resurrection."[86] "Liturgy is mission in prophetic dialogue," as Stephen Bevans and Roger Schroeder describe it. "It needs to be celebrated with deep awareness of the context of the community—its experiences, its cultures, its social location(s), its struggles and its victories. It needs to be celebrated with an 'eye to the borders', recognizing that for one or two or more in the congregation, the liturgical action can be a moment of evangelization (whether they are part of the community already or those 'on the edge')." This understanding of an evangelism-minded liturgy may be described as "inside out" or "church without walls."[87] Thus, evangelism does not start with doing evangelism, but with being a worshipping while context-sensitive community.

This specific focus on the church as "the evangelistic strategy" or as "hermeneutic of the gospel" does not amount to looking for a perfect church. Although it is important to state that "a community of people that lives by God's ways, that has learned to place love, humility, compassion, forgiveness, and honesty right at the centre will make people think,"[88] Christians have to admit that they fail too often in all these things. Until the end of time, the church remains *sub conditione peccati*, under the condition of sin. There is no such thing as a perfect community. Mission and evangelism remain patchwork, always and everywhere, patchwork with regard to God's kingdom.[89] Thus, it is important to remind ourselves that God's kingdom is the foundation and aim of the church, but never its product.[90] The church is neither the kingdom of God nor the gospel that Christians proclaim. With regard to its witness, the church remains a "defective testimony. But it is not therefore ineffectual—quite the contrary."[91]

---

86. See paragraph 58 of "To the Ends of the Earth: A Pastoral Statement on World Mission," drafted by the National Conference of Catholic Bishops in the United States in 1986. Cited in Bevans and Schroeder, *Constants in Context*, 363.

87. Ibid., 364ff. See also Moynagh and Harrold, *Church for Every Context*, 366.

88. Tomlin, *Provocative Church*, 14.

89. Sundermeier, *Mission*, 111.

90. Christoph Schwöbel, *Gott in Beziehung: Studien zur Dogmatik* (Tübingen: Mohr Siebeck, 2002), 190ff.

91. Lesslie Newbigin, *The Light Has Come: An Exposition of the Fourth Gospel* (Grand Rapids: Eerdmans, 1982), 20.

The apostle Paul speaks of a "treasure in clay jars, so that it may be made clear that this extraordinary power belongs to God and does not come from us" (2 Cor. 4:7). Here, he makes a paradigmatic statement for all Christian mission and evangelism. It may be called "the classic definition of mission."[92] Weak and fallible human beings are elected by God to proclaim the good news of God's mercy. This has, of course, a deeper meaning, because it is not the fascinating appearance of human beings or congregations that make the dynamic of the gospel, but God and God's Spirit. This considered, "it may be said without fear of contradiction that the greatest hindrance to evangelism in the world today is the failure of the church to supply evidence in her own life and work of the saving power of God."[93] There remains a tension until the end of times, but within or despite this ambivalence, God's Spirit is acting until Christ comes.

To focus on the ecclesial aspect of evangelism could be identified with a church's self-concern or self-preservation of trying to restore its former power and influence on politics and society in Europe. The solution cannot be a return to the traditional model of a Christendom church and society, which was the model for Europe for around 1,600 years. A marginalized church is called to listen to the gospel and to find its place in society anew. In such a process the understanding of "mission from the margins"[94] is an important aspect that European churches have to learn from churches in other regions of the world, which have been in a minority situation always.[95]

4.3.4 Evangelism for the inside and the outside

Although evangelism has been defined "as the proclamation of salvation in Christ to all who do not believe in him,"[96] this understanding should not be taken as ignoring the mixed nature of the church. Looking at the New Testament's use of *euangelizein* (cf. ch. 1.2.2, above), it is impossible to limit evangelism to just unbelievers. "Paul employs the word-group to cover the whole range of evangelistic and teaching ministry—from the initial proclamation of the gospel to the building up of believers and grounding them firmly in the faith."[97] The church itself is "always being evangelized" (*ecclesia semper*

---

92. Lesslie Newbigin, *Mission in Christ's Way: Bible Studies* (Geneva: WCC Publications, 1987), 24.
93. John Stott, *Favourite Psalms* (London: Angus Hudson, 1988), 68.
94. WCC, *Together*, 36–38.
95. Philip L. Wickeri, "Mission from the Margins: The Missio Dei in the Crisis of World Christianity," *International Review of Mission* 93, no. 369 (April 2004): 182–98.
96. Bosch, "Evangelism, Evangelization," 153.
97. Peter T. O'Brien, *Gospel and Mission in the Writings of Paul: An Exegetical and Theological Analysis* (Grand Rapids: Baker, 1993), 62ff.

evangelizanda).[98] A wider understanding of evangelism has to include church and believers as well. "It is a narrow view of evangelism that confines it to the activity whereby people are brought to faith; the nurture of converts and the establishment of congregations that they comprise are equally important as part of the task."[99]

Therefore, reconsidering evangelism leads to a specific focus on the need for evangelism inside the church. "The church is evangelized by the Holy Spirit again and again in the echoing word of Jesus inviting us to receive the reign of God and to enter it."[100] This happens not in a black-and-white way, as if all belief were in the church and all unbelief outside. The last words of Martin Luther with reference to Jesus' parable of the Pharisee and the tax collector in Luke 18 were: "We are beggars. This is true."[101] Any simple dichotomy between insiders and outsiders needs to be dialectically questioned. Paul Hiebert's distinction between the church as "bounded set" and as "centered set" may help to overcome a static dualism and to focus on a more dynamic understanding of church.[102] "We must make people more important than programmes, give relationships priority over order and cleanliness, and spend more time in prayer than in planning."[103]

While reflecting on the Apostles' Creed and taking up Karl Barth's distinction between a "heathen church" and "heathens outside the church," Eberhard Busch puts it this way:

> In solidarity with the heathens inside the church and with the heathens outside it, we will seek to hear and to understand in entirely new ways the gospel which is announced to all of us. We will encounter those whom we do not yet recognize as our brothers and sisters in such a way that we express our hope that they will become and can be our brothers and sisters. We will be all the more credible witnesses of Jesus Christ for them, the more we take to heart

---

98. Michael Herbst, *Missionarischer Gemeindeaufbau in der Volkskirche*, 5th ed. (Neukirchen-Vluyn: Neukirchener Theologie, 2010), 345; see also Sundermeier, *Mission*, 112ff.

99. I. Howard Marshall, *New Testament Theology:Many Witnesses, One Gospel* (Downers Grove, IL: InterVarsity, 2004), 709.

100. Guder, *Missional Church*, 96.

101. Quite often D. T. Niles is quoted here: "Evangelism is witness. It is one beggar telling another beggar where to get food. The Christian[s] do not offer out of [their] bounty. [They have] no bounty. [They are] simply guests at [their] Master's table and, as evangelists, [they] call others too." Usually only the sentence of the beggar is quoted. The longer passage can be found in Norman E. Thomas, ed., *Readings in World Mission* (London: SPCK, 1995), 158.

102. Paul G. Hiebert, "The Category 'Christian' in the Mission Task," in Hiebert, ed., *Anthropological Reflections on Missiological Issues* (Grand Rapids: Baker, 1994), 107–136.

103. Ibid., 134.

the profound statement of the Jewish theologian Franz Rosenzweig: "Christians should seek primarily not to convert others but to convert themselves, 'the heathen Christians'."[104]

Thus, evangelism is not just bringing those from the outside into the church. The gospel is a message of repentance for *all*, whether they are in the church or not. "The gospel of the kingdom of God is a call to repentance and faith for those on the outside and for those within—and for those in the uncertain middle ground."[105] Following this understanding the church becomes "a converted and thus a converting community."[106]

4.3.5 The church as an evangelistic theatre

John Calvin saw creation as the theatre of God's glory and he called Christian worship "the glorious theatre," in which God comes down to act before the eyes of the world. Thus, the church appears as a theatre, where God's glory can be seen.[107] This is a wonderful thought to reflect upon when we think about the link between church and evangelism.

The American theologian Kevin Vanhoozer combines this understanding of the church with the idea of theatre by Peter Brook, who revolutionized the modern Western understanding of theatre in his book *The Empty Space* (1968). According to Brook's understanding there is no need for buildings or big stages to start a theatre. Every empty space can be named a naked stage. "A man walks across [an] empty space whilst someone else is watching him, and this is all that is needed for an act of theatre to be engaged."[108] The empty space is a location where creative processes are needed and fixed solutions do not fit anymore. This could be an interesting metaphor for a church in a post-Christendom situation losing power and influence—increasingly being marginalized. The church is not about buildings or programmes. The given location for the church is the "empty space." Here the church "plays" the gospel. "The church is the theatre of the gospel, its members the company of performers.

104. Eberhard Busch, *Credo: Das Apostolische Glaubensbekenntnis* (Göttingen: Vandenhoeck & Ruprecht, 2003), 256. Karl Barth made this distinction in his presentation "Theologie und Mission in der Gegenwart" at the Brandenburg Mission Conference of 1932, where he referred to God's mission (*missio*). In the 1950s *missio Dei* became the key term of a new understanding of mission.
105. Harald Hegstad, *The Real Church: An Ecclesiology of the Visible* (Eugene, OR: Pickwick, 2013), 84.
106. Guder, *Continuing Conversion*, 152.
107. Peter Opitz, ed., *Calvin im Kontext der Schweizer Reformation: Historische und theologische Beiträge zur Calvinforschung* (Zürich: Theologischer Verlag Zürich, 2003), 197.
108. Peter Brook, *The Empty Space* (New York: Atheneum, 1968), 9.

. . . The theatre of the gospel requires . . . a *playerhood* of all believers in which every member of the church plays an important role."[109]

According to Brook, theatre is *représentation* and not just *répétition*. In a performance, the script is not just played, but it is made present. Theatre is "presentation" in the original sense of the word. Could it be the challenge of the church to make Christ present in such a way? This takes up Dietrich Bonhoeffer's understanding of "Christ existing as church." In the church, God reveals Godself and is recognized as personal. Thus, God can be found in the church.[110] Phrased in Brook's terminology, we may say that in the church the *représentation* of Christ happens. To be clear, Christ and church are not identical, but the church is a specific form of existence, in which Christ reveals himself or is made present.

Again following Brook, *représentation* is only possible with the help of others. Brook here reverts to the French understanding of going to a theatre: "*j'assiste à une pièce*" ("I assist in a piece"). Theatre becomes an interactive process where the play is not fixed once and for all, but is created time and again by the interaction between players and audience. Again, this can be taken up theologically. "God's conversation can't be locked up between the walls of the church, because from the beginning it has been directed to the whole creation, which has its being from God's word." The church doesn't bring the world a foreign word.[111]

4.4 Conclusion

Interaction between church and world is not only possible, but crucial. Evangelism depends on the willingness and openness of the other to interact. And as the missionary experience throughout history teaches, "the fundamental missionary experience is to live on terms set by others" (cf. ch. 8.2.2, below).[112] There is no one-directional communication, but an encounter with new, even surprising, discoveries on both sides. On the basis of a dialogical communication of the gospel, an interactive relationship is built. Within this interaction

---

109. Vanhoozer, *Drama of Doctrine*, 413ff.
110. Christiane Tietz-Steiding, *Bonhoeffers Kritik an der verkrümmten Vernunft. Beiträge zur historischen Theologie 112* (Tübingen: Mohr Siebeck, 1999), 252ff.
111. Schwöbel, *Gott in Beziehung*, 472.
112. Andrew F. Walls, *The Cross-Cultural Process in Christian History* (Maryknoll, NY: Orbis, 2002), 41.

Christ is present; the gospel speaks to all.[113] Such interaction opens a space for spiritual testing or a fluid belonging that seems to be a characteristic of the late- or postmodern European society. Christine Lienemann-Perrin calls this "temporary informal conversion."[114] The traditional understanding of evangelism first, then conversion, then belonging to a church has to be thoroughly rethought. Maybe it is just the other way around. Here again, a paradigmatic aspect for any communication of the gospel and for evangelism has to be highlighted. "To serve life rather than death, the will to truth must be accompanied by the *will to embrace the other, by the will to community*."[115] This is evangelism in Christ's way.

---

113. Vanhoozer, *Drama of Doctrine*, 414ff.
114. Christine Lienemann-Perrin, "Konversion im interreligiösen Kontext: Eine missionswissenschaftliche Perspektive," *Zeitschrift für Mission* 3 (2004): 223ff.
115. Miroslav Volf, *Exclusion and Embrace: A Theological Exploration of Identity, Otherness, and Reconciliation* (Nashville: Abingdon, 1996), 257.

CHAPTER 5

Gerrit Noort

Theological Perspectives on Evangelism

Introduction

Now that chapter 4 has provided a general overview of the contemporary discourse on evangelism, we will turn our attention to contributions on the specific understanding of evangelism in three confessional families, specifically, the Eastern Orthodox, the Roman Catholic, and the Pentecostal traditions. These contributions should enable the reader to grasp more fully confessional articulations of Christian witness in Europe. A full representation of confessional perspectives is not intended. Sections 5.1 through 5.4 below serve to illustrate the range of theological perspectives on evangelism and articulations that stand out.

In section 5.1 Dimitra Koukoura discusses evangelism in the framework of Eastern Orthodox theology. The section illustrates that the concept of the transformation of the faithful during liturgy, and the transmission of the light of Christ through a liturgical ethos in society, result in a highly spiritual perspective on evangelism. What stands out is that witness is directly rooted in the celebration of divine mystery. It is the "liturgy after the Liturgy" that transforms and leads people into communion with God.

Donna Orsuto's contribution (section 5.2) provides a clear picture of the understanding of new evangelization in Roman Catholic theology. It specifically discusses the understanding of evangelism in the papal exhortation *Evangelii Gaudium*, reflecting on the frequent use of the word *joy* and its implications for the way we share the gospel.

The final two contributions in chapter 5 are written from a Pentecostal perspective. The first, written by Wonsuk Ma (section 5.3), offers a systematic biblical-theological treatise of evangelism. It includes a section on the practice of Pentecostal evangelism, which highlights the spiritual nature of witnessing. The author articulates the work of the Spirit in evangelism and the understanding that evangelism is foremost a demonstration of God's power. Finally, in Kwabena Asamoah-Gyadu's contribution on (Nigerian) reverse evangelism in Ukraine (section 5.4), we find a contribution that is both a case study and a theological reflection on African Pentecostal evangelism. Apart from the insights on Pentecostal reverse evangelism, this contribution raises some theological and practical questions concerning evangelism and unity.

The contributions offered in this chapter (and in part 2 as a whole) are intended to offer a set of theological perspectives that will enable the reader to better evaluate the case studies contained in part 3 of this study.

5.1 Liturgy and Evangelism in Orthodox Theology

Dimitra Koukoura

5.1.1 Introduction

> Then we went on to Greece, and the Greeks led us to the edifices where they worship their God, and we knew not whether we were in heaven or on earth. For on earth there is no such splendour or such beauty, and we are at a loss how to describe it. We know only that God dwells there among men, and their service is fairer than the ceremonies of other nations. For, we cannot forget that beauty. Every man, after tasting something sweet, is afterward unwilling to accept that which is bitter, and therefore we cannot dwell longer here.[1]

In the year 987 the "pagan" Russian prince Vladimir the Great (958–1015) sent out envoys to research and study the religion of neighbouring nations. Having experienced how different peoples worshipped God, the envoys proposed to their leader to embrace not Islam or the Jewish religion, but the Eastern Orthodox Christian tradition. The reason for their choice was the beauty of its divine worship, as experienced in the majestic temple of Hagia Sophia in Constantinople. What they witnessed there and passed on to their ruler was the wonder and the surprise of an indescribable splendour: the uncreated and timeless God enters time and space and communicates with humanity. The envoys saw the reflection of this unimaginable spiritual experience in monuments of culture: the texts of the divine worship, the prayers (language and style), the hymnography (poetry and melody), the architecture and iconography, and the ritual of divine worship.

The Russians were baptized and thereby became Christians. Their choice to embrace the Eastern Orthodox Christian tradition in the end transfigured their entire culture, their thinking, their customs, their laws, and their artistic

---

1. Samuel Hazzard Cross and Olgerd P. Sherbowitz-Wetzor, eds., *The Russian Primary Chronicle: Laurentian Text* (Cambridge: The Mediaeval Academy of America, 1953). See http://www.mgh-bibliothek.de/dokumente/a/a011458.pdf.

creation. In this section I will look at the Orthodox understanding of liturgy (worship) and relate this to its implications for evangelism.

5.1.2 Christian worship
Creation and transformation of worship

Christian worship[2] was created in the Jewish environment, just as Christianity itself. Christ himself taught his disciples to pray (Luke 6:12; 22:30-45; Matt. 5:44; 6:5-8, 41), gave them the model of prayer (Matt. 6:9-13), delivered the mystery during the mystical supper (Matt. 6:26-28; Mark 14:22-24; Luke 22:17-20; 1 Cor. 11:23-25) and ordered them to baptize in the name of the Holy Trinity (Matt. 28:19), while he himself participated in the worship of the Jewish temple and in the prayer of the Hebrew synagogue. After their expulsion from the synagogue, Christians were confined to their own assemblies, fostering the consciousness that they were the new Israel, the heirs of the promises and of the true worship. The Old Testament was the holy book for the readings and preaching. The Psalter was their hymnal. They selectively upheld the feasts as well as many religious customs, which were given Christian content (e.g., Easter [Pasha], Pentecost).

Christian worship transformed the way the Jewish community worshipped, giving it a new theological content. Culturally, it incorporated elements from the Hellenistic context, such as the Hellenistic Greek *Koiné*, the Roman calendar, and the beginning of the calendar year. From the New Testament we can learn about worship of the early Christians in apostolic times (Acts; Eph. 5:24; 1 Tim. 3:16; Phil. 2:5-11; Acts 20:7; 1 Cor. 16:2; Revelation 10). We also learn from *The Didache* of the apostles. This text refers to the teaching of the apostles and also to the divine worship (baptism, agapes, the eucharist, fasting, times and ways of prayer), which from the outset reflected the faith of Christians (*lex orandi* and *lex credendi*).[3] Regarding the period of persecution, we learn through the works of Gentile historians such as Pliny the Younger (98–117) and the works of Christians such as Justin Martyr (*1 Apology*) and Pope Hippolytus of Rome (*Apostolic Tradition*) that there were organized local churches with bishops, elders, and deacons. There are also testimonies of an

---

2. See Ioannis M. Fountoulis, *Leitourgiki I Eisagogi sti Theia Latreia* (Publishing house, according to Dimitra: Ed. Mydonia), chs. 1 and 7, passim.
3. The church is first and foremost a worship community. Worship comes first. Dogmatic teaching and ecclesiastical order flow from it. The rule of prayer (*lex orandi*) has a preferential priority in the life of the Christian church. The rule of faith (*lex credendi*) is based on the devout experience and the vision of the church. George Florovsky, "The Elements of Liturgy," in Constantin G. Patelos, ed., *The Orthodox Church in the Ecumenical Movement* (Geneva: WCC Publications, 1978), 172.

oral worship that was intended, according to the ethos of this trying period, to hide the sacred mysteries of the church from outsiders to the Christian faith (*disciplina arcana*).

The pinnacle of worship

The pinnacle of Christian worship began in the 4th century and peaked during the next three centuries. The Edict of Milan (313) secured religious freedom for Christians, and Christianity was recognized as the official religion of the Roman Empire at the end of the same century. At this time great teachers of the church emerged with excellent secular and religious education,[4] monasticism was developed, and hymnography was cultivated. The great cities of the Empire—Rome, Alexandria, and Antioch—became major operating centres for large liturgical families of undivided Christendom. Many monks were attracted to Palestine and Sinai after the finding of the Holy Cross and the Holy Sepulchre in Jerusalem there. The monastic communities of Palestine and Sinai contributed to the creation of a liturgical centre, which influenced the liturgical practice of local churches by the formation of feasts and rites. Similar activity occurred in Constantinople, the new capital of the Roman Empire (330), where the liturgical traditions of Thrace, Asia Minor, and Antioch were merged together. In this way a liturgical formula was formed that prevailed throughout the Orthodox churches, with the Divine Liturgy of St John Chrysostom being predominant. This text, shorter than others, is a real masterpiece of art and linguistic style and is a fervent witness to the content of the faith. From the capital of the Eastern Roman Empire, it was disseminated to all missionary Orthodox churches that emanated from Constantinople. The ancient liturgical forms remained in use only in the ancient Eastern churches (Armenian, Coptic, Syro-Jacobite). Similarly, the Roman liturgical practice, having processed elements of ancient ritual types of the West, prevailed in the spiritual jurisdiction of the church of Rome and, after the schism (1054), in the Roman Catholic Church. The ancient liturgical forms, such as the Ambrosian, Galician, Mozarabic, the Celtic (United Kingdom), and the Punic, were confined to the cathedrals of the cities where they either developed or disappeared over time.

---

4. Basil the Great from Cappadocia and John Chrysostom from Antioch drafted texts of the Divine Liturgy during the 4th century, which until today are used by the Orthodox world and have been translated into all languages of the people who have accepted the Orthodox tradition.

Timeless God, time of creation and liturgical time

In liturgy, Orthodox churches celebrate that the immortal God became a mortal man in order to save human nature. It is the act of divine economy to which the liturgy testifies and that calls all people to celebrate and to participate in the mystery of salvation.

The concepts of space and time, which are inherent in the theology of incarnation, dominated the philosophical thinking of the first Christian centuries. The theology of incarnation gave rise to heresies as well. Those who incited these heresies knew the teaching of scripture, but they tried to interpret the mystery of the divine economy with human logic. The basic question of the heretics is clear: If Christ is God, how then can he be a man also? And the answer of the church is even clearer: If he is not an immortal God, how can he save the human nature, which he has engaged in his divine nature, from mortality?

The teaching of the Orthodox Church is based on the Bible and the empirical experience of salvation in Christ as recorded in the discourses of the great teachers of the 4th century and onward. It was codified in a clear and simple way by the first two ecumenical councils in Nicaea (325) and Constantinople (381) and the Nicene–Constantinopolitan Creed. That which is indisputable is the distinction between the uncreated, timeless, and placeless triune God and the created creation.[5] God created everything: space, time, the world, and people, which, however, do not come from God's essence. If they did, then they would also be gods, because they would have had neither a beginning nor an end. God is the source of life and creates the world with the divine will and creative energy. God is not a distant God, but is involved in creation: from nonexistence God gave it existence and constantly enriches it with the unspent deity, so as to continue to exist and so that it can participate in the divine glory.[6]

God is revealed in human history through the bodiless Word of the Old Testament (John 12:41; 1 Cor. 10:1), who is incarnated in the New Testament (Matt. 16:16) "by the Holy Spirit and the virgin Mary,"[7] in order to save humans from futility and mortality. Since the very good creation with the first creatures, free will was corrupted to evil and was driven to death (Matt.

---

5. Nikos A. Matsoukas, *Dogmatiki kai Symboliki Theologia* (Thessaloniki: Pournaras Publications, 1999), ch. 1, passim.
6. Jacques Paul Migne, ed., S. *Gregorii Nyssensi: De Vita Moysis—Patrologia Graeca*, vol. 44 (Paris: Vives, 1863), col. 333b.
7. From the Nicene–Constantinopolitan Creed.

9:13; Luke 5:31). Through incarnation, divinity is united with humanity. The timeless and placeless God, with the divine will, enters into time and space for everything to be rewarded by God's presence and by grace to become partakers of God's divine glory. That is the good news that is celebrated and of which all people, by grace, can become partakers.

This faith of the church, this great and inconceivable miracle, is depicted in the worship of the church during the first Christian centuries. Created time, which measures the temporality of people and constitutes a shadow of things to come (Col. 2:16-17), is full of feasts and liturgical services so as to be transfigured into a type of the future. It is to be "flowing": the present world which is changing and corrupted[8] is to be a foretaste of eternity.[9] Every day of the year becomes a feast day. Each day takes on a sacred content and Christians participate in an unending feast. In this way Christians live on earth and become subjects of heaven,[10] while cosmic time records decay and death; the liturgical service thus becomes a foretaste of eternity. In liturgical time the historical events of divine economy are experienced as in the present, here and now.

The kingdom of heaven is experienced in liturgical time,[11] in the present, where the past and the future are experienced. When the church sings, "Today the virgin gives birth to the transcendent One," "today" we experience the eschatological event that happened approximately two millennia ago. The last days (*eschata*) began with the coming of Christ, when he came to save the world through the mystery of the church and will end when he will come again to judge the world, to judge who accepted the message of salvation and who rejected it. Within the church we experience the eschatological perspective as a liturgical present. Liturgy is directly related to the salvation of humanity and, therefore, is inextricably related with the mission and evangelism of the church. Liturgy by its very nature is evangelistic.

In the cycle of feasts of the year, Easter (Pasha) holds a foremost place. In the cycle of weekdays the same is true for the day of the Lord,[12] when so

---

8. Everything is passed and is accompanied with defection from God and from sin, "For the present form of this world is passing away" (1 Cor. 7:31).

9. Eternity is the condition, which does not change, where believers take part by grace in the glory of the risen Christ, in his glorious presence. S. Gregorii Nazianzeni, *Oratio 17—Patrologia Graeca*, vol. 35, col. 969 BC.

10. Anonymi, *Epistola Ad Diognetum—Patrologia Graeca*, vol. 2, col. 1175C: "They busy themselves on earth, but their citizenship is in heaven."

11. Georgiou G. Galiti, "Apokalypsi kai Ekklesia. Eisigíseis sto Theologikó Synédrio tis I. Mitropóleos Ileías," 2006, http://www.apostoliki-diakonia.gr/gr_main/catehism/theologia_zoi/themata.asp?cat=dogma&main=EK_texts&file=6.htm.

12. *Kyriaki* in Greek = "of Kyrios/Lord." "Domenica" in Italian, "domingo" in Spanish, "dimanche"

eminently the Divine Liturgy is celebrated. This is related to the day on which the resurrection[13] of Christ took place, the new day after Saturday. The Lord's day was called the "eighth day" during the early Christian centuries, since Saturday, the sabbath of the Jews, was repealed with its fulfillment and its perfection by the day of the Lord.[14] Sabbath, the seventh period of creation, is God's day of rest from God's work. The apostasy of humanity from the source of life was noted in it, however, resulting in the fall and in death.[15] The new day began at the dawn of the resurrection and knows no end. It is illuminated by the transforming light of the risen Christ, which Christians experience when they participate in the holy mysteries (baptism, holy communion). The eighth day in the worship of the church obtained an eschatological and a transcendent meaning and was theorized to be a symbol of the future judgment of the kingdom of God and of eternity.[16]

The Divine Liturgy

The pre-eminent symbol of the kingdom of God is the holy eucharist, the mystery of the coming of the risen Christ and of the meeting with him, where the Lord gives those who stayed close to his trials the right to eat and drink at his table (Luke 22:29). God deifies the human being, who partakes by grace of the divine gifts. Our mind cannot comprehend this great mystery. But those who have the experience of Christ see him with faith[17] continuously present. That which they live is light, peace, hope, joy, love, life itself, since "He is God not of the dead, but of the living" (Matt. 22:32).

Through a symbolic, iconic, and mystical (sacramental) way, people can become partakers of the whole mystery of the divine economy.[18] Texts, symbols, hymnography, frescos and portable icons, the architecture of the temples, and the ritual acts bring to mind all stages of the earthly life of Christ, from

in French are all derived from the Latin *dies Domini* ("day of the Lord").

13. In Russian the word *Vashkrisenie* (= resurrection) for Sunday refers to this reality.

14. Jean Daniélou, "Le dimanche comme huitième jour de la semaine," *Lex Orandi*, vol. 39 (Paris: Éditions du Cerf, 1956), 72 sq.

15. See S. Maximi Confessoris, *Capita Ducenti—Patrologia Graeca*, vol. 90, col. 1101B.

16. The origin of the name consists a subject of extensive theological research. See Francis H. Colson, *The Week* (Cambridge: Cambridge University Press, 1926), 88; Jean Daniélou, *The Bible and the Liturgy* (Notre Dame, IN: University of Notre Dame Press, 1966), 255ff.; Willy A. Rordorf, *Sunday: The History of the Day of Rest and Worship in the Earliest Centuries of the Christian Church* (London: SCM Press, 1968), 277. In the worship of the church its symbolism has great importance for the experience of the end (*eschata*) in the present.

17. "Oh, taste and see that the Lord is good; happy are those who take refuge in him" (Ps. 34:9).

18. Alkiviadis C. Calivas, *Essays in Theology and Liturgy, vol. 3: Aspects of Orthodox Worship* (Brookline, MA: Holy Cross Orthodox Press, 2003), 23–52, passim.

the incarnation until his second coming. All the events that led to our salvation take place in the present and he becomes our contemporary, to bathe us with the light of his uncreated energies. All of this so as to become, by grace, partakers of his divine nature (2 Pet. 1:4).

Our liturgy transfers us to the threshold of another world, where we cross and we find God, the source of life. It is an experience that does not fit in the mind and is not expressed with words. It is true, however, and imbues the daily life of every believer in his path throughout history. It gives meaning to life and determines a responsible life position opposite the world's problems. It gives inspiration to the struggle for peace and justice and strengthens the hope for life's various impasses.

When we consciously participate in the Divine Liturgy, we live the unconditional love of God who created the world not out of necessity but out of love, who gave all the talents to human beings who, when they distanced themselves from the divine, Godself came to look for in the dark tomb, to retrieve the light of the new creation.[19] The experience of this reality is transformative and leads us to follow his own example: sacrificial love and a silent offer to humanity and to society and respect for the natural environment.

The Divine Liturgy is more than texts and words, motions and gestures, and rubrics. In the Orthodox Church we sing: "As we stand in the temple of your glory, we think we stand in the heavens."[20] It is clear that not only time is transformed, but space also. The holy altar is simultaneously both earthly and heavenly. The worshipping community mystically represents the heavenly forces (who mystically represent the cherubim), offering the holy gifts of the bread and wine to be altered through the invocation (*epiclesis*) of the Holy Spirit into the holy body and holy blood of Christ. Consequently, the faithful supplicate God to deem them "worthy to partake of your heavenly and awesome mysteries from this holy and spiritual table with a clear conscience; for the remission of sins, forgiveness of transgressions, communion of the Holy Spirit, inheritance of the kingdom of heaven, confidence before you, and not in judgment or condemnation."[21] And after the faithful commune they chant: "We have seen the true light; we have received the heavenly Spirit; we have found the true faith, worshipping the undivided Trinity, for the Trinity has saved us."

19. "Prayer of the Anaphora," in *The Divine Liturgy of Our Father among the Saints—John Chrysostom* (Oxford: Oxford University Press, 1995), 31.
20. A hymn of the church which is chanted during the matins of Great Lent.
21. "Prayer before Holy Communion," in *Divine Liturgy*, 38–39.

This light is the priceless treasure. It must be shared and proliferated. And those who spread it, as messengers of the gospel, emerge as worthy workers of the kingdom of God (Matt. 25:15-28). Celebrating the mystery of the gospel is the victory of life over death, over falsehood, hypocrisy, and fraud, so that those who experience it must pass it to every human being, those near and far, to the ends of the earth (Prov. 1:1-8).

When the Orthodox celebrate the resurrection of Christ, late at night, the celebrant takes the light from the sleepless oil lamp that shines on the altar, lights a candle, and then invites all those present to come together in order to take light from the eternal light and glorify the resurrected Christ. Consequently, one transmits light to another, so that everyone holds a lighted candle. The night thus shines as the day by candlelight, symbolizing the light that the myrrh-bearing women saw at the empty tomb of Christ and that Jesus' disciples saw on Mount Tabor with their own eyes. The uncreated and unapproachable light of divinity is partaken and approachable through grace to the "pure in heart" (Matt. 5:8; John 8:12; 12:36), to those who believe in the light and become children of light.

5.1.3 Liturgy after the Liturgy

We now come to the transmission of the celebrated light to those who are "outside" the church. Those who have seen the true light, which redeems human beings from the darkness of death, hatred, injustice, and despair, transmit the miracle that they experienced to others who did not partake in the celebration of the Liturgy. They perform the "liturgy after the Liturgy"[22] in their daily lives. To transform an entire life as a liturgy, to make every workplace an altar and work of the Liturgy, where the soul and the body of every believer will be offered, is "a living sacrifice and pleasing to God."[23]

During the Divine Liturgy the faithful are transformed according to the model of Jesus Christ with the power of the Holy Spirit. Christ became a sacrifice for the world. And the believer who follows in his footsteps must imitate him: to strive constantly to expel the forces of evil, injustice, exploitation, falsehood, disrespect toward human dignity and the natural environment, so that falsehood and fraud are revealed. The works of his disciples are bright and the

---

22. See Archbishop Anastasios (Yannoulatos), *Mission in Christ's Way: An Orthodox Understanding of Mission* (Brookline, MA: Holy Cross Orthodox Press, 2010), 94–98. The archbishop offers here clarification of the well-known phrase, "The liturgy after Liturgy," which he penned in 1975, though subsequently other authors used it and claimed it as their own. See Ion Bria, "The liturgy after Liturgy," *International Review of Mission* 67, no. 265 (1978): 86–90.
23. Archbishop Anastasios, *Mission*, 95.

light of truth must shine in the world to glorify the name of God the Father (Matt. 5:15-16).

The liturgical ethos of Christians is manifested in society with an active interest toward alleviating human pain, an effort which constantly increases and takes on unprecedented dimensions as long as heartlessness and the greed for profit of the powerful of the earth remains uncontrolled. *Diakonia* (Mark 10:45) to the numerous "least of these who are members of my family" (Matt. 25:40) is proof *par excellence* of compliance of people with Jesus. He identifies himself with all sufferers. Certainly, offering love does not mean absence of the prophetic voice or of criticism on the causes that bring about suffering in human societies.

5.1.4 Mission—witness

As it is the aim of liturgy to celebrate the divine mystery and to partake in his grace, so it is the aim of mission to make all people partakers of the glory of God and participators in God's kingdom—so that nobody will be left who has not learned that God manifested Godself and became a human being, died, and rose from the dead, and thus people at the end of times can expect the resurrection of the dead. Likewise, they may also have a foretaste of it here and now through the mystery of the Divine Liturgy as a present event (Acts 1:8). All human history is a revelation of God's glory.[24] This glory exists before the creation of the world (John 17:5), is revealed in the Old Testament (Exod. 3:2, 6; Isaiah 6), and is revealed in the incarnation of Jesus through the mouths of the angels ("Glory to God in the highest . . ."), through his miracles "manifesting his glory" (John 2:11; 11:4). During the transfiguration, the light of the glory of his face was revealed, as a portent of the transfiguration of humanity and the whole of nature. In the high priestly prayer, the view of Christ's glory underlines the ultimate aim of society with Christ: "Father, I desire that those also, whom you have given me, may be with me where I am, to see my glory, which you have given me because you loved me before the foundation of the world" (John 17:24).

The Son was sent by God into the world to manifest the divine glory; the Son sends his apostles and they themselves send their own disciples in order to continue the witness of God's glory throughout the ages: "You belong to Christ, and Christ belongs to God" (1 Cor. 3:22-23).

---

24. Ibid., 54–55, passim.

In an old Slavonic manuscript of the Divine Liturgy, on its first page the calligrapher-copier has reflected the principles of Orthodox witness to the nations with bright colours, symbols, and forms that are moving. It depicts Saints Cyril and Methodius, with halos around their faces, who go forth while people follow behind them. One of the two missionaries and illuminators of the Slavs holds in his hand a candle, and the other holds the Bible, and both are moving forward. The display is eloquent in its silence: the enlightened disciples transmit the light of Christ. The light is transmitted by the preaching of the gospel in the language of the recipients. The call is so that people believe that Christ is the envoy of the Father, the one who reveals God the Father to the people and connects them again with the source of life (John 17:3, 9).

Successive questions of the apostle Paul are still relevant: "But how are they to call on one in whom they have not believed? And how are they to believe in one of whom they have never heard? And how are they to hear without someone to proclaim him?" (Rom. 10:14). In the middle of the 9th century the church of Constantinople, at the request of the ruler of the Slavs in western Moravia, sent the Thessalonian brothers Saint Cyril and Methodius to his country to preach the gospel, to translate it into their language together with the liturgical and canonical books, to develop local clergy, and to convey the experience of the resurrection to the Moravians. Subsequently, the great missionaries and their disciples conveyed the experience of the resurrection to the rest of the Slavic world. During this process of transmitting the gospel to the Moravian Slavs, the missionaries respected the Slavs' cultural traits, which were given new content and thus transformed. In this way evangelism led to the creation of a new culture.

At the end of the late 20th century, the totalitarian regime in Albania collapsed and the most ruthless persecution against Christians, which had drowned almost every trace of their worship and faith, ceased. Those Orthodox who survived torture sought the church of Constantinople to reconstitute their Orthodox Church, which lay in ruins.[25] The envoy, who had been a prominent hierarch missionary on the trail of Christ,[26] arrived in the country at the ruins of one temple and asked everyone to light one candle and chant the hymn of the resurrection in Albanian.[27] He then commenced the preaching of the

---

25. The Ecumenical Patriarchate has this task within the Synodal System of the Orthodox Churches.
26. At that time the envoy was Metropolitan of Androussa Anastasios Yannoulatos, professor of the history of religions and missiology at the University of Athens, missionary in Africa, pioneer of the awaking of mission in the Orthodox world in the 1960s through his theological reflection and paradigm.
27. *Kristi Ungjial* ("Christ is risen . . .").

gospel, the celebration of the Divine Liturgy, and the liturgy after the Liturgy for the reconstruction of the church and the resurrection of hope to the fearful faces of the oppressed Christians. The church, as he noted, does not preach deliverance but offers redemption.[28] The church transmits the joyous news of salvation in Christ to those near and far and invites them to become members of Christ's body, to enter the church through baptism, and to succeed in the faith with sanctified grace that is offered through holy communion.

The message is transmitted by the missionaries, clergy and laity, men and women, younger and elders in age, who go to meet the nations to the ends of the earth or even within the midst of a modern multicultural society, which perhaps once knew something more about Christ but today hardly recognizes him. There are countless people who even today have not heard of Christ. Constantly increasing is the number of those who need to hear about him again. This means that Christian churches in traditional Christian countries, such as those of Europe, have a double imperative debt for the evangelization and re-evangelization of society so that the light of Christ shines, along with his peace and justice. Thus, those who seek the truth in the midst of the moral crisis can face it embodied in the person of Jesus Christ.

The question is, How this can be done? In what way can Christians bear witness to the Light so that all people through them might believe (John 1:7)? They can when they utter a speech of truth, peace, and reconciliation, when they engage in social and educational initiatives, when they alleviate human suffering, or when they respect human dignity. What they do needs to be consistent with what they teach; they need to become servants in the footsteps of Christ. In this way the gospel can transform modern culture, can give it meaning and make it more fair and true.

---

28. Archbishop Anastasios, *In Albania: Cross and Resurrection* (Athens: Livanis Publications, 2011).

5.2 New Paths of Evangelization in Roman Catholic Theology

Donna Orsuto

5.2.1 Introduction

The apostolic exhortation *Evangelii Gaudium* ("The Joy of the Gospel"), published on 24 November 2013, provides an excellent point of departure for grasping the current theological understanding of evangelization in the Roman Catholic Church. This recent document has been dubbed the Magna Carta of both evangelization and of church reform for today. In order to appreciate the full impact of the new paths of evangelization in Roman Catholic theology suggested here, the first part of this section will offer a brief historical overview of how evangelization has been understood in recent years. I will then, in the second part, provide a brief theological overview of how these new paths of evangelization are presented in *Evangelii Gaudium*.

5.2.2 New paths of evangelization: A historical overview

From the day of Pentecost and throughout history, communicating the good news of Jesus Christ, witnessing to the gospel, or evangelization has been an integral part of the Christian message.[1] At the same time, because of various colossal changes in the world that have taken place in recent years, Roman Catholic Church leaders have come to recognize that new and creative ways of communicating the gospel are necessary.[2]

The first and most incisive insights after the Second Vatican Council into new pathways of evangelization came from Pope Paul VI in *Evangelii*

1. In Roman Catholic theology, evangelization is best understood in the context of a theology of mission. For more on this topic, see the following books: Stephen B. Bevans and Roger P. Schroeder, *Constants in Context: A Theology of Mission for Today* (Maryknoll, NY: Orbis, 2009); idem, *Prophetic Dialogue: Reflections on Christian Mission Today* (Maryknoll, NY: Orbis, 2011). Also useful is Stephen B. Bevans, ed., *A Century of Catholic Mission: Roman Catholic Missiology 1910 to the Present* (Oxford: Regnum Books International, 2013).

2. The Pontifical Council for Promoting the New Evangelization has published a helpful tool that provides key texts related to evangelization from 1939 to 2012: Pontificio Consiglio Per la Promozione Della Nuova Evangelizzazione, *Enchiridion Della Nuova Evangelizzazione: Testi del Magistero pontificio e conciliare 1939–2012* (Vatican City: Libreria Editrice Vaticana, 2012).

Nuntiandi.[3] Described by Pope Francis as "the greatest pastoral document that has ever been written to this day," this apostolic exhortation from 1975, which has "lost nothing of its timeliness," is quoted 13 times in *Evangelii Gaudium*. Even today, it is an inspiring and practical handbook for evangelization.[4]

Evangelization, according to Paul VI, should not be understood in a "partial or fragmentary" way[5] and refers broadly to the mission of the church in its totality. Specifically, it means "to bring the good news into all areas of humanity, and through its impact, to transform that humanity from within, making it new."[6] This broad and multifaceted understanding of evangelization (cf. ch. 1.4.2, above) also includes both a proclamation of Jesus as Lord,[7] and an explicit witness to Christ by both the individual and the community.[8] In an insightful and often quoted remark, Paul VI says that people today listen more to witnesses than to teachers, and if they do listen to teachers, it is only because they witness to the gospel by their lives.[9] Ultimately, the church's "deepest identity" is linked with evangelization[10] and an integral part of its mission is to evangelize cultures. Specifically, Paul VI notes that "[t]he split between the gospel and culture is without a doubt the drama of our time, just as it was of other times. Therefore every effort must be made to ensure a full evangelization of culture, or more correctly of cultures. They have to be regenerated by an encounter with the gospel. But this encounter will not take place if the gospel is not proclaimed."[11]

Another pivotal moment for Roman Catholic theological reflection on evangelization occurred on 7 December 1990, when Pope John Paul II released the encyclical letter *Redemptoris Missio: On the Permanent Validity of the Church's Missionary Mandate*.[12] The date had a particular significance: it marked the 25th anniversary of the Second Vatican Council's Decree *Ad Gentes*, which

---

3. Pope Paul VI, "Apostolic Exhortation: *Evangelii Nuntiandi*," 8 December 1975, *Acta Apostolicae Sedis* 68 (1976): 5–79. See also James H. Kroeger, "Exploring the Rich Treasures of Pope Paul VI's Evangelii Nuntiandi," *SEDOS Bulletin* 46, no. 5 (November 2014): 227–34.
4. Cf. Kroeger, "Exploring," 227, for more detail. The document *Evangelii Nuntiandi* also had its critics. For an overview of critical comments, see Avery Dulles, *Evangelization for the Third Millennium* (Mahwah, NJ: Paulist, 2009), 18–22.
5. Pope Paul VI, *Evangelii Nuntiandi*, par. 17.
6. Ibid., par. 18.
7. Ibid., par. 22.
8. Ibid., par. 21.
9. Ibid., par. 41.
10. Ibid., par. 14.
11. Ibid., par. 20.
12. Pope John Paul II, "Encyclical Letter: *Redemptoris Missio*," 7 December 1990, *Acta Apostolicae Sedis* 83 (1991): 240–49.

already had evangelization as its theme.[13] In that encyclical letter, John Paul II referred to the "New Evangelization" 16 times.[14]

Although not used explicitly, the concept of a "New Evangelization" was already hinted at by Paul VI 15 years earlier in *Evangelii Nuntiandi* when he wrote about "a new period of evangelization."[15] In a perceptive article written in 1991, the Jesuit theologian Avery Dulles comments:

> In my judgment the evangelical turn in the theological vision of Pope Paul VI and John Paul II is one of the most surprising and important developments in the Catholic Church since Vatican II. This development . . . did not take place without a degree of preparation in Vatican II and pre-conciliar kerygmatic theology. But Paul VI went beyond the Council in identifying evangelization with the total mission of the church. John Paul II, with his unique familiarity with world Catholicism, assigned the highest priority to evangelization in the mission of the church.[16]

Following the path of his predecessors, Pope Benedict XVI took two practical steps to place evangelization yet again at the top of the church's agenda. First, on 21 September 2010, he established the Pontifical Council for Promoting the New Evangelization, a Vatican Curia department (dicastery), with a mandate to encourage "reflection on topics of the new evangelization, and by identifying and promoting suitable ways and means to accomplish it."[17]

13. See Stephen B. Bevans, "Mission at the Second Vatican Council: 1962–1965," in Bevans, *Century*, where he says, "When one thinks of how the Council treated the church's mission . . . ,one naturally looks to its 'Decree on Missionary Activity', entitled *Ad Gentes*. . . . This would be correct, of course, but it is also important to note that "mission" or "evangelization" is really at the heart of everything that the Council was about . . ." (101). See also Stephen B. Bevans and Jeffrey Gros, *Evangelization and Religious Freedom: Ad Gentes, Dignitatis Humanae* (New York: Paulist, 2009).
14. Pope John Paul II, "Encyclical," 2–3, 30, 33–34 (2 times), 37 (3 times), 59, 63, 72–73, 83, 85–86.
15. Pope Paul VI, *Evangelii Nuntiandi*, par. 2.
16. Avery Dulles, "John Paul II and the New Evangelization: December 4–5, 1991," in Dulles, *Church and Society: The Laurence J. McGinley Lectures, 1988–2007* (New York: Fordham University Press, 2008), 96. As Dulles notes in Dulles, *Evangelization*, 3: "Vatican II did in fact make evangelization one of its central themes, but this shift was scarcely noticed by the early commentators, most of whom interpreted the work of the Council in traditional Catholic categories." Already during the Second Vatican Council, the term "to evangelize" was used 18 times and the term "evangelization" 31 times. See Rino Fisichella, *The New Evangelization: Responding to the Challenge of Indifference* (Herefordshire, UK: Gracewing, 2012), 18.
17. See Pope Benedict XVI, "Apostolic Letter in the form of a *Motu Proprio Ubicumque Et Semper* of the Supreme Pontiff Benedict XVI establishing The Pontifical Council For Promoting The New Evangelization," 2010, http://www.vatican.va/holy_father/benedict_xvi/apost_letters/documents/hf_ben-xvi_apl_20100921_ubicumque-et-semper_en.html. See also Fisichella, *New Evangelization*, esp. ch. 1.

Second, he called a synod of bishops that met from 7 to 28 October 2012 to discuss the theme "*Nova evangelizatio ad christianam fidem tradendam*—The New Evangelization for the Transmission of the Christian Faith."[18] He presided over the synod, but resigned as pope on 28 February 2013 before a postsynodal document was produced. His successor, Pope Francis, had the responsibility of drafting and issuing the apostolic exhortation *Evangelii Gaudium* on 24 November 2013. Although Pope Francis focussed on the theme of the synod, he chose not to title it as a "postsynodal" apostolic exhortation. The result is that, though he followed the theme of the synod, he exercised a certain freedom in how he incorporated the propositions suggested by the synod participants into the final document.[19]

In these three pontificates, there is a clear theological continuity with regard to the necessity of finding new ways of evangelization, but at the same time there has been a slight shift in emphasis between Francis and his immediate predecessors, John Paul II and Benedict XVI. All three agree that there is an urgent need to find a new way of evangelization today. One only needs to consider the vast social changes that have happened in the last 50 years—economic crises, scientific and technological developments, and civic and political upheavals—to realize the challenge facing the church in this mission of evangelization.

John Paul II saw these vast changes and, indeed, lived through them personally. It is significant that he mentioned the phrase "New Evangelization" for the first time at the Shrine of Morila in Nova Huta (Poland), a place of deep personal significance for him. Already as Archbishop of Cracow in 1973, he had celebrated Christmas Mass at midnight in an open field with thousands of faithful, despite the resistance of civil and military authorities. When he returned to this shrine as pope in 1979, he said:

> Where the cross is raised, there is raised the sign that that place has now been reached by the good news of man's salvation through love. . . . The new wooden cross was raised not far from here at the very time we were celebrating the Millennium. With it we were given a sign that on the threshold of the new millennium, in these new times, these new conditions of life, the gospel

---

18. See Synod of Bishops, *The New Evangelization for the Transmission of the Christian Faith. Instrumentum Laboris* (Vatican City: Libreria Editrice Vaticana, 2011).
19. Humberto Miguel Yañez, "Tracce di Lettura dell'Evangelii Gaudium," in Yañez, ed., *Evangelii gaudium: il testo ci interroga. Chiavi di lettura, testimonianze e prospettive* (Roma: Gregorian & Biblical Press, 2014), 9.

is again being proclaimed. A new evangelization has begun, as if it were a new proclamation, even if in reality it is the same as ever. The cross stands aloft above the world as it turns on its axis.[20]

During his 27-year pontificate, this was a recurring theme. He was convinced that "the moment has come to commit all of the church's energies to a New Evangelization and to the mission *ad gentes*."[21] He used the expression the "New Evangelization" multiple times over the years. A major question, as raised by Rino Fisichella, the president and archbishop responsible for the Pontifical Council for the Promotion of the New Evangelization, is this: Was John Paul II referring to a "new evangelization" or to "re-evangelization"?

In order to answer this question, we have to take two things into account. On the one hand, John Paul II remarked, at a celebration in Haiti to mark the 500th anniversary of evangelization in Latin America (1983), "The commemoration of the half-millennium of evangelization will have its full significance if there is a commitment on your part as bishops, together with your presbyterate and with your lay faithful, a commitment not to re-evangelization, but to a new evangelization. It will be new in its ardour, new in its methods and new in its expressions."[22] Clearly, in this passage, John Paul II recognizes that in a changed social context, the past methods of communicating the gospel need to be renewed. In this speech delivered in Haiti, it seems that the pope is proposing not a re-evangelization, but a new evangelization.

On the other hand, in the document of greater theological weight already cited, the 1990 encyclical *Redemptoris Missio*, John Paul II distinguishes between three diverse situations that call for evangelization. First is the proclamation of the gospel to those who have not yet heard it, which is considered

---

20. See Pope John Paul II, "Homily at the Sanctuary of the Holy Cross, Mogila, Poland, 9 June 1979," in *L'Osservatore Romano, Weekly Edition in English* (16 July 1979), 11; and *Acta Apostolicae Sedis* 71 (1979): 865. Even before this time, the Latin American bishops had used the phrase at their Puebla Conference: "New situations, which arise from sociocultural changes and call for a new evangelization: emigrants to foreign countries: human urban conglomerations in our countries; the masses in every social stratum whose faith-situation is precarious; and those most exposed to the influence of sects and ideologies that do not respect their identity and that provoke confusion and divisiveness." El Consejo Episcopal Latinoamericano, "Final Document of the Third General Conference of the Latin American Episcopate (Puebla de Los Angeles, Mexico, 27 January–13 February 1979)," in John Eagleson and Philip Sharper, eds., *Puebla and Beyond: Documentation and Commentary* (Maryknoll, NY: Orbis, 1979), 174.
21. Pope John Paul II, "*Redemptoris Missio*," par. 13.
22. Pope John Paul II, "Discourse to the XIX Assembly of CELAM (9 March 1983)," in *L'Osservatore Romano, Weekly English Edition* (18 April 1983), 9; and *Acta Apostolicae Sedis* 75 (1983): 778.

the mission "*ad gentes* properly speaking." The second group includes those Christian communities "which have adequate and solid ecclesial structures" who are invited to what is sometimes referred to as a continual evangelization. The third group is "in countries of ancient Christian tradition, but at times also in younger churches, where entire groups of the baptized have lost the living sense of the faith or even no longer recognize themselves as members of the church, leading to an existence which is far from Christ and from his gospel. In this case there is a need for a 'new evangelization' or a 're-evangelization'."[23] The challenge for this third group is to rekindle the faith in those who have fallen away.[24]

The neologism "re-evangelization," according to Fisichella, has a wide variety of meanings that leaves it open to numerous interpretations. For this reason, he suggests that it is best to speak of "the new evangelization as the form by means of which one and the same gospel from the beginning is proclaimed with new enthusiasm, in a new language which is comprehensible in a different cultural situation and with new methodologies which are capable of transmitting its deepest sense, that sense which remains immutable."[25]

The phrase "New Evangelization" also occurs in Pope Francis's apostolic exhortation *Evangelii Gaudium,* but only a total of 12 times, including both the body of the text and footnotes. As Stephen Bevans perceptively notes, "Pope Francis's document, while acknowledging the New Evangelization, seems to broaden its perspective in such a way that its understanding of evangelization is perhaps better expressed by the concept of 'missionary discipleship'. . . . Other terms, such as 'new chapter,' 'new phase,' 'new paths' and 'new processes' of evangelization are used to describe how the church must proclaim the gospel today."[26]

5.2.3 New paths of evangelization in Evangelii Gaudium: A theological overview

"The Joy of the Gospel" (the English title of the apostolic exhortation *Evangelii Gaudium*) is a challenging document that deserves much careful study and meditation. In this section, only three of its multifaceted themes will be highlighted. First, what is the joy of the gospel? Second, who is called to share

23. Pope John Paul II, "Encyclical," 33. See Fisichella, *New Evangelization,* 21–23.
24. Dulles, *Evangelization,* 68.
25. Fisichella, *New Evangelization,* 23.
26. Stephen B. Bevans, "The Apostolic Exhortation *Evangelii Gaudium* on the Proclamation of the Gospel in Today's World: Implications and Prospects," *International Review of Mission* 103, no. 2 (November 2014): 297–308.

the good news with others? And finally, how is the joy of the gospel to be communicated?[27]

What is the joy of the gospel?

Evangelii Gaudium begins with an invitation to share the good news of Jesus Christ with others. Using the word *joy* 59 times, Pope Francis suggests that the joyful living of the gospel is the heart of evangelization in general, and any new paths of evangelization in particular. In order to be credible witnesses of Christ in today's world, the starting point is a personal encounter with the person of Jesus Christ. Pope Francis boldly invites "all Christians everywhere, at this moment, to a renewed personal encounter with Jesus Christ." No one is excluded, he says, "from the joy brought by the Lord." Furthermore, "the Lord does not disappoint those who take the risk: whenever we take a step towards Jesus, we come to realize that he is already there, waiting with open arms." With disarming simplicity and immediacy, he invites Christians right now to say: "Lord, I have let myself be deceived; in a thousand ways, I have shunned your love, yet here I am once more to renew my covenant with you."[28]

Authentic communication of gospel joy is born out of a personal encounter with Jesus Christ. Pope Francis is not referring to some abstract concept, but to a person who is the centre of history. On the one hand, it is the same Jesus we proclaim, "yesterday, today and forever." On the other hand, his invitation is to be creative in presenting the gospel today. Above all, this "new chapter" of evangelization begins with one's own personal encounter and communion with Christ. The desire to share the good news with others thus arises out of a personal experience or encounter. Quoting Pope Benedict, Francis says, "Being a Christian is not the result of an ethical choice or a lofty idea, but the encounter with an event, a person, which gives life a new horizon and a decisive direction."[29] This is what brings joy and this is the heart of evangelization. As the English poet William Wordsworth once remarked, "what we have loved, others will love, and we will teach them how."[30]

---

27. Cf. the extensive discussion of the apostolic exhortation by Catholic scholars in "*Evangelii Gaudium* and Ecumenism," *International Review of Mission* 104, no. 2 (November 2015); 155–92.

28. Pope Francis, *Evangelii Gaudium—The Joy of the Gospel: Apostolic Exhortation on the Proclamation of the Gospel in Today's World* (London: Catholic Truth Society, 2013), 7–8 (par. 3).

29. Ibid., 9–10 (par. 7).

30. Ernest de Selincourt, ed., *Wordsworth: The Prelude or Growth of a Poet's Mind* (Oxford: Clarendon Press, 1926), 496. See Michael J. Himes, "Communicating the Faith," in Robert P. Imbelli, ed., *Handing on the Faith: The Church's Mission and Challenge* (New York: Crossroad, 2006), 129.

Who is called to share the good news with others?

The task of evangelization is given to the whole people of God. It would be a mistake to think that the new paths of evangelization are the responsibility merely of the pope and bishops, of religious and priests, or of certain lay ecclesial movements in the church. Pope Francis presents it as the responsibility of every baptized Christian.

> In virtue of their baptism, all the members of the people of God have become missionary disciples (cf. Matt. 28:19). All the baptized whatever their position in the church or their level of instruction in the faith, are agents of evangelization, and it would be insufficient to envisage a plan of evangelization to be carried out by professionals while the rest of the faithful would simply be passive recipients. The new evangelization calls for personal involvement on the part of each of the baptized. Every Christian is challenged, here and now, to be actively engaged in evangelization; indeed, anyone who has truly experienced God's saving love does not need much time or lengthy training to go out and proclaim that love. Every Christian is a missionary to the extent that he or she has encountered the love of God in Christ Jesus . . . we are . . . 'missionary disciples'.[31]

This places a particular accent on the role of the laity in the mission of the church. Perhaps in the past Catholic laity have tended to be more passive with regards to evangelization. For example, a survey was done some years ago in the United States asking whether spreading the faith was a priority in their parishes. The results (according to Avery Dulles in his reading of Nancy Ammerman's 2005 book *Pillars of Faith*) are eye-opening: "75 percent of conservative Protestant congregations and 57 percent of African-American congregations responded affirmatively, whereas only 6 percent of Catholic parishes did the same. Asked whether they sponsored local evangelistic activities . . . only 3 percent of Catholic parishes responded positively."[32] It is obvious that laypeople need to be more involved in evangelization. The challenge is to find creative ways to help them realize that this is an integral part of their Christian vocation.

---

31. Pope Francis, *Evangelii Gaudium*, 63 (par. 120).
32. Avery Dulles, "Foreword," in Timothy E. Byerley, *The Great Commission: Models of Evangelization in American Catholicism* (Mahwah, NJ: Paulist, 2008), ix.

How is joy of the gospel to be communicated?

Pope Francis's understanding of evangelization touches not only individual members of the church as part of the people of God, but also the very essence of the church's *being*. He writes, "I dream of a 'missionary option', that is, a missionary impulse capable of transforming everything, so that the church's customs, ways of doing things, times and schedules, language and structures can be suitably channeled for the evangelization of today's world rather than for her self-preservation."[33]

Evangelization today requires, first of all, a greater openness to others. It means literally being accessible to others, having an "open door" ready to welcome all. Pope Francis goes so far as to say that Christians should think about leaving church buildings open, so that a seeker would never face a closed door.[34] This openness reflects a church that is like "a mother with an open heart"[35] and the church as a place "of mercy freely given, where everyone can feel welcomed, loved, forgiven and encouraged to live the good life of the gospel."[36] Tenderness, mercy, and love are key words to be used in this communication of gospel joy.

Evangelization also requires the baptized to "go forth from their own comfort zone in order to reach all of the 'peripheries' in need of the light of the gospel."[37] Specifically, this involves both being evangelized by the poor and evangelizing the poor, who are "the privileged recipients of the gospel."[38] To be evangelized by the poor is to discover Jesus in them, to listen to them, to become their friends, to understand not only their suffering but also the wisdom they have to teach us. It also means to "lend our voice to their causes."[39] Ultimately, Francis is convinced that this will lead to "a church which is poor and for the poor."[40] To evangelize the poor is to take seriously the social dimension of the gospel that includes not only the inclusion of the poor in society[41] but also working for the common good and peace in society.[42]

---

33. Pope Francis, *Evangelii Gaudium*, 19–20 (par. 27).
34. Ibid., 28–29 (par. 47).
35. Ibid., 28 (par. 46).
36. Ibid., 59–60 (par. 114).
37. Ibid., 16 (par. 20).
38. Ibid., 29 (par. 48).
39. Ibid., 99–100 (par. 198).
40. Ibid.
41. Ibid., 94–107 (par. 186–216).
42. Ibid., 107–114 (par. 217–237).

The new paths of evangelization also include creating a "peaceful and multifaceted culture of encounter."[43] It embraces specifically an invitation to enter into dialogue with others. This includes dialogue with states, with society, with other Christians, and with people of other religions. With regard to states and society, while promoting in a clear way "the fundamental values of human life and the convictions which can then find expression in political activity,"[44] the church does not presume to have all the answers.[45] This dialogue with society also involves dialogue with cultures and sciences.[46]

The emphasis on ecumenical dialogue is crucial because the fact is that the lack of Christian unity is an impediment to the sharing of the gospel with others. Specifically, Francis says that "[t]he credibility of the Christian message would be much greater if Christians could overcome their divisions. . . . We must never forget that we are pilgrims journeying alongside one another. This means that we must have sincere trust in our fellow pilgrims, putting aside all suspicion or mistrust, and turn our gaze to what we are seeking: the radiant peace of God's face."[47] Christians can no longer be "indifferent" or complacent about our lack of Christian unity. Efforts to restore unity are not merely "a matter of mere diplomacy or forced compliance, but an indispensible path to evangelization."[48] Without Christian unity, Christians cannot offer a credible witness of the gospel.

Finally, following a long tradition of postconciliar teaching, Pope Francis asserts that "evangelization and interreligious dialogue, far from being opposed, mutually support and nourish one another."[49] While remaining "steadfast in one's deepest convictions" and "clear and joyful in one's own identity," Christians are invited to be open to understanding others, while recognizing that "dialogue can enrich each side."[50] Here, evangelization is used in its broader sense of being synonymous with the mission and life of the church. Interreligious dialogue is presented as an integral part of that mission.[51]

---

43. Ibid., 107–108 (par. 220).
44. Ibid., 115 (par. 241).
45. Bevans, "Apostolic Exhortation," 307.
46. See Bevans, "Apostolic Exhortation," where he briefly develops these two themes. See also Pope Francis, *Evangelii Gaudium*, 116 (par. 243).
47. Ibid., 116 (par. 244).
48. Ibid., 117 (par. 246).
49. Ibid., 119 (par. 251).
50. Ibid.
51. This is a very subtle point that could be easily misinterpreted. Interreligious dialogue is not seen here as a tool of evangelization. Some helpful distinctions can be found in "Dialogue and Proclamation, Reflections and Orientations on Interreligious Dialogue and the Proclamation of Jesus Christ"

5.2.4 Conclusion

In conclusion, two key theological points emerge from this brief survey of postconciliar teaching and focus on Francis's *Evangelii Gaudium*. First, the new paths of evangelization should be understood in the broader context of the mission of the church: it is multifaceted and integral, focussing on how the good news can influence every strata of society. Although it includes an explicit proclamation of the gospel, it is also much more. Second, the new paths of evangelization imply a joyful message of mercy, tenderness, and love that is experienced by and reflected in the lives of those who share the good news. It is a message rooted in solidarity with the poor, marked by great openness to others, and inclusive of dialogue. The paths of evangelization, indeed, are about "a joy ever new, a joy which is shared,"[52] a responsibility of all the baptized, who are called to be "missionary disciples."[53]

(cf. 8–10), the 1991 document co-published by the Congregation for the Evangelization of Peoples and the Pontifical Council for Interreligious Dialogue, cf. http://www.vatican.va/roman_curia/pontifical_councils/interelg/documents/rc_pc_interelg_doc_19051991_dialogue-and-proclamatio_en.html. This builds on an earlier document published in 1984 by the Secretariat for Non-Christians (renamed the Pontifical Council for Interreligious Dialogue in 1988) entitled "The Attitude of the Church towards the Followers of Other Religions: Reflections and Orientations on Dialogue and Mission," http://www.cimer.org.au/documents/DialogueandMission1984.pdf. James Kroeger, in his article "Exploring the Rich Treasures of Pope Paul VI's *Evangelii Nuntiandi*," notes that "these two sources have considerably clarified the Catholic understanding of missionary evangelization, because the 'principle elements' are specifically named. Thus, mission and evangelization are composed of: (a) presence and witness; (b) commitment to social development and human liberation; (c) interreligious dialogue; (d) proclamation and catechesis; and, (e) liturgical life, prayer and contemplation (cf. DM 13 and DP 2). In a word, the one evangelizing mission of the Church is composed of several component elements and authentic forms. Succinctly, this is integral or holistic evangelization—the wide view of evangelization promoted by Paul VI in 'Apostolic Exhortation: *Evangelii Nuntiandi*'" (cf. Kroeger, "Exploring," 232).

52. Pope Francis, *Evangelii Gaudium*, 7 (par. 2).
53. Ibid., 63 (par. 120).

5.3 A Pentecostal Perspective on Evangelism

Wonsuk Ma

5.3.1 Introduction

Evangelism can be defined and described in various ways. According to *Together towards Life*, the World Council of Churches' mission affirmation (2013), evangelism is an "explicit and intentional articulation of the gospel," including "the invitation to personal conversion to a new life in Christ and to discipleship."[1]

Helpful illustrations of evangelism are found throughout the Bible. For example, 2 Kings 7:3-20 offers a story of four lepers outside of Samaria. The people are starving, as an Aramean army surrounds the city. These four men, who are not permitted to enter the city gate, are also starving. In their desperation, they decide to surrender to the enemy. But when they approach the enemy camp, to their surprise it has been completely deserted, with abundant supplies left behind. They experience unexpected deliverance from starvation and expected death. When they finally return to their senses, one says, "What we are doing is wrong. This is a day of good news; if we are silent and wait until the morning light, we will be found guilty; therefore, let us go and tell the king's household." Thus, they walk to the city gate and tell this good news to the starving people in the city (2 Kgs. 7:9-10).

"Good news" and "gospel" are English translations of one Greek word, *euangelion*. The verb form *euangelio* means "to bring or to proclaim good news" (see ch. 1.2.2, above). Its Old Testament counterpart was used many times, including secular usage, such as for news of victory in war (e.g., Is. 52:7). More importantly, God's plan to restore God's people (and ultimately the whole creation) to Godself is as old as human history.

In this brief discussion, several key words and concepts emerge in relation to evangelism. This section is intended to explore a biblical teaching of evangelism from a Pentecostal perspective by further studying some of the main themes: the nature of the "good news" (message), the messenger or "evangelists," the motivation for (or the "why" of) evangelism, and the methods (or the

---

1. World Council of Churches, *Together towards Life: Mission and Evangelism in Changing Landscapes* (Geneva: WCC Publications, 2013), par. 81.

"how") of evangelism. The discussion will often reach back to the Old Testament and move to its full picture in the New Testament. As the expansion of today's Christianity owes mostly to the active evangelistic work of Pentecostal believers, it is important to have this perspective in this book. The theological basis of evangelism as understood by Pentecostal Christians can be an important contribution. In a limited way, this section will also interact with World Council of Churches' *Together towards Life*.

5.3.2 *What's so good about good news?*

The New Testament is full of the "good news" brought by Jesus. For example, Mark opens his gospel with "The beginning of the good news of Jesus Christ, the Son of God" (Mark 1:1). And Matthew introduces the initial ministry of Christ: "Jesus went throughout Galilee, teaching in their synagogues and proclaiming the good news of the kingdom and curing every disease and every sickness among the people" (Matt. 4:23). More importantly, Jesus himself describes his work as "bringing good news": "The Spirit of the Lord is upon me, because he has anointed me to bring good news to the poor. He has sent me to proclaim release to the captives and recovery of sight to the blind, to let the oppressed go free, to proclaim the year of the Lord's favor" (Luke 4:18-19). The good news is good because it addresses "bad" situations, and announces liberation from these situations. The end of the enemy's seige, in 2 Kings 7, is good news to the people of Samaria because they were attacked and surrounded by a hostile enemy force.

The record of God's creation of the world was full of goodness: "God saw everything that he had made, and indeed, it was very good" (Gen. 1:31). It is through the Spirit of God that everything was created and given life (Gen. 1:2). This creation, however, was quickly corrupted by sin through the wilful disobedience of the first humans, as detailed in the painful record of Genesis 3. When sin comes into the creation, death comes into every life. By the sin of the humans, the climax of God's creation, the entire creation has been severed from the Creator and Giver of life. As the "wages of sin is death" (Rom. 6:23), all, including every creation, are under the curse of sin and death. Paul comes right to the point by plainly stating, "All have sinned and fall short of the glory of God" (Rom. 3:23). To this hopeless and dreadful bad situation, the good news is offered.

If the opposite of God's creation is death, then it is not difficult to understand that the heart of God's creation is fullness of life, with an intimate loving relationship with the Creator. After sin entered, God immediately began God's plan to bring the whole creation back to the living, loving, and saving relationship with Godself. As the gift of life comes through the Spirit of God (e.g., Job 33:4), renewal of life (e.g., Is. 32:15) is brought about by the same Spirit. In fact, one can enter into the kingdom of God only through a rebirth of water and Spirit (John 3:5).

God's plan for restoration involves a "man," just as sin entered through one man (or "first Adam"). Humans, as bearers of God's image (Gen. 1:26) and God's breath (Gen. 2:7), occupy a central place in God's creation and also in God's plan for restoration. In Paul's words, "The first man, Adam, became a living being; the last Adam became a life-giving spirit" (1 Cor. 15:45). Even though humans willfully lay enmity between themselves and God, God, by the divine will, places enmity between humans and their seducer: "I will put enmity between you and the woman, and between your offspring and hers; he will strike your head, and you will strike his heel" (Gen. 3:15).[2]

The gospels point to Jesus as the "last Adam," the Messiah, the Son of God who comes to the world to save us. God's love, the main motivation for God's whole creative work, is more explicitly expressed in God's loving relationship with God's people. Israel is often called "my people" (e.g., Ex. 7:16) or "my beloved" (throughout the Song of Solomon), and by the metaphor of a marriage relationship (Hos. 2:19-20). Israel is compared with the wife of a loving husband (God). This love urged God to "[give] his only son, so that everyone who believes in him may not perish but may have eternal life" (John 3:16). The Son is given so that he would die the ultimate atoning death to overcome our sins and death: "Let the same mind be in you that was in Christ Jesus, who, though he was in the form of God, did not regard equality with God as something to be exploited, but emptied himself, taking the form of a slave, being born in human likeness. And being found in human form, he humbled himself and became obedient to the point of death—even death on a cross" (Phil. 2:5-8). Jesus thus is the Passover Lamb of God who bears all our sins. His life, teachings, and works bear witness to his redemptive death. His resurrection not only declares the sufficiency of his sacrifice on our behalf, but also the complete victory over sin and its consequence, death. In another fitting metaphor, John describes the coming of Christ to make life flourish: "The thief comes only to steal and kill and destroy. I came that they may have life, and

---

2. This divine realignment of enmity is viewed as the prototype of the "good news" (*proto-evangelium*).

have it abundantly. I am the good shepherd. The good shepherd lays down his life for the sheep" (John 10:10-11). Jesus not only brings good news; he *is* the good news! God's gift of restored life through Jesus is the heart of the good news offered to the whole of humanity.

5.3.3 God's people, the bearers and heralds of the good news

From the beginning, humans have occupied a special place in God's creation and history. The first Adam is called "a living being," while the last Adam is referred to as "a life-giving spirit" (1 Cor. 15:45). The elaborate way in which the creation of human beings is described in Genesis 1 and 2 strongly suggests their special place in God's world. They are the bearers of God's image (Gen. 1:26), and a "living being" through the gift of God's breath (Gen. 2:7). This makes them God's suitable companions for a meaningful relationship. In fact, God seeks out the first humans in the garden "at the time of the evening breeze" (Gen. 3:8). This special status comes with a special responsibility. They are to "fill the earth and subdue it" (Gen. 1:28). While the humans are to represent the Creator to the whole creation, they are also the representatives of the entire creation to God. That is why their sin has an effect on the whole creation (Gen. 3:17b-18).

The special place of the humans continues in God's restoration plan. Then who is called to bring this good news to the world under sin and death? God's response to the eternal condemnation of the entire creation is the creation of God's own people. They serve as the sign of God's redemption, and also as God's agent to bring the good news to others.

Through the election of Abraham, God's blessing is to be known to all the families of the earth (Gen. 12:3). When Israel is chosen to be God's people, the nation is also to serve as a "priestly kingdom and a holy nation," set aside for service to God (Ex. 19:6). Its privileged status comes with a responsibility: that the nations will know and experience God through God's people. Often Israel fails to be a special people throughout its history, but this does not stop them from being witnesses to God. For example, in the household of Naaman, an Aramean commander, an Israelite slave girl takes pity on her master's suffering of leprosy. She knows that a prophet in Samaria can cure him, and she is eager to share this with her master (2 Kings 5).

The prophets of the Old Testament exemplify a tradition of preachers who speak on God's behalf. Their calling is to preach repentance to the people to bring them back to God. Isaiah, a prophet with passion, urges God's people:

"Come now, let us argue it out, says the Lord: though your sins are like scarlet, they shall be like snow; though they are red like crimson, they shall become like wool" (Is. 1:18). Micah, the 8th-century prophet, however, struggles with false prophets who refuse to point out the nation's transgression: "But as for me, I am filled with power, with the spirit of the Lord, and with justice and might, to declare to Jacob his transgression and to Israel his sin" (Mic. 3:8). In fact, for a long time there has been an expectation that one day every one of God's people would be a "prophet": "Then afterward I will pour out my spirit on all flesh; your sons and your daughters shall prophesy, your old men shall dream dreams, and your young men shall see visions. Even on the male and female slaves, in those days, I will pour out my spirit" (Joel 2:28-29).

God's people, as individuals and groups, are called to bear witness to God's good news. As in the case of the Israelite girl, each one of God's people is to be an active herald of the good news. This becomes explicit in the New Testament. First of all, Jesus calls his disciples to proclaim the coming of God's kingdom: "From that time Jesus began to proclaim, 'Repent, for the kingdom of heaven has come near.' As he walked by the Sea of Galilee, he saw two brothers. . . . And he said to them, 'Follow me, and I will make you fish for people,'" (Matt. 4:17-19). The disciples are regularly sent to announce the good news by word and deed: "Cure the sick who are there, and say to them, 'The kingdom of God has come near to you'" (Luke 10:9). In his priestly prayer before his death, Jesus defines the nature of Christian life in the world: "I am not asking you to take them out of the world, but I ask you to protect them from the evil one. . . . As you have sent me into the world, so I have sent them into the world" (John 17:15, 18). Each disciple of Christ is now being sent into the world to be a witness to God's offer of salvation. After his death and resurrection, in various times, he commissioned his disciples and followers to preach the gospel. Before he ascended to heaven, in what is called the Great Commission, he sent out his people to bring the good news: "All authority in heaven and on earth has been given to me. Go therefore and make disciples of all nations, baptizing them in the name of the Father and of the Son and of the Holy Spirit, and teaching them to obey everything that I have commanded you. And remember, I am with you always, to the end of the age" (Matt. 28:18-20).

The early church, as the new people of God, is born through the coming of the Holy Spirit (Acts 2:1-4), just as the life-giving Spirit brings about the creation. Just after a community of believers has been shaped, the first sermon preached by Peter is purely "evangelistic"! His presentation of the life, redemptive death, and vindicating resurrection of Christ produces a conviction of sin, and a cry, "Brothers, what should we do?" (Acts 2:37). Peter responds with an invitation: "Repent, and be baptized every one of you in the name of Jesus Christ so that your sins may be forgiven; and you will receive the gift of the Holy Spirit. For the promise is for you, for your children, and for all who are far away, everyone whom the Lord our God calls to him" (Acts 2:38-39). This clear presentation of the gospel is not just the privilege of the apostles. In fact, the coming of the Holy Spirit fulfills the ancient prayer that every one of God's people would proclaim the good news. One of Christ's last promises is the empowering work of the Holy Spirit: "But you will receive power when the Holy Spirit has come upon you; and you will be my witnesses in Jerusalem, in all Judea and Samaria, and to the ends of the earth" (Acts 1:8). As a result, for example, some who flee the persecution in Jerusalem preach the good news not only to Jews but also to Greek-speaking Gentiles. This is how the church in Antioch was established (Acts 11:19-21).

In the New Testament, "evangelists" are listed along other formal titles and offices of the early church (e.g., Eph. 4:11; cf. ch. 1.2.2, above). It parallels with the prophets in the Old Testament who are specifically called to convey God's message to people and nations. Although every believer is called to actively proclaim God's good news, the church has a specifically recognized "office" to carry out evangelism as a main function of the church. In the Jerusalem church, Philip is called an "evangelist" (Acts 21:8). His work, recorded particularly in Acts 8, illustrates the life of an evangelist. Paul also urges Timothy to fulfill the work of an evangelist (2 Tim. 4:5).

In closing this discussion, a word on the church may be helpful. John Stott observes a certain "evangelistic sequence" in how the Thessalonians received the gospel. Paul writes to the church in Thessaloniki: the "message of the gospel [first] came to [them]" (1 Thess. 1:5), then they "received the word with joy" (1:6), and then "the word of the Lord . . . sounded forth" from them (1:8).[3] A local congregation as part of the body of Christ is called to be a preaching community, while demonstrating the power and conviction of the gospel.

5.3.4 Motivations of evangelism

As we have affirmed that evangelism is the work of every person who belongs to God's kingdom, then what should motivate and continually energize God's

---

3. John Stott, *Through the Bible, Through the Year: Daily Reflections from Genesis to Revelation* (Oxford: Lion Hudson, 2006), 350.

people to be faithful in this call to evangelism? This discussion also helps the church to understand how to equip believers to carry out ministries (Eph. 4:12).

Love

The first motivation is the love of God, which has been shown and manifested throughout history as God carefully plans and executes to bring the fallen creation back to God. God's deep love and passion for God's own people is graphically illustrated in the book and life of the prophet Hosea. Israel is God's handicraft, lavished with love, care, protection, and provision. Yet, the wayward nation willfully goes after its own "lover" (e.g., Hos. 2:2). God's deep love for Israel causes God to hinder her way (Hos. 2:6), even ruin her supplies (Hos. 2:11-12). But soon, God "lures" her back with tender love, until she finally acknowledges God's lordship and love, and calls God "my husband" (Hos. 2:16).

God's love in the New Testament is shown in the forgiveness of our sins and the gift of salvation through the death and resurrection of Jesus. The first epistle of John defines the highest form of God's love: "God's love was revealed among us in this way: God sent his only Son into the world so that we might live through him. In this is love, not that we loved God but that he loved us and sent his Son to be the atoning sacrifice for our sins" (1 John 4:9-10). The same love is fulfilled by Jesus through his obedience: "We know love by this, that he laid down his life for us" (1 John 3:16). And because of this lavish love of the Father, now we are called "children of God" (1 John 3:1; John 1:12). Because of our salvation that comes from God's love through the sacrifice of Christ, we are now called to love one another (1 John 4:11). In fact, love of God and love of neighbour are the full summation of God's commands (Matt. 22:37-40). And the highest form of love which God's people should show to the world of hopelessness is sharing the good news of God's love for salvation and restoration. In fact, Christ sends his disciples to the world as the bearers and witnesses of the good news, as the Father has sent him to the world (John 17:18). It is God's love that compels Jesus to complete our salvation. And it should be the same love that God's people have experienced through their own salvation to urge them to bring the good news to the uttermost parts of the world.

Urgency

The second motivation is urgency, accompanied by compassion, in light of the eternal condemnation to which the whole humanity and creation is subjected without the good news of salvation and restoration. To be separated from the source of life means death, and that is the exact state of humanity and the whole creation after sin enters in. The biblical record repeats the cycle of human rebellions against God and God's punishment with a plan for a new people as God's own and as God's agent for the restoration of God's world. Sodom and Gomorrah, in the book of Genesis, epitomize the extreme sinfulness of humanity away from God. They are "wicked, great sinners against the Lord" (Gen. 13:13; 18:20). Thus, the cities are to be destroyed by God. Upon learning this impending destruction, Abraham begins to intercede for the sake of the cities and their people, including his nephew Lot. His urgent desperation leads him to engage in a hard "negotiation" with God so that even a small number could be saved. Abraham knows not only the impending judgment of God, but also its consequential severity. For this reason, Paul is urged to proclaim the gospel (1 Cor. 9:16).

God's good news for salvation through Jesus is now offered to "everyone who believes in him," so that they "may not perish but may have eternal life" (John 3:16). Jesus' command, therefore, to his followers is to "preach to the people and to testify that he is the one ordained by God as judge of the living and the dead" (Acts 10:42). Thus, evangelism is the heart of Christian living, and in the proclamation of God's good news we must "be persistent whether the time is favourable or unfavourable" (2 Tim. 4:2). This urge is grounded in Christ Jesus, who is "to judge the living and the dead" (2 Tim. 4:1). The appearing of his kingdom is at hand (2 Tim. 4:1). The universal offer of the good news calls God's people to adopt two important attitudes. The first is deep compassion toward people destined to eternal condemnation, while God's salvation is presented to them. Paul expresses his deep desire for his fellow Jews, the chosen people of God, that they may know Jesus as God's Son and their Saviour (Rom. 9:1-5). According to him, it is Christ's love that urges him to go on in his preaching (2 Cor. 5:14). This compassion for the perishing people is also found in Moses, when he pleads to God not to destroy Israel for their sins. He even asks that his name be removed from the book (of life), if God would not forgive the sins of God's own people (Ex. 32:32). The second attitude is a genuine perspective that God is also "their" God, not just ours. The blessed life of an evangelist is often affirmed by an ancient passage: "How beautiful upon the mountains are the feet of the messenger who announces peace, who brings good news, who announces salvation, who says to Zion, 'Your God reigns'" (Is. 52:7). Although there is no doubt that the herald or watchman is God's servant, the good news he proclaims to the city is "Your God reigns." The good news is offered to those who would otherwise perish, and yet, God is *their* God and Jesus is *their* Saviour after all.

Power of the gospel

The scripture claims that there is power in the good news. Paul declares, "For I am not ashamed of the gospel; it is the power of God for salvation to everyone who has faith, to the Jew first and also to the Greek" (Rom. 1:16). The root of this power is that Christ is the good news himself. The Father reconciles humanity and the creation to Godself through the sacrificial death of God's Son. Through the Holy Spirit, everyone who believes in Christ is now born again and becomes God's own child. Because of this radical impact of the good news, God's people can share their own experience of the power of the gospel with confidence, conviction, passion, and compassion. This also means that there is no other way to spread this good news of God's great work of salvation than through Christ; only those who have experienced this are called to evangelism. This unparalleled value of the good news leads Paul to confess: "I regard everything as loss because of the surpassing value of knowing Christ Jesus my Lord. For his sake I have suffered the loss of all things, and I regard them as rubbish, in order that I may gain Christ and be found in him, not having a righteousness of my own that comes from the law, but one that comes through faith in Christ, the righteousness from God based on faith" (Phil. 3:8-9).

This ultimate grace, which the gospel brings to God's people, results in joy. This in turn generates "the delightful and comforting joy" in evangelism, as "goodness always tends to spread."[4] Christ's church was born through the coming of the Holy Spirit, as he empowers each believer to be witness to Christ's death and resurrection (Acts 1:8). The joy and empowerment produces at least two important attitudes toward evangelism. The first is a deep sense of obligation to share the good news or indebtedness to those who still wait for someone to bring this good news. Paul expresses his own sense of this sacred duty: "If I proclaim the gospel, this gives me no ground for boasting, for an obligation is laid on me, and woe to me if I do not proclaim the gospel!" (1 Cor. 9:16).

---

4. Pope Francis, *Evangelii Gaudium—The Joy of the Gospel: Apostolic Exhortation on the Proclamation of the Gospel in Today's World* (London: Catholic Truth Society, 2013), 10 (par. 9).

The second is an ability to overcome hardships and difficulties for the cause of evangelism. Stephen's bold proclamation of this good news is a fine example. In his martyrdom for evangelism, he was "filled with the Holy Spirit, he gazed into heaven and saw the glory of God and Jesus standing at the right hand of God" (Acts 7:55). He even uttered the same prayer of forgiveness as the Lord did. Many Christians in the early church consider their suffering in witnessing to Christ as "the sharing of his sufferings by becoming like him in his death" (Phil. 3:10). Evangelism sometimes costs dearly, but the joy and power of the gospel empowers God's people.

Holy Spirit

The Spirit of God is the creator and giver of life, as pointed out above. In fact, the special relationship between God the Creator and humanity is marked by the presence of God's Spirit as the source of life in humans. The loss of this "life" through sin is expressed in the form of the temporarily limited presence of God's Spirit in humans: "My spirit shall not abide in mortals forever, for they are flesh; their days shall be one hundred twenty years" (Gen. 6:3). The full restoration of the creation, including humanity, is to be the work of the same life-restoring Spirit (Is. 32:15).

This promise is fulfilled through Jesus. His whole life is marked by the presence of the Holy Spirit: from his baptism, miracles, his obedience to the cross (Heb. 9:14), and resurrection. He opens the way for anyone to experience rebirth through the Holy Spirit. As he ascends to heaven, he promises the outpouring of the Holy Spirit upon his followers. In the Gospel of John, his work is sustaining God's people to be victorious in their daily life in the world. He is the Paraclete, or Advocate, who will teach, encourage, comfort, or give words for witnessing (e.g., John 14:26). In the book of Acts, the Holy Spirit is more directly associated with witnessing. The disciples were commanded not to leave Jerusalem but wait for whom the Father had promised to come, the Holy Spirit (Acts 1:4-5). The disciples would receive power through the outpouring of the Holy Spirit comes and they would be Christ's "witnesses in Jerusalem, in all Judea and Samaria, and to the ends of the earth" (Acts 1:8). The whole book of Acts is the record of God's people empowered by the Holy Spirit to preach the good news of Christ to the ends of the earth. The power of the Holy Spirit is manifested not only in healing and miracles, but also in courageous confrontations of evil and injustice, and bold proclamation of Jesus' lordship over all the earth.

5.3.5 Practice of evangelism

This last part discusses the practical side of evangelism, including various forms of evangelism (see more elaborately in ch. 8.2, below). It has been said already that only God's people who have experienced God's good news of salvation can testify this to others. It is true, however, that in the Bible, in exceptional cases through God's infinite wisdom, some who are not God's own people are used nonetheless. One example is Cyrus, the Persian king, called "my shepherd" (Is. 44:28), who historically allowed the Israelites to return to Jerusalem and rebuild the temple and the city walls.

The most common form of evangelism is verbal proclamation of the good news of Jesus Christ. It is more than mere explanation of one's experience in Christ. One who is sent by God as God's herald or prophet comes in the name of the sender, and in God's authority. In fact, Jesus prefaces his Great Commission with an important promise: "All authority in heaven and on earth has been given to me" (Matt. 28:18). Based on this promise ("therefore"), the disciples are to go and make disciples of all nations (Matt. 28:19). Stephen's courageous proclamation of Christ's lordship to the hostile Jewish crowd (Acts 7:2-53) is attributed to the empowering presence of the Holy Spirit. He is described as "a man full of faith and the Holy Spirit" (Acts 6:5). Where did his courage and boldness come from? In the face of an imminent death, Stephen is reported to be "filled with the Holy Spirit, he gazed into heaven and saw the glory of God and Jesus standing at the right hand of God" (Acts 7:55).

It is also legitimate, however, to share one's experience of God's grace. The hearer is invited to encounter the truth of Christ: "Philip found Nathanael and said to him, 'We have found him about whom Moses in the law and also the prophets wrote, Jesus son of Joseph from Nazareth.' Nathanael said to him, 'Can anything good come out of Nazareth?' Philip said to him, 'Come and see'" (John 1:45-46). Communication of the good news to others often involves "going," an intentional action to make evangelism possible. The Great Commission takes "going" as a critical part of evangelism (Matt. 28:19; Mark 16:15). As discussed earlier, the evangelist's enthusiasm and conviction for the good news, and love for the lost, should make evangelism a work of joy. The Bible, however, records a reluctant evangelist, Jonah. Yet, through his preaching, the entire city of Nineveh repents, including animals, and God withdraws divine judgment (Jon. 3:6-10).

A second aspect of witnessing is the role of the expression of God's love. The same love which motivates evangelism will cause God's people to show compassion to those who suffer. The Old Testament is clear that one's healthy relationship with God is to be reflected in a compassionate relationship with neighbours. The Jerusalem church takes the care for the needy as a serious part of its life. Feeding the hungry, healing the sick, and clothing the naked are not only natural actions of God's people, but also testimony of people saved through the work of Christ, who now live by the empowering presence of the Holy Spirit. The expansion of the Jerusalem church is attributed to eager verbal witness and testimonies of good work: "All who believed were together and had all things in common; they would sell their possessions and goods and distribute the proceeds to all, as any had need. Day by day, as they spent much time together in the temple, they broke bread at home and ate their food with glad and generous hearts, praising God and having the goodwill of all the people. And day by day the Lord added to their number those who were being saved" (Acts 2:44-47).

The third is the demonstration of God's power. In the same book, there are numerous reports of miracles, which provide unique opportunities to verbally communicate the good news. The healing of a lame man in Jerusalem by Peter and John illustrates several important elements in evangelism. First, Peter presented Christ as the healer and saviour: "I have no silver or gold, but what I have I give you; in the name of Jesus Christ of Nazareth, stand up and walk" (Acts 3:6). Second, it is the empowering work of the Holy Spirit in the disciples that made this possible. Third, this provided a unique opportunity to proclaim the good news to a larger crowd who were "filled with wonder and amazement at what had happened to him" (Acts 3:10). There was a ready audience as "all the people ran together to them . . . utterly astonished" (Acts 3:11). Peter seized the occasion and presented Jesus first as the healer, but soon as the saviour (Acts 3:13-26). This was followed by their arrest and defense of the same message in the Sanhedrin (Acts 4:1-22). Their release was motivated by the clear proof of God's presence in them through the healing: ". . . finding no way to punish them because of the people, for all of them praised God for what had happened" (Acts 4:21). Finally, this further strengthened the church in its commitment to evangelism. The apostles offered a prayer after their release with the Jerusalem church: "'And now, Lord, look at their threats, and grant to your servants to speak your word with all boldness, while you stretch out your hand to heal, and signs and wonders are performed through the name of your holy servant Jesus.' When they had prayed, the place in which they were gathered together was shaken; and they were all filled with the Holy Spirit and spoke the word of God with boldness" (Act 4:29-31).

The fourth aspect of evangelism is the everyday life of God's people as a powerful avenue for witnessing. In Joseph's story, in the midst of unjust imprisonment, his life earned the trust of the authorities, and eventually that of the king. After the interpretation of his dream, the king confessed to his servants, "Can we find anyone else like this—one in whom is the spirit of God?" (Gen. 41:38). In each period, God's people are sent with a call to witness. In the prayer of Jesus, it is clear that his followers are to remain in the world, but not for the Father to take them away from it (John 17:15). Rather, his followers who form the church, his own body, through the Holy Spirit, are sent to the world for witness. For this reason, the church is a clear "sign and portent" of God's kingdom that has already come. This discipleship is at the heart of the Great Commission: to "make disciples of all nations," and this lifestyle of witness includes dying as observed in Stephen's above.

The fifth is the reality that evangelism is essentially spiritual in nature. As discussed in the beginning, sin is the fundamental issue in evangelism and it is a spiritual state of humans in relation to God. Physical, emotional, material, and relational degeneration seen in our life are all attributed to sin, according to our Christian faith. This spiritual nature, therefore, demands a spiritual approach to evangelism, while friendship, reasoning, and love all are surely helpful and necessary. It means in evangelism that various spiritual forces are at work, including the Holy Spirit. Therefore, prayer plays an indispensable role. Several areas of prayer may be mentioned. An intercessory prayer for the people in mind for evangelism is important. Praying for God's help through the Holy Spirit and confronting evil forces at work on the people's life are equally vital. Christian assurance is found in that "the one who is in [us] is greater than the one in the world" (1 John 4:4).

The last point is the role of discernment in evangelism. Often, a visible human need may be only a symptom of a much deeper problem. This is well observed in Jesus' encounter with the Samaritan woman. His insight led their conversation to a deeper spiritual issue. The net result is the conversion of the whole community to living faith. Discerning God's leading is also crucial. Acts records Paul's missionary plan, which was "forbidden by the Holy Spirit" (Acts 16:6). Instead, a vision led him to Macedonia (16:9). We may not know the exact nature of God's revelations to Paul, but it is clear that he discerned God's will.

5.4 Reverse Evangelism: An African Pentecostal Perspective

J. Kwabena Asamoah-Gyadu

5.4.1 Introduction

This section will provide a Pentecostal perspective on reverse evangelism in Europe. In order to do this, I will look specifically at the history, spirituality, development, and evangelistic ministry of the African immigrant "Church of the Embassy of the Blessed Kingdom of God for all Nations" (briefly referred to as "Embassy of God"), based in Kiev (Ukraine). All of this will then be discussed in the broader context of the changing paradigms in Christian mission and evangelism.

Embassy of God was, until a few years ago, the single largest Christian church in Europe. Its founder is Nigerian-born immigrant pastor Sunday Adelaja, who has formed congregations in eastern Europe and has sent many Ukrainian "born-again" Christians on mission to North America. Adelaja's ministry has, within the last two decades, raised hundreds of indigenous eastern European pastors to help him with the work. The main assembly of Embassy of God in Kiev is now down to a few thousand members, for reasons that I will explain in the course of this essay. In spite of this decline, I will argue that Sunday Adelaja remains important both as an individual and as a leader of the single largest congregation in the history of Christianity in Europe. In the years of its massive growth from the late 1990s, this ministry, as an independent Pentecostal/charismatic church led by an African immigrant, had a complicated relationship with Orthodox churches in Ukraine,[1] as being Orthodox is closely related to Ukrainian identity and nationality. Patriarchates are also defined in geographical terms. Because of the relationship of Ukrainian and Orthodox identity, the leadership of the Orthodox churches was uncomfortable with foreign missionaries and new churches trying to establish congregations in

---

1. Ukraine has three Orthodox churches: the Moskow Patriarchate, the Kiev Patriarchate (since 1992), and the Ukrainian Autocephalous Orthodox Church.

Ukraine. For them, Ukrainians automatically carried the Orthodox religious identity, even if this was in name only.[2]

This particular context, in which Orthodox Christianity is historically linked to the development of cultural and national identity, contributed to the social, religious, and political challenges of Embassy of God. Managing the relationship between religious tradition and religious change has been difficult and painful. Pastor Sunday Adelaja managed to bring many powerful public figures and politicians into Embassy of God, and it is through their influence that, in spite of protests, Adelaja finally secured citizenship and permission to acquire permanent properties for his church. Embassy of God was regarded as an "alien sectarian" organization that had come to siphon members away from the Orthodox Church and alter their national religious identity.[3] In several quarters the leader was perceived as a "foreign-financed charlatan," given to the use of brainwashing and hypnotizing techniques to fleece gullible Ukrainians of their wealth.[4] In this particular case it was not the membership that was alien but, rather, the leader of the organization and the Pentecostal/charismatic spirituality of the ministry he started. Sunday Adelaja represents a new form of reverse mission in which Africans have founded churches abroad, but with time also have returned to establish branches in their home countries.

When a self-taught Nigerian pastor establishes a church in Ukraine that then sends Ukrainian believers to other countries—to bring the word of salvation and Pentecostal experiences to others—it is, as Catherine Wanner writes, no longer a case of the core exerting influence on the periphery. It is then also a case of the "colonized" missionizing the "colonizer," as Ukrainian members of Embassy of God started doing in Russia under Pastor Adelaja's leadership.[5] This is but one example that demonstrates the changing dynamics of Christian mission as a global enterprise now led by those from the underside of history.

At the heart of the new type of mission, led by people from the southern continents to the northern continents, is the power of the Holy Spirit. The Spirit is the single most important factor in the growth of Pentecostalism. The experience of the Holy Spirit breaks down hierarchical forms of ecclesial

2. Catherine Wanner, *Communities of the Converted: Ukrainians and Global Evangelism* (Ithaca: Cornell University Press, 2007), 136.
3. J. Kwabena Asamoah-Gyadu, "Unwanted Sectarians: Spirit, Migration and Mission in an African-led Mega-Size Church in Eastern Europe," *Evangelical Review of Theology* 34, no. 1 (January 2010): 71–78.
4. Afe Adogame, *The African Christian Diaspora: New Currents and Emerging Trends in World Christianity* (London: Bloomsbury Academic, 2013), 186.
5. Wanner, *Communities*, 212.

structures, making it possible for ordinary believers to share their faith wherever they find themselves, and it explains why most immigrant church communities are also from the Pentecostal/charismatic streams of the faith. The developments we discuss here could be considered as a practical outworking of Paul's submission that God chooses the weak, lowly, and despised things of this world to shame the strong and wise so that no one might boast before him (1 Cor. 1:27-29).

5.4.2 Changing paradigms in immigrant Christianity

African immigrant churches in the West, as many studies have shown, have helped to reverse mission as a one-directional practice from the North to the South.[6] The existing paradigm of African immigrant Christianity is constituted by Africans, both in terms of leadership and membership. The Kingsway International Christian Centre in London, a charismatic church led by another Nigerian, Pastor Matthew Ashimolowo, is a useful example of such a church. It brings together African immigrants and black British citizens with others drawn from the Caribbean. In most of Europe and North America, the typical African immigrant church would consist of African migrants, both in leadership and membership. A number of them are branches of denominations located in Africa. Many of them even use indigenous languages as spoken in their home countries—Akan, Yoruba, Igbo—because in addition to the church services, the new churches also offer social and economic safety networks that help with survival in the physically and spiritually precarious diasporas of the North.

A lot of times there is little or no attempt in immigrant churches to reach out to indigenous host populations. Those situations, although not ideal, do not necessarily negate Christian mission, because the witness of *presence* that these immigrant churches bring to their new contexts is also important. But for them, many beautiful cathedrals would be standing idle or converted for other mundane uses. We must also not place all such problems at the doorstep of these African immigrant churches creating "religious ghettos," because sometimes Western Christians are themselves not comfortable with the sort of Christianity that is being mediated. African Christian approaches to the Bible are often very literalist, and so preachers would freely speak out against alternative sexual lifestyles and challenge certain notions of gender equalities within the context of Christian marriage. In one African Pentecostal church,

6. See, for example, Gerrie ter Haar, *Halfway to Paradise: African Christians in Europe* (Cardiff: Cardiff Academic Press, 1998).

with multiple branches in large European and North American cities, women must still respond to their husbands as *me wura,* the Akan of Ghana expression for "Lord," because that is how Sarah addressed Abraham. A number of these practices, justified on the basis of biblical interpretation, go against the grain of developments in modern Western societies and often offend social sensibilities. In some extreme cases, Christians in host societies in the developed world treat immigrant Christianity in general, and African Christianity in particular, as an aberration of "authentic Christianity" as honed in the West and transported across the Atlantic by missionaries.

The Embassy of God represents a different kind of immigrant church. Only its leader, his family, and a handful of internationals, amounting to no more than 2 percent of the congregation, constitute its immigrant membership. The enormous size of the Embassy of God and its initial phenomenal growth and dynamism has contributed to its visibility. In addition to all these, however, as Wanner has noted, Embassy of God represents "a compelling example of innovative missionary dynamics and conversion practices at the dawn of the 21st century."[7] Thus, this church is best understood as an African-led, independent Pentecostal/charismatic ministry that has become a classic example of the sort of dynamism, exuberance, and commitment with which ordinary African Christians live their faith abroad. When given the chance, these ordinary African Christians leaders demonstrate the power of the gospel within contexts in which the processes of *militant* secularization are used to nudge the church of Jesus Christ out of the public sphere. Through the formation of nondenominational fellowships, they bring people together. Almost without exception these fellowships later become churches. That is how Embassy of God also started: a Nigerian Christian graduate student felt called by God to bring the salvation message into a European context that, he stated, had ceded too much ground to secularization, deemed an activity of the devil.

5.4.3 History

Pastor Sunday Adelaja founded Embassy of God, headquartered in Kiev (Ukraine), in 1994. He came to Soviet Belarus as a graduate student in journalism in 1986. His ministry as an evangelist started upon arrival in eastern Europe. He became a popular yet also despised street preacher, calling for the public to "come to Christ." Three years later, in 1989, during the collapse of the Soviet Union, he turned his evangelical fellowship of foreign students into

---

7. Wanner, *Communities,* 212.

the Word of Faith Church in Belarus. The limitations of growing a church in Belarus led Sunday Adelaja to relocate to Ukraine in 1993. He continued his open-air evangelism in Kiev, combining that activity with a Bible-study fellowship of fewer than ten people. The open-air evangelism here was a little more successful and, by 1994, Sunday Adelaja had restarted his Word of Faith Church, which had at least 50 members. It took less than a year for the membership to bloat to about 1,000 people. It was in 2002 that the name of the organization changed to the "Embassy of the Blessed Kingdom of God for All Nations." The name of the church was chosen to reflect the understanding of Embassy of God and its missionary influence as stated in one of its official brochures:

> The Church is the representative of God on the earth—His "Embassy." Therefore, we—children of God—are the citizens of His Divine Kingdom and not citizens of this world! The Blessed Kingdom of God [is] a place of destruction of curses. At the head of every kingdom is a king. Our King is Jesus Christ! He is the Lord of all nations; . . . Jesus Christ is the Savior for everyone, irrespective of his age, color or skin, nationality and social status.[8]

Embassy of God is a contemporary Pentecostal/charismatic church that shares all the characteristics of Christian communities belonging to that stream of Christianity—charismatic leadership, belief in speaking in tongues and other manifestations of the Spirit, an attraction for urban youth, extensive uses of modern media, internationalism and a gospel of success, possibility, and prosperity.

From about the mid-2000s, Embassy of God started to lose its popularity for several reasons. First, the leader's message took on a "prosperity gospel tone," with a materialistic dimension. This brought him into conflict with other conservative evangelical Christian leaders in eastern Europe. Embassy of God and its leaders therefore became isolated from the Evangelical Protestant community. The breakdown of these ecumenical relations meant that the leader was left to deal with his problems alone, with the exception of his transnational cooperation with several leading North American televangelists. The Evangelical churches in Ukraine at some point even issued public statements denouncing some of the prosperity teachings of Embassy of God. Second, the leader got involved in the Ukrainian Orange Revolution, and he even wrote a book

---

8. Stated in the church's eighth-anniversary brochure, 5.

about his involvement. When the political tables turned in opposite directions, his political connections suffered badly and that affected his social standing as a religious leader. Third, a little over six years ago Embassy of God also started having problems with the state over a financial pyramid scheme promoted by its founder that went wrong. The government opened criminal proceedings against the leadership and many people, especially those affected negatively by the scheme, along with their families and friends, left the Embassy of God. Until these developments, the Embassy of God was a megachurch that brought together in a single location more than 10,000 worshippers every Sunday. It also had a number of satellite congregations scattered around Eastern Europe.

Until the Embassy of God started going through the crises described above, which were also related to financial accountability, its total membership was quoted at about 25,000 adults. Figures relating to the membership of religious organizations can be notoriously deceptive. Nevertheless, the patrons of the church of the Embassy of God stated that at the height of its popularity, the membership would not have been too far from the indicated numbers. In March 2004, during an evangelical procession dubbed "Jesus March," I had the occasion to observe for the first time the numerical strength of the church. The march started at the Dynamo Kiev Stadium and made its way through the city, proclaiming Jesus Christ as Lord, and negotiated its way to the city's public square where the world's media was waiting. At the end of the procession there were fervent prayers and singing, and further preaching and narration of testimonies of people who had been delivered from various powers of addiction ranging from alcoholism and hard drugs to sexual perversions. The march was led by a group of young men and women, first-time converts to the Pentecostal faith from previous lives as drug addicts, prostitutes, alcoholics, and gangsters. They were "born again" and baptized in the Holy Spirit, most of them spoke in tongues, and now, with megaphones in hand, proclaimed through the streets: "'Ukraine is choosing Jesus'; 'There is a way out and it is Jesus'; 'Jesus is the answer to AIDS'; 'Jesus is the answer to narcotics'; 'God is blessing Ukraine'; 'Choosing Jesus will protect Ukraine from AIDS.'"

The Jesus marches are a testimonial to faith and symbolic re-enactments of the biblical "Jericho march" recorded in Joshua 6. Under the leadership of Joshua, God instructed Israel to march around Jericho once a day for six days and on the seventh day to do so seven times. At the blast of trumpets and shouting at the final round, the walls of the city came down. These activities, amounting to enchanted "noises"—that is, screaming, shouting, stamping of feet, and clapping of hands—have been reinvented in certain Pentecostal contexts as ways of fighting enemies and taking control of spaces illegally occupied by the "enemy." Noisemaking is how, according the biblical account, Jericho was conquered. In its modern-day re-enactments, Pentecostal/charismatic pastors lead their members to "take possession" of lands and properties that they intend to acquire, or, if they have already been acquired, before actual occupation takes place.

The vision of the founder, Nigerian-born and bred charismatic pastor Sunday Adelaja, was not necessarily to bring "African Christianity" to postcommunist Europe. His vision, as he understood God's specific mandate to him, was to bring a particular type of Christian experience into a context in which lives were being wrecked by social evils, particularly drug addiction, alcoholism, crime, and sexual promiscuity. He preached a clear message of the Billy Graham type that emphasized the born-again experience, adding to that the infilling of the Holy Spirit, leading to a Spirit-empowered and victorious Christian life. It is Pastor Adelaja's success with the transformation of lives into "new temples" or "vessels of honour" and the physical evidences of success that propelled him into public significance as an immigrant Christian pastor who was building an African-led, eastern European, Pentecostal/charismatic church. An important aim of the Embassy of God, Pastor Adelaja explains, is to "reverse the current secularization of eastern Europe," which for him was as shocking as the region's declining economic fortunes and social structures when he first arrived as a student in the then Soviet Union in 1986.[9]

According to Catherine Wanner, the transition from the church's previous name, "Word of Faith," to the "Church of the Blessed Embassy of the Kingdom of God for all Nations" signalled the leader's new mission to establish a public role for religion and to bring the faith to "all nations" through extensive missionizing.[10] When Pastor Adelaja relocated from Belarus to the Ukraine, he established himself there as an advocate of a particular type of conversion. An "advocate" is what Lewis R. Rambo calls the person who "assesses the potential target audience and formulates persuasive tactics to bring converts into the religious community."[11] Pastor Adelaja's own conversion, anointing in the Spirit, and subsequent redemptive uplift in material terms have become paradigmatic

---

9. Alyona Dobrovolskaya, ed., *Olorunwa: The Roads of Life—There Is God: Portrait of Sunday Adelaja* (Kiev: Fares Publishing House, 2007), 63–64.
10. Wanner, *Communities*, 211.
11. Lewis R. Rambo, *Understanding Religious Conversion* (New Haven: Yale University Press, 1993), 2, 66.

for the movement he leads. Every single testimony I have heard from Embassy of God concludes with gratitude to God for bringing Pastor Adelaja to deliver the speaker from a destructive habit. Although in principle all born-again believers are able and entitled to *embody* the Holy Spirit, as Birgit Meyer points out, Pentecostal/charismatic pastors are prime exponents of divine power.[12] Pentecostal/charismatic pastors impart such Holy Spirit power to others either through various anointing services or, more frequently, through the imposition of hands in prayer, shaking hands with people, or even touching them.

5.4.4 Missionizing and internationalism

The breakup of the Soviet Union in the early 1990s brought with it some socioeconomic and cultural dislocations that left people looking for answers to the void that socialist ideologies had failed to fill. Many sought refuge in Evangelical Protestant traditions like Pentecostal churches, which affirmed the importance of experience in individual and collective religious lives. Religion became "a refuge, a meaningful identity and mode of living in an alternative moral universe, in defiance of the numerous risks and penalties involved."[13] The narratives of conversion in the Pentecostal church Adelaja went on to found in response to this spiritually malnourished society, as he saw it, reveal much about this type of experiential religion. Significant numbers of its members have long histories of drug addiction, prostitution, and alcohol-related problems. Their stories underscore the Pentecostal understanding of conversion as a process of transformation, particularly as it relates to the experiences of the Spirit, the use of the physical body, dominion over the earth, and the relationships among these. In this new type of transnational Pentecostalism, the born again no longer retreat among themselves in order to maintain the purity of their beliefs and their moral rigour. Far from the temptations and corruption of the "world of sin," "salvation is now resolutely this-worldly and the evidence of new life has become as much material as spiritual."[14]

In other words, salvation is expected to be physically evident. A person must look well, take control of resources channelled away from previously wasteful lifestyles, seize opportunities in education and business, and be prosperous in life's endeavours through the application of the principles of "sowing

---

12. Birgit Meyer, *Religious Sensations: Why Media, Aesthetics and Power Matter in the Study of Contemporary Religion* (Amsterdam: Vrije Universiteit, 2006), 11.

13. Wanner, *Communities*, 2.

14. André Corten and Ruth Marshall-Fratani, eds., *Between Babel and Pentecost: Transnational Pentecostalism in Africa and Latin America* (Bloomington: Indiana University Press, 2001), 7.

and reaping," commitment, and hard work. Sunday Adelaja emerged in a period of economic and social uncertainty in eastern Europe, in Ukraine in particular. His message of upward mobility therefore served as a great attraction for upwardly mobile young people and professionals because, among other spiritual benefits, these are places where people can be offered new hope using the message of a certain type of motivational Christianity. One convert in the Ukraine, a young man in his 30s, pointed to his new blue-black blazer, grey trousers, red flying necktie, and shiny black shoes, telling me, "Look, Jesus has made me fine; I am a new temple."

Pentecostal/charismatic Christians have come to adopt Jesus marches and reinterpret them to suit contemporary situations partly because of the ardent belief in the existence of territorial demons. Marches for Jesus are symbolic in ridding society of demons, witches, and evil spirits, who are said to account for the ills of society, including the breakdown of the moral order, political instability, stunted economic growth, and crisis and secularization.[15] It must be understood that the conscious attempt to secularize society, and to persecute Evangelical Christians in particular, led to the demonization of communism as a political ideology. These territorial demons controlling the destinies of countries, according to the conservative Evangelical imagination, not only lead people away from God into social vices and rejection of the gospel, but they can even control the fortunes of nations by contaminating the land. Emeka Nwankpa, a Nigerian Pentecostal, has gathered some of these thoughts in the book *Redeeming the Land: Interceding for the Nations.* The title is suggestive enough. In it he opines: "Satan expanded his hold over the earth by deploying his principalities and powers to cause and spread spiritual wickedness in this world." "[Satan] strengthened his hold over families, communities, cities and nations," he says, "but Jesus Christ came into the world to destroy the works of the devil, not only to save man but to redeem everything. We must therefore deal spiritually with the [satanic powers] in order to redeem the land so that people can live even more abundant lives."[16] The belief in territorial demons is not necessarily an African phenomenon, as one finds similar ideas in the writings of Americans like Peter Wagner, and much of it has become part of the sort of global charismatic culture of which Embassy of God is a part.

---

15. Adogame, *African Christian Diaspora*, 188.
16. Emeka Nwankpa, *Redeeming the Land: Interceding for the Nations* (Achimota: Africa Christian Press, 1998), 9, 11.

5.4.5 Mission, migration, and diaspora

People move for different reasons, and in our 21st-century world, the migration of people both within and across continents has become a topical issue. International migration in particular is often motivated by the desire to acquire an academic degree or the search for a better life, or more often than not, by natural disasters or one of the many political crises facing a number of regions of the world. Those who migrate either embrace new religious ideas or carry their old faiths with them. Evangelical Christianity in particular is a stream of the faith that challenges its adherents to consciously "win souls for Christ." The spread of Evangelical Christianity—with its emphasis on active Christian witnessing, a life of holiness, and an ardent commitment to the reading of scriptures—accounts in part for the emergence of immigrant churches across the world. With increasing global trends in migration, Christianity in Africa has now gone international. To that end, religious communities like Embassy of God have become powerful globalizing forces that help Ukraine move beyond its socialist past.

In African hands mission and evangelization have truly gone international, and African diaspora Christianity is at the forefront of the new initiatives. Originating in the Jewish biblical tradition, the term *diaspora* now enjoys growing importance in the study of religion precisely because of some of the developments relating to the dispersal of African Christians in the modern West. For many of these people, however, the word *return* usually associated with the diaspora does not exist in their vocabulary. A majority of Africans in Europe are economic migrants, although it is possible to encounter a significant number who may fall within the categories of academic and political migrants. Migration is something that takes place all the time and has been part of human history through the ages, and religion has always been a significant aspect of it. What we learn from Sunday Adelaja's effort, in spite of its failures, is the impact that a single African migrant with the right motivation in mission can have on societies that have known and practiced Christianity for centuries. Into whichever category they fall, African migrants have always carried their faith with them to the diasporas, and Adelaja remains a classic example of this. One of the testimonials to the mission work of Embassy of God is the institutionalization of social-intervention programmes through the organization of soup kitchens and medical clinics for the poor and homeless.

Unlike the cries of diaspora Jews, who out of exilic despair could not fathom singing the Lord's song in a foreign land, modern migrants are doing just that with the formation of churches. It is not insignificant that Africa, a continent despised, deprived, trampled upon, marginalized, and shamed in many ways, has emerged as the beacon of Christian mission and evangelization in the global spread of the faith. This does not render European Christianity irrelevant, but rather it shows that at a time when the faith is under siege in its former heartlands, God has placed its destiny in the hands of the people of the South. Thus, for many African Christians in the diaspora like Adelaja, the recession of Christianity among Westerners is a call to evangelism and the re-establishment of kingdom values in the lands of 19th-century missionaries. Mission is in reverse.

5.4.6 Varieties of churches in mission

African-led churches in Europe come in different varieties and categories. The earliest ones began as fellowships among migrants who felt unwelcome in the established churches of Europe on racial grounds. These interdenominational fellowships served a second purpose of making up for the spiritual and liturgical poverty of worship life in the European church. As the churches of the missionaries continued to lose their spiritual fervour and sense of the supernatural, the Africans took their spiritual destinies into their own hands and reconstituted fellowships into churches where faith could be expressed in ways that resonated with African and biblical pieties. In western Europe the rise of African immigrant churches and other non-Western Christian congregations has been noted to be dramatically visible because of the stark contrast between the dynamism of new immigrant Christian groups and the often-moribund tone of the traditional churches.[17] The first African immigrant churches to form in Europe were the African independent churches, known in Ghana as Spiritual churches and in Nigeria and South Africa as *Aladura* ("praying people") and Zionist churches, respectively. African members of mainline denominations in their home countries initially joined similar denominations in Europe, particularly so in the United Kingdom and Germany.

Within the last quarter of the 20th century, the range of churches filled with African migrants has broadened widely. African-based classical Pentecostal churches, such as the "Ghana Church of Pentecost" and Nigerian William F. Kumuyi's "Deeper Christian Life Bible Church," have brought together their own and established congregations throughout Europe. In more recent years, African neo-Pentecostals have also taken Europe by storm. Ashimolowo's

---

17. Jehu J. Hanciles, *Beyond Christendom: Globalization, African Migration, and the Transformation of the West* (Maryknoll, NY: Orbis, 2008), 150.

Kingsway International Christian Centre and Adelaja's Embassy of God belong to this category but, as stated earlier, the former attracts mostly Africans and the latter is filled with Europeans. Neo-Pentecostal churches that have burgeoned in Europe include A. A. Adeboye's "Redeemed Christian Church of God" and many other autochthonous charismatic churches that are completely transforming the European religious landscape through the mission of *presence*. The primary intention of these churches is not to establish congregations for only Africans, so those belonging to the independent category usually cast themselves as international churches. Thus, my preferred designation for the religious initiatives of people like Adelaja is "African-led churches in Europe" in order not to create the impression that these communions are not intended for non-Africans.

The questions of ethnic and cultural identities are important for people in the diaspora, but African immigrant Christians see themselves as international churches, thereby consciously labelling themselves in inclusive terms. African Christians in the Netherlands generally identify themselves first and foremost as Christians and only secondly as Africans or African Christians. In their own view, their public adherence to Christianity constitutes the most important element of their identity. There is no questioning the fact that the immigrant churches in Europe founded and dominated by Africans provide for members a social safety net from the harsh immigration conditions that are worsening by the day, due to the reconstitution of the European Union. For many of them, however, their religion helps them to achieve a degree of security and inner strength within a hostile European environment. Jesus Christ's own life and ministry included the travail of a refugee, the pain of uprootedness, and the alienation that comes with being a stranger.

5.4.7 Conclusion

The painful experiences therefore notwithstanding, African Christians and African-led churches in Europe interpret their presence in terms of a call to mission and evangelism. Thus, Adelaja's mission has included providing religious and social services, desperately needed within a society that, in their thinking, had proven inept at coping with social evils such as alcoholism, drugs, and prostitution. Christian mission has to do with knowing what the Creator-Redeemer is doing in the world and allowing God to engage one in the enterprise. I use mission and evangelism as synonymous expressions encapsulating the active prosecution of an agenda to restore and reconcile a broken world to God in Christ. That has been God's business. African-led immigrant churches in Europe like Embassy of God are serving deep-seated religious needs that lie neglected in the evangelism efforts of the churches belonging to the former heartlands of Christian mission. The Spirit of God seems to have chosen the church in Africa and African Christian leaders for a spectacular advance. I believe that the ministries of immigrant churches are serving the purposes of the Spirit in God's work of renewal and mission.

We can observe several reasons for the reverse in mission as exemplified in the ministry of Sunday Adelaja. First, Christianity in African hands serves to challenge the moral relativisms in European culture by getting people to offer their lives to Christ in ways reminiscent of what occurs in the biblical Acts of the Apostles. The people that have been reached by Sunday Adelaja's Embassy of God are, as stated before, predominantly former drug addicts, prostitutes, and leaders and members of mafia gangs who have now, under the powerful influence of the Spirit, turned to Christ.

Second, through these churches, the Bible has returned to the life of the church as the authoritative word of God. It is the main book from which preaching is done and it is considered sufficient for teaching, rebuking, and training in righteousness. In the use of the Bible, African immigrant churches do take African worldviews of supernatural evil seriously as far as pastoral care is concerned. Thus, African Christians find ample evidence for their beliefs in the Bible, which represents forces of good and evil, as having power over life and death. African churches in the diaspora, irrespective of their particular per-suasion, address the issue of spiritual forces explicitly. Right from missionary times, Western missionaries described African worldviews of mystical causality as psychological delusions and the figment of people's imagination. Not so with African churches in Europe, which irrespective of whatever abuses that may be associated with those worldviews, do take them seriously and articulate Christian responses to them in ways that may look alien to Western rational and cerebral Christianity. The sense of fear, uncertainty, and insecurity asso-ciated with being an immigrant makes the ministry of spiritual warfare an important aspect of the mission of diaspora churches.

Third, the reverse in mission has implications for liturgical renewal. African churches generally prefer worship life that is experiential, expressive, exuber-ant, and dynamic in nature. Although informal liturgical services character-ize Pentecostal worship, in African hands things move notches higher, and this is evident in the life of the Embassy of God. Whether they belong to the

Pentecostal/charismatic stream of Christianity or not, renewal seems to be an important element in the lives of these churches, the point being that the active presence of the Spirit is what gives the church of Jesus Christ its identity.

Fourth, the churches in the diaspora provide much needed moral and physical support for their fellow aliens in the foreign lands of Europe. The African immigrant at the present time lives within a very precarious and difficult European world, and spiritual and material support from the churches cannot but be considered a high priority on the church's agenda. In that respect, these churches have chosen a path of evangelization that is not discontinuous with what we encounter in the Acts of the Apostles, where the believers bonded together to provide for each other's needs in the spirit of Christ.

Finally, perhaps one of the greatest lessons we learn from the ministry of *presence* associated with the African diaspora initiatives is that through these immigrants God may be preserving the life of the church. It recalls the days of Jesus' birth when his infant life came under threat from Herod and his henchmen. Under the direction of the divine messenger, the child and his parents took refuge in Egypt until the time when it was considered conducive for mission to resume. In African hands, Christianity has virtually returned "home" to the continent that granted refugee status to the Lord of mission when his life was in danger. With the recession of Christianity in the modern West and the siege under which the faith has sometimes come, immigrant churches may well be the institutions through whose efforts God would like to keep God's presence active in the West.

PART THREE

Evangelism and Its Practice

CHAPTER 6

Francis Brienen

Trends and Developments in Evangelism: An Overview

6.1 Introduction

Speak to an ordinary member of a local church and it will not take long to discover that evangelism has an image problem. It may be seen as something practiced by a specific group within the mainline churches or by particular churches (free, Evangelical, Pentecostal) and associated with a specific approach, often linked to the evangelical revivalist approaches of the 19th century and the crusades of Billy Graham from the 1950s to 2005.[1] Yet, that is only partly the reality of evangelism. It could be argued that today the evangelism scene is more diverse, innovative, and dynamic than ever, involving many denominations and individual Christians, deploying many different methods and approaches. In addition to that, for many churches evangelism is no longer a niche activity but has moved centre stage.

1. Billy Graham conducted 417 crusades in 185 countries. His first campaign in western Europe was in 1954, in England, the Netherlands, West Germany, France, Denmark, Finland, and Sweden. His first campaigns to the former Eastern Bloc were in Hungary in 1977 and in the Soviet Union, East Germany, and Czechoslovakia in 1982. Between 1947 and 2005 his campaigns reached 210 million people worldwide.

These changes can be explained by a number of factors, two of which stand out. The first was the realization in the 1980s that Billy Graham–style campaigns were losing their effectiveness in a changed spiritual context.[2] The second was accelerated church decline after 1980, which led many denominations to a deep questioning about the way forward in how to share faith and connect with contemporary culture. This culture, across Europe, was increasingly marked by secularism and "believing without belonging," a phrase Grace Davie coined to indicate that people still adhere to certain beliefs without translating this into belonging to the church. Danièle Hervieu-Léger added further nuances by introducing "belonging without believing," referring to the fact that church members remain so for traditional and cultural, rather than faith, reasons. Hans Raun Iversen, focussing on the Danish Lutheran Church, speaks of "belonging without even believing in belonging." David Voas captured the changes in contemporary culture with the phrase "fuzzy fidelity" to describe the religious inclinations of the majority of European populations: they are neither regular churchgoers nor self-consciously nonreligious; they believe in something "out there"; they retain some residual involvement and some loyalty to Christian values and tradition.[3]

The churches found themselves in a new and often bewildering context. Yet, this also led to an opening up to new opportunities for evangelism and for reimagining what it means to be followers of Christ and to be church. In France, Germany, and the United Kingdom there was a growing realization that they were now mission countries and that the Christian faith had to be inculturated in new ways. Consequently, mission and evangelism found their way back onto the agenda with renewed urgency. The French Catholic Bishops' *Proposer la Foi dans la Société Actuelle*, published in 1997, set out to enable Catholics to perceive better how faith could still be lived out and proposed, regardless of the changes in culture. In Germany the Evangelical Lutheran Church published *Das Evangelium unter die Leute bringen*, not long after the Catholic Bishops' document, *Zeit zur Aussaat*.[4] Both documents

---

2. John Finney, *Emerging Evangelism* (London: Darton, Longman and Todd, 2004), 70–72.
3. Grace Davie, *Religion in Britain since 1945: Believing without Belonging* (Oxford: Blackwell, 1994); Danièle Hervieu-Léger, *Pilger und Konvertiten: Religion in Bewegung* (Würzburg: Ergon, 2004), 34; Hans Raun Iversen, "Leaving the Distant Church: The Danish Experience," in Mordechai Bar-Lev and William Shaffir, eds., *Leaving Religion and Religious Life* (Greenwich, CT: JAI Press, 1997), 157; David Voas, "The Rise and Fall of Fuzzy Fidelity in Europe," *European Sociological Review* 25, no. 2 (2009): 155–68.
4. Les Évêques de France, *Proposer la Foi dans la Société Actuelle: Lettres aux Catholiques de France* (Paris: Éditions du Cerf, 1997); Evangelische Kirche in Deutschland, *Das Evangelium unter die Leute bringen: Zum missionarischen Dienst der Kirche in unserem Land. EKD—Texte 68* (Hannover: EKD,

focussed the churches' attention outward and highlighted evangelization as the normal, everyday duty of the whole people of God. Mission was the heartbeat of the church.[5] In the United Kingdom a major development was the Anglican Communion's Decade of Evangelism, launched in 1988 and embraced by the churches in Britain in the 1990s. While the decade did not reverse numerical decline, it did produce an important change in mindset about evangelism. Whereas in 1985 evangelism still meant for many the big meeting and the imported speaker, by the end of the Decade it meant the small group, the ordinary member of the congregation, and the continuous work of the church. Similar accents could be found in a major study document of the Community of Protestant Churches in Europe, published some years later, called *Evangelising/Evangelisch Evangelisieren*, which aimed at developing and strengthening evangelism in its 105 member churches.[6]

The arrival of migrant Christians in Europe in relatively recent years also had a major impact both on the shape of Christianity in Europe and on the churches' view of evangelism. In the same way that a massive missionary movement attended earlier European migrations, recent migration into Europe is also marked by tremendous missionary activity.[7] Not only did this result in the planting of many new churches, migrant Christians' fresh and positive views of evangelism also enabled local churches to rediscover a passion for mission and evangelism. Migrant Christians' buoyant spirituality, their knowledge of what it means to be church on the margins, and a zeal to share their faith story influenced and shaped the search for new ways of evangelism in Europe and continue to do so.

This chapter will describe some of the trends and developments in recent years in the practice of evangelism. One chapter cannot do justice to the diversity and complexity of the continent of Europe nor to the many ways in which churches and individual Christians engage in evangelism. It is recognized that most trends and developments discussed here are based on knowledge and experience of the northwest European and Protestant context in particular.

2001); Sekretariat der Deutschen Bischofskonferenz, ed., *Zeit zur Aussaat, Missionarisch Kirche Sein* (Bonn, 2000).

5. A phrase introduced by Eberhard Jüngel, speaking at the General Synod of the German Evangelical Church (EKD) in Leipzig in 1999.

6. Michael Bünker and Martin Friedrich, eds., *Evangelising: Protestant Perspectives for the Churches in Europe* (Budapest: Community of Protestant Churches in Europe, 2007).

7. Jehu J. Hanciles, "Migration and Mission: The Religious Significance of the North-South Divide," in Andrew Walls and Cathy Ross, eds., *Mission in the Twenty-First Century: Exploring the Five Marks of Global Mission* (London: Darton, Longman and Todd, 2008), 121.

Other chapters in this volume, as well as some of the case studies, will explore more deeply developments in other traditions and in other parts of Europe.

The proliferation of approaches in evangelism that can be seen in recent years all represent different ways in which churches interact with their community. Churches do so by being attractional, engaging, or by being contextual/incarnational. Attractional churches relate to the world on a "you-come-to-us" basis, while engaged churches go into their communities in loving service, often hoping that the people they serve will be drawn into the church on Sunday. Contextual or incarnational churches go into the surrounding context and grow new churches within it.[8] This threefold distinction provides the framework and organizing principle for describing the trends and developments in evangelism in this chapter.

6.2 Attractional Developments

6.2.1 Invitation

Religion in Europe is in decline. Although there are some minor differences in the speed of the decline (the most religious countries are changing more quickly than the least religious), the magnitude of the fall in religiosity from the early to the late 20th century has been remarkably constant across the continent.[9] This has not meant a decline in interest in spirituality, however, merely a declining interest in structured and institutionalized religion.[10] The *Mission-Shaped Church* report published in the United Kingdom in 2004 estimated that 60 percent of the population were beyond the reach of the way most churches go about sharing their faith.[11] And it was expected that with every generation the number of those "out of reach" would increase.[12] Yet, the report also noted that there was a significant proportion of people who were within reach of the church: 10 percent of the population came to church regularly (at

8. See Michael Moynagh, *Church for Every Context: An Introduction to Theology and Practice* (London: SCM Press, 2012), xvi. Moynagh draws on the work of Michael Frost and Alan Hirsch for the distinction between attractional and incarnational/contextual churches, and on the work of Bob Hopkins and Michael Breen for the engaged approach.
9. Voas, "Rise and Fall," 155–68.
10. Steven Croft et al., *Evangelism in a Spiritual Age: Communicating Faith in a Changing Culture* (London: Church House Publishing, 2005), 129.
11. Church of England's Mission and Public Affairs Council, *Mission-Shaped Church: Church Planting and Fresh Expressions of Church in a Changing Context* (London: Church House Publishing, 2004).
12. This was borne out by Voas's research in 2008.

least once a month), 10 percent came occasionally (at festivals or very occasionally), and 20 percent used to come and were open to coming back. This finding was affirmed by research into churchgoing in the United Kingdom in 2007, sponsored by the relief agency Tearfund, which also found that a significant number of people would come to church if only they were asked.[13] These reports encouraged the churches in Britain to engage in a number of new initiatives in attractional and invitational evangelism, based on the active involvement of ordinary church members.

One such major initiative was "Back to Church Sunday," which was started in the United Kingdom in 2004. It is based on the simple idea of one person inviting another person to come to church with them on the last Sunday of September. "Back to Church Sunday" has grown beyond all expectations and it is now the largest single local-church invitation initiative in the world, taking place in churches across denominations worldwide. The organizers recently expanded "Back to Church Sunday" to a "Season of Invitation," encouraging church members to invite a friend to church on five occasions, from Harvest Sunday (at the end of September) to Christmas. The change was based on the finding that people are much more likely to come to church and keep coming if they are invited several times.[14]

Invitation and attraction also mark the "New Evangelization" in the Roman Catholic Church, which was introduced during the pontificate of Pope John Paul II and which had a strong, though not exclusive, focus on those who were baptized but did not practice (cf. ch. 5.2.2, above). This is continued in *Evangelii Gaudium*, the first major document of Pope Francis's pontificate.[15] It identifies three principal settings in which evangelization is carried out: in ordinary pastoral ministry to the faithful; in new evangelization of the baptized who lack a meaningful relation with the church (lapsed Catholics); and in primary proclamation to those who do not know Jesus Christ. Inactive baptized people are called to reconnect with the church and the Catholic faith, and the faithful are urged to invite them by sharing their joy, as "it is not by proselytizing that

---

13. Jacinta Ashworth and Ian Farthing, *Churchgoing in the UK: A Research Report from Tearfund on Church Attendance in the UK* (Teddington, UK: Tearfund, 2007). The research suggested that three million people would come to church if they were invited.

14. A Season of Invitation, "Back to Church Sunday," http://www.seasonofinvitation.co.uk/about/back-to-church-sunday.

15. Pope Francis, *Evangelii Gaudium—The Joy of the Gospel: Apostolic Exhortation on the Proclamation of the Gospel in Today's World* (London: Catholic Truth Society, 2013), 7 (par. 3).

the church grows, but 'by attraction'."[16] In England and Wales this has led to the development of the Crossing the Threshold project, which is aimed at the four million baptized Catholics who rarely or never visit their local Catholic parish. The project supports every parish to make ministry and outreach to non-churchgoing Catholics a priority.[17]

6.2.2 Welcome

In *Transforming Mission: Paradigm Shifts in Theology of Mission,* the South African theologian David J. Bosch (1929–1992) describes persuasively the importance of the life and witness of the church in the apostle Paul's mission, both as authenticators of his mission and as foretaste of the kingdom. Through their unity, mutual love, exemplary conduct, and radiant joy, churches become missionary by their very nature. Evangelism is only possible when the community that evangelizes is a radiant manifestation of the Christian faith and exhibits an attractive lifestyle.[18] Referring to Hans-Werner Gensichen's criteria for a missionary church, the witness of life of the believing community prepares the way for the gospel.[19] The link between *communio* and *missio* is also made in the German Bishops' *Zeit zur Aussaat,* Pope Francis's *Evangelii Gaudium,* and in the World Council of Churches' new statement on mission and evangelism, *Together towards Life,* which states: "Authentic Christian witness is not only in *what* we do in mission but *how* we live out our mission."[20]

Churches are rediscovering that the life of the witnessing community and the act of evangelizing are inextricably linked. This is not just a matter of practicality or tactics. Increasingly, churches are discovering that hospitality and welcome are central to their Christian calling and go to the heart of Christian community living. The quality of the life of the witnessing community is a key factor in evangelism. As a consequence, there is a strong emphasis in contemporary evangelism on enhancing the hospitality and welcome of the local church. Through courses, literature, and seminars—such as Bob Jackson's and Mike Fisher's *Everybody Welcome* course developed in the United Kingdom,

16. Ibid., 15, quoting Pope Benedict XVI, "Homily at Mass for the Opening of the Fifth General Conference of the Latin American and Caribbean Bishops" (13 May 2007), Aparecida, Brazil, *Acta Apostolicae Sedis* 99 (2007): 437.

17. For more information on the "Crossing the Threshold" project, see http://www. cbcew.org.uk.

18. David J. Bosch, *Transforming Mission: Paradigm Shifts in Theology of Mission* (Maryknoll, NY: Orbis, 1991), 414.

19. Hans-Werner Gensichen, *Glaube für die Welt: Theologische Aspekte der Mission* (Gütersloh: Gütersloher Verlagshaus Gerd Mohn, 1971), 170–72.

20. World Council of Churches, *Together towards Life: Mission and Evangelism in Changing Landscapes* (Geneva: WCC Publications, 2013), 29.

which draws on biblical inspiration as well as the insights of the hospitality industry—churches are helped to look at their life, to become more intentional about being open and welcoming, and, by doing so, to overcome the sense of embarrassment some have about their lacklustre life and witness.[21] Churches are also becoming aware that welcoming people into membership of the community of Christ and nurturing them into Christian discipleship can only be achieved when the quality of the life of the whole church measures up to the task in hand. In addition to that, there is a realization that increasing the retention rate of people trying the church out is the most powerful way in which churches grow, and more churches are becoming aware that failing to do so weakens the power of evangelistic approaches.[22]

But does improving one's welcome and hospitality go far enough? Some would argue that in an increasingly multicultural context it does not, and that churches need to move beyond merely welcoming and giving hospitality. In his book *Exclusion and Embrace*, Miroslav Volf challenges churches to go beyond learning to live with one another and to take the dangerous and costly step of opening themselves to the other and to readjust their identities to make space for them.[23] Stephanie Spellers's book *Radical Welcome* provides a practical theological guide for congregations that want to move beyond mere inclusivity toward becoming a place where welcoming "the Other" is taken seriously and issues of power and patterns of inclusion and exclusion are addressed.[24] Spellers's work has inspired the "God Is Still Speaking" campaign of the United Church of Christ in the United States, an initiative which has generated interest in a number of European churches as well.

6.2.3 Inquiry and nurture courses

The rise of the nurture group is a phenomenon, which has had a massive impact on the church in the United Kingdom and, increasingly, on the church worldwide. Nurture groups are small groups aimed at helping inquirers and new

---

21. Bob Jackson and George Fisher's Everybody Welcome course is an example. It helps churches to look at making the church more visible in the community, making the premises more inviting, making the people more welcoming, helping newcomers to belong, and how to train a welcome team. Jackson and Fisher, *Everybody Welcome: The Course Where Everybody Helps Grow Their Church* (London: Church House Publishing, 2009).

22. Ibid. See also Ron Kallmier and Andy Peck, *Closing the Back Door of the Church* (Surrey, UK: CWR Publishing, 2009).

23. Miroslav Volf, *Exclusion & Embrace: A Theological Exploration of Identity, Otherness, and Reconciliation* (Nashville: Abingdon, 1996).

24. Stephanie Spellers, *Radical Welcome: Embracing God, The Other, and the Spirit of Transformation* (New York: Church Publishing, 2006), 11.

Christians to explore faith and to do so in a supportive environment where priority is given to asking questions and sharing spiritual experiences. It can be argued that nurture groups have been more evangelistically effective than many more high-profile movements.[25] They can be traced back to catechism or confirmation groups and membership classes, which had been a normal part of church life for generations. It was recognition of the differences in the evangelistic context, however, which led to the start of the nurture groups in the United Kingdom. Key factors that played a part in the development of the nurture group included the need to focus on adults in faith formation, and the realization that the initiation of an individual into faith is complex and requires something deeper and more extensive.

A major step toward the development of the nurture group was taken by the Billy Graham campaigns of the 1980s. It was felt that, because many British people were so far away from the faith, after making a decision in the stadium, they needed to be steered toward a small group for learning and integration into the church. These groups proved their worth: research after the campaigns showed that 72 percent of people who went to a nurture group went on to full membership of their local church, while only 23 percent of those who did not join such a group made that transition.[26] A significant boost came from the Decade of Evangelism, which identified the nurture group rather than big evangelistic campaigns as the main emphasis for evangelism in England. Local churches were encouraged to set up their own nurture groups to draw in those outside the church. This was based on two insights: that building relationships is crucial to evangelism and that conversion is a journey to faith, a process, rather than a sudden decision.

It was this context that produced one of the most remarkable developments in the evangelism scene in the United Kingdom and beyond: the rise of courses like Alpha, Emmaus, and others, all of which are designed to help inquirers to explore faith in small groups over a period of weeks. Of these courses, Alpha has become the most well known and most widely used.[27]

Alpha is a series of interactive sessions that freely explore the basics of the Christian faith. It runs in churches, bars, coffee shops, and homes all around the globe. Typically, Alpha has around ten sessions and includes food, a short talk,

---

25. Finney, *Emerging Evangelism*, 73–88.
26. Ibid., 76.
27. Mike Booker and Mark Ireland, *Evangelism—Which Way Now? An Evaluation of Alpha, Emmaus, Cell Church and Other Contemporary Strategies for Evangelism* (London: Church House Publishing, 2003), 9.

and a discussion at the end. Alpha began as an introduction to the Christian faith—effectively a nurture course—for new Christians attending the Anglican Holy Trinity Brompton Church in central London. When curate Nicky Gumbel took over the running of Alpha at Holy Trinity Brompton in 1990, he noticed its appeal to those who would not describe themselves as Christians and he revised the course to make it more directly evangelistic. Alpha became increasingly popular and, after the first training conference for church leaders in 1993, began running in other churches in the United Kingdom and around the world. Worldwide Alpha was embraced by 165 churches across a very wide denominational spectrum, and is often run as an ecumenical initiative between churches or in an ecumenical context like a prison chaplaincy. Since the start of Alpha, 27 million people have done the course in 169 countries and 112 languages.[28] It has grown from being one church's nurture course to a worldwide movement with a high public profile.

Alpha has been critiqued for its standardization (some call it "McDonaldization") and lack of contextualization, its theology, and for using power evangelism as its underlying model.[29] There is also the risk that churches will reduce their evangelism to running Alpha at the expense of other less fashionable and more difficult forms of evangelism, such as ministry in the community. Nevertheless, Alpha became the biggest evangelistic tool of the 1990s and has helped many hundreds of thousands of people around the world to come to Christian faith.

Early research, in 1999, into the effectiveness of Alpha and other inquirer/nurture courses in the Anglican Diocese of Lichfield in the United Kingdom showed that 61 percent of parishes were offering one or more of such courses and 39 percent of them used Alpha. Of those attending, 21 percent had "come to Christian faith, commitment or confirmation."[30] At the same time there was a noticeable decline in the number of parishes holding traditional missions. Other research has produced evidence that churches running Alpha are less likely to show decline in attendance, particularly if they have been running Alpha for three or more years.[31]

---

28. Since 1993, 3.3 million people have taken part in Alpha courses in the United Kingdom. Alpha attracted 299,000 people in 2012.

29. Booker and Ireland, *Evangelism*, 23.

30. See Mark Ireland, "A Study of the Effectiveness of Process Evangelism Courses in the Diocese of Lichfield with Special Reference to Alpha" (Master's thesis, University of Sheffield, 2000). However, research by Stephen Hunt suggests the figure is slightly lower, at 17 percent; Hunt, *Anyone for Alpha? Evangelism in a Post-CHRISTIAN society* (London: Darton, Longman and Todd, 2001), 97.

31. Research by Peter Brierley, *Church Growth in the 1990s: What the English Church Attendance Survey Reveals* (London: Christian Research, 2000), quoted in Booker and Ireland, *Evangelism*, 16.

The number of churches running Alpha in the United Kingdom plateaued after the year 2000, suggesting that by then the market was saturated. Another reason, however, was the explosion in the number of other courses that have been published since Alpha. One of these is Emmaus, which, though not as well known as Alpha, has now also been used widely beyond the United Kingdom. Based on an earlier course, *Christians for Life*, the Emmaus course was developed by Stephen Cottrell, Steve Croft, John Finney, Felicity Lawson, and Robert Warren in the Anglican Diocese of Wakefield and was first published in 1996. If Alpha's strength lies in helping interested inquirers to commit their lives to Christ, then Emmaus aims to start further back, at the first contact stage, and to continue further on, fully initiating new believers into the life of the church. Its three phases go from contact to nurture to growth. Influenced by the rediscovery of the early church's practice of adult catechumenate in both the Roman Catholic and Anglican traditions, Emmaus draws on a variety of its features, including rituals of response, stages on the journey, and enough material to last a group for four years.[32] The stress which the early church put on proper Christian initiation and the effort and prayer which was required is seen as a guide for the 21st-century church, when once again people are coming to faith who have no Christian background at all. The four principles underlying the course are: (1) entry into faith is a process of discovery, (2) the process is best practiced as an accompanied journey, (3) the process affects the whole of our lives, and (4) effective initiation affects the life of the whole church. In contrast to Alpha, Emmaus's starting point is the inquirer's experience rather than doctrine or apologetics.

Alongside Alpha and Emmaus, many other process-evangelism courses have been developed.[33] These include lesser-known, prepackaged courses, as well as homemade programmes, devised by churches themselves. The courses represent a major development in evangelism and have shaped churches' understanding of, and engagement in, evangelism in significant ways:

Charles Freebury's comparative study of Alpha and Emmaus in the Methodist Disctrict of Plymouth and Exeter and the Anglican Diocese of Bath and Wells in 2001 comes to a similar conclusion: the number of people coming to faith increased significantly for those who had run the course four times or more. See Charles Freebury, "A Comparative Evaluation of the Alpha and Emmaus Courses" (Master's thesis, University of Sheffield, 2001).

32. Note that this tradition was never lost in the Orthodox tradition.

33. Such as the "*Glaubenskurse*" in Germany, developed by the Arbeitsgemeinschaft Missionarische Dienste.

1. They have helped churches to move from event-based evangelism toward process evangelism.[34]

2. They are based on an understanding of faith as a journey of discovery and growth and of conversion as a process. This broadens the focus of evangelism to a much longer-term process of discipleship.

3. They have deepened the understanding of the relationship between believing and belonging. The majority of people belong before they believe and many may well believe while no longer belonging to a church.[35]

4. They have highlighted the importance of the small group, friendship, and relationship in evangelism.

5. They have given the privilege and responsibility of evangelism back to ordinary church members.

6. They can become discipleship courses for church members as well, thus demonstrating that evangelism is not just a practice *ad extram* but *ad intram* as well.[36]

6.3 Engaging Approaches

While many churches have moved to approaches to evangelism that are more attractional and invitational, the most common way in which churches interact with their community is by engagement, that is, by going into their communities in loving service or evangelistic action, hoping that the people they reach will be drawn into the church. This can take the form of short-term or one-off events, but more often it is part of an understanding of mission (rather than evangelism) that is integral to all that the church does, and that leads to long-term engagement with the community, taking the church beyond its walls and combining evangelism with loving service (*diakonia*) or social action.

---

34. "Process evangelism" is a term coined by Gavin Reid, in Booker and Ireland, *Evangelism*, 63–64.
35. John Finney, *Finding Faith Today* (Swindon, UK: Bible Society, 1992).
36. Martin Reppenhagen, "Trends and Perspectives in the European Context." Unpublished paper delivered at the World Council of Churches' consultation on the elaboration of an ecumenical handbook on teaching evangelism in Europe, June 2014, Bossey, Switzerland.

6.3.1 Evangelistic action

The most common way in which churches have traditionally reached out to their communities is through short-term, one-off evangelistic campaigns, often led by an evangelist. Although there has been a shift to mission as an ongoing focus of the life of the church, there is still a significant place in the evangelistic work of the church for the long tradition of special mission events and special evangelistic people.[37] For many people this approach still works. Increasingly, however, churches that still run such events do so as part of an array of ways of reaching out into the community. The evangelistic event as the only tool for evangelism is in serious decline, as its effectiveness has decreased significantly. This can be explained by factors such as the absence of residual faith in the hearers and unfamiliarity with the church, but, most importantly, with how faith and conversion are understood in terms of journey and process.

Yet, it is also because the journey of faith is a process that there is room for one-off evangelistic events. Within that process of discovering faith there may be important crisis points and major steps forward, as conceptualized by James F. Engel and others.[38] An evangelistic event can help people to take these significant steps. At a time when the gulf between the church and the world around it has widened, a short event can play a major part in raising questions and arousing interest. An example of this is "The Passion" in the Netherlands, a contemporary musical retelling of the passion story aimed at making it accessible to every person in the Netherlands. Staged in a different city each year, with well-known actors and singers, and broadcast live on television, the event attracts much attention, admiration, and debate.[39] Major community events, even when not intentionally evangelistic, such as the German Kirchentag or the Taizé community's New Year gatherings, can have similar impact.

---

37. This tradition can be traced back to the apostle Paul, through to the travelling prophets mentioned in the *Didache*, Celtic missionaries, medieval preaching friars, and the preachers of the 18th-century evangelical revival. Since then a continuous tradition of open-air preaching and travelling evangelism can be traced up to the late 20th century, with the greatest impact made by the Billy Graham campaigns. Booker and Ireland, *Evangelism*, 62–64.

38. The Engel Scale resembles a number line, depicting a series of steps from "awareness of a supreme being and no knowledge of the gospel" to "communion with God and stewardship." The Engel Scale and its adaptations have been much critiqued for depicting the faith journey as a cognitive process and underplaying its emotional and relational aspects. Moynagh, *Church for Every Context*, 339.

39. "The Passion" is supported by a website (http://www.thepassion.nl) which points visitors to Bible readings, an online course about searching for God, ways of engaging with other believers, and tips on how to pray.

6.3.2 Evangelism and social action

The most common way in which churches interact with their community, however, is by going outside their walls in loving service and social action. Social engagement is not new. Throughout history, churches and individual Christians have tried to follow the example of Jesus, who proclaimed the good news in words and actions. Monasteries in the Middle Ages, 19th-century inner-city missions, and the Salvation Army are but a few examples of Christians proclaiming and living out the good news. Christians' involvement did not stop at practical caring for the needy and the relief of suffering. During the 19th century in particular, Christians were at the forefront, for example, of seeking to break the chains of injustice and oppression, pushing for the abolition of slavery and the slave trade, and for reform in housing and education.

Today, too, Christians are involved in a significant and wide variety of crucial activities in society across Europe. Through individuals, churches, clergy, and religious orders, the church provides a range of services to the community and society. Many Christians are engaged in campaigns for social, political, and economic justice. Many also volunteer in secular organizations and are crucial to their functioning. What is worthy of note is that it is increasingly local churches that get involved in one-off and long-term community involvement rather than leaving it to specialist bodies and agencies, as they might have done in the past. And so it is local churches providing lunch clubs and other activities for the elderly, organizing winter shelters for homeless people, offering debt counselling and benefit advice, caring for lonely people by befriending and keeping in telephone contact, creating events for parents and toddlers, and much more.

What is also notable is that much community-based engagement takes place ecumenically. Greater unity in mission action is a discernable trend in much of the churches' work, in the United Kingdom and elsewhere. In the United Kingdom, 420 foodbanks, serving over one million people, are run by churches and communities working together. Street Pastors, an initiative set up to make the nighttime economy and communities safer by engaging with and helping people on the streets, works with local teams representing at least four different denominations. Winter shelters for homeless people tend to be run by groups of churches in a local area, so that they can share the burden of providing facilities, food, and volunteers.

In the United Kingdom parachurch agencies play an active and important role in enabling such ecumenical cooperation. An example is "HOPE," an agency which provides resources for local churches of all denominations to work together, in word and action, focussing on the Christian festivals and major events, such as the centenary of the First World War. Another parachurch agency, "More Than Gold," facilitated ecumenical action around the London Olympics and Paralympics in 2012. This helped churches and Christian agencies to work together by offering hospitality and service, sharing faith, and speaking out on social issues connected with such events, such as sex trafficking and child labour. For example, the Baptists brought in mission teams, the Salvation Army handed out cups of water to the spectators, Christians of all denominations offered home stays to athletes who did not have the means to stay in the Olympic Village, various Pentecostal denominations handed out free Bibles, and churches of all persuasions organized community festivals. Similar ecumenical action took place around the FIFA World Cup in Germany.

6.3.3 Integral mission

What is often problematic for the engaged church is to hold evangelism and social action together as integral to mission. Speaking about the United Kingdom, Mike Booker and Mark Ireland contend that as churches engage in ministry and mission in the community, a clear and coherent partnership between evangelism and social action seldom emerges.[40] Many projects are undertaken not with evangelism in mind, but as a form of service or Christian presence. Where churches are deeply involved in community projects it is at times difficult to detect that these are activities done by or in the name of a church. There is a deep-rooted hesitancy about overt evangelism, for fear of it being exploitative or insensitive. Many feel it is not appropriate in our increasingly multifaith societies.

In this, the United Kingdom churches are not alone. Across Europe, many local churches and denominations will have separate committees or departments for *diakonia* and for mission/evangelism. Many will be able to echo Anne Marie Kool, who, when speaking about the churches' work in Central Europe among the Roma community, noted that the evangelistic perspective was absent. Yet, she comments, it is exactly the transformational power of the gospel that has changed lives.[41] A recent evaluation of the "HOPE" initiative

---

40. Booker and Ireland, *Evangelism*, 93.
41. Annemarie Kool, "Evangelism in Theological Education and Missiological Formation: A Central and Eastern European Perspective with a Hungarian Focus." Unpublished paper for a consultation on Evangelism in Theological Education and Missiological formation arranged by the World Council of Churches, 28–31 October 2012, Bossey, Switzerland.

in the United Kingdom found that in the churches' ecumenical outreach to the community in word and action, the social-action aspect had worked well but faith sharing had not.[42]

Yet, it can be argued that both in the church's thinking and practice there is a growing awareness that word and action, witness and service are part of holistic or integral Christian mission. In the words of David Bosch: "The word may . . . never be divorced from the deed, the example, the 'Christian presence', the witness of life. It is the 'Word made flesh' that is the gospel."[43] Christopher Wright, writing from an Evangelical perspective, also argues for a more holistic understanding of the church's mission, preferring to speak of the ultimacy rather than the primacy of evangelism. Missional engagement may not always begin with evangelism, but the ultimate purpose for all mission activity is evangelistic proclamation of the gospel.[44]

This shift toward holistic or integral mission can also be perceived in the major Evangelical, ecumenical, and Catholic documents of recent years. In the Evangelical movement the first major document, the *Lausanne Covenant* of 1974, could still confidently state that "in the church's mission of sacrificial service, evangelism is primary."[45] The second major document, however, the *Manila Manifesto* of 1989, while still seeing evangelism as primary, clearly recognizes that true mission should always be incarnational.[46] The third document, *The Cape Town Commitment* of 2010, provides a refocussed emphasis on evangelism and the integral mission of the church, stating that all mission must reflect the integration of evangelism and committed engagement in the world. Integral mission proclamation has social consequences as people are called to love and repentance in all areas of life, and social involvement has evangelistic consequences as it witnesses to the transforming grace of Jesus Christ.[47]

A shift can also be observed in *Together towards Life*, which represents a move from a separation of social action and evangelism, as was visible in the Melbourne conference in 1980, to an understanding of the integral nature of the two.[48] Identifying social action and evangelism as key activities in the life

---

42. Theos Think Tank, *A Year of Mission: An Evaluation of HOPE 2014* (London: Theos, 2015).

43. Bosch, *Transforming Mission*, 420.

44. Christopher J. H. Wright, *The Mission of God: Unlocking the Bible's Grand Narrative* (Downers Grove, IL: Intervarsity Press, 2006).

45. The Lausanne Movement, *The Lausanne Covenant* (Lausanne, 1974), paras. 4–6.

46. The Lausanne Movement, *The Manila Manifesto* (Manila, 1989), section 4.

47. The Lausanne Movement, *The Cape Town Commitment* (Cape Town, 2010).

48. The World Council of Churches' commission on World Mission and Evangelism's conference in Melbourne, 1980, focussed on the theme "Your Kingdom Come." While the necessity of proclamation was clearly recognized, the cries of the poor, the hungry, and the oppressed predominated.

of local congregations, it goes on to say that evangelism is sharing the good news both in word and action. While evangelism through verbal proclamation is profoundly biblical, our words have to be consistent with our actions for evangelism to be authentic. "The combination of verbal declaration and visible action bears witness to God's revelation in Jesus Christ and of his purposes."[49]

Evangelii Gaudium devotes an entire chapter to the social dimension of evangelization.[50] It states clearly that evangelizing is to make the kingdom of God present in our world. Leaving out the social dimension constitutes a distortion of the authentic and integral meaning of the kerygma: "From the heart of the gospel we see the profound connection between evangelization and human advancement, which must necessarily find expression and develop in every work of evangelization." The mission of proclaiming the good news of Jesus Christ has a universal destination and its mandate of charity encompasses all dimensions of existence, all individuals, all areas of community life, and all peoples.

British community theologian Ann Morisy, in her book *Beyond the Good Samaritan*, notes that community ministry, defined as "a distinctive process which links together practical social responsibility and active, purposeful mission in a manner which does not abuse the vulnerable," is achievable for most church-run projects. Community ministry responds to an issue of local concern, but in this recognizes that Christians have something worth sharing. It takes the experience of faith seriously, believing that faith makes a difference to one's life. The challenge is not to abuse a sensitively established relationship with those who are vulnerable. Because community ministry is also underpinned by the belief that the poor and marginalized play a key part in the purposes of God, and that they are likely to be the means of conversion of those who show concern for their need, it offers a strategy for integral mission. Furthermore, it calls out people's involvement in their community and invites them to embrace a struggle wider than their own and to express venturesome love (Karl Rahner). This is at the heart of discipleship and helps them to link private faith with public action. It is from this that the potential for new insights, including a recognition of the significance of the gospel, can dawn. So, community ministry opens up the journey to faith in several ways: it offers Christians an opportunity to act in faith and thereby to arouse people's interest in their motivation; it also creates structures of participation for those in and

---

49. World Council of Churches, *Together*, 86.
50. Pope Francis, *Evangelii*, 89–90 (par.178), 91–92 (par. 181), 93 (par. 183).

outside the church.[51] Partnership in action may be the starting point. As people share with Christians in the work of the gospel, the journey of discipleship is begun even before faith is owned.

6.4 Contextual or Incarnational Developments

The latest and perhaps most exciting development in evangelism is the emergence of contextual or incarnational churches, that is, churches which go into the surrounding context and grow new churches within it. New expressions of the church are springing up in many parts of Europe. They are a response to changes in society and to the new post-Christendom context that the church faces in the global North. These emerging expressions have every appearance of being one of the most significant missional movements in the history of Christianity in the United Kingdom and in other parts of Europe. In his book *Church for Every Context*, Michael Moynagh uses "new contextual church" as the umbrella term to describe them. They are Christian communities that serve people mainly outside the church, belong to their culture, make discipleship a priority, and form a new church among the people they serve.[52] In other words, they are missional, contextual, formational, and ecclesial.

6.4.1 New contextual churches

Moynagh identifies four overlapping streams from which new contextual churches are emerging: (1) church planting, which has a long history in the United Kingdom going back as far as the Industrial Revolution and which had a resurgence in the 1990s; (2) the "fresh expressions" movement in the United Kingdom; (3) the existence of communities in mission, that is, groups that seek to combine rich life in community with mission; and (4) the "emerging-church" conversation which originated in the United States.[53]

---

51. Ann Morisy, *Beyond the Good Samaritan: Community Ministry and Mission* (London: Continuum, 1997), ix.

52. Moynagh, *Church for Every Context*, x.

53. Robert Doornenbal notes that emerging churches have sprung up in response to the adaptive challenge to the church in the face of church decline, increasing pluralism, consumerism, and postmodernity. They are grassroots communities that are consciously contextual, both culturally as well as geographically. See Robert Doornenbal, *Crossroads: An Exploration of the Emerging-Missional Conversation with a Special Focus on "Missional Leadership" and its Challenges for Theological Education* (Delft: Eburon Academic Publishers, 2012). Moynagh notes that many emerging churches have developed alternative forms of worship to re-engage Christians who find existing church alien, while others connect with people further from the church. Emerging churches are generally outside the

Within each of these four streams there are groups that tap into a new monasticism. Within these there are three different groups that can be identified: "those inspired by monks and nuns who gather for prayer in disused pubs, youth clubs, in places of natural beauty and elsewhere; those who identify with the friar tradition and move into an area either as single households of pioneers or as intentional communities; and a growing number of 'friar monks' who are inspired by both monk and friar traditions."[54]

6.4.2 Fresh expressions

Perhaps the most influential stream for the European context has been "fresh expressions." The term was first used in print in 2004 in the Church of England's report, *Mission-Shaped Church*, which has been highly influential.[55] The report was published by a working group, which had been tasked with reviewing the 1994 report *Breaking New Ground: Church Planting in the Church of England*, to assess progress and to consider new developments. The *Mission-Shaped Church* report recognized that the missionary context in Britain had changed. Communities, the report noted, are now multilayered, comprising neighbourhoods and a wide variety of networks, ranging from the relatively local to the global. What is called for in this new landscape is new proclamation of the gospel and the shaping of contextual faith communities within the different social structures of which people are part (family, job, leisure, politics, education, etc.). The report also noted that our diverse consumer and post-Christendom culture will never be reached by one standard form of church and therefore recommended a variety of integrated missionary approaches—in other words, a mixed economy of parish churches and network churches.

The *Mission-Shaped Church* report also described some of the new forms of church already in existence or emerging, such as alternative worship communities, churches arising out of community initiatives, network-focussed churches, seeker churches, traditional church plants, and youth congregations. These new forms, or fresh expressions, embrace two realities: existing churches that are seeking to renew and redirect what they already have, and others who are

---

denomination and highly critical of them. See Moynagh, *Church for Every Context*, xi. For communities in mission, see Bob Hopkins and Mike Breen, *Clusters: Creative Mid-sized Missional Communities* (Sheffield, UK: 3D Ministries Publications, 2007), 29–41.

54. Ian Mobsby, "The Importance of New Monasticism as a Model for Building Ecclesial Communities out of Contextual Mission," in Graham Cray, Ian Mobsby, and Aaron Kennedy, eds., *New Monasticism as Fresh Expression of Church* (London: Canterbury Press, 2010), 13–15.

55. Church of England's Mission and Public Affairs Council, *Mission-Shaped Church*.

intentionally sending out planting groups to discover what will emerge when the gospel is immersed in the mission context.

The report resulted in an ecumenical movement supported by a team, which has as its aim to encourage and support the development of fresh expressions of church in the United Kingdom.[56] Fresh expressions of church have multiplied across the participating denominations. In recent years they have also been embraced by a number of denominations across Europe, with fresh expressions and new forms of church now emerging in Switzerland, the Netherlands, Germany, and elsewhere.

In the United Kingdom the number of fresh expressions continues to multiply. In 2010, the Methodist Church found that 14 percent of its local churches had fresh expressions associated with them.[57] In 2011, the Church of England identified at least 1,000 parishes (6 percent of the total) with a fresh expression of church. Research published in 2014 into church growth in the Church of England found that four times as many initiatives were being started by 2012, compared to 2003 (80 compared with 20). Of the fresh expressions surveyed, the research found that 56 percent met in a wide variety of venues that were not church buildings; they mostly attracted people who do not otherwise go to church; just half of those coming were under 16 years of age; 52 percent were led by laypeople, most with no formal training for the role and 40 percent taking on the role in their spare time; 50 percent of fresh expressions were led by men and 50 percent by women.[58]

Of special note within fresh expressions, and perhaps its most popular form, is "messy church." "Messy church" is a form of church for children and adults that involves creativity, celebration, and hospitality. It is primarily for people who do not already belong to another form of church and meets at a time (and sometimes in a place) that suits them. "Messy church" was started in 2004, at an Anglican Church near Portsmouth (United Kingdom), by Lucy Moore and others. Since then "messy church" has spread across denominations and countries in Europe and beyond.[59] John Walker, reporting on church

---

56. "Fresh Expressions" is the name of the team in formal partnership with the Church of England, the Church of Scotland, the Congregational Federation, the Methodist Church of Great Britain, the Salvation Army, and the United Reformed Church.

57. *Are We Yet Alive?* (London: The Methodist Church, 2011), 14.

58. David Voas et al., *From Anecdote to Evidence: Findings from the Church Growth Research Programme 2011–2013* (London: The Church of England, 2014), http://www.churchgrowthresearch. org.uk/UserFiles/File/Reports/FromAnecdoteToEvidence1.0.pdf.

59. Within Europe, "messy church" can be found in Belgium, Denmark, Germany, Iceland, Ireland, Norway, Poland, Portugal, Spain, Sweden, Switzerland, and The Netherlands. See http://www. messychurch.org.uk.

growth in the Diocese of Canterbury, notes that research shows the supreme importance of childhood engagement with faith for the future health of the church's mission. He concludes that fresh expressions in general, and "messy church" in particular, are showing a demonstrable ability to address this issue.[60]

6.4.3 Mixed economy

Fresh expressions have changed the ecclesial landscape as well as denominational strategies. Rowan Williams has helpfully coined the phrase "mixed economy" to indicate that they can exist alongside traditional church and that there is a need for a range of different kinds of churches to reach into different sections of the population.[61] It is this very notion of mixed economy, however, that has been critiqued vigorously by Andrew Davison and Alison Millbank, who regard the concept as undermining traditional Anglican ecclesiology, which has its basis in the parish system. Regarding fresh expressions as no more than special-interest groups, they argue that if "Fresh Expressions is as equally valid a form of life for the Anglican Church as the parish, then what is common to both forms, the defining minimum of our identity, is greatly contracted."[62] This is not the only area of debate around fresh expressions. Ecclesiology (e.g., When does a small group of people become church?), sacramental theology (What about communion and baptism in fresh expressions?), leadership (Can anyone start/lead a fresh expression?), accountability (How does a fresh expression fit within the structure of the denomination and to whom are they accountable?), sustainability (Are they just a fad? Are they financially viable?), and fresh expressions' ability to connect with the multicultural church are all areas that generate lively and ongoing discussion.[63]

Nevertheless, it is beyond doubt that fresh expressions are connecting where traditional church is failing to connect. In 1995 Robert Warren identified "from doctrine to spirituality" as one of the enriching trends during the Decade of Evangelism. In many fresh expressions we are seeing Christians trying to engage with people in their spiritual search in new ways. They provide

---

60. John Walker, "Achieving sustainable growth in the Diocese of Canterbury. A shorter report," 20 March 2012, https://www.canterburydiocese.org/media/missionministryandgrowth/walkershort-draftreport.pdf. See also John Walker, *Testing Fresh Expressions: Identity and Transformation* (Farnham, UK: Ashgate, 2014).

61. Steven Croft, ed., *Mission-Shaped Questions: Defining Issues for Today's Church* (London: Church House Publishing, 2008), 3.

62. Andrew Davison and Alison Milbank, *For the Parish: A Critique of Fresh Expressions* (London: SCM Press, 2010), viii.

63. For a full list of questions about fresh expressions, see http://www.freshexpressions.org.uk.

"tents" along the way, small worshipping communities that concentrate on practical discipleship by serving their contexts and drawing others into faith.[64]

Fresh expressions also provide helpful lessons for traditional churches as they develop their evangelism. Tim Sumpter, in his book *Freshly Expressed Church*, lists what churches can learn: they embody the life of Christ in their lives, they prioritize human relationships by sharing meals together, they prioritize testimony as a central way of sharing faith verbally, they move away from intellectualizing faith toward communicating truth in a more reflective and interactive way, and they meet intentionally in places where people naturally interact and make friends.[65]

6.5 Conclusion

In this chapter I have explored a variety of ways in which churches and individual Christians engage in evangelism. Although not comprehensive, and focussed largely on the experience of local churches, the overview shows that evangelism in Europe is alive, dynamic, and ever changing. From our discussion of attractional, engaging, and contextual approaches a number of trends seem to emerge.

First of all, churches are increasingly recognizing that mission and evangelism are their core business. There is a greater awareness of the church's role in the *missio Dei* and perhaps also a greater confidence in the church as a vehicle of the gospel. In the words of *Together towards Life*: "To fulfil God's missionary purpose is the church's aim."[66] Mission is indeed the heartbeat of the church and evangelism its task.

Second, laypeople, ordinary church members, are increasingly moving centre stage in evangelism. Many churches and individual Christians are rediscovering the biblical notion that the call to share one's faith is extended to all. This is recognized in all major mission affirmations of recent years. *Evangelii Gaudium* notes: "Every Christian is challenged, here and now, to be actively engaged in evangelization. . . . Every Christian is a missionary to the extent that he or she has encountered the love of God in Christ Jesus: we no longer

---

64. Moynagh, *Church for Every Context*, 69, 363.
65. Tim Sumpter, *Freshly Expressed Church: Lessons from Fresh Expressions for the Wider Church* (Cambridge, UK: Grove Books, 2015).
66. World Council of Churches, *Together*, 57.

say that we are 'disciples' and 'missionaries', but rather that we are always 'missionary disciples'."[67]

Third, evangelism is moving from a separate activity to being integral to life and part of a wider discipleship. Evangelism is a way of life, taking place at anytime, anywhere, and under any circumstance. It happens in the ordinary activities in one's life and in the life of the church. We see this in particular in the new contextual churches.

Finally, we see a shift toward greater unity in mission and evangelism. From nurture courses to running night shelters to pioneering we see increased ecumenical cooperation. Christians increasingly assume to do mission and evangelism together, often in new ways. What is emerging can be described as "a new ecumenism," focussing less on the search for structural unity and more on common mission action. The call to greater unity that rings through all major mission affirmations of recent years is in Europe, in part at least, becoming reality.

It is beyond doubt that the church in Europe faces an immense challenge to be faithful to the call to share the gospel in a rapidly changing context. What is required is a transformation of the ways in which churches have traditionally shared the good news. What this overview has shown is that the church is responding to this challenge with courage, creativity, and hope. This transformation is not yet complete and much will be asked of the church's capacity to be flexible and to respond to change in the future. In doing so, however, it may be confident that God is faithful and through the Holy Spirit will continue to renew and empower the church for witness in this world.

---

67. Pope Francis, *Evangelii*, 63 (par. 120).

Gerrit Noort

Evangelism in Case Studies and Practices

Introduction to the Case Studies

Now that the preceding chapter has provided an overview of trends and developments in the ministry of evangelism, we can turn to the actual practice of evangelism. Chapter 7 therefore offers eight case studies which describe how Christian churches, communities, and organizations shape their witness in different contexts. The case studies do not offer an exhaustive portrait of existing models and practices in evangelism, but they are nevertheless a fair illustration of its range.

As this publication discusses evangelism in the European continent, the geographical locations of the case studies intentionally vary. They range from Russia to the United Kingdom and from Italy to Sweden. Of course, this implies that the cultural and religious contexts of the described cases are substantially different as well. The chapter also offers a variety of "confessional locations," as across Europe confessional representation differs greatly. The studies therefore show a variety of settings in Eastern Orthodox, Roman Catholic, Protestant, and Pentecostal ministries of evangelism. A few case studies, however, are not rooted in a specific confessional tradition, but have ecumenical cooperation of churches and mission in unity as their identity.

The case studies can be loosely grouped in pairs of two. In the first two case studies, on the street pastors in the United Kingdom (ch. 7.1) and the online church in the Netherlands (ch. 7.2), evangelism in the context of British nightlife and of the postmodern Dutch quest to "enjoy life" is described. The next set of case studies, on the Roman Catholic community Sant'Egidio (ch. 7.3) and the ecumenical Taizé community (ch. 7.4), illustrates the important relationship of Christian community and evangelism. These studies are followed by two cases about Christian witness in the Orthodox Churches in Russia (ch. 7.5) and Bosnia Herzegovina and Serbia (ch. 7.6). These studies show that formal religious education is an important tool for evangelism and that culture, shaped by Christianity, can be a surprisingly evangelizing influence itself. The last two case studies refer specifically to the role of evangelism in multicultural ministries. The first of these, on the International Christian Fellowship in Rotterdam (ch. 7.7), shows that migration has an impact on evangelistic ministries of traditional churches and leads to a renewed emphasis on the missionary nature of the congregation. The second, on reverse mission in Sweden (ch. 7.8), takes a different perspective as it focusses on the involvement of Christian migrants in evangelism in Europe and maps what their contribution entails.

Most of the case studies have a similar structure, which should help the reader to reflect fruitfully on essential issues in the practice of evangelism and to identify topics for further analysis. The structure, as such, is provided by the use of a more or less fixed set of seven frames that provide (1) the general history of the case being studied, (2) a description of its context, (3) an account of its identity and "culture," (4) a sketch of the theological inspiration that has proven relevant for the development of the project, (5) an explanation of the structure of the project and the available means to sustain it, (6) a clarification on the ideas about leadership, and, finally, (7) a section on lessons that were learned in the described ministry of evangelism.

7.1 Street Pastors: A Case Study from the United Kingdom

Francis Brienen

7.1.1 General description and history

Dalston, in the London borough of Hackney, is a lively neighbourhood with a multicultural population. Social and economic deprivation is high, but in recent years there has been a significant degree of gentrification as a result of the 2012 Olympic and Paralympic Games. At night the area is popular with students and young urban professionals who frequent the many bars and clubs in the area. This Friday night is no exception, and the street is buzzing with young people out for a good time. At the end of the road, at the local Baptist church, four people also gather. They include a teacher, a retired church worker, a retired housewife, and a charity worker. They are Street Pastors, volunteers from local churches, who patrol the streets ready to talk, listen, and help wherever needed. After catching up with one another, praying together, and calling the police to say that they will be patrolling the area, they are on their way. It is 11 PM. They walk slowly, smile, and say hello to everyone they pass. Soon conversations start: with roadworkers repairing potholes in the road, with people queueing up at a nightclub, with people they pass on the pavement. At the entrance to a shop, two Street Pastors start talking with two older men. One tells them about his struggle with alcohol and how he would like to give it up. The others strike up a conversation with three friends on a night out. It ends with praying for two of them. Walking along the busy, noisy main road, the street pastors are greeted by nightclub doormen, police, and people who have encountered them before. Someone asks what they are about. Only on one occasion does someone act in an intimidating way, but his friends calm him down. Outside one of the larger clubs in the area, the team gets into conversation with a group of friends, most of them Muslim and one of them Christian, and animated conversations follow about Jesus, about the Bible, and the Qur'an. One of them tells his life story to one of the Street Pastors. It ends with the promise of prayer. On the way back to base, the Street Pastors notice a loud argument in the street between two 19-year-old women. One threatens to abandon the other, leaving her alone and vulnerable. After lengthy negotiation, the Street Pastors manage to effect some kind of reconciliation and send them home in a taxi. The Street Pastors continue on their way, clearing up glass bottles as they go along. The evening ends back at the church just after 2 AM with their comparing notes and praying for the people they have encountered.

This fairly typical evening in the life of a Street Pastors team is now replicated in more than 270 locations in the United Kingdom. There are 11,000 trained Street Pastors, and about 2,000 of them are out on any Friday or Saturday night, between 10 PM and 4 AM.[1] They are the church on the street, not out to evangelize, but to work together with other partners in the nighttime economy to make communities better and safer. They carry bottles of water and foil blankets for revellers who have become dehydrated or cold, and flip-flops for those no longer able to walk on high-heeled shoes. They help, they listen, they care, and when asked, they pray. They are there to pick up the pieces amid drunken fights and accidents, bringing a softness to streets that can be hard and mean.

From the very beginning Street Pastors were concerned that street preaching or explicit evangelism would not be on the agenda. This sprang from the fundamental belief that the right to share the gospel has to be earned, both from the people in the street and from local authorities and the police. Nevertheless, even if there is not an explicit evangelistic intention, there is a clear evangelistic dimension to the work of Street Pastors.[2]

The Hackney team is normally made up of about eight people.[3] They are a mixed team: men and women, black and white, varying in age from 30s to 70s and representing five different denominations. They are committed Christians who all belong to a local church and who have undergone the rigorous Street

1. Figures quoted by Les Isaac in Stephen Tomkins, "Saturday night and Sunday morning, an interview with Les Isaac," *Reform Magazine* (October 2014).
2. See Hans-Werner Gensichen, *Glaube für die Welt: Theologische Aspekte der Mission* (Gütersloh: Gütersloher Verlagshaus Gerd Mohn, 1971). Gensichen uses "missionary intention" to refer to an explicitly missionary act, something that is primarily intended to be an expression of the love of God and of the church to the outsider. "Missionary dimension" denotes that the church's entire nature is missionary. The church must in all circumstances be missionary, but is not in every moment missionizing. Street Pastors' approach to evangelism offers a thought-provoking example of the creative relationship between these two concepts.
3. On the night described, four were absent.

Pastors training. What characterizes them is a strong concern for others, their local community, and society; a willingness to engage with people; and an ability to understand them without judgment.

Like all Street Pastors teams, the Hackney team is supported by prayer. This is essential to their work. Some Street Pastors teams include prayer pastors who stay at the base on the nights that they are out and pray for the team and the situations that they encounter. In the case of others, churches and individuals pray for them and the wider Street Pastors network wherever and whenever they can.

So, how did it all begin?

Street Pastors was launched in London in January 2003. The driving force for the initiative was Les Isaac, a pastor in the Ichthus Christian Fellowship, and for him it was the culmination of a journey that had led him through racist violence, gang warfare, Rastafarianism, conversion to Christianity, and becoming a church minister, to this point.

In 1993 Les Isaac had founded the "Ascension Trust," which aimed to see churches involved in mission in their context, through social action and sharing the gospel. From the outset Isaac had been deeply concerned about violence, particularly in urban contexts and among the Caribbean community. When the issues of gangs, drugs, and violence seemed to get worse, the Trust organized a "Guns on our Streets" tour, in conjunction with "Operation Trident" (the Metropolitan Police's special unit that deals with gun crimes within the black community). Alongside Isaac, Detective Constable Ian Crichlow and Baptist Minister David Shosanya, a trustee of the Ascension Trust, played key roles. The road show visited London, Manchester, and Birmingham, and the main speakers included pastors Bobby Wilmot and Bruce Fletcher from Jamaica, who talked with church and community leaders about the realities of drugs, guns, and gangs.[4]

The road show met with a mixed response, but the shooting of four teenage girls in Birmingham on New Year's Day 2003 was a turning point. From then on, people began to take the issues seriously, recognizing that they were complex and deep-seated. Street Pastors was launched three weeks later, in

---

4. Around the time of the tour, Isaac and other Trustees also began to walk around communities and discovered that there were two critical times: between 2 and 6 pm, when young people come out of school, and between 10:30 pm and 3 am, when pubs close and alcohol takes effect, leading to crime and antisocial behaviour. They began to see that the work that needed to be done would be outside a building and within these nighttime hours.

January 2003, and the first team of 18 people went out on the streets of Brixton (in the London borough of Lambeth) and in Hackney in April of that year. In 2004 a Street Pastors team started in a third London borough, Lewisham. In the same year Street Pastors also started in Birmingham and Manchester.

Since then, the growth of Street Pastors has been rapid. The good reputation of Street Pastors has led to requests from churches, local councils, and the police to start new teams all over the United Kingdom. In his book *Faith on the Streets*, Les Isaac notes that beyond the first areas of Lambeth, Hackney, Lewisham, Birmingham, and Manchester, where they were aware of the great need for Street Pastors, the Ascension Trust has never instigated the initiative in an area.[5] Teams have always been started on the initiative of others.

In recent years, Street Pastors has spread beyond the United Kingdom and teams are now active in Australia, the Channel Islands, Gibraltar, Ireland, Nigeria, the United States, Antigua and Barbuda, Jamaica, Trinidad, and Tobago. New developments in United Kingdom's Street Pastors include School and College Pastors and Response Pastors.

7.1.2 Context

Street Pastors first arose in the context of inner-city, predominantly Afro-Caribbean, communities where gun crime and gang violence among young people was high. These were areas marked by lack of opportunity in education, poor housing, conflict with the police, deprivation, family breakdown, and a sense of hopelessness. Les Isaac notes that Street Pastors offers people an opportunity to reconnect with organic, working-class communities, which the church in Britain has failed to reach.[6]

The initiative, however, is now working in many different contexts: in regional cities, small towns, rural areas, and coastal resorts. Kenwyn Pierce, area coordinator for Hackney and Southwark, puts it down to the Street Pastors' basic position of availability, which is adaptable to every context.[7] He notes that Street Pastors is about the church getting out there, being where people are, making human contact, and being open without prejudice, willing to listen, and able to provide practical help. This is how Street Pastors go out in

---

5. Les Isaac and Rosalind Davies, *Faith on the Streets: Christians in Action through the Street Pastors Movement* (London: Hodder & Stoughton, 2014), 192.
6. Les Isaac and Rosalind Davies, *Street Pastors* (Eastbourne, UK: David C. Cook Kingsway Communications, 2009), 24.
7. Interview with Kenwyn Pierce, Street Pastors area coordinator for Hackney and Southwark, conducted on 29 April 2015.

any context or country. Because they leave the initiative with the people they meet, the adapting to context happens organically.

In many places the presence of Street Pastors teams has had a visible impact on the levels of crime and antisocial behavior.[8] This has meant that Street Pastors are increasingly valued as a "good fit" with the aims of the police, the local council, and other groups. As a result, Street Pastors can and do get involved in projects that extend their work. For example, in the London borough of Southwark, the British Transport Police invited Street Pastors to work alongside them in an empty shop, which they had set up as a place for people to sober up before travelling home.[9]

7.1.3 Identity and culture

Street Pastors is an ecumenical venture and cannot be associated with one church in particular. A basic condition for setting up a Street Pastors "area" is that this must be supported by at least four different Christian denominations in the area. This makes it robust and credible. The Hackney team of eight volunteers represents five different denominations. This is fairly typical for other Street Pastors teams, too.[10] Kenwyn Pierce notes that being on the street on behalf of *the* church rather than *my* church presents an incredibly powerful message: "That is the moment when people on the streets click that we are not a recruitment team, but have come together for something beyond ourselves."[11]

For the Street Pastors founders it was clear from the beginning that for the church to make an impact on the community, the crossover between theological and traditional boundaries needed to happen. This was a matter as much of theological conviction as of practicality. In Les Isaac's words:

---

8. In the first 13 weeks of operation in three South London boroughs, there was a noticeable impact, with a 30 percent reduction in crime in Lewisham, a 95 percent reduction in Camberwell, and 74 percent in Peckham (figures from 2004–2005, quoted in *Street Pastors, caring, helping, listening*, an Ascension Trust information booklet). In Lincoln there was a 7.5 percent reduction within the first six months. Research conducted in Portsmouth found a 62 percent reduction in alcohol-fuelled violence against persons in the period July 2007–2008, following a concerted campaign combining various initiatives (Isaac and Davies, *Street Pastors*, 69). The report acknowledges Street Pastors' contribution to this improvement. A 2012 presentation at the Carlisle city-centre group mentions Street Pastors as one of the factors contributing to a 45 percent drop in violent crime in the city (Isaac and Davies, *Faith on the Streets*, 103). The Ealing borough commander recently commented that when Street Pastors are out, crime is 50 percent lower (quoted by Kenwyn Pierce).
9. Other examples include the "Safe Space Bus" in Aberdeen, and "Door Watch schemes" in Reading, Newcastle, and elsewhere (Isaac and Davies, *Faith on the Streets*, 105).
10. The Reading team of 52 volunteers represents 22 denominations.
11. Quoted from interview conducted on 29 April 2015.

I strongly believe that no one denomination or stream of church can deal with or respond to the problems and challenges that we are facing today in the twenty-first century. . . . When I think of the Catholic Church and the many good works that it has done over the years, I am truly encouraged. Likewise the Anglicans and various other mainstream churches. . . . Then I think about the African and Caribbean community, and the work that they are doing in terms of Saturday schools, supplementary education (much of it largely unnoticed), and I always come to the same conclusion: imagine what the impact would be if there was collective thinking and a joined-up strategy? If that was happening, how much more could we impact communities?[12]

Bringing about that partnership was not easy, and Isaac and the other founders encountered considerable misgivings or lack of enthusiasm on the part of the churches. In the early days they found most support in the newer Pentecostal and Baptist churches, and that background shines through to this day, most notably in a deeply pragmatic approach. Over time, however, other denominations have embraced the initiative, too, and this is visible in the make-up of local Street Pastors teams as well as in the governance of the Ascension Trust.

Because Street Pastors does not specifically preach the gospel, theological differences have not carried the weight that they do in many ecumenical projects, and, as such, Street Pastors has brought churches together at a grassroots level in a very significant way. Street Pastors has been hailed "the new ecumenism," representing a way of working together that has as its aim partnership in mission rather than visible unity.[13] And perhaps this is what is most remarkable about the initiative.

7.1.4 Theological inspiration

Kenwyn Pierce, area coordinator for Hackney and Southwark, summarizes the theological vision underlying Street Pastors in three points:

The church is called to do mission Jesus' way

It is churches and individual Christians who are called to mission. Parachurch organizations, like the Ascension Trust, have their role to play, but they exist alongside churches to support them. Churches and local Christians are

12. Isaac and Davies, *Street Pastors*, 160.
13. Rev. Dr Pat Took, regional minister team leader for the London Baptist Association, quoted in ibid., 166.

called to give their faith practical expression in their communities. The motivation for this is both practical and biblical. The vision behind Street Pastors is inspired by the life and work of Jesus. Jesus provides a clear example of meeting people's needs where they are, had a passion for the poor and the marginalized, and showed that salvation and "abundant life" have practical as well as spiritual implications. It is this Jesus who calls Christians to be light and salt and to show the love of God in practical and tangible ways. It is the life and work of Jesus that has inspired Street Pastors' holistic approach, aimed at caring for the whole person. A story that illustrates this approach well is the parable of the Good Samaritan, a passage often quoted in Les Isaac's book *Street Pastors*.

The value of human life

The value of human life features high in the work of Street Pastors. This shines through particularly in the core values that were formulated in the early days of Street Pastors, when thought had to be given to what churches were being asked to do. The five core values are both theologically and culturally relevant, rooted as they are in the concept of God's likeness in every human being and in the African concept of Ubuntu. The five core values include:

1. The sacredness and sanctity of human life

2. The importance of valuing and honouring the community

3. Being a person of integrity

4. Taking personal responsibility

5. The growth and development of the individual to their fullest potential[14]

The core values continue to express the ethos to which every Street Pastors team commits when it goes out onto the streets, whatever the needs of the community.

The value of partnership

Foundational to Street Pastors is the conviction that the church needs to be in partnership with other community agencies. The issues facing society are so big that no single group or organization can tackle them successfully. This was a key insight Les Isaac gained from Ray Bakke's book *The Urban Christian*. Bakke did some analysis of the city of Chicago and what different groups of

14. Ibid., 104.

people brought to the community. Particularly effective were the Irish immigrant groups, who had knowledge of and influence in three sectors of society in particular: politics, policing, and the church.[15] This convinced Isaac that they also needed this tripartite base of church, police, and local government for the benefit of the community. Bakke calls it "the urban trinity."

Kenwyn Pierce, however, notes that the emphasis on partnership goes beyond the concept of the urban trinity and extends to the wider community. It can include passers-by or nightclub doormen who give street pastors a tip-off when someone is in trouble. In order to be in partnership like that, one has to be available to others and to be able to let go of control. This can be counter to how churches go about mission, tempted as they may be to have their own initiative which they control and deliver.

7.1.5 Structure and means

The fast growth of Street Pastors has posed a lot of challenges for the Ascension Trust. The trust started out doing Street Pastors itself, but the expansion of the initiative soon forced a rethink of the relationship between the administrative hub and the dispersed local teams. The Ascension Trust is now an umbrella organization, working in partnership with local entities who deliver Street Pastors locally. Street Pastors is, therefore, a network of charities rather than one charity.

Each Street Pastors area has a management committee with representation from at least four churches. The management team and the initiative as a whole are accountable to the churches in the area, as well as to the Ascension Trust. All Street Pastors areas are independent entities and some are charities in their own right (if their income is over 5,000 British pounds). They have to sign a license agreement with the Ascension Trust, which covers all the rules and regulations, and Ascension Trust representatives help areas to set up and deliver part of the training (especially key is session one, on roles and responsibilities).

Each Street Pastors area has a coordinator who is accountable to the local management committee.[16] The coordinator's role includes managing the volunteer teams; drawing up the patrol rotas; liaising with the team leaders; networking with churches, the police, and the local council; and finding new recruits.

---

15. Ray Bakke, *The Urban Christian: Effective Ministry in Today's Urban World* (Downers Grove, IL: Intervarsity Press, 1987).

16. An area coordinator can be a part-time volunteer or someone employed by the local area. Some area coordinators are directly employed by the Ascension Trust.

Every Street Pastors team has a team leader or senior Street Pastor who is accountable to the area coordinator. The team leaders are responsible on the night of the patrol. They organize the team into balanced pairs, make sure the police are informed, decide where they will patrol, lead the briefing and debriefing, and ensure that information about the patrol is passed on to the area coordinator.

Funding streams into Street Pastors vary. Locally, Street Pastors depend on giving from churches; grants from the police, local authorities, local businesses (such as the bigger clubs), or contributions from individuals. Street Pastors trainees are encouraged to pay for their own training and uniform, but the Hackney Area coordinator tries to get grants to cover 50 percent and then asks the volunteers to get the other 50 percent from their church. This creates accountability and ownership.

Nationally, Street Pastors have received funding from the home office to develop their training programme and manual. Every Street Pastors area agrees in the license agreement that they will give 15 percent of their income back to the Ascension Trust to cover the costs of running the office.

7.1.6 Leadership

It is beyond doubt that the visible face of Street Pastors is Les Isaac, who is now the chief executive officer of the Ascension Trust. The story of Street Pastors, however, shows that from the beginning this was a group initiative, and this continues to be the case. Kenwyn Pierce characterizes the organizational leadership style as directive, practical, and vision-driven. There is strong quality control from the Ascension Trust/Street Pastors centrally, but this does not preclude a great degree of freedom in local operations once the criteria are met. Locally, leadership styles vary significantly, with leaders who are either entrepreneurial, focussed on maintaining structure and quality control, or pastoral in their approach.

The Street Pastors teams are made up of mostly laypeople, though there are ministers and professional church workers, too. Overall, there are more women than men. Some Street Pastors teams find that those street pastors who are most easily accepted into tense situations on the street are female and older. It is known as the "granny factor."

7.1.7 Three main lessons

So how would Street Pastors describe the three main lessons from their work? In the words of area coordinator Kenwyn Pierce:

1. God works when we make ourselves available.

2. The church can be and is appreciated by the wider public.

3. People do want to respond spiritually. We do not have to push the faith element of what we are doing. If we give people proper attention they are ready to engage.[17]

This final lesson is confirmed by Les Isaac in his book *Faith on the Streets*, where he notes that an estimated 75 percent of the people he meets as a Street Pastor ask him to pray for them.[18] The percentage may not be as high as that for the Hackney team, but it is beyond doubt that they are accepted as people who inspire informal spiritual engagement. As such, Street Pastors can be a link in the chain of an individual's spiritual journey. As Pierce notes: "The Street Pastors project is not evangelistic in its intention, but making the church visible in practical, caring ways and being intentional about treating people as we think Jesus would, can have evangelistic outcomes."

---

17. Interview conducted on 29 April 2015.
18. Isaac and Davies, *Faith on the Streets*, 156.

7.2 MyChurch: Shaping an Online Faith Community

Gerrit Noort

7.2.1 General description and history

In October 2013 the Protestant Church in the Netherlands launched "mijnkerk.nl" (MyChurch.com), a missional website that is intentionally contextual. The site is all about "enjoying life, sharing beautiful moments, finding support in difficult moments, discovering and sharing important things in life, celebrating the abundance of life and making life more beautiful."[1] MyChurch is not just another informative website; rather, it intends to create a community of people who share life stories. The idea to start an online church certainly isn't new,[2] yet it has generated a lot of media interest.

How did it all begin?

The Protestant Church in the Netherlands, instituted in May 2004 as the result of a lengthy unification process of three Reformed and Lutheran churches, acknowledged its missionary nature and calling from the very outset. General Secretary Rev. Dr Bas Plaisier, a former missionary in Indonesia, stressed that the unification wasn't intended to realize a stronger ecclesial organization, but to ensure "that the gospel message could be communicated in a more powerful way."[3] The synod paper "What contributes to Christian witness" (2004), discussed by the synod, presbyteries, and staff of the national office, led to a challenging process of redefining and reimagining the missional calling of the church.

As part of that process in the years 2006–2008, the Protestant Church in the Netherlands also started to rethink the missionary structure of its 1,571

---

1. See http://www.mijnkerk.nl.
2. See Christian Harwig, "Wie zitten er in mijn kerk?" (Master's thesis, Vrije Universiteit Amsterdam, 2015), 30–31. For a broader context on online Christian communities, see Tim Hutchings, "Creating Church Online: Networks and Collectives in Contemporary Christianity," in Pauline H. Cheong et al., ed., *Digital Religion, Social Media and Culture: Perspectives, Practices and Futures* (New York: Peter Lang, 2012); Simon Jenkins, "Rituals and Pixels—Experiments in Online Church," *Heidelberg Journal of Religions on the Internet* 3, no. 1 (2008): 95–113.
3. Marion Stenneke, "PKN gaat voor 'zending,'" *Friesch Dagblad*, 14 May 2004.

local congregations.[4] Influenced by developments in the Church of England, specifically its influential report *Mission-Shaped Church* (2004) and its consistent emphasis on so-called fresh expressions of church, the Protestant Church in the Netherlands' leadership gave instruction to write a report on the possible need for a renewed emphasis on church planting in the midst of secularized and postmodern Dutch society. This report was instrumental in establishing a new department in the national Protestant Church in the Netherlands' office that focussed on initiating pioneering evangelistic projects in the Netherlands.[5] One of the first projects focussed on church planting in Amsterdam. A missionary pastor was appointed with the specific assignment to establish a new Christian community in the borough of IJburg, a newly built part of the city that houses thousands of inhabitants, but without any visible representation of the Christian tradition and church life.[6]

The Protestant Church in the Netherlands' general synod, facing serious decline in membership and the rapid breakdown of traditional structures for transmitting the Christian faith to younger generations, stated in its 2012 vision document *The Heartbeat of Life* that "faith does not come to somebody automatically." Therefore, the church "will continue looking for ways and means to reach the general public with media campaigns and by new media." In an ensuing paragraph, on the forms of being a congregation, we read: "New challenges also force us to reflect upon new ways of being church, with all due consequences. Experiments with new forms and ways of being a church will be given the opportunity, like local group congregations, pioneering ministries and home congregations."[7]

It was therefore boldly decided that initiative should be taken to establish 100 pioneering projects in the years 2012–16. These projects should aim to shape new missional communities in creative ways that could have significance and meaning for the dechurched and unchurched. The project team responsible for realizing this vision understood that the Internet is a place for

---

4. Ronald Bolwijn and Harm Dane, *Statistische jaarbrief 2014 van de Protestantse Kerk in Nederland* (Utrecht: Expertisecentrum Protestantse Kerk, 16 April 2014), 11.
5. Gerrit Noort, "Adviesnota nieuwe christelijke gemeenschapsvorming" (unpublished report, Utrecht, 2007).
6. Church membership in Amsterdam is significantly lower than elsewhere in the Netherlands. See Derek Schippers and Clemens Wenneker, *Religie in Amsterdam: Gelovigen en plaatsen van samenkomst* (Amsterdam: Gemeente Amsterdam—bureau onderzoek en statistiek, 2014), 8.
7. Arjan Plaisier, *The Heartbeat of Life: Memorandum concerning the Vision for the Life and Work of the Protestant Church in the Netherlands* (Utrecht: Protestant Church in the Netherlands, 2012), 32–33. Eng. trans.: http://www.protestantsekerk.nl/overons/protestantse-kerk/missie-en-visie/Paginas/Visienota-2012.aspx.

pioneering as well, next to tangible and visible places in dechurched cities and suburban areas. A creative plan was written, a content strategist was consulted, and a professional MyChurch team was put together, consisting of an Internet pastor, a community manager, and a web editor. Facebook and Twitter accounts were opened, while the website went online after intensive consultations with the content strategist. By March 2015, one and a half years after its launch, MyChurch attracted many visitors and numbers were growing quickly. The site had 8,750 unique visitors monthly, two to three new blogs were posted by some 25 bloggers each day, the Twitter account had 2,000 followers, and the closed Facebook group had 448 members.[8] The initiative generated a lot of media coverage, even on national television.

7.2.2 Context

Developing a website for the large number of dechurched and unchurched people in the Netherlands posed a number of serious challenges for the project team. Statistics made clear that church membership was declining rapidly. In 1899 only 2.3 percent of the Dutch population was not religiously affiliated.[9] In 1970 church membership had dwindled to 75 percent, and it decreased to 45 percent in 2005.[10] It is projected that by 2020 about 72 percent of the population will have no religious affiliation. Christians will then constitute 14 percent of the population and Muslims 8 percent.[11] These percentages are now a reality for the generation that was born after 1975. This is not the place to delve deeper into discussions on statistics about church membership and religious affiliation. It just goes to show that the Protestant Church in the Netherlands' missional project was imagined and shaped in a context of secularization and dechurched Dutch citizens.

These statistics, however, still left a question unanswered: What exactly was the intended target audience of MyChurch? About half of the Dutch population may be dechurched, but they are by no means a homogeneous group that can be approached as one target audience. To respond to this challenge, the Protestant Church in the Netherlands made use of a values-and-lifestyle research tool that provides target-group classification and related approaches.

---

8. "Tussenrapportage MijnKerk.nl," (Utrecht, 30 March 2015), 1 (unpublished report, at http://www.MijnKerk.nl).
9. Joris van Eijnatten and Fred van Lieburg, *Nederlandse Religiegeschiedenis* (Hilversum: Verloren, 2006), 330.
10. Jos Becker and Joep de Hart, *Godsdienstige veranderingen in Nederland: Verschuivingen in de binding met de kerken en de christelijke traditie* (Den Haag: Sociaal en Cultureel Planbureau, 2006), 29.
11. Ibid., 52–53.

The tool, developed by the Dutch research firm MotivAction, segmented eight "mentality" groups in Dutch society: "traditionals" (13%), "modern mainstream" (22%), "cosmopolitans" (13%), "new conservatives" (8%), "postmodern hedonists" (10%), "social climbers" (15%), "convenience oriented" (10%), and "postmaterialists" (9%).[12] It was decided that the project would focus on "modern mainstream," as this group would probably respond most favourably to the missional content of the website. It is also the biggest of the eight segments identified and comprises about 2.8 million Dutch citizens.

According to MotivAction, people who belong to "modern mainstream" are characterized by an intention to find a balance between traditional standards and modern values. In doing so, they are quite conformist in their attitudes, they regard the nuclear family as the cornerstone of society, and they value authority and rules. In their lifestyle they avoid risk taking and opt for a secure job, financial security, and enjoying life. The wish to enjoy life is important for this group. While they may have personal problems, most of the modern mainstreamers will stress that they have a pleasant life. Materialism and consumerism are characteristic of this segment. According to a report by Sabel Online, produced at the request of the Protestant Church in the Netherlands, "people who belong to modern mainstream feel it is important to belong, they value enjoying life, property and consuming, they like to be entertained and cushioned."[13] It is a group that highly values support and care, rituals at key moments in life, and sharing collective experiences.

Modern mainstreamers want to enjoy life, but they also look for inspiration. Believing there is a powerful "something," they like to relate to that higher power but are not sure how. Basically, they have a positive attitude to faith, religion, and spirituality and they have maintained some curiosity about Jesus. Although many do not have a positive image of the church because of negative experiences, they sometimes have nostalgic ideas about being part of a small and engaged community.

7.2.3 Identity and culture

MyChurch intends to be an online community for "people who don't go to church anymore, simply because that is how things in life came to be." In doing so, MyChurch focusses on people who believe there is more to life and

---

12. See Martijn Lampert, "Mentality," http://www.motivaction.nl/en/mentality/mentality-segmentation. On the website each of the mentality groups is described in detail.
13. Sabel Online, "Twee of drie in Mijn Naam. Het digitale Lichaam van Christus," (9 November 2012), 8.

that there is "something" which they still call God. The missional intention is to shape a community that connects people with one another and with God. As modern mainstreamers highly value enjoying life, the logo of the website is therefore a four-leaf clover, symbol of happiness and luck. MyChurch intends to be a "safe place" where people can come to their senses, find recognition, and enjoy life. The website accommodates its message to modern mainstreamers. This is clear in the choice of the four themes offered: life, nature, music, and faith.[14] The pages about "life" have feel-good items, such as a story about baking pies for other people, a poem about springtime, and a message of good wishes to all mothers (on Mother's Day). But there is also an item about the joys and anxieties of being a mother, and one about a candle lit for somebody who was reanimated. The "nature" pages offer, for instance, an item on the shades of light in the forest and the emotions they evoke.

The website doesn't just embrace happiness and beauty, but it also relates, in an easygoing manner, to serious issues in life: "Next to beautiful, nice and funny moments in life (humour), MyChurch also offers space for the other side: trouble, sorrow, illness or dying. In that way people really get to meet each other, based on respect for the other, and contact from heart to heart can grow."[15] MyChurch intends to act as a guide for daily life in that process. Faith is an integral part of the website and it is offered in a generous and friendly way: through blogs that reflect on life and, of course, through the contributions of the two Internet pastors, Fred Omvlee and Janneke Nijboer. They are prominently visible for everyone who visits the site. They make themselves known in blogs and ultra-short "video sermons," and they can be contacted through email, Facebook, Twitter, or cell phone.

As MyChurch focusses on modern mainstreamers, the team had to make choices with regard to the identity, themes, and language used on the website. As modern mainstreamers are risk-averse and prefer a pleasant life, MyChurch doesn't stress "difficult" political issues, such as the impact of migration on European and Dutch society, ecological issues like the effects of global warming, or the sustainability of our consumerism. Instead, it stresses that we may enjoy the good things of life and that is related to faith and stewardship. The style is open, inviting, and inspiring, pointing to Jesus in a very basic way. It is about God's love for everybody. The blogs and themes are not a treasure trove for academics, keen on thorough reflection but, rather, are more about showing what the good news of Jesus can mean in our lives.

14. See http://www.mijnkerk.nl.
15. Sabel Online, "Twee of drie in Mijn Naam," 11.

These starting points imply that the identity of the website is not defined by a theological position that functions *a priori*. In the words of Adrie Stemmer, editor of the website: "It is mostly about listening and looking. What motivates and drives people? What are the defining moments in their lives? How do they look for comfort, for something to hold onto, for meaning?"[16] In doing all that, guidance can be offered by giving meaning to life events. Guidance is not offered in a dogmatic way, but it is offered as an opinion: "Could it be that . . . ?" As many visitors of the site are dechurched, many resist a normative approach. Negative experiences with the church as a powerful institution or with a strict Christian upbringing make it undesirable to start from the normative. It could easily lead to alienation of the website's visitor. The open approach is a conscious missional choice.

Stemmer readily admits that the method to relate to modern mainstreamers is not well established, but it is a continuous process of trial and error, of listening closely and looking for bridges that enable communication and witness. That is why the team closely monitors which pages and blogs are well visited and responded to. This process of monitoring led the initiative also to start offline meet-ups for site visitors. As one visitor said, "It is nice to light a candle online, but you don't feel its warmth." One of these offline meetings was about wine tasting, another on baking pies together. A third was a "Top 2000 Church Meet-up," in which fans of pop music can meet "in a relaxed atmosphere" where they can talk about favourite pop songs and "what the songs mean in your personal life."[17]

7.2.4 Theological inspiration

The above already makes clear that the theological inspiration for the Protestant Church in the Netherlands' pioneering projects was primarily found in the missional renewal of the Church of England and its "five marks of mission."[18] This Anglican influence is explicitly acknowledged in a recent policy paper (2015) of the Protestant Church of the Netherlands' missionary department, which states that is was the "renewal in the United Kingdom" that helped to create more space for pioneering in the Protestant Church.[19]

---

16. Interview with Adrie Stemmer, conducted on 8 May 2015.

17. See Anton van Dijken, "Top 2000 Kerk Meet Up—Kick-off Stadstheater," http://www.mijnkerk.nl/meetups/top2000kerk-meetup-kick-off-stadstheater-zoetermeer.

18. The five marks: (1) to proclaim the good news of the kingdom; (2) to teach, baptize, and nurture new believers; (3) to respond to human need by loving service; (4) to transform unjust structures of society, challenge violence of every kind, and pursue peace and reconciliation; and (5) to strive to safeguard the integrity of creation, and sustain and renew the life of the earth.

19. Martijn Vellekoop, "Ontwikkelingen rondom pionieren" (Utrecht, 30 March 2015). (unpublished Protestant Church in the Netherlands' policy paper).

MyChurch is based on the conviction that visitors of the website, people who are dechurched or unchurched, should hear about the gospel of Jesus Christ. As the Protestant Church in the Netherlands is a mainline church, a range of theological voices has shaped the project. Stemmer, a journalist with theological training, underscores that MyChurch is an intentionally evangelistic project. To MyChurch she brings her experience of a church-planting project in the city of Amersfoort, which she helped initiate in 2009. Her ministry is linked with Urban Expression, a "mission agency that *recruits*, *equips*, *deploys* and *networks* self-financing teams, pioneering creative and relevant expressions of the Christian church in under-churched areas of the inner city."[20] Urban Expression's core values underline that the gospel creates a new community that is not only about individual conversion but also about peace and justice for the city.[21]

Fred Omvlee, one of the two pastors of MyChurch who works as a Navy chaplain as well, argues that the beautiful theological tradition of the Protestant Church in the Netherlands is "too much, too deep, too high, too emotional, too much Jesus, too abstract for modern mainstream."[22] Christian faith, he states, has to be "authentic, personal, and understandable." In his work for MyChurch he builds on his ministerial experience with a "light-footed" approach, focussing on popular culture. In doing so, he became known for his "Elvis chapel," worship services in which he combines his love for the music of Elvis Presley and his love for the gospel. Participants are invited to sing gospel songs with Elvis, and Omvlee preaches about Elvis as "sinner and saint."[23] His approach, he recognizes, is not always welcomed by the three main theological schools in the Protestant Church in the Netherlands. Conservative Protestants think his approach is too superficial, the Evangelicals see it as "worldly," and modern theologians often find it "trite." But Omvlee is convinced that reaching modern mainstreams with the gospel demands a new approach that creates new space and appreciation for other convictions.

Richard Niebuhr's study *Christ and Culture* is an important source of inspiration for Omvlee.[24] Niebuhr describes five different relationships that a Christian can have with local culture: "opposition," "agreement," "Christ above

20. See Urban Expression, "Urban Expression: Creative church planting in the inner city," http://www.urbanexpression.org.uk. "Urban Expression" was founded in the United Kingdom by Stuart Murray, lecturer at Baptist College in Bristol and chair of the Anabaptist Network.
21. See Urban Expression, "Geloof: wat is onze bron?," http://www.urbanexpression.nl.
22. Fred Omvlee, e-mail messages to the author, 5 and 6 May 2015.
23. See http://www.elviskapel.nl.
24. Richard Niebuhr, *Christ and Culture* (New York: Harper & Row, 1951).

culture," "tension," and "transformation." Omvlee applies these categories to online culture as well. For him, the world of information technology is an extension of God's good creation, which has great potential. Christians are called to contribute toward transformation. In the midst of the effects of sin, they can create new space for people and for the gospel. As a second source of inspiration Omvlee mentions the work of the Dutch practical theologian Andries Baart, who developed a theory of presence that is focussed on "creating just and loving human relationships, especially where it concerns people who are overlooked, poor, socially superfluous." Baart's approach underlines the importance of both critical distance from interventionism and faithful proximity to the other.

7.2.5 Structure and means

MyChurch is an initiative of the Protestant Church in the Netherlands and the appointed team reports to its department for missional work. As such, the department specifically focusses on mobilizing resources (finances, training, and communication) for pioneering missional work in the Netherlands. The MyChurch team is small. Paid staff now consists of a part-time editor (18 hours a week) and an Internet pastor (a freelance contract for about 12 hours weekly). The team also works with volunteers (volunteer contracts). Rev. Janneke Nijboer is one of the volunteers; four deputy editors work as volunteers as well. As offline meetings are becoming regular, the meet-up leaders will also be given volunteer contracts.

Finances for MyChurch were pledged by the Protestant Church in the Netherlands for a period of three years, thereby following the usual practice for new pioneering initiatives. The church supported first-generation projects with 100,000 euros a year (until 2013), but due to the growing number of pioneering projects[25] and limited finances, the church decided that financial support for second-generation pioneering projects (after 2013) should be capped at 15,000 euros a year.[26] This means that projects should aim to be self-supporting as soon as possible and should develop a sustainable structure. Though "self-financing" is a classic notion in foreign mission,[27] the Protestant Church in the Netherlands realizes that this is ambitious, as pioneering projects are by

---

25. Some 40 new pioneering projects are now in an advanced stage of preparation. See Vellekoop, "Ontwikkelingen," 2.

26. Ibid., 2, 4.

27. In the mid-19th century, mission strategists Henry Venn (1796–1873) and Rufus Anderson (1796–1880) developed their influential ideas about young indigenous churches, which should become self-supporting, self-governing, and self-propagating.

definition small and vulnerable. An evaluation of first-generation pioneering projects has furthermore shown that three years is not enough to create a viable new faith community, so there is a renewed discussion about the period that financial support should be given. Should it be eight years, while funding is gradually diminished?

As MyChurch started in 2013, support for a next phase now has to be negotiated, as the project doesn't generate income. Continued funding for the online project will be available, but the means will be considerably lower than in previous years. This means that the project will have to rely on volunteers even more.

7.2.6 Leadership

Formally, the MyChurch team reports to the Protestant Church in the Netherlands' missional department. The missional department takes care of finances and ensures policy development within the structures of the church, but in practice the MyChurch team works quite independently. Rev. Fred Omvlee serves as an important source of inspiration for the project and coaches the meet-up leaders. He "creates a flow in which he inspires people to move."[28] His leadership is inspirational and not hierarchical.

7.2.7 Three main lessons

The team feels that the project is still in an early phase of its development. Yet, they mention some lessons they have learned in the past three years.

When MyChurch started, the project plan was very open. It was felt that starting an online faith community was like charting hitherto unknown territory and that the plan therefore shouldn't be too detailed. With hindsight, the team states that the project would have benefitted from a clearer sense of direction. Too much was too unclear. The choice to opt for a radical contextual approach was not shared by all on the initial project team. One team member was alienated by the integration of Facebook and Twitter symbols in online liturgy, which could possibly have been prevented if from the outset there had been a clearer sense of theological direction and of the contextualization model that would be used.

The team acknowledged that they underestimated the importance of the closed Facebook group for the creation and growth of an online community. As the number of participants in the group rose to over 400, the team considered

---

28. Interview with Adrie Stemmer, conducted on 8 May 2015.

splitting the Facebook group in two. This plan, however, led to strong reactions from the group participants. Remarks like "We have been together so long already" showed that a much stronger sense of community had grown than was expected.

Finally, the importance of offline meetings was initially underestimated. Although an authentic sense of community had grown in the Facebook group, this didn't mean that people had the feeling the online meetings could altogether replace face-to-face meetings. Offline meet-ups have therefore started and are still in development. Offline and online meetings turn out to be complementary.

7.3 Community of Sant'Egidio: A Case Study from Italy

Donna Orsuto

7.3.1 General description and history[1]

Trastevere, in the heart of historic Rome, is the oldest Roman neighbourhood. It is also where the first Christians gathered in the city.[2] In the past it was considered the place where the "real" Romans lived, old families who had made their home there for centuries. Although some remained, today this neighbourhood also draws an eclectic medley of people, including foreigners out for an evening meal at one of the chic restaurants, Roma who fill the piazzas with their colourful clothes, and the homeless seeking money for the next meal. The neighbourhood might have changed over the years, but one constant is the evening prayer of the Sant'Egidio community that has continued every day since 1973. Yes, *every* day, without interruption.

The prayer occurs each evening at 8:30 in the stunningly beautiful basilica of Santa Maria in Trastevere.[3] All are welcome, without exception. As the church bells ring, an empty church is suddenly filled with people of every age and nation, though the majority are Italians. The daily liturgy includes chanted psalms, a gospel reading, and reflection followed by prayers of intercession. Many have come to the prayer directly after work in other parts of the city

1. For further reading, see Andrea Riccardi, *Sant'Egidio, L'Évangile au-delà des frontières: Entretiens avec Dominique Chivot* (Paris: Bayard Editions, 2001).
2. Trastevere "was a strategic quarter of ancient Rome. Located outside the walls, it was the city's port, a feature that it retained till Rome became the capital of Italy (in 1871). Very much the 'people's quarter', in Roman times it was inhabited by workers, artisans, and merchants, a majority of them 'Orientals' (Greeks, Africans, Syrians, Egyptians, Jews). . . . These Jews were probably among the first to adhere to Christianity. The first Christian community in Trastevere seems to have gathered where the basilica of Santa Maria stands today." See Andrea Riccardi, *Sant'Egidio, Rome and the World* (London: St Pauls, 1999), 33.
3. Originally, it began in the little church of Sant'Egidio, just around the corner. As Andrea Riccardi explains, "And so in 1973 we opened the church for the first time in our history. We hadn't been at Sant'Egidio very long. We opened the church and began to experience prayer as a moment of meditation as well. It was important, because in that moment we went from being a community that was warm but to some extent closed . . . to a language of welcome, of openness, to a community that becomes an opportunity for others too and that finds its paths crossed and itself questioned by others." See Riccardi, ibid., 39–40.

before heading home for a late dinner. Most have spent at least some time that day or week in the service of those in need: the poor, the homeless, the elderly, and the disabled. Sant'Egidio community members seem to be everywhere: in Rome and beyond, wherever the poor can be found. As Pope Francis said, when visiting the community on 15 June 2014: "To pray in the centre of the city doesn't mean to forget the human and urban peripheries. It means to listen and receive the gospel of love to go forth and encounter the brothers and sisters on the fringes of the city and the world!"[4]

The commitment to "go out" and to share the good news of Jesus Christ by serving the poor is epitomized by the annual Christmas luncheon in that same basilica. Each year, since 1982, on 25 December, the pews are moved out and banquet tables are set up for a festive meal with the elderly and the poor of Rome. The tradition started with just 20 guests the first year, but now the banquet has widened to welcome hundreds from Rome as well as from other parts of the world. What is the significance of this Christmas extravaganza? The community of Sant'Egidio explains it in this way:

> The community is a family gathered by the gospel. Therefore at Christmas, when all over the world families gather around the table, the community celebrates with the poor, who are our friends and relatives. Saint Francis used to say that Christmas is "the feast of the feasts," which means that it should embrace everybody . . .
>
> At Christmas, all over the world, families gather, buy presents to exchange with each other under the tree, prepare the table for the feast: but for those who don't have anybody this feast, more than all others, turns into a very sad day.
>
> This is the reason why the community wishes, on the very day Jesus was born, poor for the world's salvation, to gather as a big family where everybody can feel at home. It is the most beautiful image, which explains to the world eloquently the community way of staying among the people and particularly with the poor.[5]

---

4. See Libreria Editrice Vaticana, "Address of Pope Francis to the Sant'Egidio Community," 15 June 2014, https://w2.vatican.va/content/francesco/en/speeches/2014/june/documents/papa-francesco_20140615_comunita-sant-egidio.html.
5. Community of Sant'Egidio, "Christmas 1982–2002. Twenty Years Having Lunch Together," http://www.santegidio.org/en/pranzodinatale/pagina01.htm.

The heart of the Sant'Egidio community is that all would understand, both those who are served and those who serve, that they are all part of God's family, each with gifts to share with one another. What is the community of Sant'Egidio and how did it begin? How is the community directly involved in evangelism? These are the questions this case study will address.

What is the Community of Sant'Egidio and how did it begin?

Sant'Egidio is the name both of the 10th-century Roman saint, Egidius (St Giles), and of the church where the headquarters of the community of Sant'Egidio is now located. Founded in 1968 by Andrea Riccardi with a group of Roman Catholic teenagers, it is now a movement of laypeople with more than 60,000 members who are dedicated to "evangelization and charity" both in Rome (Italy) and in more than 73 other countries. Although it was launched quite simply as a communal effort of a group of teenagers to listen to the gospel and put it into practice in the city of Rome, especially in the periphery, the mission has expanded while maintaining its initial inspiration.[6] The Vatican website offers a succinct description of the community:

> From the outset, specific features of the community have been service to the very poor and defence of human dignity and human rights, together with prayer and the communication of the gospel. It has created ways of helping and extending friendship where there is poverty, both in its old and new forms (elderly people living alone and unable to cope, immigrants, homeless people, terminally ill and AIDS sufferers, children at risk of delinquency and social out-casting, itinerants and physically and mentally disabled people, drug addicts, war victims, inmates and people under sentence of death). The poor are the daily companions of life and of the work of the members of the community, as their friends and part of their family. It is precisely this friendship that has given Sant'Egidio a clearer understanding of the way that war is the mother of all forms of poverty, and hence their explicit commitment to working for peace.[7]

---

6. Massimo Faggioli, "The New Elites of Italian Catholicism: 1968 and the New Catholic Movements," *The Catholic Historical Review* 98, no. 1 (January 2012): 18–40.
7. Libreria Editrice Vaticana, "Pontifical Council for the Laity: International Associations of the Faithful. Directory," 2006, http://www.vatican.va/roman_curia/pontifical_councils/laity/documents/rc_pc_laity_doc_20051114_associazioni_en.html.

This description highlights the basic pillars of the community: (1) personal and communal prayer; (2) a commitment to communicate the gospel (i.e., evangelization); and (3) solidarity with the poor. These basic works flow into activities ranging from peace negotiation to both ecumenical and interreligious dialogue. The diverse activities of this community are vast, and their website in eighteen different languages offers regular updates. The purpose of this case study is to focus specifically on the community's approach to evangelism.

The Sant'Egidio community's approach to evangelism can be summed up in the words often wrongly attributed to St Francis of Assisi: "Preach the gospel always. Use words only when necessary."[8] The community attracts people to Christ through offering them a positive experience of Christian love and an experience of community and friendship.

7.3.2 Context

The community of Sant'Egidio was born in a period of countercultural upheaval that was sweeping over western Europe and other parts of the world in the 1960s and 1970s. It also developed immediately after the Second Vatican Council with its call for renewal within the Roman Catholic Church and a greater openness to the world.

How did the Second Vatican Council affect the community of Sant'Egidio? Andrea Riccardi suggests that the link, at first, was somewhat indirect: "I think we were struck by much of the spirit of the Council. I say that retrospectively. In fact, when the life of the community just started out, the Council was an atmosphere, something more general, intersection and ideas rather than specific texts: the need to change, to reform, the church of the poor, the primacy of the Word of God."[9] As the community began to read more documents, the Second Vatican Council became a "compass" for moving ahead.[10]

7.3.3 Identity and culture

The community of Sant'Egidio considers "communicating the gospel" as the heart of its mission. In fact, the first goal of the community is to evangelize. This is clearly stated in the community's statutes:

---

8. Franciscan scholars suggest that the idea echoes the Franciscan ideal even though the wording is not exactly found in St Francis's writings. For example, in the Rule of 1221, Francis writes, "Let all the brothers preach by their deeds." See St Francis of Assisi, *Regula non bullata* (1221), ch. 17.
9. Riccardi, *Sant'Egidio, Rome and the World*, 29.
10. Ibid.

The first goal of the community of Sant'Egidio is evangelization, the "essential mission of the church". . . . The community realizes that the Word of God, "I must bring the good news to the poor" (Luke 4:18), applies to its life. And it makes its own the thought of the apostle Paul, "For if I preach the gospel, that gives me no ground for boasting. Woe to me if I do not preach the gospel!" (1 Cor. 9:16). The community lives this commitment of evangelization especially to those who are far away, so as to form with them a single family around the table of the eucharist, in mutual charity and the Spirit of the Lord.[11]

The specific way that the community of Sant'Egidio evangelizes is, first of all, by experiencing the gospel itself as the good news through a prayerful encounter with the word of God. Out of this encounter flows a commitment to communicate that message to others. This call to share the good news with others is not an optional activity; it is an intrinsic part of their Christian call. They consider the gospel as a "precious treasure," as a "light that cannot be hidden." At the same time, the gospel is not considered in any way as something they possess: it is both a gift and a responsibility. They realize that the gift has been given and is meant to be shared with those whom they encounter.

In Sant'Egidio's experience being disciples and living and sharing the gospel are synonymous. It is an experience of joy and celebration, as in the gospel according to Luke, when the 72 came back full of joy saying: "Lord," they said, "even the devils submit to us when we use your name" (Luke 10:17). It is the experience of each disciple and of each one in the community of Sant'Egidio, which has led, during these years, to our living a 'missionary brotherhood' in many parts of the world.[12]

This short passage offers three key ideas about the Sant'Egidio way of evangelism. First of all, evangelism is about sharing the gospel. It is about communicating the good news of Jesus Christ who came that we might have life. Second, no distinction is made between living and sharing the gospel. The joy of a personal encounter with Jesus Christ and a communal celebration of this encounter is already a way of evangelizing. Does this mean that Sant'Egidio is

---

11. Andrea Riccardi, "Statutes of the Community of Sant'Egidio Association," in Riccardi, ibid., 50ff.

12. Community of Sant'Egidio, "Communicating the Gospel," http://www.santegidio.org/pageID/14/langID/en/Communicating-the-Gospel.html.

not involved in explicit evangelism in the traditional sense? No. The very fact that the community has grown and is in so many parts of the world is a sign that their "method" of evangelism works. It attracts others to Christ by revitalizing their faith. An encounter with members of the community enkindles in those who participate in the prayers and activities a desire to cultivate this friendship with Christ and others. Third, a distinctive characteristic of this evangelism as practiced by Sant'Egidio is the living out of a missionary fraternity in various parts of the world. Sant'Egidio evangelizes by inviting people to experience the joy of community, the joy of fellowship with others. They befriend others, especially the poor, and invite them into this missionary fraternity where each person becomes a protagonist in the sharing of the gospel.

7.3.4 Theological inspiration

What are some of the key theological ideas that inspire the Sant'Egidio community? First of all, the community began when a group of young people started reading the Bible together seriously. Listening daily to the word of God, especially the gospels, is fundamental for responding to the call to follow Jesus. Thus, the first focus is on the centrality of the word of God. Riccardi also acknowledges that St Francis of Assisi inspired him and his early companions in their journey toward founding Sant'Egidio:

> St. Francis has always been a treasured companion along the way, above all because he wanted to be a layman, living alongside everyone else, in humility, as a "minor" among minors. St. Francis stands for the gospel straight out, friendship with the poor, and in the last years, dialogue with Islam, at Damietta (Egypt), with the rejection of the other-as-enemy that marks the spirit of the crusades. Francis of Assisi and his story vividly teach us how the gospel can be the source of renewal for Christian life.[13]

In addition, the *Rule of Benedict* was an important document because it is a "fundamental text for community life in the church." This rule, originally written for monks, has a meaning that goes beyond the confines of religious life. It has a message for the "organization of the church community as a whole, especially for the affirmation of the primacy of the Word of God in Christian life."[14] The themes of *ora et labora* (prayer and work) and hospitality as described in the *Rule of Benedict* helped to inspire the Sant'Egidio way of life.

13. Riccardi, *Sant'Egidio, Rome and the World*, 12.
14. Ibid.

7.3.5 Structure and means

Sant'Egidio is, paradoxically, both a structured and a flexible community. The community has statutes and is recognized by the Roman Catholic Church as an international public association of laypeople. Following the Code of Canon Law in the Catholic Church, these statutes are approved by the Pontifical Council for the Laity. The community not only has ecclesial standing, but also it is recognized as a nonprofit organization that fosters projects of cooperation in international development.

Every four years an electoral assembly, consisting of 40 representatives from various communities, elects both the president and a council who guide the community. In addition, according to its statutes, a general ecclesiastical assistant is appointed by the Pontifical Council for the Laity. This priest is chosen from three names submitted by the community to the Pontifical Council for the Laity.

Although Sant'Egidio has a clear structure in place, it is also said to be quite flexible and fluid. As Riccardi has said, "The frontiers of the community are not rigid."[15] Community members, friends, and others take part in prayer, service activities, and, where appropriate, in taking responsibility. Although those ultimately responsible for the community are the president and the council, many others have roles of responsibility. For example, for certain ministries, the leaders consult all of those involved and often a coordinating committee emerges naturally to focus on specific projects.

How are the activities of the community financed? According to their website, the work of the community is carried out thanks to volunteers and is financed by collection, contributions, and donations, both public and private.[16] The majority of people who belong to Sant'Egidio are volunteers. They are not paid for their services; rather, they share their own time and resources with those whom they serve.

7.3.6 Leadership

The founder of Sant'Egidio is Andrea Riccardi, who served as its leader until 2003. The current leader, elected in 2003, is Marco Impagliazzo, a full professor of contemporary history at the University for Foreigners in Perugia (*Università per Stranieri in Perugia*). Every four years the electoral assembly elects both the president and a council. The purpose of this council is to orient the

---

15. Ibid., 53.
16. Community of Sant'Egidio, "Help us to help, you can make the difference for many," http://www.santegidio.org/index.php?langID=en.

community, while various local committees are involved in directly organizing activities in their specific geographical areas.[17]

7.3.7 Three main lessons

What does the Sant'Egidio community teach us about evangelism? First, prayer is at the heart of effective evangelism. Effective evangelism takes place only when individuals and communities are open to cultivating a personal relationship with Jesus Christ. This is why prayer is such an anchor for each member of the community. They are encouraged to pray daily, both individually and, if possible, as a community. Scripture reading and a strong sacramental life are also an integral part of their spirituality. These means help them to embrace the call to follow Jesus, to become his disciples in the midst of the world.

Second, evangelism has a social-commitment component. Those who enter into a personal encounter with Jesus Christ are called to reach out to others in need. As Pope Francis has emphasized in *Evangelii Gaudium*, we share the gospel of joy by our practical commitment to the poor and the vulnerable. There can be no credible witness to the gospel without service to the poor. This means that some practical commitment to serve the poor is an essential part of sharing the gospel of joy with others. The community of Sant'Egidio is a good example of how to put this teaching into practice.

Third, community matters. Building up friendships among members, with the poor, the disabled, prisoners, and people of other religions is a key component of the Sant'Egidio spirituality. The community members are not merely involved in an active service of the poor; they become genuine friends of those in need, engaging them in a real experience of community. The elderly, the disabled, Roma, and prisoners all experience this bond of fraternity and friendship that makes them feel spiritually connected to community members and to God. There is a collective energy when the community gathers to pray, to feast, to share burdens and joys.

The experience of Sant'Egidio also teaches that evangelism is not opposed to dialogue. Part of Christian discipleship includes building up relationships with people from other religions, especially in efforts at peacebuilding. For example, the community helped organize the historic 1986 meeting in Assisi between Pope John Paul II and religious leaders from around the world and since then has sponsored a yearly meeting for peace "in the spirit of Assisi." The first meeting included 50 representatives of other Christian churches and

---

17. Riccardi, *Sant'Egidio, Rome and the World*, 51.

60 representatives of other religions. The inspiration behind this was to bring people together in the city of St Francis, to pray for peace and stand beside each other in an appeal to stop the horrors of war. Since 1987 the community has organized an annual meeting of "People and Religions" in different cities of Italy and other countries. An integral part of evangelism is a willingness to dialogue with others, to work together to promote peace.

Finally, the community of Sant'Egidio epitomizes many of the trends in evangelism in the Roman Catholic Church today. Strongly rooted in prayer and the word of God, the community aims to respond personally and communally to the call to follow Jesus Christ. This experience impels them to share the good news with others through concrete service of those in need. Gradually, though, the distinction between those serving and those served fades as family bonds develop. People experience the joy of the gospel in community and this binds them together and flows out to others. Evangelism also includes creating a culture of encounter and dialogue. No one is excluded from the love of Christ that overcomes every barrier.

7.4 The Taizé Community in France

Brother John

7.4.1 General description and history

Who would have imagined that a Christian community rooted in the monastic tradition would become a place of evangelization for tens of thousands of young adults from across the world? In examining the history and practice of the Taizé Community, our too-facile distinctions between prayer and contemplation, on the one hand, and Christian mission and outreach, on the other, are called into question. These pages will hopefully shed light on the link between what we might call the inward-looking and outward-looking dimensions of the Christian faith, in the history and practice of Taizé.

The story of Taizé begins with one man, Roger Louis Schutz-Marsauche, known today to many as "Brother Roger of Taizé." Born in 1915, as the son of a Reformed pastor in French-speaking Switzerland, Roger early on felt called to be a writer. Following his rediscovery of faith after an adolescent religious crisis and a long bout with tuberculosis that brought him close to death, Roger decided to study theology, more in accordance with his father's wishes than with any desire to become the pastor of a parish.

The young Roger was deeply concerned about the growing individualism in society that was leaving its mark on the church as well. In addition, he was convinced that transmitting the message of Jesus Christ by words alone was not enough. Although in Europe everyone by now was familiar with the figure of Jesus, his message, and his church, this knowledge seemingly no longer had the power to move mountains. What was needed, according to Roger, were concrete signs that would manifest the truth and beauty of the gospel. This led him to examine the age-old tradition of intentional community life in the church and its possible relevance for our time.

When the Second World War broke out and the North of France was occupied by the Nazi armies, Roger felt called to leave neutral Switzerland and settle in France, where his mother originally came from. In August 1940 he found an abandoned house for sale in the small, isolated hamlet of Taizé, in

Burgundy, and purchased it. His reasons for coming to Taizé were twofold. On the one hand, he was still envisaging the creation of a community inspired by the monastic tradition. And on the other, he wanted to be close to those who were suffering from the war. Quickly, he began to welcome and hide refugees, notably Jews, fleeing from the Nazi persecution, and helped them cross over into Switzerland. This double motivation shows clearly how the two dimensions of faith came together in his life: the search for God in prayer and work, in community with others, and the outreach to those most in need.

Monasticism was a peculiar interest for a Reformed theology student, and yet the future founder of Taizé was never interested in community life merely, or even primarily, for the sake of those who would join. It is striking to realize how, from the very beginning, he justified this life on the basis of its sign value. In a small book published in 1944, when the nascent community numbered only four members, he wrote: "The preaching of the Word must always be completed by that of example. Thus, a resident community could be, in the church, an image of the Christian community, an image that is alive, with clear contours, and in this way more accessible to the individualistic outlook of our century."[1] In a later work, he used Jesus' parable of the leaven in the dough (Matt. 13:33) to illustrate how community life could affect church and world:

> Today as never before, if it is filled with the sap proper to it, if it overflows with the freshness of brotherly life that is its reason for being, community life is a leaven in the dough. It contains within itself a potentially explosive force. It can raise mountains of indifference and bring to people an irreplaceable quality of Christ's presence. In the darkest periods, very often a small number of women and men, spread across the world, were able to reverse the course of historical evolutions, because they hoped against all hope. What seemed doomed to disintegration entered instead into the current of a new dynamism.[2]

Brother Roger's vision of community life thus unites, in ways reminiscent of the Johannine writings in the New Testament, mutual love among believers in Christ and a universal outlook. The two realities are not in tension, as if one had to choose which one to give priority to, nor are they simply two separate dimensions of a life of discipleship. Communion among believers is

---

1. Roger Schutz, *Introduction à la vie communautaire* (Geneva: Labor et Fides, 1944), 28–29.
2. Roger Schutz, *Unanimité dans le pluralisme* (Taizé: Les Presses de Taizé, 1966), 13–14.

primordial, since it expresses the basic meaning of their Christian identity (cf. John 13:34-35). This communion is shown most visibly, as we see in the biblical Acts of the Apostles, by spiritual and material sharing among the disciples of Christ, who consider themselves members of one and the same family—in short, by life in community. And this life should be as far as possible a parable that speaks for itself without explanations; it is, beyond any verbal preaching, the most effective proclamation of the Christian message. A Christian community thus exists not for itself, but for the church and for all humanity. Or, more exactly, its deepest rationale is to give expression to human relationships of goodwill and kindness which are rooted in a relationship with God through Christ, and which contain a dynamism that inexorably extends outward to "the whole world" (cf. 1 John 2:2).

7.4.2 Context: Brothers on mission

Despite this universal outlook present from the start, during the first years of its existence the Taizé Community was in practice a rather modest affair. A small group of brothers committed for life to material and spiritual sharing and to celibacy, coming from different European countries and from different Protestant backgrounds—Reformed, Lutheran, and, later, Anglican. Today, the makeup of the community has broadened but has not changed dramatically: there are 100 brothers from over 25 different countries on all continents, with, since 1966, the addition of Roman Catholics as well.

At first all the brothers lived in Taizé. Soon, some brothers were sent out on mission, first to urban centres in France and across Europe, where secularization had made strong inroads, then later to other continents. Today, small groups of Taizé brothers live in Brazil, Bangladesh, South Korea, Kenya, Senegal, and Cuba. In addition to these relatively permanent groups, brothers travel constantly to make visits and to prepare gatherings of young adults.

The Rule of Taizé, a short text written by Brother Roger in 1952–53 to sum up the community's aims, describes the spirit of their presence: "Like the disciples, sent out two by two, brothers on mission are witnesses to Christ. They are called to be a sign of his presence among all people and bearers of joy."[3] The brothers do not go out with an agenda set in advance; they do not begin by organizing social-service projects, going on a preaching tour, or founding a congregation. Their first priority is to enter into the life of the local people by getting to know them and by listening to them. As in Taizé, their existence is

---

3. Roger Schutz, *The Rule of Taizé* (London: SPCK, 2012), 95.

centred in community prayer and in life together. They live out this prayer and this life in the midst of the local population, with no ulterior motives, in order to be a sign of Christ's love and concern for all human beings. Two of these groups, in Bangladesh and in Senegal, are located in predominantly Muslim countries, and thus offer a wonderful opportunity for an interreligious presence on a grassroots level.

As one might expect, the friendships created locally and the needs perceived often lead to different forms of active collaboration. In Mymensingh, Bangladesh, the brothers noticed that youngsters with disabilities were seen as objects of shame and hidden away by their families. They began to visit these families and get to know them better; this eventually led to the creation of sharing groups for the mothers of these children. These women, of Christian, Muslim, and Hindu backgrounds, discovered that beyond their religious differences they had much in common, and they found great support in these groups. Could this undertaking not represent a neglected form of interreligious dialogue, parallel to the more theological endeavours—people from different origins meeting together to share questions of vital concern to their lives?

In addition, the brothers in Bangladesh have developed relationships with homeless youngsters who live at the railway station. They invite them to their home and organize activities with them. In similar fashion, the brothers in Alagoinhas, Brazil, work a lot today with mothers and their young children. In a neighbourhood that has become increasingly violent due mainly to drug dealing, they have created a safe space where the children and their mothers can spend the day together. Finally, the brothers in Dakar, Senegal, also try to help the many neighbourhood children, both Christian and Muslim, who are unable to afford the school fees; they have organized a kind of alternative education for these children, with many different kinds of activities to widen their horizons.

All these activities are not an end in themselves and, indeed, can and do change as the situation evolves. The Taizé Community is not a nongovernmental organization (NGO). The community looks for ways of entering into the lives of local people and collaborating with them, placing their gifts at the disposition of others. It has often happened that, when local people are willing and able to assume responsibilities for an endeavour begun by the community, the brothers pull back and allow the indigenous leadership to take over. Their presence in these places is not necessarily permanent, and certainly does not wish to replace what people can do for themselves. As is true of many people who go out on mission, the brothers feel that in the final analysis they receive more than they can give.

Where is the work of evangelism in this form of presence, one might ask? It consists in inserting a life of communion, for the sake of Christ and the gospel, in the dough of a human environment often marked by poverty or exclusion. The brothers do not hide the reason for their existence as a community and for their coming; their worship, open to all, makes it clear that they are living and acting out of faithfulness to Jesus Christ. They are confident that the yeast of the gospel can transform their own lives and the lives of those around them in ways they cannot imagine. Or, to take another of Jesus' parables, they trust that the seed that falls into the earth and may seem insignificant will sprout and grow in God's own good time, though they know not how (cf. Mark 4:26-32).

7.4.3 Identity and culture: A place for the young

From the beginning, then, the Taizé Community sought not to live for itself alone, but to go toward others and witness to God's universal love. But it was in the 1960s that the major change occurred which was to turn Taizé into the phenomenon that many are familiar with today. Those years were marked by the postwar generation, the "baby boomers," coming of age and beginning to ask serious questions about their life in society and church. Among the places they visited was the hill of Taizé. Brother Roger had always been interested in the young, remembering the difficulties he had as a young person in discovering his way and in finding a listening ear on the part of his elders:

> When I was young, I was surprised that young people were made to keep a certain distance from their elders. I respected that distance, I don't think I suffered from it, but it still astonished me. . . . And I wondered: does there exist, here on earth, a way to understand everything in another person? . . . I said to myself: if such a way exists, begin with yourself and commit yourself to understanding everything in every human being. . . . I think it was then that I began to listen to young people. . . . I say to myself again and again: in my own youth, deep within myself, I would have wanted to be listened to in the same way that I listen.[4]

During the 1960s, the community organized some small work camps for the young, and soon the numbers of participants began to mushroom. These

4. Rex Brico, *Taizé: Brother Roger and His Community* (London: Collins, 1978), 187–88.

participants told their friends, and Taizé soon became known as a place where their concerns were taken seriously and where they could meet other like-minded persons. For his part Brother Roger, despite misgivings on the part of many at a time of increasing polarization between the generations, was more and more convinced that this influx of young adults was a sign of the times and needed to be taken seriously. He did all he could to find ways of making the young more welcome on the hill of Taizé, often at the cost of shaking up the habits and customs of the community. The clearest sign of this was the decision made at Easter 1972 to tear down the façade of the "Church of Reconciliation," which had been inaugurated only ten years earlier, and to attach a circus tent to it in order to welcome the thousands of young people coming to Taizé for Holy Week. What clearer sign could be found to show that people are more important than buildings?

In many ways, the Taizé brothers were not prepared for this work of welcoming the young. They were not trained in youth ministry, and had to learn by doing. The basic thrust of their response, however, lay at the heart of their life from the beginning—the Christian and monastic value of hospitality. What Taizé has always tried to do when faced with the arrival of so many young people has simply been to make them feel welcome. And welcoming someone means not just offering him or her a bed and something to eat; it involves sharing what is most important in one's own life. So, the brothers did all they could to allow the visitors to enter into their own priorities: the search for a relationship with God in prayer and reflection on the Bible, and the importance of creating community beyond divisions of nationality, language, and religious affiliation.

7.4.4 Theological inspiration: Praying, listening, and sharing in simplicity

Gradually, the international young-adult meetings in Taizé took on a clearer shape. Participants were—and still are—encouraged to arrive on Sunday and stay a week, since entering into a rhythm of life so different from the frenetic chaos of the surrounding society takes time. Those who come for a day or two for the first time often leave still disoriented by the experience. At the centre of life on the hill, for the young pilgrims as well as for the brothers, is the experience of common worship: prayer services three times a day lasting between 30 and 45 minutes, classical in form, made up of psalms, scripture readings, intercessions, and, at the heart, a long period of silence. When the numbers of young visitors began to grow, the community sought ways of making the prayer more accessible to them, while maintaining the sung, biblical, and meditative quality which had always characterized it. The Bible readings were shortened, chosen for their comprehensibility, and read in many languages. Instead of long psalms and hymns sung in French, the community developed the short repetitive refrains now associated throughout the world with the name of Taizé. Although the original motivation for this was a practical one, the community soon came to see that, as in many religious traditions, the repetition helped people to go beyond superficial rationality and come closer to the core of their being. And the eight minutes or so of silence at the heart of every prayer service offers an island of peace in a busy and noisy world. The experience of sitting in prayerful silence with thousands of young people from across the world never fails to touch participants deeply.

A second important dimension of the young-adult meetings in Taizé is reflection on the word of God. Each morning, brothers of the community or one of the sisters who collaborate with us give a short introduction on a Bible text to try and make it more accessible. Following this short talk, participants break into small groups and discuss what possible light the text can shed on their own life. Sharing questions about the meaning of life and faith with others from a great variety of backgrounds and experiences, discovering that beyond the differences there are most often common aspirations and common frustrations, is an experience that never fails to have a deep impact on people. It gives concrete and specific content to expressions like "the global village" or "one human family."

A question the community is sometimes asked is this: Are the young pilgrims to Taizé led to commit their lives to God or to Jesus Christ? What "results" come out of this experience concerning evangelization, in the classic sense of the term? It should be clear from the above that Taizé does not employ a "hard-sell strategy" in communicating the gospel. Brother Roger always insisted that God does not force anyone to believe, and no one who comes to Taizé feels pressured to make a choice. It is also true that those who take part in the gatherings organized by Taizé are quite diverse, ranging from Christians already deeply committed in a church to those who are searching without yet being sure of what they believe. Nonetheless, it is clear that for many, a stay in Taizé is far more than a transitory experience. It is not uncommon for those who return, sometimes after many years, to tell the brothers that the time spent in Taizé awakened questions and desires that eventually led to a radical change in their life. As a result, some began to attend church regularly; others became more involved in a particular ministry; still others made a more radical commitment, such as deciding to undertake missionary work or to attend seminary. No statistics are kept on such things, and indeed, this would be impossible. But years of experience have convinced the community that God uses it to touch the hearts of many, in ways that they themselves may only fully understand much later.

7.4.5 Structure and means: Practical tasks and experience of simplicity

In Taizé, the worship and reflection take place in the context of community life. All the participants are given a practical task to do in order to make life together possible. The fact that there is no hard-and-fast division between "staff" and "visitors" is an essential part of the experience. The young people realize that they are not targets of a mission strategy or passive consumers, but are invited for a few days to become part of an international and ecumenical Christian community where they, just like the more permanent members, can give as well as receive.

A final dimension of life in Taizé that the community wishes to share with the pilgrims is the experience of simplicity. This was first of all necessary for practical reasons. Life in Taizé is simple because that is the only way that the community can welcome so many people. With no sources of funding beyond the modest contributions of the participants and the work of the brothers, the material side of life must be kept basic. The young sleep in cabins with bunk-beds or in tents; the food is wholesome without being fancy. And yet, many young people are struck positively by this simplicity of life, which offers them a refreshing alternative to societies drowning in excess, where nothing ever stops. They discover that it is possible to be happy without an overabundance of consumer goods; they enjoy being together without being burdened by expectations to meet or busy schedules to follow.

7.4.6 Lessons learned: A pilgrimage of trust

It is true in any case that an experience of Christian community outside of one's ordinary life must of necessity deal with the question of returning home, the relationship between the experience and daily life. Taizé has always refused to create a movement centred on itself, preferring to send the young visitors back to their local churches. But in order to make the link clearer, for years now the community has been organizing gatherings similar to those in Taizé in cities throughout the world. In particular, a "European meeting" brings together tens of thousands of young adults to a large European city at the end of every year. For five days, participants have an experience similar to that in Taizé in the churches of the city, together with people of all denominations. An important dimension of these gatherings is the hospitality offered by families, a very concrete way of creating understanding between people of diverse backgrounds.

To sum up: the Taizé Community, which began in the wake of the Second World War as a handful of men attempting to live the monastic life in today's world, never wished to separate the search for God in prayer and outreach to one's fellow human beings. The brothers wished first of all to witness to the gospel by the form and the quality of their life together. Open to the promptings of the Spirit, they were led to journey across the world to live their life in the midst of the most varied human realities. They were also led, somewhat unexpectedly, to share their faith and to open their community life to young people who, for over 40 years now, have been visiting them by the tens of thousands. Their music and prayer style has touched many more. Although no one could have foreseen it, God has been able to use the tiny mustard seed of one man's faithfulness to allow multitudes to enter into a deeper contact with the good news of Jesus Christ.

7.5 PIMEN and Evangelization as Education in Post-Soviet Russia

Vladimir Fedorov and Gerrit Noort

7.5.1 General description and history

The subject of this case study is the work and experience of the Orthodox Institute for Missiology, Ecumenism and New Religious Movements (PIMEN).[1] This institute was established in 1994 in St Petersburg (Russia). Its founders[2] were impelled by their wish to identify and analyze particularities of evangelization in atheist (1917–1991) and post-atheist Russia (1991–2015). Through research on faith in Russia and working ecumenically, the institute intends to contribute to developing models for doing evangelism in Russia.

Although Vladimir Fedorov, co-author of this case study, and those who participate in the institute are Russian Orthodox, many Orthodox Christians may not acknowledge that PIMEN is typical for evangelism in the Orthodox Church in Russia. This has to do with the institute's ecumenical outlook on evangelism. PIMEN is deeply convinced that the future of the Orthodox mission can only be promising and fruitful if they cooperate ecumenically and interconfessionally.

For a long time many Western missiologists and evangelists assumed that Orthodox churches were "liturgical" churches and as such indifferent to mission and missional activities. James Stamoolis, however, has decisively shown that this is a misunderstanding. In his remarkable book *Eastern Orthodox Mission Theology Today* (1986), he provided many examples of missionary initiatives by Russian Orthodoxy and described specific characteristics of Eastern Orthodox evangelization.[3]

---

1. PIMEN is the Russian acronym for *Pravoslavny Institut Missiologii, Ekumenizma i Novykh Religioznykh Dvizhenii.*
2. Father Fedorov was the main founder of this ecumenical institute, which organizes conferences and publishes studies on the religious situation in Russia.
3. A fundamental contribution to the Orthodox missiology were numerous reports, lectures, papers, and books by His Beatitude Anastasios (Yannoulatos), Archbishop of Tirana, Durrës, and All Albania. See, for example, Yannoulatos Anastasios, *Facing the World: Orthodox Christian Essays on Global Concerns* (Yonkers, NY: St Vladimir's Seminary Press, 2003).

The present case study on the ministry of PIMEN highlights two significant aspects of evangelization, namely evangelization via culture and via education. Culture was a significant form of preaching in atheist and post-atheist Russian society. Related to this form of preaching through culture, this case study will address education as a mission of the church. In Orthodox understanding, Christian education is a moving force of culture, a process of transmitting human experience and knowledge from one generation to another. This process of transmission is living tradition.

History: Evangelization in Russia, 1917–1991[4]

As a result of the revolution of 1917, communists came to power in Russia. With them they brought their rigid atheist ideology. The mass closing down of churches and monasteries that followed deprived the church of its strongest Orthodox missionary resource, namely liturgy.[5] For it is in the liturgy, Orthodox churches hold, that the spiritual life and labour culminate and from which "liturgy after the Liturgy" (witness, service, and vocation in the wider society) flows. In that understanding, being deprived of liturgy implies being deprived of the liturgical sending of Christian witnesses, who testify as faithful disciples in everyday life.[6]

Between 1927 and 1940 the number of functioning Orthodox churches in Soviet Russia dropped from 29,500 to fewer than 500. Thousands of priests were arrested and martyred. Although the number of open churches was higher after the Second World War,[7] this was still only a drop in the ocean of millions of Russians. The deep process of "atheization" under the former communist regime implied a breakdown and lack of any system of religious education. In spite of these adverse conditions, the Russian Orthodox Church continued its mission. During these years many citizens, brought up before the revolution, tried to keep the familial faith and church traditions alive. Especially women (mothers and grandmothers) played a crucial role in the process of continued faith transmission, but this was far from being general practice in the communist context.

---

4. See Walter W. Sawatsky and Peter F. Penner, eds., *Mission in the Former Soviet Union* (Schwarzenfeld: Neufeld Verlag, 2005).

5. On the role of liturgy in mission, see James J. Stamoolis, *Eastern Orthodox Mission Theology Today* (Maryknoll, NY: Orbis, 1986).

6. Ion Bria, *The Liturgy after the Liturgy: Mission and Witness from an Orthodox Perspective* (Geneva: WCC Publications, 1996).

7. The number of open churches reached 22,000 in the year 1957, but in the 1980s only 7,000 open churches remained due to forced closure of church buildings.

Especially in the 1960s and 1970s, when the strength of the communist ideology was slowly fading out, the gospel was communicated through culture and the arts. Evangelization was possible by virtue of some cultural treasures that had survived atheist ideology intact. It enabled people to familiarize themselves partially with Christian values, with elements of the church history and with fragments of the holy scripture. Fine arts (such as painting, music, literature, poetry), the Russian religious philosophical thought of the early 20th century, museums and libraries, the détente, and possible contacts with the Western world culture proved a true breeding ground for young people to reflect on their *raison d'etre* and to search for the truth.

In this context we need to mention that the communist control in Russia was not as total as it was in China or Albania. Famous museums, like the Moscow Tretyakov Gallery or the Russian Museum in Leningrad, could still expose icons. Scientific state libraries, including the libraries at pre-revolutionary universities, saved and conserved religious philosophical literature (of course, with certain exceptions). Programs of the concerts at philharmonic halls started to include spiritual and church music, first Western masses and requiems, but later also Orthodox church music. This dissemination of fragments of the gospel in society, though limited in scope, should be regarded as evangelization through culture. The following examples can serve as illustrations of the effects of this type of evangelization.

In the early 1970s a student at the Orthodox Theological Academy in St Petersburg told Vladimir Fedorov that he came from a nonbelieving family. After listening to Mozart's *Requiem* at a concert, he began studying Latin and Russian' texts. As he was intrigued, he then started to read theological literature, which eventually led him to enroll as a student in one of the three remaining Orthodox seminaries.

In that same period another student said his first encounter with religious philosophy occurred while reading verses by the famous Russian intellectual Vladimir Solovyov (1853–1900). He obtained Solvyov's writings after noticing that the equally famous poet Alexandr Blok (1880–1921) quoted him. When he started to read Solovyov's collected works, he came to understand that this was a brilliant religious thinker and the founder of a new school of philosophical thought. The study of his work instilled in him the desire to become a student of theology and prepare for ministry in the church.

Another priest told that he was an art critic before entering the seminary. He studied the history of icon painting, gradually took an interest in the controversy between iconoclasts and icon venerators (iconodules or icono-philes), and finally became interested in the theology of the icon and theology of the name. Thus, he was evangelized by culture and slowly drawn into the mystery of faith.

The previous examples show that Russian culture brought forth philolo-gists, historians, and other intellectuals who were deep religious thinkers and who could draw people to the tradition of the church. One of these thinkers was Sergei Averintsev (1937–2004), whose lectures on the history of literature and world culture were almost homilies. They were not the kind of homilies we hear in church, but they would give the listeners "horizons of divine revela-tions" and make them look for opportunities to read the holy scripture and commentaries.[8] In this way, not only a novelist like Fyodor Dostoyevsky, but also many other Russian authors helped the young people to follow their own way toward the truth. Culture can be a vehicle of evangelism, as Russia never lost interest in its Byzantine culture and heritage, which was shaped by Chris-tian faith. This national heritage evangelized Russian intelligentsia. Of course, not only the intelligentsia was congenial to culture. But in an atheist society where religion was stigmatized as obscurantism, the authority of intelligent believers was important.

In the late 1980s, at the time of *perestroika*, several graduates from the philosophical faculty of the Leningrad University came to realize the shortages of the alternative Marxist framework in the field of humanities. Influenced by Russian religious culture and freed from the Marxist atheist blinkers of the state ideology, they pioneered to establish a nongovernmental institution for higher education in the country. In 1989 their school opened in St Petersburg, under the ideologically neutral name "Higher Courses for the Humanities." In 1991, after the communist ideology lost its state position, they renamed it the "Russian Christian Institute for the Humanities" (RCIH).[9]

The decision to change the name was based on the founders' strong conviction that Christian faith helps young people to appreciate the values of European and world culture and that it provides a basis for integral and wide education in the humanities. They thought that the state educational

---

8. In his report "Christianity in the History of European Culture," which he wrote at the Moscow College of Culturology in 1990, Sergei S. Averintsev dwelt on the specificity of Christianity as compared to Judaism, Islam, and paganism, on the meaning of dogmas, on characteristics of each of the four gospels, etc. See Sergei S. Averintsev, "Christianity in the History of European Culture: Report," http://royallib.com/read/averintsev_sergey/hristianstvo_v_istorii_evropeyskoy_kulturi.html#0.

9. See its website, Russian Christian Institute for the Humanities, http://www.rhga.ru.

institutions were running the risk of producing narrow-minded professionals, as they didn't acknowledge the Christian roots of Russian culture.

7.5.2 Context: Evangelization in the post-Soviet situation (1991–2015)

The revolution of 1991 was about liberalization. It also destroyed, however, an awareness of the need for ideological and moral standards. While the freedom of speech was regained, the revolution also resulted in decreasing respect for traditional culture. Atheism ceased to be the communist state ideology in Russia, and a wide range of the most diverse evangelistic activities emerged. The sudden influx of many Western evangelists who came to Russia, bringing their own churches and confessions, created a perplexing problem for the Orthodox Church. The Western style of living and believing influenced many Russians in new ways. Notorious were public evangelistic gatherings organized by Protestant preachers, held in huge auditoriums, where holy scriptures and religious literature were distributed. At that time it was hard to understand what was going on in the churches in Russia.

It was in this particular context that initiative was taken to establish PIMEN. A priest, who was among the Russian Christian Institute for the Humanities' founders and lecturers, also served as a professor at the Orthodox Theological Academy in St Petersburg. Inspired by the new prospects for the development of the Russian Christian Institute for the Humanities, he suggested that within its framework an Orthodox institution for missiology, ecumenism, and new religious movements should be established. This new institute (PIMEN) was started in 1994 under the leadership of Vladimir Fedorov.

The above-mentioned context of confusion and uncertainty about faith in Russia was the reason why PIMEN started its specific research on the shape of belief and faith practices in Russia. The results made clear that the majority of Russians regard being a member of the Orthodox Church as a national identity marker, but that only a minority of them are practitioners who attend church worship and have knowledge of the Christian faith.

Based on these results, PIMEN called for a strong emphasis on Christian education in the missionary work of the Orthodox Church, as teaching future priests and laypeople was urgent in order to respond effectively to the challenges of a changing society. This was the very reason the institute produced a handbook on religious education and tried to convince the government that a course on Russian culture and Orthodox Church should be part of the curriculum.

Orthodox leaders in the post-Soviet period were largely focussed on the restoration of local churches and founding new parishes in order to safeguard the continuity of the Christian tradition. But they now set up educational structures such as Sunday schools in the parishes, nongovernmental Orthodox high schools, gymnasiums, and higher-educational institutions.

7.5.3 Identity and culture

Characteristic for the way PIMEN has worked is the unusual (in Orthodox Russia) but stimulating practice of cooperation of Orthodox professors and students with members of other denominations. The institute has reflected on mission in cooperation with representatives of Protestant communities such as the Lutheran and Presbyterian churches, as well as with members of Baptist and Pentecostal churches.

The following may serve as a good example of the interchurch cooperation in evangelism. Protestant churches, springing up everywhere after the collapse of the USSR in 1991, needed educated pastors to lead their new faith communities. There were, however, practically no Russian educational institutions with cultural and religious curricula that suited the needs of Protestant communities. In this context Protestants welcomed the opportunity to be educated at state-accredited educational institutions, like the Russian Christian Institute for the Humanities and the Institute for Missiology.

The course of events has shown that, even when some lectures were delivered by a professor who was confessionally strict, adherents to other confessions had space to bring their religious identity into the conversation. This was the result, first, of the lecturer's awareness of the confessional diversity represented in his audience, and, second, because the lecturer realized his obligation to be truthful, honest, and unbiased.

Practice has shown that joint courses, such as "History of Christianity," resulted in mutual and interconfessional interest. Likewise, studying the history of iconoclasm and theology of the icon allowed Protestant students to see the meaning of icon veneration. The context of the post-Soviet period, with its increasing diversity and growing need for good education, is a clear sign that ecumenical cooperation in Christian mission and evangelism is much needed. The founders of the Russian Christian Institute for the Humanities and PIMEN believed that Orthodox preaching should be rooted in interconfessional dialogues and even in dialoguing with nonbelieving scholars. They were inspired by St Teresa Benedicta of the Cross (1891–1942), a Roman Catholic saint who sought new paths for philosophy and theology, who said: "God is truth. Anyone who seeks the truth seeks God, whether or not he is aware of it."

7.5.4 Theological inspiration

As the founders and lecturers of the Institute for Missiology are members of the Orthodox Church, their understanding of evangelism is shaped by the Orthodox theology of mission. As far back as the early 1990s they came to understand that evangelization isn't limited to the important task of preaching or attempts to convert others. Because of 70 years of aggressive atheism, Russian citizens are inept in religious matters and do not easily respond to preaching or calls to conversion. The words of Archimandrite Makary (1792–1847) taught us: "If you do not know how to be a catcher of men, then catch fish to feed the catchers of men."[10] Missionary action through preaching may not catch many humans, but developing a truly Christian answer to contemporary problems in word and action may catch the fish.

PIMEN is convinced that evangelistic action is more effective when it works through culture and education. This implies that the development of various educational structures, clerical and secular, has to be part and parcel of the mission of the church. As Ignatius IV, patriarch of Antioch (1920–2012), stated: "it is our task to 're-orient culture from within.'" Contemporary Russian culture still bears the marks of Christian faith and of evangelism in earlier times. Therefore, Orthodox spirituality reveals itself in society, and evangelism can relate to a culture shaped by Orthodox faith. It evokes a new understanding of revelation and truth.

In this framework evangelism is thus understood as a task of Christian enlightenment, as the gospel teaches that "Christ is the light of the world" (John 8:12). In Russian, the word *enlightenment* is primarily understood as having or giving somebody knowledge or understanding. In Russian everyday usage, this term is not associated with the age of Enlightenment and is often preferred to the word *education*. In our Orthodox worship and prayers we often hear reference to en-light-enment: "The light of Christ shines for all!," "Christ is joyful light," "Christ is the sun of righteousness." So, it comes quite naturally to the Russian mind to understand all kinds of education as enlightenment, as preaching the word (light) of God.

The above makes clear that Orthodox churches regard "enlightenment"— pedagogics, upbringing, and education—as exceptionally important for

---

10. Makary Nevsky, *Complete Sermons of His Eminence Makary (Nevsky), Archbishop of Tomsk and Altai* (Tomsk, 1910), 492.

evangelization. This is especially true for the country about which the great Russian Orthodox writer Nikolai Leskov (1831–1895) said: "Rus [ancient Russia] was baptized but not enlightened." Some Orthodox dignitaries may object to this judgment, but Patriarch Alexii II (1990–2008) explicitly referred to these words when he reflected on the mission of Orthodoxy after 1991 and stated that in evangelism the work of enlightening people should be given its proper place. It is the mission of the church to enlighten people, so that they can understand the language of revelation more and more. If in mission and evangelism we want to avoid the Scylla of modernism and the Charybdis of fundamentalism, that will only be possible by cultivating profound knowledge of the history and tradition of the church as well as a sincere personal faith.

Cultivating this knowledge (education) is a process of transmitting experience from one generation to another. In Orthodox understanding, tradition is Holy Tradition, that is, theological or religious education or teaching religions. It is a missionary task to assist secular education to attain a historical perspective on culture and to enable the search for the fundamentals and laws of the created world. This type of evangelism guides the search for the Logos as the universal principle of the world and the true science of overcoming chaos.

This means that Orthodoxy holds that the mission of education and the service of enlightenment are sacral. To illustrate this we can use a vivid expression analogous to the one used for *diakonia*. If *diakonia* is called a "liturgy *after* Liturgy,"[11] then education can be referred to as a "liturgy *before* Liturgy."[12] Religious education, evangelization, catechization, and preparing believers for eucharist are worship: a "liturgy before the Liturgy."

Those who conceptualized the curricula of the above-mentioned Russian Christian Institute for the Humanities took their starting point for evangelization in Jesus Christ's life and way as the central event in world history. Consequently, they underscored the fundamentality of Christianity in the cultural history of mankind: "Christianity is not a total of some frozen images and theological doctrines, but a spiritual revolution that occurred and that ever

---

11. The first to coin this image more than 40 years ago was the present-day head of the Albanian Orthodox Church, Archbishop Anastasios Yannulatos. Later, it was frequently used by Father Ion Bria. He would say that the liturgy is not a self-centered service and action, but is a service for the building of the one body of Christ within the economy of salvation, which is for all people of all ages.

12. For more on this topic see Vladimir Fedorov, "Orthodox View on Theological Education as Mission," *Religion in Eastern Europe* 25/3 (2005): 1-37; condensed in Peter F. Penner, ed., *Theological Education as Mission* (Schwarzenfeld: Neufeld Verlag, 2005).

since has been going on in the people's minds and hearts, an energy that creates a new man and thus, a new cultural and historical reality."[13]

7.5.5 Structure and means

The Institute for Missiology is closely related to both the Russian Christian Institute for the Humanities and the Orthodox Theological Academy. Research fellows are recruited from the graduates and the staff of the Russian Christian Institute for the Humanities. Within the structure of PIMEN, space was created for an additional Institute of Religious Pedagogics, which specifically researches "Education as mission."

PIMEN, as such, functioned independently since it was established in 1994, but in 1998 it became part of the Interchurch Partnership "Apostolic City Nevskaya Perspectiva" in St Petersburg. Its former president, Mrs Marina Shishova, who also served as researcher at the missiological institute, is now the chief of staff to the rector of the Russian Christian Institute for the Humanities. Interchurch Partnership (established 1998) conducts activities directed at church and society. Its objectives are:

- finding new ways of evangelization,

- developing structures of religious and peace education and enlightenment,

- completing an analysis of the interrelationship between the society, churches, and religious communities,

- completing the study of the religious situation in Russia,

- the analysis of the problems of church life and finding ways to resolve them,

- assuring peace and unity while overcoming religious conflicts and animosity.[14]

The Russian Christian Institute for the Humanities, as such, competed successfully with state educational schools because of the quality of its education. This contributed to the prestige of the institution, which is not confined to confessional belonging to any religious tradition. So, among its students

---

13. D. K. Burlaka, "Programma Russkogo Hristianskogo Gumanitarnogo Instituta: istoriya, filoso-fiya pragmatika novoi modeli gumanirarnogo obrazovaniya," *Vestnik RHGI*, Spb 1 (1997): 13.
14. See Pax Christi International, "Interchurch Partnership Apostolic City-Nevskaya Perspetive," http://www.paxchristi.net/member-organizations/russia/146.

there have been Christians and nonbelievers, as well as members of so-called new religious movements (in Russia not infrequently referred to as "sects" or "cults"). The 25-year history of the school shows that students who previously had no association with church life or were initially drawn by exotic religious and pseudo-religious movements, joined Christian communities they found agreeable. This happened without any Orthodox pressure.

In St Petersburg there were several Protestant schools and a Roman Catholic seminary, besides the Orthodox educational institutions. It was the growing sense of needed cooperation between the theological schools and secular educational institutions that led to the plan to establish the Interchurch Partnership "Apostolic City," which focusses on nonprofit education.

7.5.6 Main lessons

Continuous learning is needed not only to comprehend the revelation of holy scripture and tradition, but also in order to perceive God's revelation as discernible in nature, the sciences, and social structures. In Orthodox understanding, being a well-educated person is a virtue. A neglectful attitude toward education moves one further away from God, because ideally, education should prepare one for meeting Christ, for thanksgiving, for eucharist, and for grateful service to our Lord. Therefore, evangelism can't do without education.

7.6 Religious Education as Evangelism in the Serbian Orthodox Church

Darko Djogo

7.6.1 Introduction: A personal experience

For the Serbian Orthodox Church, religious education is a significant and primary method of evangelization. The best way to show this is to tell you my personal story. It will make clear how the introduction of religious education in the schools of the war-torn Republic of Srpska (Serbia) affected its pupils. I recall my first class of religious education very well. The primary school which I attended was the only building with electricity in the town of Pale, to which we were evacuated after the war broke out. As pupils we stayed in it from dawn until dusk, not so much because we were diligent and hardworking but because it was warm and relatively safe there. And also because, as medieval scribes, we copied the necessary material with our own hands, as proper printed manuals were not available. Deeply worried about our fathers on the battlefield, we focussed on our mathematical problems in order not to think about the rest of the world. We were learning about the rainforests, monkeys, and pandas, thereby preventing ourselves from thinking about tanks, guns, and the news.

In that wartime situation we received religious education. When I, now a professor of theology, look back to these first courses it is easy to complain about the professional skills of our first teacher of Orthodox religious education. Nevertheless, even today I remember how we learned our prayers by heart for the whole duration of a full school hour, which is 45 minutes. In the year 1992–93 I was in the third grade of primary school and all of that year we just prayed. We prayed like the thirsty man drinks water. Everything we had to say was a prayer. The comic side of the situation was that when our teacher finally decided do give us marks on the prayers we had learned, he gave me a 4+ (B+), which is quite average. It certainly was not a very promising beginning for my professional theological career, and I am quite sure that my students would be very satisfied to hear this little piece of information.

7.6.2 Historical context

Let us look at the way formal religious education was shaped in the Republic of Srpska, and Bosnia and Herzegovina. Religious education was first introduced in the schools of the Republic of Srpska in December 1992. Then, up to the summer of 1993, it was introduced in the schools in what is today the federation of Bosnia and Herzegovina. At that time, today's federation was split into two large territories: the first was the Republic of Bosnia and Herzegovina, predominantly controlled by the Muslim Bosnian Army, and the second was the Republic of Herzeg-Bosna, controlled by the Catholic Croatian Army. All territories considered it important to introduce religious education in their primary-school educational systems. The reason for this was the same: each of the warring parties had abandoned the communist ideology and turned to a new one, which can be called a nationalistic ideology.

There were different understandings of this new nationalistic ideology. Some referred to the term *nationalistic* in a pejorative manner as chauvinism, while others understood it as patriotism. Each of the governments wanted to leave behind the no-longer-useful concepts of the Yugoslav "brotherhood and equality" of nations, broken by the harsh realities of history. They considered it their primary task to restore religious education as both a method of social engineering and as a reminder of the precommunist times when religious education also was a proper subject in all public and private schools. Being rooted in the Orthodox tradition and being primarily familiar with the history and content of the Orthodox religious education in today's Bosnia Herzegovina, I will limit myself to a discussion of religious education in Orthodoxy. We have to keep in mind, though, that while the Orthodox, Catholic, and Muslim traditions are quite different, the same phenomenological characteristics related to the introduction of religious education can be found in all three faith traditions.

7.6.3 Identity and culture

Although it may look like heresy for 99 percent of the traditional believers of our Serbian Orthodox Church in Bosnia Herzegovina, the very concept of the church as "a keeper of ancient traditions" represents one of the major obstacles for broader evangelization. Traditionalism is still very much alive in former Yugoslavia. One of the main reasons can be found in the social structure of the former Yugoslav population. Yugoslavia experienced an intensive transformation from a predominantly rural society between 1918 and 1945, to a society with a strong urbanized population in 1990. Yet, reminiscences on the old rural way of life are still very much alive in a major portion of the urban population, not to mention in still-existing rural environments. Nowadays, we even talk about the increasing "rural-mode-of-life nostalgia" among the urban population faced with economic problems. It is important to note that in rural religiosity it has never been clear what is exactly Christian truth and what is mere traditional folklore. There is a blurred line between tradition and religiosity which goes back to Ottoman rule (1463–1878). During those times it was important to survive and yet keep your own religious identity. Therefore, popular tradition generally preserved some elements of Orthodox religiosity.

A problem emerges, however, when this historically shaped tradition is declared the ultimate religious way, the first and the last word of Orthodoxy, as a synonym for Orthodoxy itself. A driving instructor once told me that it is much easier to teach a person who has had no previous driving experience than to teach a young boy who has been illegally driving for a couple of years. In the same way, it is easier to explain, for instance, the meaning of the eucharist or baptism to a newly converted urban intellectual who is baptized in his 20s or 30s than to explain its meaning to a traditionalist who always had his children baptized "because my forefathers were doing that as well."

In the past 20 years different social aspects of religious education have been researched and we can therefore observe some of the effects of religious education in the societies of the former Yugoslav republics. Generally speaking, it is obvious that in all of these the tendency for people to identify themselves as a believer is still very high. This, of course, cannot only be explained by the influence of religious education, as it is also related to the old practice of stating your national identity by means of your religious identity and affiliation. To say "I am an Orthodox believer" means that I respect the Orthodox tradition as a part of my Serbian or Macedonian identity and heritage. The same could be said for the Muslim identity of the Bosnjaks or the Catholic identity of the Croatians. Although this is the case, figures show that the percentage of people in our societies who practice their faith is relatively high compared to western Europe as a whole or even in comparison to a highly religious society such as the United States.

Interpretation of such data in our societies is very often a matter of political or sociopolitical debate. There are two main opposed groups: those who advocate a liberal interpretation and those who favour a conservative approach. The liberal interpretation sees religious education only as a problematic issue which cherishes nationalism and which is an obstacle to fully establishing the European model of civil society in the countries of southeastern Europe. For the supporters of the liberal view, religion is the private matter of each individual and, as such, it should not be taught in schools. Their conviction is, of course, rooted in their perspectives on the role of religious communities in the war of the 1990s. According to the liberal interpretation, the role of religion was always negative and even diabolical. Also, they hold that religious education leads to an undesired segregation of pupils, especially so in those communities where pupils of various ethnicities attend the same school. Those in favour of the liberal interpretation lately advocate that a course on "culture of religions" should substitute for classic religious education.

The conservative interpretation views religious education as a symbol of classical, European, and Christian (or Muslim) values, as one of the main achievements of civil societies; and as one of the fundamental human freedoms, namely the freedom to educate your child in your own religious tradition in the public educational system. It is almost self-evident that the supporters of this point of view oppose the introduction of the "culture of religions" as a substitute for religious education.

Both the liberal and the conservative approach are highly ideological and make one great hermeneutical mistake: they understand religious education through the lens of their ideologies. They see religious education as a symbol of their concerns about values and not as a living process with children and persons of "flesh and blood" who are involved in it. In general, they see religious education only as a method of social engineering. Even on that level they fail to see that religious education has other, socially needed components as well. Yes, it is true that religious education promotes religious identities, but what would happen if we shove religious identity aside? The former Yugoslav educational system provides a good example of what would happen in that case. Back then all high school and university students were obliged to attend classes on Marxism. Yet, this did not prevent them from slaughtering each other during the war, despite the fact that for four, and up to eight, years they had learned that "nation" is an obsolete concept that would soon be abandoned in the "kingdom of proletarians." It taught them that scientific socialism could only tolerate religion as a remainder of the old regressive system. Basically, religious education filled in the ethical and axiological hole when the old socialist system collapsed.

Nevertheless, the big-style comeback of religious education can be critiqued. Especially during the first couple of years after its introduction, communities were delighted about the restoration of religious education, but they hardly knew what to do once it was reintroduced. The content of religious education was not yet clear. Certainly, this greatly improved over time. Important and practical issues of evangelization emerged: What should we do with the many adults who rushed into the churches during the 1990s? How could we educate them? In response to these emerging issues, the Serbian Orthodox Church didn't develop a broad and general strategy on evangelism. It was primarily left to the individual parishes and priests to decide whether they would organize some basic teaching for the newly baptized persons or not. In this context the question surfaced of what the basics of the faith actually are. In response to this, some authors, priests, and teachers looked to the image of the Orthodox theology as it is given in the neopatristic movement (or more specially, as it is given by Metropolitan Zizioulas[1]) for guidance. This was understood as fundamental and necessary basics for Orthodox Christians. But then, the next question is how the basics should be taught in religious education to young people. My 12-year-old cousin, living in Belgrade, asked me some time ago to help her out with her homework for religious education. I agreed to do that, but was highly astonished when I realized that she was struggling to understand the hypostatical union of the two substances in Christ. To explain this to a 12-year-old teenager is certainly not an easy task. It made me wonder about the required minimum of theological content in our books on religious education. The issue, of course, is what it takes to convey the essence of the Christian tradition to the next generation and to those adults who turn to the Christian tradition.

My teaching experience tells me that some theological content is quite popular among the pupil-student population, such as an emphasis on divine love, or the concepts of community and solidarity. These can act as bridges to convey the basics of Christian faith. Also, which may come as a surprise, our teenagers love the liturgical and sacramental life. They do so for various reasons. Some love it because liturgical and sacramental life is old and gives them a sense of antiquity. Others do so because this life is quite liberal and does not have strict rules of conduct.

Interestingly, we observe that teenagers and even children evangelize their parents and elderly relatives, because they at least have some idea of religion,

---

1. Johannes Zizioulas (b. 1931) is the Eastern Orthodox Metropolitan of Pergamon.

whereas elderly people have not. If we keep this fact in mind, the question of the content of evangelization in religious education becomes even more interesting. We have observed that adults are more interested in formal aspects of faith. They ask questions like "What is a proper liturgical act?," "What is the proper moral behavior?," and so forth. But teenagers and children are more interested in the "ontological" questions. They ask, "Is there a God?," "How can we make contact with God?," "What is the meaning of eucharist?," and the like. The difference can be explained by pointing to the fact that our middle-aged generation is tired of ideological faith. They are depressed because of the war and economic catastrophes. The older generation seeks the easier way to "ensure the eternal life," while the younger generations are interested in, as Dostoyevsky called them, "eternal damned questions."

7.6.4 Structure and means

As previously mentioned, during the entire school year of 1992–93 we did not have any proper manuals for religious education. The war and its sad circumstances, of course, had their share in this. In 1993–94 the situation changed a bit: as pupils we noticed that our teacher of religious education had a book in his hands. For me, it was thrilling to realize that this volume was one of my favorite Orthodox books: a tiny publication called *The Faith of the Saints*, written by St Nicolai Velimirovic of Zica and Ohrid (1880–1956). Basically, this is a classic "catechism" with questions and answers, but if you keep in mind the fact that we were 10 years old at that time, it suited us quite well. It provided us with basic liturgical and theological content of our faith in quite a nice and unobtrusive manner. One of the reasons for its adoption as a manual was that it was one of the rare "catechetical" or "theological" books printed in the former Yugoslavia.

Nevertheless, this catechism did not stay in use for a long time. It was replaced by another catechism called *There Is No Nicer Faith than the Christian*, written by the prominent bishops Danilo Krstic (1927–2002) and Amfilohije Radovic (b. 1938). This catechism kept the question-and-answer structure, but it was more theological than the first one. It is obvious, for instance, that neopatristic theology had its influence on this book. The eucharist was therefore not considered as only one of the mysteries/sacraments, but as a central one. One of the questions, considering the history of the church, was, "Who were the Philocalists?," and the answer tells the story about St Nicodeme the Agiorite (1749–1809).

It was only in the late 1990s and the beginning of the new millennium that junior classes got their proper, functionally written manuals. One of them is called *Our Life with God* (translated from the English). The "theological" content is presented through drawing and games, thereby making it a very suitable manual for educational purposes.

In Serbia, due to the historical context, religious education was not introduced until the year 2004. Unlike the newborn countries (the former Yugoslav republics), the Communist Party in Serbia changed its name to the Socialist Party and virtually controlled the country up to 5 October 2000. Although the opposition, which took control of the country on that date, generally tended to uphold civil freedoms, a large debate arose about the issue of whether or not the freedom of religious education was a part of civil freedoms. Many who opposed the idea of civil freedoms were former communist dissidents who changed their allegiance from the communist ideology to an extreme left-wing European ideology. Thanks to a gentlemen's agreement between the late prime minister of Serbia (Zoran Djindjic) and the late patriarch of the Serbian Orthodox Church (Pavle), religious education was finally introduced in 2004.

The *ad hoc* character of this solution, however, has resulted in some bad consequences even today. Let me just mention some of them. Religious education is now taught both in primary and secondary schools, but it is not an obligatory subject. Children may choose between religious education and "Civil Society Education" (CSE). Since CSE is predominantly taught by professors of philosophy, sociology, or technical education, most schools tend to prefer it to religious education, that is, most school directors suggest to the parents that their children should take these classes. Second, marks given on the classes of religious education cannot be included in the final average mark. Because of that, many pupils and students regard classes on religious education as a nice break between the "true subjects" (courses that count for the final mark) or even as "lost time." And third, teachers of religious education will only be employed by the school for one academic year, meaning that the teachers' contract always lasts just one year and never more. This makes the organization of the educational process as well as the labour status of the teacher of religious education tough and uncertain. The teachers are predominantly educated theologians or students of theology. Yet, there are still many cases where a pious teacher of history, with the blessing of local bishop, teaches religious education as well.

In the Republic of Srpska the senior grades (grades 6 to 9) now have their own manuals, written by persons appointed by the catechetical board of the Serbian Orthodox Church. The manuals cover the general history of the church (6th grade), history of the Serbian Orthodox Church (7th grade), and some basics of Orthodox liturgy and Christian ethics (8th and 9th grades). Although these manuals are not perfect and many things can be improved, they are helpful for transmitting the Christian faith to the younger generation.

Thus, religious education in the Republic of Srpska and Bosnia Herzegovina is taught in primary schools and it is an obligatory subject, unless the parents declare in writing that they do not want their children to take these classes. This happens rarely, however. Marks given in the classes of religious education, unlike the situation in Serbia, are included in the final average mark of a child. It has to be acknowledged, however, that teachers of religious education tend to give only 4's and 5's (A's and B's), very much like the teachers of artistic disciplines and sports. Second, and finally, teachers of religious education have finished their studies at the theological faculty. They are appointed by their bishops and, unlike the situation in Serbia, they have the same labour status as any teacher of other subjects.

7.6.5 Lessons learned

Some lessons learned are evident and obvious. First of all, we have observed that religious education in the realms of the formal educational system (as one of the subjects among the others) is a good way to evangelize children and youth, but we learned as well that it cannot replace evangelism that is directed to the middle-aged generation (born in the 1950s, 1960s, and 1970s). The middle-aged generation is "stuck" in an ethical, social, and ideological vacuum, as it was brought up in the spirit of socialism. Although socialism may have lost its influence over people's lives, this generation was raised without substantial religious education. They only have some knowledge of the "Orthodox traditionalism," which mistakenly is understood as "Orthodox religion." From time to time, the Serbian Orthodox Church has therefore undertaken smaller short-term initiatives for evangelism among adults, but none of these was part of overall Serbian Orthodox Church programmes and they did not last for a longer period. This type of evangelism was, and still is, laid into the hands of individual priests and religious-education teachers. This implies that evangelism in the Serbian Orthodox Church is not regarded as a responsibility of the church as such, but that it depends on the evangelistic zeal, capacity, education, or good will of the individual. An overall special programme of evangelism is therefore very much needed.

Second, we have learned that a programme of evangelism obviously can't be uniformly applied in different social environments. Priests, religious-education teachers, and local Christians will find themselves in the different contexts of a two million-person metropolis, of a small town in Serbia or the Republic of Srpska, or in a half-destroyed village in Croatia or the federation of Bosnia Herzegovina. That means that we will have to be sensitive to the context and develop more than one "general" programme of evangelism in the Serbian Orthodox Church.

Third, we have learned that theological accents in these future programmes of evangelism will have to be sensitive to the language of the modern world, yet at the very same time have to be authentic and consistent with the faith of the church and the fathers. It is not enough just to translate patristic texts and to write theological studies. We need to develop forms of written evangelism that were already present in the precommunist Serbian culture. For instance, we need to reintroduce the method of the theological essay, which nowadays is almost absent from present-day theological publications. At the same time, we need to develop new forms of addressing people. Television shows and social media are new realities we have to take into account, but we should not do this in an unsystematic and chaotic way. We need to strategize about what we want to convey in our evangelism and how we want to address the world.

Finally, we have learned that although about 5 to 7 percent of the urban population professes a certain level of repulsion toward "religion," they mainly have its traditional form in mind. Through experience we have learned that at least some of the people who say they are "not religious" in fact mean that they are "not traditional," or "not traditionally religious." Being "spiritual but not religious" is not only a characteristic of northern European societies, but it is more and more present in the modern Serbian social context as well. One of the primary tasks of the Serbian Orthodox Church in her future evangelization efforts must therefore be to find proper ways to mediate between these two concepts in order to be, in Paul's words, "all things to all people, that I might by all means save some" (1 Cor. 9:22).

7.7 Evangelism in the International Christian Fellowship in Rotterdam

Gerrit Noort and Stefan Paas

7.7.1 General description and history

The buzzing city of Rotterdam, with its port and maritime industry, attracts many migrants, sailors, students, and businesspeople. Christian newcomers to this city established around 130 Christian faith communities, next to already-existing indigenous churches.[1] A small number of these indigenous churches, realizing the massive demographic shift in the past 30 years, looked for ways to shape welcoming communities for people from other nations. One of the results of this search was the founding of the International Christian Fellowship (ICF), a newly established faith community[2] that developed a ministry with remarkable emphasis on evangelism.

The ICF started as an interdenominational initiative. Members of several Reformed denominations wanted to offer a home to English-speaking fellow citizens. English worship services were therefore offered in the Christian Reformed Church in Rotterdam-Charlois, starting in November 1998. Volunteers organized and facilitated the services, while an interdenominational board took responsibility for the activities. Amongst these volunteers was Theo Visser, who later became the first pastor of the ICF.

Despite good intentions, not many people turned up for these English worship services. This changed, however, when in the year 2000 Visser and his family decided to move into the multicultural *Tarwe*-borough and Visser became the visible promotor of the new initiative. Under his leadership the project developed a strong missionary focus and soon an international faith community started to grow.

The growth of the ICF made it necessary to reconsider its relation to the churches. Was it to be an independent interdenominational congregation or could formal relations to an existing denomination be established? It

---

1. Robert Calvert, *Gids voor Christelijke Migranten Gemeenschappen in Rotterdam* (Rotterdam: SKIN-Rotterdam, 2007).
2. See http://icfrotterdam.nl.

was decided to establish a formal relationship with the Christian Reformed Churches in the Netherlands. The local Christian Reformed congregation entered into partnership with the new faith community and both were acknowledged as Christian Reformed congregations. In January 2001 the faith community was instituted as a new Christian Reformed congregation with 30 members and three elders. This meant that the interdenominational board was dissolved, as it transferred responsibility to the newly shaped church council. When the older Christian Reformed congregation had to be closed due to decline in "white" membership, the ICF became the only Christian Reformed congregation in the neighbourhood.

7.7.2 Context

The International Christian Fellowship is rooted in Rotterdam-Charlois, a municipality located in the south of the city. Until the 1950s people in this part of town were churchgoers. There were a large number of church buildings, filled to the brim on Sundays. Nowadays most of these churches are no longer in use. In 1940 some 19 Reformed congregations were active in Rotterdam South, but now not even five of these faith communities remain. The same applies to other Protestant congregations as well, as their members moved out of the city to surrounding suburbs. In recent decades migrants have moved into the city. The International Christian Fellowship has its meeting place in the Tarwewijk borough. This township has a very mixed population. Roughly 70 percent of the inhabitants are migrants and only a negligible percentage is churchgoing.

Because of the demographic shift, churches in Rotterdam South can only be relevant to society if they cross ethnic boundaries. The ICF realizes this and accepts its calling to share the gospel cross-culturally and to foster a sense of cohesion. This is not an easy endeavour. The ICF recognizes that in this context people come and go, that cultural differences are difficult to bridge, and that the migratory experience may have been painful. Visser often refers to the metaphor of the field hospital. "Life in this world," he said, "resembles a battlefield. Many fall victim to injustice and the hardships of migration. The faith community resembles the field hospital. Its mission is to respond to urgent needs and it excels in doing so, but it is not equipped to offer the sophisticated services of an academic hospital. It provides first aid, temporary care and shelter."

When the ICF was no longer in its pioneering phase, it realized the limitations of the metaphoric field hospital. The image instilled a sense of division:

the "caretakers" and the "victims." After 2008 the leadership started to under-score the importance of participation. Not just the "caretakers" are called to serve, but the calling to grow in love and service for God and our neighbours (Matt. 22:36-40) applies to all.[3] The ICF's vision statement (2014) says: "We build together, we cry and laugh, work and serve. We sing and pray, and say goodbye after some time." While the ICF accepts this temporary character of being together as a matter of fact, its goal is not only to "equip everybody to walk his or her personal path of life together with God," but also "to send them out as committed followers of Jesus Christ."[4]

The pioneering phase of the faith community showed remarkable growth. During this period, between 2001 and 2008, membership grew exponentially from 30 to 260 members.[5] The growth included some 80 adults, from diverse ethnic backgrounds, who were baptized. New believers were ethnically often Kurdish, but others came from countries like Sierra Leone, Nigeria, Sudan, and Lebanon. About 54 percent of the membership had Dutch parents. Of the other members, Africans were the biggest group, followed by Asians and migrants from the Middle East. Since 2008 a growing number of eastern Euro-peans participate in the ICF's activities. Through its worship services, home groups, and programmes it reaches around 400 people regularly. In 2014 five new believers were baptized and about 20 people participated in Alpha courses. People who want to be baptized take catechism classes for one year, so that they have good knowledge of the Christian tradition before baptism.

In 2004 the ICF initiated a diaconal programme in the neighbourhood. This was a direct response to a government report, which stated in sharp words that the six churches in the neighbourhood did not have any social relevance for its inhabitants. "The churches," the report said, "were mainly working for their own people and their own purposes." In 2003 the ICF started talks with the municipality about taking responsibility. "House of Hope," a "safe place for adults and children,"[6] was opened in 2004 as a diaconal project of the ICF intended to provide support to citizens as well as a place to meet. Its purpose was to promote participation in society and the ability to cope. This should result in growth of cohesion in society.[7]

3. "Visie en richtingbepaling," in *Handbook ICF Rotterdam* (3 December 2013), 2.
4. See ICF Rotterdam, "Our Vision: 'Passion for God, Compassion for People'," http://icfrotterdam.nl/?page_id=27.
5. The ICF struggles with the concept of membership, as many are involved in the faith community but see no use in membership as such. This means that the actual number of people involved is much higher than the actual number of members.
6. See http://www.houseofhope.nl.
7. Ibid.

House of Hope receives financial support from the municipality. About 225 volunteers support House of Hope in its activities, which include running a food bank, providing legal advice, visiting people at home, providing marriage counselling, and organizing neighbourhood events. Sometimes participation in these activities leads to an interest in faith and the faith community, but the social project operates independently from the ICF. Its primary goal is aiding people in need, with no strings attached and without an intention to Christianize. In 2014 the initiators of House of Hope were awarded the municipal Erasmus decoration for their continued and outstanding service to "living together" in Rotterdam.

For the Christian Reformed churches, which had little experience with missional church planting, the ICF constituted a somewhat unusual presence in their midst. With its unusually high membership of non-Western migrants and its divergent congregational structure, its exceptional reach in society and its unorthodox methods, the new faith community initially invited critical questions. But the developments in the ICF ensured that missional issues were discussed by the Christian Reformed Church's synod. In 2004 the synod made two decisions that were of great importance for the development of the ICF. First, the synod introduced in its church order the so-called mission congregation. Faith communities that resulted from evangelism and that (partially) consisted of new believers could be given the status of mission congregation. This meant that this congregation had ample space, within the framework of the church order, to operate closely to its missional context and to respond without hindrance to its challenges. Second, in this type of congregation the denomination could appoint an evangelist who was given special exemption to administer the sacraments as needed in the missional work and in the faith community. It was deemed undesirable for the missionary work that, in case of baptism, an—to the new believer—unknown ordained Christian Reformed minister should come to administer the sacrament. Both synodical decisions have become a reality in the ICF. As of May 2005 the ICF has the status of being a mission congregation, and in January 2006 Theo Visser officially became its evangelist.

7.7.3 Identity and culture

According to its mission statement the International Christian Fellowship wants to be "a fellowship, shaped by people from all over the world, which gathers around God in worship."[8] Reference is made to Isaiah 56:7 and Mark 11:17, where we read about a house of prayer for all peoples. That is what the ICF intends to be. Prayer and worship are mentioned as a first priority. "Everything that we are and want to reach, starts with His dreams and His will. We may pray together and based on that we can work together in His kingdom."[9]

The ICF affirms that interaction with multicultural society is especially relevant for Christian mission and ministry. It is seen as a biblical calling. Christian faith is not limited to one specific culture, but it enters into many cultures and takes contextual shape. A multicultural church enables people to create mutual exchange between adherents of different cultures. The ICF welcomes this exchange positively as it enriches communal life and faith. It is exactly this multicultural identity that made the ICF effective in evangelism. Of the new believers who were baptized, 75 percent came from a wide diversity of ethnic groups. A monocultural church may not have reached these people.

These convictions and experiences led to a particular blend and mix of people. If you were to visit the ICF on Sunday afternoon, you would find up to 40 different nationalities present. That is fascinating in itself, yet it also creates challenges. Differences in style of clothing, colour of skin, language, and ways of expressing oneself may easily be noticed, but less visible are other differences—for instance, the way people experience the style of worship, what is expected of the pastor, how people think about other ethnic groups, and so forth. And, of course, there are theological differences. This is obvious when we look at the denominational backgrounds of those who are involved in the ICF. Some are born into a Christian Reformed family, but the majority comes from other denominations, such as Roman Catholic, Anglican, Baptist, Methodist, and Pentecostal. Next to that, Muslim-background believers comprise about 10 percent of the membership.

In the context of this rich diversity in ethnicity and theology, the ICF aims for unity. This unity is found in teaching and accepting a number of core convictions, like trust that God is our shelter, being a child of God, guidance of the believer through the Spirit, and authority of the Bible. Reformed identity markers such as sin and grace, election and covenant, and conversion and sanctification play a role in the life of the community. But other issues are discussed as well, such as gifts of the Spirit, prayer for healing, and the priesthood of all believers. These issues are to a much lesser extent part of the Reformed tradition. When sensitive issues are raised, such as baptism, the stance of the

8. "Visie," par. 1.
9. Ibid., par. 4.1.

Reformed tradition is made clear, but always respectful of others who may hold different views.

The ICF has convictions, but intends to tread carefully. Deep is the conviction that the New Testament speaks with authority on multicultural aspects of being a faith community. The congregations in Jerusalem, Antioch, Ephesus, Corinth, and Rome all had a membership that consisted of people from diverse social and religious backgrounds. Yet, they assembled around the good news of Christ. In those communities tensions arose. When that happened they opted for tolerance, not separation. Paul taught believers they have to accept each other in love, as Christ accepts us. Having convictions, being respectful, and not irritating your sister or brother are essential ingredients for communal life. The ICF underscores these New Testament values, based on the conviction that only through these values can unity in diversity be realized. Such a reconciled community, celebrating diversity as well as unity, is an exemplary witness in a world that is deeply divided by ethnicity and religion.

Members of the ICF realize that there can be tangible tension between cultures, and that the predominant Dutch culture should take care not to make its own values the yardstick for true faith and life. The ICF certainly has characteristics of Dutch ecclesial culture, as is clearly visible in its emphasis on supervision and orderliness. The Dutch have some values which may not be easily accepted elsewhere: equality of all people, strong debate, and a sense of shared responsibility when it comes to executing tasks. The ICF upholds these values, but other cultures have uplifted new values such as respect for elders and pastors, hierarchical leadership, upholding the honour of others, staying in relationship, faith in the power of prayer, tithing, the use of fasting, and making use of mediators. The ICF values these influences and understands their importance for mission and evangelism in a multicultural context. Accepting that being a multicultural church is not only about teaching but also about continuously learning together implies that the culture of the faith community is somewhat fluid.

The ICF intentionally became an international church, as that was an effective way for evangelism. It is not a Dutch church that provides hospitality for migrants, but it is a faith community for and of all peoples. The word *of* is essential. As long as non-Western visitors do not experience ownership, they will continue to feel and act as guests. Involvement flows from the experience that the church, the programmes, and activities are really theirs.

In 2008 the step was taken to transfer leadership from Visser to a multicultural team consisting of three people from Ghana, Pakistan, and the Netherlands. This was intended as a next step in realizing shared (multicultural) ownership. The team acted as an executive committee of the church council and was highly visible in church activities. In the church council, as such, the balance of Dutch and non-Dutch members was carefully guarded. This resulted in a different style of conducting the council meetings. More time was taken for prayer, and decision making was to reflect other cultural values as well. The shaping of a multicultural leadership team, however, was not the golden key for ownership, as will be shown below.

7.7.4 Theological inspiration

Migrant churches in the Netherlands have a long history. French-speaking Wallonian congregations and Scottish churches were shaped centuries ago, while Moluccan churches came into existence in the 1950s. But international churches—intentionally multiethnic—are a relatively new phenomenon in the Netherlands. Only slowly is missiological and practical theological reflection on their praxis emerging. Not surprisingly, much more work has been done in this area by churches in, for instance, Australia and the United States, as these countries have had a long tradition of immigration. The Presbyterian Church of the United States of America (PCUSA) and the Presbyterian Church of America (PCA) have developed viable multicultural ministries.[10]

The vision of the International Christian Fellowship in Rotterdam was strongly influenced by the Presbyterian Church of America, more specifically, by Redeemer Presbyterian Church in New York, pastored by the rev. Dr. Tim Keller. Its influence is mainly visible in its focus on evangelism and the shaping of new missional communities. The leadership of the ICF attended several conferences that were organized by Redeemer Church and were coached by them in the initial phase of their ministry. The *Redeemer Church Planting Manual* turned out to be a useful tool for contextual evangelism and provided ample flexibility to adapt methods and instruments for local use.

The main source of inspiration for the ICF is the Bible. Especially passages like Revelation 5, about the 24 elders from all nations who glorify God, were important for the development and orientation of the evangelistic ministry.

10. See Presbyterian Mission Agency, "Who We Are: The Mission of Multicultural Congregational Support," http://www.presbyterianmission.org/ministries/multicultural/who-we-are; and Mission to North America, "Multicultural Commitment," http://pcamna.org/church-planting/church-planting-resources/multicultural/.

The ICF underscores that the future depicted in the Bible is multicultural. In God's future, segregation and ethnic divides are no more. If, according to the ICF, this multicultural future plays such an important part in what the Bible says about times to come, this should have implications for mission and evangelism in present times. Faith communities should embrace cultural and ethnic diversity.

In order to better cope with friction and the challenge of cultural diversity, the leadership of the ICF makes use of relevant anthropological and missiological literature by Geert Hofstede (cultural dimensions), David J. Hesselgrave (contextualization), and others. In recent policy meetings the ICF leadership made use of Richard D. Lewis's model for cross-cultural communication that classifies cultural norms into "linear-active," "multi-active," and "re-active." This model is used to analyze which norms are dominant and which are not sufficiently observed and acknowledged.

7.7.5 Structure

The International Christian Fellowship is a complex congregation due to its multicultural character. The community is organized around three levels and five goals. At the micro-level it organizes home groups. Around 90 percent of the membership takes parts in these meetings in private homes. The leader of the home group is not only responsible for fostering spiritual life, but is also the initial contact for pastoral and diaconal needs. The purpose of the home groups is to share daily life. An average group has about 10 to 12 participants. People who do not profess the Christian faith are encouraged to take part in the meetings. The groups are intentionally multicultural. Some use Dutch in their meetings, others English.

At a meso-level, community is shaped by meetings of the linguistic-ethnic groups. These groups are bigger than the home groups. People speak their own language. In years past there were ethnic meetings in Chinese, Turkish, Kurdish, English, and French. Seminars and recreational activities are also offered at meso-level. At the macro-level, members meet in the Sunday worship services. This is where the unity and diversity of the faith community are celebrated.

The activities and tasks of the community are based on Matthew 22:36-40 and 28:18-20. The calling of the congregation is, first, to love God and to love one's neighbour; and, second, to invite all peoples to discipleship and teach them about God's ways. Based on this twofold calling the ICF states five goals of the communities' activities, namely worship, service, evangelism, fellowship, and discipleship.[11] To these goals, or much rather values, a sixth goal was later added: financial sustainability.[12]

The first goal, worship, is all about giving thanks to God for the good news in Christ. The related activity is the organization of the Sunday services. Its intentions are to stipulate that God is honoured through our lives and to foster an attitude of prayer. Serving others is a core value, as many in the neighbourhood have below-average income. This results in a need for solid diaconal programmes. The deacons look after the needy and keep in touch through the House of Hope.

Evangelism focusses on growth in being an attractive faith community. When people sign the guestbook on Sunday, they will be visited later that week. Other activities include special Christmas services, offering Alpha courses, and reaching out to ethnic groups. The ICF envisions shaping other missional multicultural faith communities. This is realized by assisting other congregations to shape new faith communities and through participating in the network of International Church Plants (ICP).

In its core value of fellowship, growth in love to one another is at stake. This value relates to organizing home groups and ethnic group meetings. Organizing counselling is part of this as well, which is done by the elders and a special team. The last goal is discipleship that focusses on growth in faith and dedication. Related activities involve accompanying new believers so that they will come to mature faith. This is done through organizing seminars, teaching modules for the home groups, and personal coaching.

Financial sustainability, finally, is an important issue for the ICF. With its specific membership the church needs to be active in raising external funding. In 2003 around 75 percent of the budget was supplied by external sources. From 59 percent in 2008 this percentage dropped to 43 percent in 2013, and 30 percent in 2014. In 2014 the accounts were closed with a surplus. This created the hope that the congregation can appoint a children's worker or an evangelist in response to the growing demands in the ministry. The ICF receives donations from partnering Christian Reformed congregations, private donors, and some companies.

---

11. "Visie," par. 2.
12. Ibid., par. 4.6.

7.7.6 Leadership

For the success of the missional project, it was of vital importance to have qualified staff: someone with a gift for mission and evangelism who could devote time to the International Christian Fellowship on a daily basis and could provide guidance for the volunteers. This person was Theo Visser, a theologian who got his degree from Utrecht University. Through earlier appointments he was experienced in cross-cultural ministry, especially with asylum seekers. When he came to Rotterdam this gave added value to the work. He built relationships in the neighbourhood and appointed co-workers who were willing to move into the neighbourhood.

The substantial growth in the years 2001–2008 slowly pushed Visser into the role of an "ordinary" pastor. Administrative tasks grew exponentially, which gave him less time for evangelism and leading the worship services. The culture of pioneering—informal decision making, little bureaucracy, a central role for the leader—was no longer productive in the phase of rapid growth. Therefore, another leader, Bram Dingemanse, was appointed part-time.[13] With his background in management of educational institutions he was well versed in governmental and administrative affairs. His task was to create a more effective organizational structure for the faith community and its activities, while Visser could concentrate on evangelism, leading the faith community, and initiating new projects.

During the years Visser served as the evangelist of the ICF, he was not the only one with an evangelistic ministry. Two elders had a specific task in evangelism as well. One of them is a Kurd who ministers fulltime to migrants of Kurdish ethnicity. He is not on the ICF payroll, but is financially supported by an independent foundation. The ICF reimburses him for the expenses related to his ministry. He is specifically involved in activities around two homestays in Rotterdam where Kurdish asylum seekers can stay from Thursday to Monday. The ICF also had a Chinese evangelist, Anton Qin, who ministered to Chinese migrants. This elder observed, however, that many Chinese hardly spoke Dutch or English, so after some time—in spite of the ICF's multicultural ideal—he started an independent Chinese-speaking church plant.

13. In 2011 Dingemanse was appointed in the leadership team of "Thuis in West" ("At home in West"), a new social project of the Christian Reformed Churches in Rotterdam-Middelland. See http://www.thuisinwest.nl. It is formally independent from the International Christian Fellowship, yet the ICF is considered as the church to which new believers can be referred. Eventually the Christian Reformed churches intend to appoint a missionary pastor for Thuis in West and Rotterdam-Centre. A new faith community can be realized by asking the ICF members, who live in that part of town, to be a part of a new church plant.

When in 2008 Visser wanted to rise to a new challenge, he stepped down as the ICF evangelist. He became the leader of the International Church Plants Network and initiated "Leef" ("Live"), a number of new interlinked and multicultural faith communities in Rotterdam South.[14] Therefore, in 2008 the decision was made to appoint a multicultural leadership team. This team consisted of three elders from Ghana, Pakistan, and the Netherlands. From 2008 until 2012 they took responsibility for the faith community. This was a demanding period for the ICF. The transition from pioneering to consolidation, from one leader to a multicultural leadership team, was not easily made. Great effort was needed to maintain the focus on the mission of the church.

The appointment of Rev. Coen Legemaate in 2013, as Visser's successor, marked the beginning of a new period that brought stability, a renewed sense of direction, and development of the missional ministry. The relationship with the Chinese community was restored, but it remained an independent church plant. The multicultural leadership team was dissolved, following external ecclesial advice, and special emphasis was given to pastoral visits at home.

7.7.7 Lessons learned

Looking back, Legemaate calls the years 2008–2013 a time of growing pains. The rapid growth in the preceding years and needed transitions led to considerable tension and instability. The adaptations, however, were needed. The flexible structures of the pioneering phase were not compatible with the new phase of consolidation. The faith community needed a different type of leadership that could strike a good balance between the missional drive, on the one hand, and the need for a shepherd of the flock, on the other. By 2008 the increased size of the community demanded a certain degree of professionalism in public worship services and in diaconal programmes. An important question for the leadership became how standards for serving the community could be raised without losing the commitment of volunteering church members.

The International Christian Fellowship learned that it is by definition a congregation of people who are on the move. In that sense, the membership is fluid and the varying composition of the community demands diverse structures and styles of leadership. In 2001 the ICF was a pioneering project. Now, it has reached maturity and advises other multicultural faith communities.

Next to that, it is observed that the multicultural leadership team ran into some serious issues. It turned out that this leadership model required double

---

14. See Leef, "Missie & Visie," http://leef.cc/over-leef/missie-visie/.

integration for migrants. Not only did they have to redefine their own identity as foreigners in a strange country while adapting to Dutch culture, but they also had to adapt to an African or Asian style of leadership, which potentially presented an equally big cultural difference. For some, this double process of adaptation proved too much and utterly confusing.

An important finding was that the home groups were the locus of trust and commitment during the period of instability. In the home groups people found encouragement and there they could work and pray together. "Now," states Legemaate, "it is time to restore the focus on evangelism." That doesn't imply that evangelism had altogether withered. Members were active in mission and evangelism in the city, and even in other countries. Visser, who still is a member of the ICF, was "sent" to continue his pioneering work for evangelism. But the challenge is now to realign the ministry for mission and evangelism in a period that requires professional mechanisms to continue the life and work of the faith community. A new metaphor is needed, one that helps the missional congregation to move from the "field hospital" to a place that recognizes the impact of injustice on the life of migrants, offers opportunity for all to be part of God's mission, and creates a shelter for all sojourners.

7.8 Evangelism by Ethiopian Christians in Sweden

Dawit Olika Terfassa

7.8.1 General description and history

The shifting center of gravity of Christianity to the global South and East challenges us to explore missiological expressions that are rooted in these contexts, cultures, and spiritualities.[1]

The wish and vision of non-Western migrant Christian communities and churches from the global South and East to be agents for the re-evangelization of the West have drawn attention during the last few decades.[2] This section, on reverse evangelism, will describe common trends, understandings, and experiences of evangelism among the migrant congregations, especially the Ethiopian Christian diaspora communities in Scandinavia. By expressing their strong commitment and their positive view of evangelism, they hope to contribute to the search for new ways of evangelism and promote mutual learning in order to develop effective evangelism that is relevant to the new landscape that migration has created in Europe.[3]

According to common understanding, until recently the West has been the main source of all knowledge on missionary and evangelism activities. Growing evidence of several evangelism activities launched by migrant Christians and congregations in Europe has been observed, however, the result of the shift of the centre of the gravity of Christianity and migration.[4] Migration is

1. World Council of Churches, *Resource Book—WCC 10th Assembly, Busan, 2013* (Geneva: WCC Publications, 2013), 74.
2. Paul Freston distinguishes between the reverse mission via diaspora churches and nondiasporic reverse mission, favouring the later as the most efficient form of reverse mission. See Paul Freston, "Reverse Mission: A Discourse in Search of Reality?," *Pentecostal Studies: An Interdisciplinary Journal for Research on the Pentecostal and Charismatic Movements* 9, no. 2 (2010): 153–74.
3. WCC, *Resource Book*, 74.
4. Babatunde Aderemi Adedibu, "Reverse Mission or Migrant Sanctuaries? Migration, Symbolic Mapping, and Missionary Challenges of Britain's Black Majority Churches," *Pneuma* 35, no. 3 (2013): 405–406; Kenneth R. Ross, "Non-Western Christians in Scotland: Mission in Reverse," *Theology in Scotland* 12, no. 2 (2005): 71–72, http://www.ctbi.org.uk/pdf_view.php?id=210; Freston, "Reverse Mission," 154–57.

one of the most influential factors that have changed the demographic, social, cultural, religious, economic, and political landscapes of our contexts.[5] A large number of people are daily on the move due to war and conflict, persecutions, economic and political problems, and natural disaster.[6] According to the United Nations, 250 million people are migrants, which is about 3 percent of the population of the world.[7] There are forced immigrants as well as voluntary immigrants. They migrate to the West both from the global South and East and it differs from country to country. Of the total number of global migrants, an estimated 106 million (49%) are Christians, 60 million (27%) Muslims, Hindus (5%), Buddhists (3%), Jews (2%), and other faiths (4%). The major destinations for Christian emigrants are Europe (38%), North America (34%), and Asia Pacific (11%).[8] As a result, the number of migrant churches and fellowships in Europe is increasing rapidly. For example, by the year 2010 there were already over 90 migrant churches just in Oslo[9] and over 1,000 congregations with an African leadership and an almost exclusive African membership in Germany.[10] In Sweden the number of migrant churches in a number of cities has grown from only 17 in the year 2000 to 67 in 2010.[11] Earlier studies have also shown that there are more than three million Christians of African origin living in Europe.[12]

The presence of a large migrant/diaspora community in Europe, with its multicultural elements, introduces diversified new ways of lifestyles, models of worship, theological insights, fresh trends, and methods of evangelism.[13] These can contribute to and shape the search for new ways of evangelism in Europe.

---

5. Adele Halliday, "Migration and Multicultural Ministries as Mission," *International Review of Mission* 101, no. 2 (November 2012): 413.

6. International Association for the Study of Forced Migration, "Mission of the IASFM," http://www.efms.uni-bamberg.de/iasfm/mission.htm; Jehu J. Hanciles, *Beyond Christendom: Globalization, African Migration, and the Transformation of the West* (Maryknoll, NY: Orbis, 2008), 176ff., 181ff.

7. Halliday, "Migration," 406–407.

8. Mélisande Lorke and Dietrich Werner, eds., *Ecumenical Visions for the 21st Century: A Reader for Theological Education* (Geneva: WCC Publications, 2013), 272–77.

9. Roar G. Fotland, "Migrasjon og den misjonale kirke: Kan dagens kirke hente inspirasjon fra amerikansk metodisme på 1800 tallet?," *Norsk Tidsskrift for Misjonsvitenskap* 68, no. 1 (2014): 40.

10. Werner Kahl, "Migrants as Instruments of Evangelization: In Early Christianity and in Contemporary Christianity," in Chandler H. Im and Amos Yong, eds., *Global Diasporas and Missions* (Oxford: Regnum Books International, 2014), 83–84.

11. Öyvind Tholvsen, *Frikyrkan flyttar: En studie av frikyrkornas utveckling i Sverige 2000–2010* (Örebro, 2011), 2–28. This is, according to the study made, mainly in the large cities of Sweden. There are many smaller fellowships/churches all over Sweden that are not covered by this study.

12. Ross, "Non-Western Christians," 77.

13. "They had brought along not only their particular languages and cultures, but also their distinct confessions, beliefs, and forms of worship" (see Kahl, "Migrants," 83).

As Knud Jørgensen says: "[W]e in the West and the North shall need all the help we can get from the global South in interpreting the implications of being the church in a multi-religious minority situation."[14]

Migrants can contribute to the understanding and practice of evangelism in Europe in three ways. First, migrants are a mission field in themselves: think of the presence and openness of thousands of migrants to hear the gospel. Second, migrants can be fresh partners and co-partners; their fresh and positive view of evangelism is a resource to the local churches. And third, migrants are missionaries to Europe.[15] Migrants bring a remarkable new dimension to the understanding and practice of evangelism in Europe. As Gerrit Noort points out, the presence of migrant churches in the West demands the rethinking of missiological understanding and practice in our changed society in order to identify missiological challenges and mission frontiers.[16] This case study therefore attempts to give emphasis to and describe the practical trends and practices of evangelism that exist among the migrant congregations, with special reference to the Ethiopian diaspora community in Scandinavia.

7.8.2 Context: Evangelism among the migrant Christians in Sweden/ Scandinavia
Recent developments

It was Saturday afternoon and I had just arrived in an area called Skärholmen in Stockholm to preach at a worship service of the Ethiopian diaspora community. Arriving about one hour early, I was sitting at a nearby public square where I suddenly heard the voice of an Ethiopian woman who was preaching through a microphone. She invited people saying, "The end of time and the world is getting closer! Therefore all of you who are sinners and would like to be saved from eternal judgment and join eternal life instead, believe in Jesus Christ as your personal saviour today. . . . He loves you and wants you to be saved and that you come close to him. . . . Take your chance which is now and here; you never know what happens next . . .". After preaching like this

14. Knud Jørgensen, "Mission in the Postmodern Society," in Kjell Olav Sannes et al., eds., *Med Kristus til Jordens ender: festskrift til Tormud Engelsviken* (Trondheim: Tapir Akademisk Forlag, 2008), 122; Hanciles, *Beyond Christendom*, 119ff.
15. See Dawit Olika Terfassa, "The Impact of Migrants on Evangelism in Europe," *International Review of Mission* 103, no. 2 (November 2014): 265–74.
16. Gerrit Noort, "Emerging Migrant Churches in the Netherlands: Missiological Challenges and Mission Frontiers," *International Review of Mission* 100, no. 1 (April 2011): 4, 11; Halliday, "Migration," 410.

for about ten minutes she started to distribute tracts and printed information about the Ethiopian diaspora community services to those in the square including me without knowing that I was a preacher whom she was about to listen to in just a few minutes.

Reading such stories of street evangelism[17] in Europe today not only surprises us and makes us wonder if such a Christendom approach to evangelism is appropriate and effective in a postmodern and post-Christendom Europe (for a discussion of these terms, see chs. 3.2.1 and 3.4.1, above), but also points to something that is generally true for most migrant Christians and churches. Most of them have a strong commitment to, as well as a fresh and long experience of, witnessing about the gospel to people with diverse backgrounds. As observed by Jehu Hanciles, their capacity "to maintain effective Christian witness in the face of religious plurality enhances their missionary capacity."[18] They know well how to reach their own people and other non-Christian immigrants, as long as they are not limited by cultural and language barriers.[19] In addition, most migrant Christians and pastors have the conviction that God has called them to be missionaries/agents of re-evangelism in the West.[20]

Many non-Western migrants do not confine their witness to their own circles. They are convinced of their call to preach the full gospel to secular Europeans as well. . . . Just as European missionaries once believed in their divine task of bringing the gospel to Africa, African church leaders in Europe are today

---

17. "[A] number of African migrant pastors tried to reach out to the indigenous population, often employing techniques they used in West-Africa, especially street evangelism. Generally, these attempts did not result in winning numbers of converts, be it from mainline churches to charismatic ministries, or from among the non-Christian population" (see Kahl, "Migrants," 83–84).
18. Hanciles, *Beyond Christendom*, 299; Beate Fagerli et al., eds., *A Learning Missional Church: Reflections from Young Missiologists* (Oxford: Regnum Books International, 2012), 4.
19. "[I]mmigrant churches model religious commitment, apply the message of the gospel directly to daily exigencies, and comprise communities that interact on a daily basis with other marginalized segments of the society" (see Hanciles, *Beyond Christendom*, 278); Jan A. B. Jongeneel, "The Mission of Migrant Churches in Europe," *Missiology: An International Review* 31, no. 1 (2003): 31–32, http://mis.sagepub.com/content/31/1/29.
20. "Mission has been understood as a movement taking place from the center to periphery. . . . Now people at the margins are claiming their key role as agents of mission and affirming mission as a transformation" (see WCC, *Resource Book*, 52); Jehu J. Hanciles, "Migration, Diaspora Communities, and the New Missionary Encounter with Western Society," *Lausanne World Pulse Archives*, 2008, http://www.lausanneworldpulse.com/themedarticles-php/975/07-2008; Kahl, "Migrants," 83–84.

convinced of their mission to bring the gospel back to those who originally provided them with it.[21]

As far as the Ethiopian diaspora is concerned, there is no well-organized structure, mission organization, or network as a migrant Christian community for the evangelism of Europe. Many in the Ethiopian Christian diaspora, however, are members and active supporters of the International Mission Society (IMS)[22] established by their mother church, the Ethiopian Evangelical Church Mekane Yesus (EECMY). In addition to the establishment of the IMS, the EECMY has recently established its own department called "Diaspora Ministry,"[23] which works closely with the IMS to mobilize and equip the diaspora community for effective evangelism in the West. One can also see a growing concern and some initial steps toward the practical implementation of the reverse mission's vision among the Ethiopian Christian diaspora. The Oromo[24] Theologians Forum held in Oslo on 6–8 March 2015 was attended by over 25 Oromo theologians and was devoted to a practical and theological reflection on the issue of contextualization and integration in order to be able to share the gospel in Europe effectively.[25] The annual conference of the Nordic Ethiopian

21. Jongeneel, "Mission of Migrant Churches," 31–32; Gerrie Ter Haar, "African Christians in Europe: A Mission in Reverse," in Katharina Kunter and Jens Holger Schjørring, eds., *Changing Relations between Churches in Europe and Africa: The Internationalization of Christianity and Politics in the 20th Century* (Wiesbaden: Harrassowitz Verlag, 2008), 240–55.

22. This society was established in 2009, and has so far sent several missionaries to central Africa and some Arab countries. It is a long-term plan of this society to send missionaries to Europe. Currently, they are working on mobilizing and organizing the diaspora community that is already scattered all over Europe. See http://www.eecmy.org/?home=ims for more information.

23. The vision of this department is to facilitate and mobilize the diaspora Christian community. Summarized by the words of the director of the EECMY's International Mission Society: "Diaspora is one of our mission forces who are already in the mission field as God sent missionaries . . . for the International Mission Society, mobilizing Diaspora is more than connecting them with their mother church and mother land. . . . Mobilizing Diaspora is unlocking their God given 'missional potential' and call for the sake of kingdom as well as for the blessings of host and sending countries" (Pastor Wondimu Mathewos, flyer for the celebration of the national mission day, 17 February 2015). Its Ethiopian Christian Diaspora conference (25–30 July 2012, Addis Ababa, Bishoftu) was attended by over 150 participants, including members and leaders of the Ethiopian diaspora churches from the United States and Europe. It was devoted to equip the diaspora Christian community for effective evangelism and mission in their respective countries.

24. See "Oromo People," http://en.wikipedia.org/wiki/Oromo_people, and "Oromo Language."

25. Oromo Theologians Forum was established and organized by the evangelical Oromo church in Oslo, which has a membership of about 250 people. The attendants of the forum were members and leaders in the Oromo congregations in Norway, Sweden, and Germany. See the following links to get more information about some of these migrant congregations: http://oromochurchtrondheim.org/index.html and http://www.oromochurchoslo.org/.

Evangelical Church Fellowship (NEFCF),[26] which took place in Sweden on 2–5 July 2015, had a panel discussion which was devoted mainly to the identification of factors that had hindered the reverse mission so far. In addition, they discussed the question of how this community can effectively reach the local people with the good news. Issues like equipping and nurturing the youth and children for future evangelism work in the West were also given much attention, because the second and third generations do not share the same challenges or limitations as the first generation when it comes to integration and language. A similar annual conference, with a predominantly Lutheran church background, "The North European Ethiopian Evangelical Church Mekane Yesus' Christians Fellowship," took place on 21–26 July 2015 in Kumla (Sweden) and was attended by more than 150 members and ministers, who also had a concern about how to carry out evangelism in Europe in a better way.[27]

Despite the absence of a well-organized network and organization, evangelistic activity is and has been carried out through networks and contacts that the migrants themselves have established in various contexts and everyday contacts. I will present some of these ways or models without claiming to present the full story.

One-to-one evangelism: Storytelling in relationships

Most migrant Christians are aware that sharing the gospel is inherent to being a Christian. It is part of their DNA and responsibility. They come from, and are in, churches where evangelism and mission are not just treated as an activity and programme assigned to a specific group, but are seen as central to the identity of a Christian (cf. ch. 1.4.2, above). Most of the migrant Christians consider themselves evangelists or disciples, called to participate in God's mission through verbal and life witness. Such a missional self-understanding plays a key role in motivating and encouraging members of the migrant churches to actively engage in evangelism. As a result, they use all possible opportunities

---

26. The conference takes place every year in different Scandinavian countries. In 2015 it took place in Sweden, and the celebration of the 30th-year anniversary of its establishment was given central place in the conference. The conference was attended by over 350 people of all ages, and included ministers and members of the various Evangelical diaspora churches in Scandinavia. The Nordic Ethiopian Evangelical Church Fellowship (NEFCF) "30th conference, special print," *Amharic magazine* (2015). See also http://www.ybcnorway.com; http://www.j-e-c.org; http://www.eecfin.org; and http://www.ebenzer-church.com, to get more information about some of these Evangelicals.
27. Interview with Mr Mengesha Tadesse (the chairperson of the North European Ethiopian Evangelical Church Mekane Yesus' Christians Fellowship), Mrs Asegedech Tikle (member of the outreach committee), and Mr Ambaye Aklilu (chairperson of the Stockholm Mekane Yesus Congregation, Kumla, Sweden), conducted on 25 July 2015.

to share their faith and witness about Christ and the importance of a personal belief in him as saviour. A Scandinavian missiologist observes that "it is the migrants and refugees themselves rather than the missionaries who bring the faith from one place to another . . . , a majority of the migrants are profoundly Christian and explicitly evangelistic."[28] Migrant Christians share their stories of the joy of being the follower of Christ to other immigrants and local people; they meet in different places, in refugee camps, schools, work places, and with friends face to face, via Internet, blogs, TV programmes,[29] and social-media sites like Facebook.[30] This type of relational evangelism has the potential of giving room to the listeners to make their own reflection and decision without feeling confronted. In order to achieve this, it assumes the cultivation of good relationships and building up trust before going to the topic of religion (personal faith in particular), which is almost a taboo in Europe today. Therefore, relational evangelism can be very effective. A former pastor of the Oromo congregation in Oslo (an Ethiopian diaspora church), who currently serves as a priest in the Norwegian Church, shares his experience:

> I meet people in different contexts. As a person working in the church of Norway as a pastor, I meet people in different arenas. Even though most of them claim their religion as Christianity, most of them are nominal in practice. I use the opportunities I get, for instance, baptism conversations, funerals, confirmation classes, Sunday services, and so on, to tell about the uniqueness of Christ. In addition, I live in Oslo in the area called "Groruddalen," where nearly half of the population is from other countries. . . . These meeting points give me an opportunity to discuss different issues, not least about our faith. I have also prepared a flyer in both Norwegian and English, which I give to people.[31]

---

28. Tormod Engelsviken, Erling Lundeby, and Dagfinn Solheim, *The Church Going Glocal: Mission and Globalisation* (Oxford: Regnum Books International, 2011), 11; see also Hanciles, *Beyond Christendom*, 6, 278.

29. The Amharic television Ministry for Ethiopia, called "The day of salvation, Yedemdanken," is an example of TV ministries. See http://www.yemedanken.fi.

30. One can see a similar understanding and practice in their home church situation. See Temesgen Shibru Galla, "The Mission Thinking of the Ethiopian Evangelical Mekane Yesus (EECMY)" (Master's thesis, MF Norwegian School of Theology, 2011), 34ff.

31. Interview with Rev. Mengesha Desalegn, the former pastor of the Oromo Congregation in Oslo and currently religious educator and project-coordinator in the Church of Norway, conducted on 16 June 2015.

Knud Jørgensen agrees with Jehu Hanciles that "every Christian migrant is a potential missionary."[32] Based on biblical and historical evidence, the Scottish missiologist Andrew Walls points to the significance of the migrant churches in forwarding the gospel, including among the local people.[33] For a migrant Christian, religion and faith in God are among the top issues of life and this makes it more natural and exciting to tell about one's faith. In addition to this positive understanding of evangelism,[34] the strong social and communal aspects of migrant societies and their lifestyles have contributed to making them courageous and interested in making contact with other people. Through one-to-one (relational) evangelism, many have heard and are hearing about Christ and convert to Christianity.

Inclusive communities, worship, networks, and diaconal ministry

Migrant Christians intend to make their church a place where everyone feels welcome, despite their diverse backgrounds, colour, and social status. Student fellowships, international coffee hours, and celebrations of some important days like "AIDS Day," "Women's Day," and "United Nations Day" have functioned as contexts of inclusive communities. Such gatherings are neutral and interesting because they make most people feel equally welcomed and involved. The social contacts they provide, as well as the soup and bread or cultural food shared in this context, are often appreciated. Many of the participants get help with practical issues like learning the language of the host country, learning how to fill out different forms, and making contact with the local authorities and offices. The participants can also make use of counselling services on different issues and engage in different family activities, mostly for mothers. Even if the migrant churches are often lacking the material and financial resources to provide diaconal service in its broader sense, they have always attempted to respond to the various needs as a demonstration of God's love following the example of Jesus.[35]

---

32. Engelsviken, Lundeby, and Solheim, *Church Going Glocal*, 11; Hanciles, "Migration."
33. "Studies on African and Afro-Caribbean churches in Europe offer insights into their significance. It is clear that these churches are among the few expanding sectors of European Christianity. It is also clear that they are beginning to have an impact on the indigenous Western population, for some of whom, being untouched by traditional culture Christianity, immigrants from Africa or Asia (and in Spain, from Latin America) provide the first contact with Christianity as a living faith." See Andrew F. Walls, "Mission and Migration: The Diaspora Factor in Christian History," in Im and Yong, eds., *Global Diasporas*, 21ff.
34. Dietrich Werner, "Evangelism in Theological Education in Europe—12 Considerations from ETC/WCC," unpublished paper for consultation of WCC/CWME in Bossey, Switzerland (2012), 8; Noort, "Emerging Migrant Churches," 12ff. See also Ross, "Non-Western Christians," 71ff.
35. World Council of Churches, "Theological Perspectives on Diakonia in 21st Century," 6 June

Providing such networks and services has often given the opportunity to non-Christians, including Muslims, to develop a sense of belonging, to make close friends and to hear about the Christian faith. Through such services and inclusive networks the dimensional aspect of evangelism has been demonstrated, although it is not the intentional plan and motive. Ross has observed the fact that "[t]he vulnerability of the migrant has often proved to be an opportunity for evangelism as, through their experience of up-rootedness, people on the move have been brought to faith."[36] Lack of understanding that both proclamation/evangelism and diaconal services are equal and complementary expressions of the gospel is a risk to look at diaconal ministry as an instrument or method of evangelism but "[t]his mission-focused method contradicts the biblical imperative of assisting people in need as a God-given mandate and an important action in itself, as clearly exemplified in the diaconal practice of Jesus."[37] In addition, making arrangements for multicultural worship programmes, providing space for the use of other languages, or organizing translation services without sticking to the exclusive use of the local language have in many cases contributed to make the newcomers comfortable enough to join the church and thereby hear the good news. Rinkeby Internationella Församling (Rinkeby International Church),[38] New Life Church,[39] Hillsong,[40] Immanuel International Church in Stockholm,[41] and the International Church of Stockholm[42] are some examples. These congregations, through their emphasis on a vision of evangelism within the multicultural contexts and their welcoming attitude to people of all backgrounds, have managed to attract other nationalities. As a result, they have become large multinational churches, although most of them started as small ethnic congregations.

2002, https://www.oikoumene.org/en/resources/documents/wcc-programmes/unity-mission-evangelism-and-spirituality/just-and-inclusive-communities/theological-perspectives-on-diakonia-in-21st-century. "To be in Christ implies being in his grace and participating in his continued and active work of love. The practice of diakonia, its ethos of inclusiveness and the mutual sharing of resources, clearly imply ethical demands, but its basis is the experience of God's grace and the gift of belonging to the communion created by God's grace." See Lutheran World Federation, *Diakonia in Context: Transformation, Reconciliation, Empowerment*, Kjell Nordstokke, ed. (Geneva: Lutheran World Federation, 2009), 29.

36. Ross, "Non-Western Christians," 80.

37. Lutheran World Federation, *Diakonia*, 84ff, n.35 supra.

38. See http://www.rinkebykyrkan.se/. Rinkeby is a neighbourhood in Stockholm where 90 percent of the residents come from different parts of the world and services are provided mainly in Swedish, Arabic, and English.

39. See http://www.newlife.nu/stockholm/.

40. See http://hillsong.com/stockholm/om-oss/.

41. See http://www.immanuel.se/international.

42. See http://www.ics-stockholm.se/International_Church_of_Stockholm.html.

Migrant's model of theological education

Theologians and theological education play a central role in equipping the members as evangelists and faithful disciples. Migrant Christians and churches are taught by leaders and pastors who have received their training mostly in theological institutions in Ethiopia[43] that integrate evangelism and mission into all fields of theological study. Evangelism and mission are lines of thought that run through the various courses. Most of the courses and curricula are shaped around the vital interrelatedness of evangelism and theological study in such a way that further knowledge of any specific topic or course leads naturally to equipping the individuals for better and more effective evangelism. Course syllabi are often connected to the vision of the organizing institutions or churches, which is to bring the good news of the gospel to all human beings.

Through a strong focus on the spiritual formation, regardless of their field, the students are equipped to be authentic evangelists and disciples who in turn are able to equip others as evangelists. Therefore, the place and attention given to evangelism and mission in theological education has an important role in producing equipped pastors and members of the church for effective evangelism. John Bowen underlines this by saying: "[I]f seminaries do not train their future pastors in evangelism, it is unlikely that the congregations they lead will ever develop a ministry of evangelism. . . . If, however, evangelism is to be an integral part of the seminary curriculum, rather than an optional appendix, a new model of theological education will have a more lasting effect."[44]

Migrant theologians have a strong belief in and a strong commitment to the practice of evangelism as the missional DNA of all Christians.[45] The majority of the migrant Christians themselves have in one way or another received some evangelistically oriented theological education through residential and distance theological courses, evening Bible-school classes, Theological Education by Extension (TEE), and nowadays through online courses via the Internet, TV programmes, or radio programmes run by different ministries or

---

43. As far as it concerns the EECMY, there are five seminaries (four regional and one national), as well as one interdenominational theological institution, from which most of the leaders and pastors in the Ethiopian diaspora community have received or are receiving their theological education. See http://www.eecmy.org/?home=mys.

44. John P. Bowen, "Towards Scholarly Evangelists and Evangelistic Scholars: The Teaching of Evangelism in Theological Seminaries," *McMaster Journal of Theology and Ministry* 6 (2003–2005), 118–19, http://www.mcmaster.ca/mjtm/pdfs/MJTM_6.6_Bowen_Evangelism.pdf.

45. For example: according to a study Jehu Hanciles made among the pastors of African immigrant churches in the United States, 70 percent of the pastors believe in evangelism/mission as the principal area of ministry. See Hanciles, *Beyond Christendom*, 364.

churches. This has equipped most of them for active engagement in evangelistic activities.

Family evangelism: The family as the space for evangelism

A majority of Christian migrants focus strongly on the devotional life of their family and the transfer of their faith to the next generation. Their tradition of regular family devotional life gives favourable chances to nonbelievers in the family, visiting guests, and neighbours to hear the gospel. In addition, these family devotions provide their children and youth with the chance to grow in their faith. Most of the migrant parents believe in what the Bible says: "Train children in the right way, and when old, they will not stray" (Prov. 22:6). Therefore, many of them give much attention and priority to introducing Christian faith to their children from an early age and pray for their upbringing as committed Christians.

Children are encouraged and taught to participate regularly in the daily devotions, church services, and Sunday school. The major challenge for migrant parents is, however, the influence of the secularization to which their children are exposed in the schools and in society, as well as a lack of knowledge and skills to make the Christian faith attractive to their children in their new context.

Kahl reflects on this common challenge from the perspective of the second-generation teenagers and young adults of the migrant Christians, by pointing out the difficulty they face because they do not feel completely at home with the spirituality and culture of their parents' congregations and are not attracted by the local churches, either. They are wandering to find congregations that celebrate and communicate the gospel in new ways that are meaningful to their life and needs.[46] This demands extra focus and a well-contextualized approach that accepts and encourages the participation of the children and youth to establish open and love-based relationships and dialogue without enforcing faith on them. This is because attempts by some migrant parents and church leaders, trying to implement the same authoritative parental mentality like at home, have resulted in driving away the youth and children from the church/faith. Marco Fibbi, who has observed such a challenge, suggests that a course for the parents on how they can communicate their faith to their children, without the risk of creating dissatisfaction with faith, could provide these parents with the necessary skills and approach.[47]

---

46. Kahl, "Migrants," 86.
47. Marco Fibbi, "A Witness from Workers in a Particularly Difficult Situation of Challenge—Youth

Prayer and the leadership of the Holy Spirit: Impulses for evangelism

The commitment of most migrant Christians to proclaim the good news of the gospel is often the result of the impulse of the Holy Spirit and the biblical motives (theological/soteriological). A majority of migrant Christians strongly believe that, without being filled and led by the Holy Spirit, no effective evangelism can take place. They identify easily with the pneumatological emphasis in the WCC's *Together towards Life*, when it says: "Life in the Holy Spirit is the essence of mission, the core of why we do what we do, and how we live our lives. Spirituality gives deepest meaning to our lives and motivates our actions. It is a sacred gift from the Creator, the energy for affirming and caring for life. . . ."[48]

Jesus' words to his disciples, "but you will receive power when the Holy Spirit has come upon you; and you will be my witnesses . . . to the ends of the earth" (Acts 1:8), and the witness of the role and work of the Holy Spirit in the books of Acts, remind us of the role and place of the Holy Spirit in evangelism (cf. chs. 5.3.2–5, above, and 8.2.2–3, below). Most migrants devote much time to prayer to be filled by the Holy Spirit and seek the Spirit's guidance as they engage in evangelism. A mission strategy, missionary courses, and mission techniques that neglect the place and role of the Holy Spirit are hard labour in vain.[49] It is only God's Spirit who creates new life and brings about rebirth (John 3:5-8; 1 Thess. 1:4-6). Therefore, it is a common practice among the Ethiopian migrants, as it is among most Christian African immigrants, to pray for the unbelievers in general or for someone with whom they have thought to share the gospel, before taking any action. Prayer for an unbelieving husband, family member, neighbour, colleague, and the like is common. It is believed that it is more effective and easier to sow the seeds of the gospel in hearts and minds that have been softened by prayer and the Holy Spirit. Such a close relationship and dependence on the Holy Spirit through regular prayer make the witness effective and powerful. "Many churches have got many new members

and Social Communication: How Is the Gospel Preached and Spread, the Liturgy Celebrated, the Creed Confessed Today?," in Rolv Olsen et al., eds., *Mission and Postmodernities* (Oxford: Regnum Books International, 2011), 112.

48. World Council of Churches, *Together towards Life: Mission and Evangelism in Changing Landscapes* (Geneva: WCC Publications, 2013), 4.

49. "The model [the translatability of the gospel] can be described as a holistic and dynamic-equivalent (re-) translation of the biblical witness of Jesus Christ into the lives of modern Europeans—in the power of the Holy Spirit and through the missionary witness of Christian churches and fellowships. John Stott highlighted the Christological center, 'The only way to be delivered from Euro pessimism is to catch a fresh vision of Christ!'" See Friedemann Walldorf, "Searching for the Soul(s) of Europe: Missiological Models in the Ecumenical Debate on Mission in Postmodern Europe," in Olsen, *Mission and Postmodernities*, 62.

from other countries; many of them exchange students and scholars. First of all, it is their spiritual life that strikes me. They bring into many churches 'fresh air' and a strong focus on genuine spirituality."[50]

Home-to-home prayer fellowships and cell groups: Witnessing through presence

The social life, love, and fellowship among the migrant Christians are among the forces that attract and invite mostly non-Christian migrants, but also local people, to Christ or the church. According to Nasser Fard, most of those who are part of the Iranian Christian community in Scandinavia have been led to Jesus by friends: "Real friendship, real concern and the communication of God's love through practical deeds are pulling people to the kingdom of God. If we wish to share our faith with Muslims, the road passes through friendship."[51]

Friendships are cultivated through Bible-study groups and home-to-home prayer fellowships on weekdays in addition to Sunday worship services. This not only strengthens and increases opportunities for evangelism, but also provides a sense of belonging, inclusion, and good self-esteem among all members, including those who feel excluded in society based on their background. The fellowships are welcoming; they are about coming together, eating together, and then going through different areas of Christian life. Members of the fellowships support one another in times of happiness, sorrow, and crisis. Seeing such love and care among the migrants, their colleagues, friends, classmates, and neighbours may become more curious to know about the migrants' faith. Often, this gives them the chance to get to know Christ. In addition, the gospel is introduced in diaconal situations since such fellowships provide help to those in need. A similar model of fellowship used by local churches to reach the unreached individuals in a secularized society is the Alpha course (see ch. 6.2.3, above, for a more detailed description of the Alpha course). So far, more than 90,000 people in Sweden have attended, and many of them have found their way to a personal faith in Christian truth.[52]

---

50. Interview with Rev. Thomas Bjerkholt, pastor of Trondheim Free Church, conducted on 16 September 2012.
51. Nasser Fard, "Global Migration: Mission to Iranians in Scandinavia—Example of a Development through Immigration," in Engelsviken, Lundeby, and Solheim, eds., *Church Going Glocal*, 11, 142.
52. Interview with Dr Klas Lundström, conducted on 10 September 2012. "Mission in Europe, therefore, means to share the biblical story of the Living God, Father, Son and Holy Spirit, with Europeans in a holistic way as an invitation to life and truth. Since European media culture is filled with moving, but imaginary stories, it is decisive that the biblical story be true, as well as life-transforming" (see Walldorf, "Searching," 81, cf. 69ff.).

7.8.3 Major challenges

There are several challenges and obstacles that hinder mutual learning between the indigenous and migrant congregations and which thus hinder the development of a renewed understanding and practice of evangelism that can promote reverse mission in a practical way.

Lack of recognition and full acceptance of migrants' role as contributors

The issue of mutual acceptance and recognition has been discussed in different forums. Practically speaking, however, migrant congregations and Christians, theologians as well as theologies, are still suffering from the absence of humble and full recognition of who migrants are and what they contribute. According to some of the pastors of the Ethiopian diaspora community in Scandinavia and previous studies[53] from broader contexts, there is a common attitude and expectation within the older Western churches for the migrant Christians and congregations to adapt completely to the local culture and system, without recognizing and accepting the migrants' identity, their prophetic voices, and their role as equal contributors.[54]

Migrants are mostly seen only as objects of the compassion and care that the European churches can provide. Often, when the issue of migration is discussed, the ethical and theological responses to the hardships and difficulties the migrants face are prioritized.[55] Without disregarding the few efforts and networks that exist to give space to the migrants, one can say that there is mistrust and prejudice against migrants, their theology, and the practice of their faith. Often, this is due to their conservative views on homosexuality, their emphasis on conversion, and their focus on spiritual experiences of healing, exorcisms, and prophecies. Anne Kubai expresses this problem by saying, "[t]he relationship between the African congregations and their host churches

---

53. Ross is pointing to the widespread testimony that suggests that European congregations are not readily accessible to incoming non-Western Christians, based on Gerrie ter Haar, who observed, "In Britain the unfriendly reception accorded to black immigrants by the established churches was the immediate reason for Africans and Afro-Caribbeans to found independent churches" (see Ross, "Non-Western Christians," 83).

54. Interview with Rev. Mengesha Desalegn, conducted on 3 September 2012; interview with Rev. Daniel Lars, leader of the Ethiopian diaspora community in Denmark (Yerusalem Evangelical Church), conducted on 4 July 2015; interview with Rev. Ephrem Demelash, leader of the Ethiopian diaspora community in Stockholm (Yerusalem Evangelical Church), conducted on 4 July 2015.

55. Dietrich Werner, "Oslo: The Future of Theology in the Changing Landscapes of Universities in Europe and Beyond," *The Ecumenical Review* 64, no. 3 (2012): 394; Adèle Djomo Ngomedje, "Christian Communities in Contemporary Contexts: A Cross-cultural Church and Mission Experience," in Fagerli, *Learning Missional Church*, 59ff.

is characterized by both accommodation and tension. On the one hand, a number of native churches in Sweden have acknowledged the need for African churches in their midst; and at the same time they are faced with the dilemma of accommodating some of the African forms of worship that they see as different from their own."[56]

In addition, the biographical and narrative theologies of many migrant Christians are by and large viewed as pre-Enlightenment and old-fashioned.[57] Developing a positive openness, fostering mutual learning, and recognizing the contribution migrants can make to the understanding of faith and being church, however, are important to come to a renewed view and practice of evangelism in Europe.[58] Establishing multicultural forums, designing innovative models of theological education and bridge programmes,[59] and forming functional networks between migrant and local congregations can contribute to develop effective and contextualized models of evangelism in Europe.[60]

Based on his study of how the Methodist church in America succeeded in evangelism and mission among its migrants during the 19th century by recognizing the migrants' culture and language and adapting to it, Roar Fotland argues that Western countries can promote integration in a better way if they recognize and encourage the migrant churches to use their own culture

---

56. Anne Kubai, "Singing the Lord's Song in a Strange Land, African Churches in Sweden—Between Segregation and Integration," 2007, http://anslag.rj.se/en/fund/36814. See also Anne Kubai, "'Living by the Spirit': African Christian Communities in Sweden," in Afe Adogame, ed., *The Public Face of African New Religious Movements in Diaspora: Imagining the Religious 'Other'* (Farnham, UK: Ashgate, 2014), 163–90.

57. Noort, "Emerging Migrant Churches," 14; Werner, "Oslo," 396; Kenneth R. Ross, *Edinburgh 2010: Springboard for Mission* (Pasadena: William Carey International University Press, 2009), 59; Dietrich Werner, "Mission and Theological Education—Suggestions for Possible Priorities in CEC for the Future," Lecture for CEC Commission Churches in Dialogue, Budapest, June 2011, 4; Ogbu U. Kalu, "Multicultural Theological Education in a Non-Western Context: Africa, 1975–2000," in David V. Esterline and Ogbu U. Kalu, eds., *Shaping Beloved Community: Multicultural Theological Education* (Louisville: Westminster John Knox, 2006), 238.

58. WCC, *Resource Book*, 115. See also Jørgensen, "Mission," 117–19. "If the churches of the North are to participate in the life of the global church, their theological seminaries need a diverse curriculum of studies which include non-Western church histories and theologies, thereby reversing the assumption that Western Christianity possesses the spiritual, theological and material resources needed by the rest of the world." See Tod Johnson and Sandra S. K. Lee, "The Changing Face of Global Christianity," http://www.bostontheological.org/assets/files/02tjohnson.pdf (28).

59. Dietrich Werner lists possible options for achieving this goal; see Werner, "Theological Education with Migrant Christians," 1 December 2010, http://www.oik-oumene.org/en/resources/documents/wcc-programmes/education-and-ecu-menical-formation/ete/wcc-programme-on-ecumenical-theological-education/theological-education-with-migrant-christians-in-the-changing-landscape-of-world-christianity.

60. Noort, "Emerging Migrant Churches," 7–15.

and language and give them the possibility of being part of the leadership and deciding bodies as equal contributing partners, not just as objects of help.[61]

Lack of contextualization and integration

The strong passion that migrant Christians and congregations have for evangelism in Europe is not enough to win the trust of their fellow Europeans. As Anne Kubai points out, "[R]elating to Swedish social values is a major challenge for members of African churches/congregations,"[62] and the same goes for other migrants. Migrants need to integrate well into European society and build good relationships in order to fulfill the dream of a reverse mission. This will provide more opportunities for an effective sharing of the gospel.[63] Not only "white" Western Europeans, but also migrants need to develop a positive openness and humility, free from spiritual superiority and prejudice. They need to understand the European culture and spirituality in order to contextualize their message and approach.[64] This demands a change of attitude, realizing that the process of evangelism in Europe does not happen as fast as the migrants are used to,[65] and that evangelism in Europe requires an understanding of both modernity and postmodernity. They need to understand that an incarnational approach, with a focus on listening, is often more successful than the attractional model with a focus on speaking. Paul wrote to the Corinthians: "I have become all things to all people, that I might by all means save some. I do it all for the sake of the gospel, so that I may share in its blessings" (1 Cor. 9:23).

Uta Andrée criticizes the reverse mission for being irrelevant to the West and proposes an alternative approach when she says, "We need a translation of the gospel by the people themselves; not based on new excitement for faith, like some programs of reverse mission try to introduce mission, but based on that rational approach that is so particular for Germany and other European

---

61. Fotland, "Migrasjon," 39–61; Walldorf, "Searching," 57.

62. Kubai, "Singing"; see also Kubai, "Living," 163–90.

63. Ngomedje, "Christian Communities," 117–18.

64. Øyvind Økland, "Intercultural Communication in Mission: A Tool or a Goal? Missionary Methodology in View of Developments in Intercultural Communication," in Tormod Engelsviken et al., eds., *Mission to the World: Communicating the Gospel in the 21st Century—Essays in Honour of Knud Jørgensen* (Oxford: Regnum Books International, 2008), 163–77.

65. "Evangelism involves more than a friendly bus stop chat. It is a journey, a process, a time consuming relationship. It requires us to share our lives, share a meal, share hardships and joyful moments. People would like to hear beautiful words, but most of all they like to see our words matching our actions." See Rita Rimkiene, "Mission and Evangelism: Case Study Incarnational Mission in Gloucester," unpublished paper for a consultation on Evangelism in Theological Education and Missiological Formation arranged by the World Council of Churches on 28–31 October 2012, in Bossey, Switzerland, 2.

countries."[66] Migrant preachers and evangelists should address European people in such a way that it attracts them, without sounding offensive or simplistic, but within the listeners' frames of reference.[67] Lack of integration and contextualization is commonly observed and is a growing problem among the migrant churches. Even if in some cases a longer stay of migrants in the country decreases their resistance against integration, challenges of integration have been observed due to a growing resistance to migration on the part of the host populations. The growing attitude of racism and discrimination that is often related to increasing numbers of migrants, joblessness, and the challenging economic situation in many European countries can be the causes of this tendency toward isolation.

In addition, as Mogens Mogensen's empirical study on conversion and baptism in Denmark has pointed out: problems of ethnic identity and the need of getting their self-esteem confirmed, the need to protect their cultural heritage, and lack of deep knowledge of the culture of the hosting countries are hindering the migrant churches from exercising their full potential to integrate themselves into the host culture.[68] Kubai, who conducted one of the first studies of African migrant churches and Christian communities in Sweden and the Nordic region, points to a similar finding:

> When it comes to the role of the churches in segregation and integration, African churches provide social, spiritual and spatial spaces for both segregation and integration of African communities in Sweden. Identity communities are built around the churches where they speak their native languages and recreate their customs and traditions, rather than integrate themselves regardless of length of residence in Sweden. . . . Also there are divergent discourses on integration which means different things to different groups and

---

66. Uta Andrée, "Presentation on Mission and Evangelism in Germany," unpublished paper for a consultation on Evangelism in Theological Education and Missiological Formation arranged by the World Council of Churches on 28–31 October 2012, in Bossey, Switzerland.

67. Kahl, "Migrants," 83–84.

68. Mogens S. Mogensen, "Migration and Conversion—The Conversion of Immigrants to Christianity in a Danish Context," in Engelsviken et al., ed., *Mission*, 70, 80–83; Roar G. Fotland, "The Southern Phase of Christianity: The Contribution of the Global South to the Church in the Global North," in Engelsviken et al., ed., *Mission*, 215–29. Similar problems have been identified by other writers. "It is apt to note that Britain's BMCs are but one case of reverse mission that, in reality, more resembles migrant sanctuaries all across the Western world. The lack of understanding of the British culture, flawed church-planting strategies, and the operational methods employed by these churches have severely hampered the BMCs' missionary endeavors in Britain" (see Adedibu, "Reverse Mission," 405).

stakeholders. The analysis of these discourses led me to the conclusion that, integration is not a priority for many members of these communities.[69]

If migrant churches are to live up to the claims of being missionaries to Europe, it is necessary for them to integrate fully into the culture and the society, without losing their distinct Christian identity.[70] The Churches' Commission for Migrants in Europe (CCME), through the MIRACLE[71] project, suggests ten ways of improving the active participation and integration of migrants in the local churches and culture:[72]

1. Integration as a two-way process, based on mutual and equal efforts by migrants and the host society/church

2. A welcoming attitude

3. The introduction of intercultural church activities

4. The improvement of social interaction among church members

5. A reflection on church structures related to aspects and attitudes that influence active participation

6. Going where the others are

7. Establishing dialogue on core issues

8. Addressing conflicts in the church

9. Creating and improving relations with associations, migrant-led churches, and traditional churches for exchanging good practices

10. Data collection on church participation.

MIRACLE underlines that integration can happen through religion, since religion and belief play an important role in immigrant societies and their individual identities. This shows that religious communities could become models for an integrated and inclusive society if they live an integrated life.[73]

---

69. Kubai, "Singing"; see also Kubai, "Living," 163–90, for detailed information.
70. Adedibu, "Reverse Mission," 418–23.
71. Models of Integration through Religion, Activation Cultural Learning and Exchange.
72. Olivia Bertelli and Doris Peschke, eds., MIRACLE: *Models of Integration through Religion, Activation, Cultural Learning and Exchange. Recommendations for Active Participation of Migrants in Churches* (Brussels: Churches' Commission for Migrants in Europe, 2010), 2–50.
73. Ibid., 6ff.; Ngomedje, "Christian Communities," 129ff.

But experiences so far, as well as some studies,[74] reveal the weakness and often even the absence of any practical implication of the conviction and claims of the majority of migrant churches and Christians to be missionaries to the West.[75] Except for the few successful examples of the reverse mission through the Nigerian-founded and -led migrant churches in Ukraine (Kiev) and the United Kingdom (London), failure to carry out evangelistic activity among the local people is a common prevailing problem among the migrant churches.[76] This is often due to lack of integration, which is closely linked with a language problem.[77] Migrant congregations are primarily ethnic-based fellowships that serve as contexts of ethnical identity, designed to fulfill the needs of a particular immigrant group, and lack long-term strategic plans to reach the local people.

These and similar experiences have been the ground for some voices echoing the fact that the only effective and promising approach for evangelism in Europe is not a reverse mission via a diaspora community, but rather a nondiaspora direct mission by outsider missionaries, like those from Brazil and South Korea.[78] But whether through a reverse mission via diaspora or nondiaspora direct mission, it is impossible to imagine the realization of a re-evangelized West without realistically and humbly addressing these main challenges that hinder mutual recognition/acceptance, integration, and contextualized effective evangelism in Europe.

7.8.4 Conclusion

The changing landscapes and the multicultural society we live in today need a renewed and contextualized view and practice of evangelism. Migrant churches and Christians bring a new dimension from their rich and diverse experience of evangelism among people of diverse backgrounds. They can offer experiences and inspirations that can develop renewed and effective practices of evangelism in Europe.

To mention some examples, most migrant Christians, and specifically the Ethiopian Christian diaspora community, come from a context where evangelism is intrinsically interrelated with discipleship (on the relationship between

74. Freston, "Reverse Mission," 154–60.
75. "The initial hope of many African migrant pastors and evangelists in a divine program of 'reverse mission' did not materialize due to a widespread inability to overcome cross-cultural communication barriers. The attempt to evangelize among indigenous Germans by migrant preachers from West African of the first generation has turned out to be a 'mission impossible'" (see Kahl, "Migrants," 83–84).
76. Freston, "Reverse Mission," 153ff.
77. Hanciles, "Migration."
78. Freston, "Reverse Mission," 160ff.

evangelism and discipleship, see also ch. 4.2.6, above) and is seen as the central identity and essence of being a Christian or a church. Almost every member of the migrant churches understands and practices evangelism with passion in everyday life, mainly in a form of one-to-one storytelling. They engage in a deliberate sharing of what Christ has done for them with the purpose of winning people for Christ. They have a deep spirituality that depends on the power of prayer and internal impulse of the Holy Spirit. Their mentality and practice of social life, community of care, love, and friendship are facilitating evangelism to a large extent. Their tradition of spiritual upbringing of their children and youth as a necessary and central part of discipleship is very strong. Since most of these activities take place among their own people or other migrants, so far evangelism among the local people has not been a priority. In order to promote a more effective and joint evangelism between the local and migrant churches, mutual recognition and learning based on genuine openness are very important. This will allow the migrants to gain all they need to contextualize their message and approach, and it will permit the local churches to be inspired by migrants' positive view and practice of evangelism.[79]

> Effective evangelization of Europeans by diaspora churches would thus presuppose both a fundamental reorientation of priorities and rethinking of strategies on the part of the diaspora churches, and fundamental attitudinal change on the part of native Europeans, in which diaspora churches and preachers would be seen no longer as fanatical or merely exotic or even in need of help, but as purveyors of a message, practices and life styles relevant to the problems in Europe.[80]

Therefore, both the Europeans, who are used to being in control in church life, theology, and mission, and the migrant churches/Christians, who claim spiritual superiority, need to leave behind their cultural, racial, historical, and spiritual pride to avoid dividing lines and prejudice. This can help to promote a positive attitude, to create a culture of closeness, and to develop models and practices of evangelism that are relevant to the diverse contexts of Europe. In this way, the rediscovery and reaffirmation of the importance of evangelism can be possible.[81]

---

79. Ngomedje, "Christian Communities," 117–18.
80. Freston, "Reverse Mission," 162.
81. WCC, *Resource Book*, 74; Halliday, "Migration," 410; Engelsviken, Lundeby, and Solheim, *Church Going Glocal*, 205.

CHAPTER 8

Gerrit Noort

Theological Issues in the Case Studies

Introduction to the Issues

What observations can we make after having read the preceding case studies? Do the described practices of evangelism raise theological questions that we need to address? The case studies have no doubt shown a remarkable variety in the practice of evangelism. In itself that is not surprising, as the studies have illustrated that the range of theological perspectives on the communication of the gospel influences and shapes the method of evangelism. In the following we shall point to five issues that stand out and which deserve our attention in this chapter.

The model and method of evangelism

It is easy to observe that the evangelistic approach of the Street Pastors in the United Kingdom is quite different from the way Ethiopian Christian migrants in Sweden shape evangelism. Whereas the first hesitate even to call their ministry evangelism at all—we read that the pastors who "take faith to the streets" are "not out to evangelize" (see 7.1.1, above)—the latter are said to have a "strong commitment" to evangelism. It is not coincidental that in this last case study we find a solid reference to the impact of "old-style" street evangelism that focusses on verbal witness (see 7.8.2, above). This raises the question about appropriate and contextual models for evangelism. Does developing an appropriate model for the communication of the gospel imply a choice between evangelism as presence and evangelism as the (explicit and verbal) call to discipleship, or can they fruitfully coexist?

In the 1970s and 1980s, adherents of these models sometimes created the unjustified impression that the models are mutually exclusive. The "presence model" was widely accepted in ecumenical and conciliar missionary movements, whereas the "witness model" was often upheld by more conservative Christians. The case studies at hand show an interesting cross-fertilization. In the evangelistic model of the Street Pastors ("presence") we can observe a remarkable role of prayer. The teams on the street are supported by it and people receive a word of prayer when they request it (see 7.1.1, above). On the other hand, we can observe that the case study on Ethiopian Christian migrants doesn't hesitate to refer to "witness through presence" (see 7.8.2, above) as an integral part of their ministry. In the International Christian Fellowship in Rotterdam we can discern the same coherence of *martyria* and *diakonia* (see 7.7.3 and 4.2.4–5, above). Whereas the call to discipleship is clear, especially so in the baptism of many adults from other faith traditions, the community is also strongly involved in community service (cf. 7.7.2, above). In this respect the missionary "model" used in Sant'Egidio is exemplary, as it explicitly and unequivocally takes together service to the poor, communal prayer, and evangelism as the single calling of the Christian community (cf. 7.3.3, above).

Next to this issue—how verbal witness and presence relate to one another and how this shapes the ministry methodically—we can also observe that Orthodox churches meticulously relate evangelism to (vestiges of) Christian culture and make ample use of this in religious education. These studies acknowledge that culture bears the imprint of the gospel and has an impact on the method of evangelism. Culture is regarded as a vehicle that may lead people to a reorientation in life. In Protestant churches, however, formal religious education and Christian vestiges in culture are only rarely discussed in relation to the ecclesial ministry of evangelism. Protestants tend to highlight the communication of the gospel as the calling of the individual evangelist (not of the teacher of religion) or as the fruit of a dedicated communal Christian life. Should Protestants reconsider the relation of evangelism and (vestiges of) Christian culture as a possible method to shape the communication of the gospel? Should Orthodox churches rethink their evangelistic methods in relation to the far-reaching consequences of the dechristianization of culture and secularization?

The role of the Christian community in evangelism

Not only the case studies on Taizé and Sant'Egidio have exemplified the importance of the Christian community as a means for the communication of the gospel. The same goes *mutatis mutandis* for the case studies on MyChurch, the International Christian Fellowship, and Christian migrant communities. They all show that evangelism can hardly be authentic when it is separated from communal Christian life. The possibility of belonging to the Christian community and of participating in its life plays an important role in the process of becoming a disciple of Christ. It is therefore an important issue in evangelism.

The case study on the International Christian Fellowship makes clear that new missional communities have to relate to the structures of the established church, the denomination that is involved in evangelism. It is not self-evident that the old structures fit with the missionary realities and their demands. The fellowship in Rotterdam therefore obtained a special status, as a missionary congregation. What are the demands that evangelism puts on traditional church structures?

The role of spirituality in evangelism

The case studies refer explicitly to the role of prayer and liturgy in evangelism. This is not only true for the Orthodox case studies, but it also applies to the case study of the Street Pastors as well as the studies on Sant'Egidio and Taizé. In the study on MyChurch we find, in addition, explicit references to the spirituality of dechurched and unchurched people. As observed above, Sant'Egidio unambiguously relates prayer to its mission: No evangelism without prayer, and no spirituality without evangelism and serving the poor. The relationship of prayer and evangelism clearly emerges in these case studies, but in ecclesial practice, prayer and spirituality are not always acknowledged as an integral part of the ministry of evangelism. This relationship of evangelism and spirituality deserves our attention.

The role of conversion in evangelism

It is quite remarkable that the word *conversion* is hardly mentioned in the case studies. In the history of mission and evangelism, conversion was central to the understanding of the goals and methods of the ministry. In the case studies we can observe that there is a certain reticence to use the term. This is certainly true for the study on the Street Pastors, though its founder is said to have converted to Christianity. In the rest of the case study, however, it is evident that "conversion," as such, is not on the minds of the street teams. That is different in the studies on PIMEN and the International Christian Fellowship, which report on people finding faith in Christ. In the study on MyChurch, the primary method is "listening" (see 7.2.3, above), not the explicit call to follow Christ. The study on Sant'Egidio notes that the ministry is about revitalization of faith, but new faith (conversion) as such is not discussed. And Brother John of Taizé states that their ministry to young people is not a "hard-sell strategy," but he underlines at the same time that many have experienced reorientation in life (see 7.4.4, above). In light of the long historical sequence of missiological publications on conversion as the goal of mission and evangelism, this raises the question about our understanding of the call to discipleship.

The role of ecumenical cooperation in evangelism

Finally, we can observe that in a number of case studies the ministry of evangelism is shaped along confessional and denominational lines. Confessionally shaped evangelism has often raised the issue of proselytism, but this is not mentioned in the case studies at all. Some of the case studies, however, explicitly mention that evangelism is best practiced in ecumenical cooperation. We can observe this in the study on PIMEN, in which we read about the conviction of its founder that an interconfessional approach is most beneficial for the ministry of evangelism (see 7.5.1 and 7.5.3, above). Ecumenical cooperation in evangelism is also mentioned in the study on Street Pastors, and it surfaces, to a lesser extent, in the study on the International Christian Fellowship, as this community provides space for Christians from many denominational backgrounds. The issue of ecumenical cooperation in evangelism not only raises the issue of the relationship of Christian witness and proselytism, but also questions practices that overemphasize doctrinal convictions instead of the aspired reorientation of life.

This chapter will address the above-mentioned issues in greater detail. The ecumenical dimension of evangelism and the search for a common understanding, however, will be discussed in the final chapter of this book (ch. 10, below).

8.1 Evangelism and the Call to Conversion

Gerrit Noort and Martin Reppenhagen

8.1.1 Introduction

The case study on Street Pastors in the United Kingdom points out that its founder, Les Isaac, converted to Christianity, became a church minister and brought "faith on the streets" (see ch. 7.1.1, above). The study shows that this conversion was an important turning point, yet the resulting ministry that brings faith to the streets is said to have "no explicit evangelistic intention" (even though evangelism happens now and then). Apparently, the ministry is not purposefully directed toward inviting people to turn to God. How can that be so in a case study in a handbook on evangelism? And, for that matter, how can it be that in the other case studies on practices of evangelism unambiguous references to conversion are scarce?

This section tries to answer these questions and looks at conversion from several perspectives. We will start by making some observations about the meaning of conversion and types of conversion in missiological writings and will then take a closer look at conversion in the case studies as contained in part 3 of this book. The final part of this contribution once more addresses conversion in ecumenical affirmations on mission and evangelism and considers its implications.

8.1.2 Conversion in missiology

Conversion in three standard missiological textbooks

It is not only in the case studies but also in recent and widely used textbooks on mission and evangelism that the term *conversion* is used less than might be expected.[1] This can be exemplified by looking briefly at standard missiological textbooks by Stephen Bevans and Roger Schroeder (Roman Catholic), Timothy Tennent (Evangelical), and David J. Bosch (Reformed Protestant).

While Bevans and Schroeder's *Constants in Context* (2004) refers to the conversion of Peter and mass conversions in the European early Middle Ages,

---

1. The 14th assembly of the International Association for Mission Studies (IAMS), in August 2016, was devoted to "Conversions and Transformations: Missiological Approaches to Religious Change."

it doesn't offer a missiological treatise on the term *conversion* as such.[2] In Tennent's *Invitation to World Mission* (2010) we find that he mentions conversion only twice and critically states that our missionary practice "has been overly privatized and focused almost exclusively on conversion as the 'end' of the missionary engagement."[3] Bosch, in his missiological work *Transforming Mission* (1991), devotes many chapters to emerging mission paradigms, but among them we do not find a chapter on "mission as [the ministry of] conversion."

That doesn't mean, however, that the authors don't discuss religious change as such. If we look at Bosch's publication in more detail, we find that he does so primarily in his discussion of the missionary paradigms of the apostles, in part 1 of his book. When referring to the Lukan paradigm he writes that Luke's Gospel and Acts "are built on the expectation of response." The witness of the missionaries, he continues, "aims at repentance and forgiveness" which leads to salvation. In their ministry they therefore insist on "repentance and conversion."[4] When writing about Paul's missionary paradigm he labels this as the invitation to join the eschatological community that reflects "the values of God's coming world" and which is "the vanguard of the new creation."[5] It is not the church, though, that is the ultimate aim of mission. Mission is about the reconciliation of the world with God through Christ's redemptive work (the salvation of humankind), so that every knee shall bow. Paul's understanding of mission is not focussed on conversion, however, but on the confession of being saved.[6] Building on his description of the missionary character of the early church, Bosch explicitly uses the term *conversion* in his chapter on the creative tension of mission and dialogue. He stipulates in that context that the Christian faith cannot surrender the conviction that God, in sending Christ, has taken a definitive course of action, "which, in turn, calls for a human response in the form of conviction."[7] According to Bosch, this call for a response is part and parcel of the Christian faith. To him, conversion is not about joining a community in order to procure "eternal salvation," but it much

---

2. Stephen B. Bevans and Roger P. Schroeder, *Constants in Context: A Theology of Mission for Today* (Maryknoll, NY: Orbis, 2004), 24, 125–26.

3. Timothy C. Tennent, *Invitation to World Missions: A Trinitarian Missiology for the Twenty-first Century* (Grand Rapids: Kregel, 2010), 81. Tennent discusses the double conversion in Acts 10, of both Cornelius and Peter (89).

4. David J. Bosch, *Transforming Mission: Paradigm Shifts in Theology of Mission* (Maryknoll, NY: Orbis, 1991), 117.

5. Ibid., 172.

6. Ibid., 178.

7. Ibid., 488.

rather points to a change in allegiance. Conversion is about accepting Christ as the centre of one's life.

Conversion in earlier missiological writings

The history of mission and evangelism shows that conversion had a prominent place in European mission theology. In classical texts on the theology of mission, conversion is emphasized as a predominant goal of mission and evangelism, mostly in conjunction with the planting of the church. "Compel people to come in, so that my house may be filled" (Luke 14:23) was widely used as a missionary mandate in the medieval period.[8] In his *Summa Theologica*, Thomas Aquinas (1225–1274) therefore discusses the nature of conversion and stresses that "infidels" should not be compelled to believe. It is Christ who compels. Believing and the act to join the Christian community should be voluntary. He therefore submits that the use of force to convert people is not a proper missionary method.[9] In Protestant writings the emphasis on conversion is already shown in the works of influential Dutch theologian Gisbertus Voetius (1589–1676), who affirmed that conversion of people to God (*conversio gentium*) was one of the primary goals of mission work, to be followed by the gathering of believers (*collectio*) and the planting of the church (*plantatio ecclesiae*). Both goals, however, are subsumed under the most important purpose of mission for Voetius: the glorification and manifestation of divine grace.[10] The importance of conversion is also evident in the *Enquiry into the Obligations of Christians: To Use Means for the Conversion of the Heathens* (1792), the "charter" for many a Protestant mission society in the 19th century. Its author, the English missionary William Carey (1761–1834), underscored that the missionary enterprise should be taken seriously, as the time had come for the conversion of the heathens.[11]

We can observe a similar emphasis in Protestant German missiology. Gustav Warneck (1834–1910), in his three-volume theology of mission, pointed to the centrality of conversion for the understanding of mission.[12] Walter Freytag

---

8. Norman E. Thomas, ed., *Classic Texts in Mission and World Christianity* (Maryknoll, NY: Orbis, 1995), 24.

9. Ibid., 24–25.

10. Huibert Antonie van Andel, *De zendingsleer van Gisbertus Voetius* (Kampen: Kok, 1912), 141ff.; See also Bosch, *Transforming Mission*, 262.

11. William Carey, *An Enquiry into the Obligations of Christians: To Use Means for the Conversion of the Heathens* (Leicester, 1792), 12.

12. See Werner Raupp, ed., *Mission in Quellentexten: Geschichte der Deutschen Evangelischen Mission von der Reformation bis zur Weltmissionskonferenz Edingburgh 1910* (Erlangen: Verlag der Evangelisch-Lutherischen Mission, 1990), 371ff.

(1899–1959) even stated that nothing can be called mission which isn't aiming at conversion and baptism.[13] Here, conversion becomes a kind of litmus test for the authenticity of mission. Roman Catholic missiologists of the Münster school of mission, such as the influential Joseph Schmidlin (1876–1944), contended that God's salvific will was manifested in the *conversio animarum* (conversion of the soul). The Louvain school of mission regarded the *plantatio ecclesiae* (planting of the church) as its manifestation, but conversions are obviously a prerequisite for planting a church.[14] The Dutch Roman Catholic missiologist Alphonsus J. M. Mulders (1893–1981) underlined that mission is about "planting, establishing and expanding the church" and submitted that converting non-Catholics was the main part of the missionary work. These conversions, however, ultimately intended to geographically expand the church.[15] As life change was the centre point or even ultimate goal in mission and evangelism, it is not surprising that Protestant mission societies in the first half of the 20th century produced a plethora of conversion histories, both biographical and autobiographical.

In that theological tradition the British mission theologian Lesslie Newbigin (1909–1998) wrote: "The calling of men and women to be converted, to follow Jesus, and to be part of his community is and must always be at the centre of mission. . . . Anyone who knows Jesus Christ as Lord and Savior must desire ardently that others should share that knowledge and must rejoice when the number of those who do is multiplied."[16] Newbigin wrote this against the backdrop of a sharp and painful ecumenical debate about the concept of salvation in the 1960s and 1970s. In the 1960s the North American missiologist Donald McGavran, having read the WCC documents for the assembly in Uppsala (1968), made a plea not to betray the two billion lost souls in this world and the effort to work toward conversion of the masses, as many in the ecumenical mission movement opted for the transformation of human life.[17] Just a few years later, at the WCC's World Mission Conference

13. Cited in Johannes Triebel, *Bekehrung als Ziel der missionarischen Verkündigung: Die Theologie Walter Freytags und das ökumenische Gespräch* (Erlangen: Verlag der Evangelisch-Lutherischen Mission, 1976), 11: "Nichts kann im biblischen Sinne Mission genannt werden, das . . . nicht auf Bekehrung und Taufe abzielt."
14. Paulus Y. Pham, *Towards an Ecumenical Paradigm for Christian Mission: David Bosch's Missionary Vision* (Rome: Gregorian and Biblical Press, 2010), 141–42; Bevans and Schroeder, *Constants*, 248–49.
15. Alph Mulders, *Inleiding tot de missiewetenschap* (Bussum: Paul Brand, 1950), 15, 166.
16. Lesslie Newbigin, *The Open Secret: An Introduction to the Theology of Mission*, 2d ed. (Grand Rapids: Eerdmans, 1995), 121, 127.
17. See Arthur F. Glasser and Donald A. McGavran, eds., *The Conciliar Evangelical Debate* (Waco, TX: Word, 1972), 233–34; Donald A. McGavran, "Will Upsala Betray the Two Billion?," *Church*

in Bangkok (1973), German missiologist Peter Beyerhaus (born 1929) and the Indian theologian Madathilparampil M. (M. M.) Thomas (1916–1996) debated vehemently about the same issue. Beyerhaus emphasized the heart of mission as the call to repentance and the justification of the sinner, whereas Thomas opted for salvation as transformation and humanization in the midst of poverty.[18] This "great debate in mission"[19] eventually evoked the formation of a worldwide Evangelical movement (cf. the issuing of *The Lausanne Covenant* in 1974), as Evangelicals felt that the unicity of Christ and the exclusive character of his redemptive work were at stake. Together with the World Evangelical Alliance they represented a more conservative approach to salvation, evangelism, and conversion.[20]

Also, in our times it is easy to observe that while for some the call to conversion is indeed the very heart of the evangelistic ministry, others advise us that "it is improper to invite adherents of other faiths or of no faith to put their trust in God through Christ."[21] There are diverging approaches to conversion and religious change that are hard to reconcile. Newbigin was concerned about the diverging approaches and wrote: "Where this desire [to share the knowledge of Christ] and this rejoicing [about multiplication] are absent, we must ask whether something is not wrong at the centres of the church's life."[22] The reasons for the feeling that a call to conversion is somehow improper are different in nature. Many people, including Christians, reason that this feeling is related to one-sided practices in mission and evangelism in the past and they therefore want to distance themselves from an overemphasis on conversion. Another, and probably more important, reason may be the feeling that an emphasis on conversion is inherently related to a truth claim that can no longer be maintained in post-Christian and pluralistic contexts. It is this feeling that is evident in Paul Knitter and John Hick's *The Myth of Christian Uniqueness* (1987).[23] It is only fair to say that not only in public debate, but also in church and mission, conversion has become a sensitive and highly controversial issue.

Growth Bulletin 4, no. 5 (May 1968).

18. Roger E. Hedlund, *Roots of the Great Debate in Mission: Mission in Historical and Theological Perspective*, rev. ed. (Bangalore: Theological Book Trust, 2002), 257–90.

19. See ibid.

20. "Towards Common Witness to Christ Today: Mission and Visible Unity of the Church," *International Review of Mission* 99, no. 1 (April 2010): 90.

21. Bosch, *Transforming Mission*, 488. Bosch writes about those who feel it is improper to do so, but this does not reflect his own position.

22. Newbigin, *Open Secret*, 127.

23. John Hick and Paul Knitter, eds., *The Myth of Christian Uniqueness: Toward a Pluralistic Theology of Religions* (Maryknoll, NY: Orbis, 2005).

Be this as it may, the pervasive sensitivity about conversion can be critically questioned as well. In today's Western world the effort to convince others of one's own views is very normal. We continuously try to "convert," to win over, others to our views: we do so in the political debate about the immigration of refugees, in talk shows in the media, in interpreting results of scientific research, and in advertising the good news of brand-new products. Large companies, like Apple or Starbucks, talk unembarrassedly about their "evangelists" and they present "testimonials" about their products. We stress our unique selling points every day and hope that others can be tempted to accept our point of view or buy our newly developed product. We do so without hesitation or reservation. It is even fair to say that in democratic societies we can't do without this effort to "convert" the other, as it is a means of making progress. What if nobody should ever be persuaded to change his or her opinion about ideas he or she holds dear? That would amount to giving up on public debate, politics, science, education, and what more? It is in the ongoing process of exchanging our views that we constantly evaluate our knowledge, adjust our opinions and find "the good" and the good way forward.

Yet, though we highly value this continuous dialogue and acknowledge that everybody advertises their good news and aspires to influence society, it has become very suspect to do this with respect to religion. European societies have wittingly or unwittingly declared that religious convictions belong to the private domain and that any attempt to call people to turn to God even infringes on human freedom. Of course, we realize that some practices of conversion have given rise to strong reservations. Nevertheless, in this chapter we take the approach that a call to conversion is neither improper nor an infringement of freedom. It is, rather, an honest endeavour to bring Christian identity in dialogue with its context. The conviction that the gospel is good news indeed invites us to share this greater good with others. This is not so different from other deeply ingrained attempts in our societies to convince the other of what is good, truthful, and beneficial.

8.1.3 Evangelism and conversion

In this section we will now look at conversion in some more detail. We will discuss conversion as a part of evangelism, types of conversion, and proselytism. We will conclude with a final section on implications of what we have discussed.

Conversion as integral part of evangelism

A survey of missiological writings shows that most of the mission theologians today wouldn't accept a definition of mission that frames conversion as its main goal. But even though most missiologists have a broader understanding of mission and evangelism, and although the term *conversion* seems to be marginalized, the concept is still present in many mission paradigms. Since evangelism includes an invitation to believe in the gospel and hopes for a response in faith, conversion as turning to God comes into focus. This is clearly visible in the WCC's *Mission and Evangelism: An Ecumenical Affirmation* (1982): "The proclamation of the gospel includes an invitation to recognize and accept in a personal decision the saving lordship of Christ. It is the announcement of a personal encounter, mediated by the Holy Spirit, with the living Christ, receiving his forgiveness and making a personal acceptance of the call to discipleship and a life of service."[24] This specific focus on conversion as "personal encounter" is later balanced by the "call to conversion, as a call to repentance and obedience, . . . to nations, groups and families."[25] Thus, evangelism doesn't only focus on change in the life of individuals, but also on transformation of the world. We are reminded of this by the words of Robert H. Schreiter, who wrote: "Good evangelization will also bring about cultural change."[26] Also, the WCC's mission statement *Together towards Life* (2013) takes this change, in both individual life and in the world, as its starting point as it states: "evangelism leads to repentance, faith, and baptism. . . . It provokes conversion, involving a change of attitudes, priorities, and goals. It results in salvation of the lost, healing of the sick, and the liberation of the oppressed and the whole creation."[27] Here again, conversion spans from the personal to the global. It includes not only turning to God, but also to our neighbour. Conversion "to the other" should, according to the WCC, be viewed as fulfillment of the missional aim "to be with the marginalized people"[28] and recognition that

---

24. World Council of Churches, *Mission and Evangelism: An Ecumenical Affirmation* (Geneva: WCC Publications, 1982), par. 10.

25. Ibid., par. 12.

26. Robert J. Schreiter, *Constructing Local Theologies*, 15th ed. (Maryknoll, NY: Orbis, 2008), 157.

27. World Council of Churches, *Together towards Life: Mission and Evangelism in Changing Landscapes* (Geneva: WCC Publications, 2013), 30 (par. 84). Claudia Währisch-Oblau observes in her discussion of *Together towards Life*'s paragraphs 84 and 89 that the document as a whole shows "a palpable hesitancy when it comes to witnessing to Christ." Rather than overflowing with joy, she contends, *Together towards Life* "seems fearful of a wrong evangelism." See Währisch Oblau, "Evangelism in *Evangelii Gaudium*, *The Cape Town Commitment*, and *Together towards Life*," *International Review of Mission* 104, no. 2 (November 2015): 266.

28. WCC, *Together*, 15 (par. 36).

the "other," who was also created in the image of God, "is not just tolerated in the kingdom of God, but has an active role to play and a unique contribution to make."[29]

The emphasis on conversion in WCC's mission affirmations is clearly expressed, while acknowledging that "evangelism in the past has been distorted and lost its credibility because some Christians have forced 'conversions' on people by violent means or the abuse of power."[30] In all evangelistic efforts it is therefore essential to be guided by ethical principles, such as are presented to us in *Christian Witness in a Multi-Religious World* (2011).[31] In the ministry of evangelism we should keep in mind the Augsburg Confession (1530), which says with regards to conversion: "where and when it pleases God" (*ubi et quando visum est Deo*). Evangelism is never the cause of conversion (only the Spirit can convert people) but, hopefully, it creates conditions that lead to conversion. Witness and invitation are the only appropriate means of evangelism. "Converting someone," however, is the work of God's Spirit and far beyond any human possibilities. Putting it into a trinitarian framework, "evangelism is God's work long before it is our work. The Father prepares the ground, the Son gives the invitation and the Spirit prompts the person to respond in repentance and faith to the good news."[32] Thus, evangelism that is faithful to the gospel respects freedom. Those interacting with the evangelist are free to respond in a positive, negative, or even indifferent way.[33]

Types of conversion

When describing the process of conversion as such, it is helpful to make use of Lewis Rambo's study *Understanding Religious Conversion* (1993), which has become a point of reference for the research on conversion.[34] According to him, conversion is a "total transformation of the person by the power of God" which entails "turning from and to new religious groups, ways of life, systems

---

29. World Council of Churches, *The 'Other' Is My Neighbour: Developing an Ecumenical Response to Migration* (Geneva: WCC Publications, 2013), 13 (par. 17).

30. WCC, *Together*, 30 (par. 82).

31. World Council of Churches, the Pontifical Council for Interreligious Dialogue, and World Evangelical Alliance, *Christian Witness in a Multi-Religious World: Recommendations for Conduct* (Geneva: WCC Publications, 2011).

32. J. Andrew Kirk, *What Is Mission? Theological Explorations* (Minneapolis: Augsburg Fortress Press, 2000), 73.

33. WCC et al., *Christian Witness*, principles 3, 6–7.

34. For a thorough treatment of conversion and its different aspects, see Lewis R. Rambo and Charles E. Farhadian, eds., *The Oxford Handbook of Religious Conversion* (New York: Oxford University Press, 2014).

of belief, and modes of relating to a deity or the nature of reality."[35] Although for many throughout church history the apostle Paul's dramatic conversion on the road to Damascus has become a paradigm for understanding conversion, Rambo concludes that conversion is usually a process with seven stages. In his understanding, conversion has a specific *context*, and it is initiated by a *crisis* and a *quest*. These are followed by an *encounter* and *interaction* with an "advocate." This is a term Rambo uses to describe followers of a religious group or vision of life. The encounter with the advocate then results in a (new) *commitment* followed by specific *consequences*. As Rambo doesn't understand these stages in the sense of a fixed chronological order, the stages could also be referred to as "dimensions" of conversion.[36]

It is evident that the term *conversion* is often equated with a sudden and ultimate experience. This shows the strong influence of the Pietistic and Methodist traditions on the practice of evangelism. It may be more helpful to use the term *conversional processes* (German: *konversive Prozesse*), which point to the process character of conversion.[37] According to Scot McKnight, for many Christians conversion was a "process of socialization."[38] If we relate this to biblical narratives on conversion, as John Finney does, for a small majority of Christians the road to Emmaus seems to be a better metaphor of conversion than the road to Damascus.[39] That, however, doesn't take away that a significant minority of those who have experienced a conversion will refer to it as a dramatic event.

The issue that is at stake here, essentially, is how one defines what it means to be a "Christian." Those who are influenced by Pietistic and Methodist traditions tend to emphasize the subjective experience as an indispensable element of intrinsic faith, while those who come from the older churches—Catholics, the Orthodox, the Reformed community—tend to stress the objective (extrinsic) elements of Christian identity, such as participating in the sacraments, belonging to the body of Christ, or being a member of the covenant. Clearly,

---

35. Lewis R. Rambo, *Understanding Religious Conversion* (New Haven: Yale University, 1993), xii and 3.

36. Scot McKnight, "Missions and Conversion Theory," *Mission Studies* 20, no. 2 (2003): 118–39.

37. Henning Wrogemann, "Wahrnehmung und Begleitung 'konversiver Prozesse': Missionarische Herausforderung kirchlicher Praxis im Kontext des Pluralismus," in Klaus Schäfer, ed., *Weltmission heute 53: Umkehr zum lebendigen Gott: Beitrage zu Mission und Bekerung* (Hamburg: Evangelisches Missionswerk, 2003), 61–79.

38. Scot McKnight, *Turning to Jesus: The Sociology of Conversion in the Gospels* (Louisville: Westminster John Knox, 2002), 1ff.

39. John Finney, *Finding Faith Today: How Does It Happen?* (Stonehill Green: British and Foreign Bible Society, 1992).

these different theological approaches of Christian identity influence how we think about conversion. Is it primarily a surprising, liberating individual experience at a crucial point in our lives? Or is it, rather, a gradually increasing sense of belonging to the Christian family, a growing certitude of being accepted by God? In the very end, it is both, even if we favour one approach over the other in the short term.

It is important not to create false alternatives here. Both approaches are (or can be) authentic representations of faith.[40] Evangelists may tend to favour the subjective view, but there is also much evidence for the wisdom of the more objective view. In the end, these different approaches may have to do with deeper theological issues, such as the objectivity of Christ's work and God's universal will of salvation on the one hand, and the subjectivity of the Spirit's work in believers and in the world at large on the other. Clearly, there can be and will be extremes at both sides, but (to repeat a point already made) it is crucial that Christians try to avoid any false dichotomies here.

Building on the distinction between more "subjective" and more "objective" approaches to Christian identity—while acknowledging that there may be many shades in between—different modes of conversion emerge.[41] A subjective approach that articulates intrinsic faith then leads to or follows "conversion through personal decision." This is a central notion in the Evangelical and Pentecostal traditions. Personal experience and decision—sometimes including references to a specific date and year—are essential. Throughout church history, until today, there have been examples that show such an understanding of conversion. In the 20th century many evangelistic campaigns were based on this understanding as well, especially those influenced by revivalism. Therefore, it shouldn't surprise us that many regard this as the one and only understanding of conversion.

Conversion through socialization is another perspective on conversion. Individual decision is not the heart of the matter here, but nurtured in a context of belonging. This is a central notion in the understanding of conversion in the older churches of Europe. In these churches we also come across a third understanding of conversion: conversion through liturgical acts. Although the term *conversion* is not often used by Roman Catholics, Lutheran or Reformed

40. See Gordon W. Allport, "The Religious Context of Prejudice," *Journal for the Scientific Study of Religion* 5, no. 3 (1966): 447–57; Lawrence A. Young, ed., *Rational Choice Theory and Religion: Summary and Assessment* (London: Routledge, 1997).
41. The following types of conversion are taken from Richard V. Peace, "Conflicting Understandings of Christian Conversion: A Missiological Challenge," *International Bulletin of Missionary Research* 28, no. 1 (January 2004): 8–14.

Protestants, and the Orthodox, rites of passage (such as adult baptism, confirmation, baptismal renewal) are always related to the notion of conversion. Based on his understanding of rites of passage, Karl Rahner therefore made a plea to embrace the idea of conversion as a conscious act of initiation.

Rambo's above-cited definition of conversion comes close to the traditional definition William James gave in his 1901–1902 Gifford lectures: "To say that a man is 'converted' means . . . that religious ideas, previously peripheral in his consciousness, now take a central place, and that religious aims form the habitual centre of his energy."[42] This definition doesn't equate conversion with a change of religion, which so often happens in popular understanding. Conversion may result in a change of religion, but that is not necessary.[43] David Plüss makes a helpful distinction in this regard when he points to "vertical" and "horizontal" conversions. While the latter is connected with a change of religion or church, the former points to a revitalization of or ritualized turning to a religious belief.[44] Henri Gooren even goes a step further and tries a new approach when speaking of conversion as a lifelong process. He even speaks of a "conversion career," "which includes all periods of higher or lower participation in one or more religious groups during a person's life history."[45]

The above implies that conversion is not only something that happens in the realm of evangelism amongst nonbelievers, but also that we may discover conversion within existing religious groups and churches. Building on this assumption, Henning Wrogemann discovers three different types of conversional processes within Protestant mainline churches in Germany.[46] In his first model, which he calls "relief by connecting with tradition," conversion takes place by participating in ecclesial rites of passage. This type of conversion usually happens to "churched" people. As members they participate in church activities and thereby experience transformation. His second model, "relief by integration," is related to seekers who find answers by attending church services

---

42. William James, *The Varieties of Religious Experience: A Study in Human Nature. Being the Gifford Lectures on Natural Religion Delivered at Edinburgh 1901–1902* (London: Longmans, Green and Co., 1929), 196.

43. See the lengthy and exhaustive working definition by Wolfgang Lienemann in Christine Lienemann-Perrin and Wolfgang Lienemann, eds., *Religiöse Grenzüberschreitungen: Studien zu Bekehrung, Konfessions- und Religionswechsel* [ET: *Crossing Religious Borders: Studies on Conversion and Religious Belonging*] (Wiesbaden: Harrassowitz, 2012), 26ff. Also Christine Lienemann-Perrin, "Conversion in a Post-Modern Context," *Swedish Missiological Themes* 95, no. 4 (2007): 443–62.

44. David Plüss, "Vertikale Konversion am Beispiel des Alpha-Kurses," in Lienemann-Perrin and Lienemann, *Religiöse*, 151ff.

45. Henri Gooren, "Towards a New Model of Conversion Careers: The Impact of Personality and Situational Actors," *Exchange* 34 (2005): 153.

46. Wrogemann, "Wahrnehmung."

or other events. He then adds a third model, referred to as "relief by reduction," in which de- or unchurched people experience transformation of life.

The "Greifswald typology of conversion," focussing on the context of older ("mainline") churches, distinguishes three models of conversion as well. It refers first to assurance (German: *Vergewisserung*), when a church member rediscovers faith; second, to discovery (German: *Entdeckung*), when faith gets a new centrality in the life of a dechurched person; and third, to a turn of life (German: *Lebenswende*), when an unchurched person starts believing in the gospel.[47]

With a focus on mainline churches, Wrogemann wonders if many conversional processes remain unexplored because no or only little help is provided to interpret these processes. If we learn to understand conversion as the "opening of a new perspective of life," this may well lead to a new appreciation and a new cultivation of conversion.[48] Following that understanding, conversion is "breaking out into the broader field."[49] Or, to quote the Canadian novelist Rudy Wiebe, "you repent, not by feeling bad, but by thinking different." Thus understood, conversion is about direction: "It involves turning the whole personality with its social, cultural, and religious inheritance toward Christ, opening it up to him. It is about turning what is already there."[50]

This turning does not imply an easy dichotomy between "old" and "new," or between world and church. It is much rather a dialectical relationship in terms of distance and belonging, as is well exemplified in the words of Miroslav Volf: "Let us assume that Christians can depart without leaving, that their distance always involves belonging and that their kind of belonging takes the form of distance."[51] It is this creative tension in which all converts have their rooting, between their specific culture and God's new world:

> Christians do not come into their own social world from the outside seeking
> either to accommodate to their new home (as second generation immigrants

47. Johannes Zimmermann and Anna-Konstanze Schröder, eds., *Wie finden Erwachsene zum Glauben? Einführung und Ergebnisse der Greifswalder Studie*, 2d ed. (Neukirchen-Vluyn: Neukirchener Aussaat, 2011), 32.

48. Henning Wrogemann, "Konvivenz, Konversion und Kirche: Eine missionswissenschaftliche Betrachtung," in Martin Reppenhagen, ed., *Konversion zwischen empirischer Forschung und theologischer Reflexion* (Neukirchen-Vluyn: Neukirchener Theologie, 2012), 173.

49. Charles Taylor, *A Secular Age* (Cambridge: Belknap Press/Harvard University Press, 2007), 769.

50. Andrew F. Walls, "Converts or Proselytes? The Crisis over Conversion in the Early Church," *International Bulletin of Missionary Research* 28, no. 1 (2004): 6.

51. Miroslav Volf, *Exclusion and Embrace: A Theological Exploration of Identity, Otherness, and Reconciliation* (Nashville: Abingdon, 1996), 50.

would), shape it in the image of the one they have left behind (as colonizers would), or establish a little haven in the strange new world reminiscent of the old (as resident aliens would). They are not outsiders who either seek to become insiders or maintain strenuously the status of outsiders. Christians are the insiders who have diverted from their culture by being born again.[52]

When missiologist Andrew Walls discusses conversion, he distinguishes between *turning* and *substituting*. He contends that conversion means turning: "It is not about substituting something new for something old. . . . Nor is it a matter of adding something new to something old. It is much more radical than either. In other words, it is turning what is already there; turning to Christ the elements of the pre-conversion setting."[53] In Walls's understanding, the substitution of something new for something old is no less than proselytism. For him, this is a uniforming process that in essence denies human and cultural differences, whereas conversion is based on the translatability of the gospel. It accepts, or even makes possible, a pluriformity of world Christianity. Conversion is not about just giving up or denying one's own cultural or individual character. In this context Walls points to the Jerusalem council in Acts 15 as the key event for the future of the cross-cultural story of the Gentile mission and for the future of the church: "Finally, after deep deliberation, the leaders of the Jerusalem community . . . accepted the essentials of Paul's argument. Though circumcised, Torah-keeping Jews themselves, they recognized that gentile believers in the Messiah could enter Israel without becoming Jews. They were converts not proselytes." Walls then concludes that "it is hardly possible to exaggerate the importance of this early controversy and its outcome," for it "built the principle of cultural diversity into Christianity in perpetuity."[54] Although Walls does not relate his discussion on proselytism to the issue of "sheep stealing" and territorial claims to "one nation—one church," and limits it to the uniforming process that denies difference, his principle of translatability and pluriformity may well have implications for this sensitive issue.

---

52. See the whole article by Miroslav Volf, "Soft Difference: Theological Reflections on the Relation between Church and Culture in 1 Peter," *Ex Auditu* 10 (1994): 15–30.

53. Andrew F. Walls, "The Mission of the Church Today in the Light of Global History," *Word and World* 20, no. 1 (2000): 21. See also his discussion of conversion in Andrew F. Walls, *The Missionary Movement in Christian History: Studies in the Transmission of Faith* (Maryknoll, NY: Orbis, 1996), 43–54.

54. Andrew F. Walls, "Old Athens and New Jerusalem: Some Signposts for Christian Scholarship in the Early History of Mission Studies," *International Bulletin of Missionary Research* 21, no. 4 (1997): 147ff.

Conversion and proselytism

Especially in contexts where a substantial number of people belong to a national church, the sensitive issue of proselytism ("sheep stealing") emerges when minority churches start specific evangelistic outreaches (cf. ch. 8.2.4, below). This is especially the case in Eastern Europe, where many Protestant evangelists have ministered in a predominantly Orthodox context. In other parts of Europe the same discussion surfaces, however, when Protestants evangelize in Roman Catholic countries, or when Baptists and Pentecostals call for conversion in predominantly Lutheran or Reformed areas. Usually, these outreaches are not aimed at members of already existing churches, as such, but nevertheless they do attract these members as well. Proselytism is regarded as "fishing in the neighbor's pond," as Miroslav Volf put it.[55] It is clear that proselytism causes tensions and clashes between churches, which has quite frequently led to mutual anathemas.

The question is: How do we respond to the fact that already baptized Christians may be attracted by evangelistic efforts of another church and do become members of that church? Especially the post-Communist reality in eastern Europe has, not without reason, been referred to as an "ecumenical meltdown."[56] Attempts to draw members of Orthodox churches toward Protestant churches led to friction and to the frustration of ecumenical relations. Here, many new Protestant evangelists coming from the West hardly recognized the value of (or didn't understand) Orthodox faith, quite often arguing that these territories were "spiritually dead." On the other hand, Orthodox Church leaders saw these new evangelistic efforts as threats to their traditional dominant position and spoke of "canonical territories"[57] where church activities of any other church were under general suspicion. Thus, they developed a somewhat problematic relationship with the notion of religious freedom, that is, the right of each citizen to choose his or her own religion. Both sides had, and even still have, some tendencies that steer away from developing ecumenical relations, resulting in difficulties with each other.

55. Miroslav Volf, "Fishing in the Neighbor's Pond: Mission and Proselytism in Eastern Europe," *International Bulletin of Missionary Research* 20, no. 1 (1996): 26–31.

56. Joseph Loya, "Interchurch Relations in Post-Perestroika Eastern Europe: A Short History of an Ecumenical Meltdown," *Religion in Eastern Europe* 14, no. 1 (1994): 1–17.

57. The understanding of a "canonical territory" goes back to the old church meaning "one city, one bishop." The term was taken up by the Russian Orthodox Church against the Roman Catholic Church planning to establish Russian dioceses. See Henning Wrogemann, *Missionstheologien der Gegenwart: Globale Entwicklungen, kontextuelle Profile und ökumenische Herausforderungen* (Gütersloh: Gütersloher Verlagshaus, 2013), 205ff. This idea was common practice on the "mission field," which quite often was divided according to the denominational missions working in this area.

The issue of proselytism in evangelistic ministry has been taken seriously in the ecumenical movement. One example of that awareness is the joint working group of the Roman Catholic Church and the WCC, which started already back in the 1960s and that published a study document titled *Common Witness and Proselytism* in 1970.[58] Here, "unity in witness and witness in unity" is highlighted and false evangelistic methods are rejected. Karl Müller argues along similar lines and concludes: "Christians divided among themselves are no genuine witness to the non-Christian world."[59] (See also ch. 5.2.3, above, in which Donna Orsuto points to the emphasis on unity as a condition for mission in recent papal documents.) WCC's *Towards Common Witness* (1997) points to proselytism, in distinction from evangelism, as "the encouragement of Christians who belong to a church to change their denominational allegiance, through ways and means that 'contradict the spirit of Christian love, violate the freedom of the human person and diminish trust in the Christian witness of the church'."[60]

In accordance with this document (almost) all later documents of the WCC focussing on evangelism rebuke proselytism or "sheep stealing," because "proselytism is not a legitimate way of practicing evangelism."[61] The involved churches are aware of the importance of ecumenical relationships between churches and of the danger in mingling evangelism with proselytism. In this context the Lausanne Movement states clearly: "We are called to share good news in evangelism, but not to engage in unworthy proselytizing."[62]

The issue of proselytism, or transfer conversion, has often been labelled as an issue between Protestant and Orthodox churches, but it has been a Catholic–Orthodox and a Protestant–Catholic issue as well, and even between Protestant denominations proselytism may cause major problems. Quite a few church members from Protestant mainline churches were attracted by

---

58. See the third report of the joint working group between the Roman Catholic Church and the World Council of Churches, especially appendix II, http://www.prounione.urbe.it/dia-int/jwg/doc/e_jwg-n3_06.html.

59. Karl Müller, "Proselytism," in Müller et al., ed., *Dictionary of Mission: Theology, History, Perspectives* (Maryknoll, NY: Orbis, 1997), 374ff. See also Peter F. Penner, "Proselytism," in John Corrie, ed., *Dictionary of Mission Theology: Evangelical Foundations* (Downers Grove, IL: InterVarsity, 2007), 321–22.

60. World Council of Churches, "Towards Common Witness: A Call to Adopt Responsible Relationships in Mission and to Renounce Proselytism," 19 September 1997, https://www.oikoumene.org/en/resources/documents/commissions/mission-and-evangelism/towards-common-witness. See also the study paper "Towards Common Witness to Christ Today: Mission and Visible Unity of the Church," *International Review of Mission* 99, no. 1 (April 2010): 100–101.

61. WCC, *Together*, par. 82.

62. The Lausanne Movement, *The Cape Town Commitment* (Cape Town, 2010), 32.

evangelistic ministries of the so-called free churches, and became members of these churches. According to their witness they weren't real Christians before, in spite of their church membership. They state that they came to new faith. Sometimes they even get baptized as adults, although they were already baptized as infants. Here, different understandings of faith and being a Christian, as well as of baptism, are in tension with each other.

One may conclude that proselytism, for different reasons, becomes an issue when a church attracts members of another church. In most cases, majority churches in Europe are affected here by the evangelistic work of dynamic minority churches. These majority churches are usually the first ones in raising the issue of "sheep stealing," while the minority churches point to the freedom of religious choice. Thus, the issue of proselytism is framed differently depending on perspective: either by stressing the importance of religious freedom or by emphasizing Christian unity and ecumenical relationships with other churches. By responding in this way, "transfer conversion" (from one church to the other) can't be banned. It will still happen, as people are free to make their own choices.

There is a still ongoing debate about what is meant by "through ways and means that 'contradict the spirit of Christian love.'" Is any evangelistic attempt which attracts other church members ("transfer conversion") evidence of proselytism? Here, one has to recognize that religious switching is a matter of fact,[63] even though it is not practiced by the majority of church members in Europe (however, migrant churches are exceptions to this rule).[64] But every attempt should be avoided to attract members of another church for the benefit of one's own, or to substitute a certain understanding of Christian teaching with another. Instead, mutual relationships between churches should be strengthened and Christians who are a member of other churches should not be encouraged to transfer membership, but to strengthen their Christian identity and faith within their own faith communities.[65]

Being aware of these tensions, one needs to acknowledge that the evangelistic call to conversion should never be confused with the practice of proselytism. To quote Bosch, "Evangelism is not a form of ecclesiastical propaganda and may never have as its primary objective the enlarging of the membership

---

63. For Great Britain, see, e.g., Jonathan A. Romain, *Your God Shall Be My God: Religious Conversion in Britain Today* (London: SCM Press, 2000).

64. In the United States it is a quite common practice, as Robert Wuthnow shows in his book *The Restructuring of American Religion: Society and Faith since World War II* (Princeton: Princeton University Press, 1988).

65. WCC, et al., *Christian Witness.*

of a particular church or the promoting of particular doctrines."[66] Yet, accepting that this is true doesn't solve the problem. Everybody will agree that false evangelistic methods are unacceptable, but the underlying issue is different understandings of the subjective and objective approach of Christian identity. While some will categorically regard an individual who is objectively affiliated with, and part of, a sacramental communion as a Christian (apart from their subjective participation), others may regard the very same individual as a nominal Christian or a "baptized heathen" (in spite of the objective church membership). While for some the old church is an agent of salvation, for others churches are primarily a means for the proclamation of the gospel.[67] Another problematic issue remains the interrelatedness of national and religious identity over against individual religious freedom. As Kwabena Asamoah-Gyadu shows in chapter 5.4.1 (above), on reverse mission in Ukraine, this is a major issue for Pentecostals in the context of Orthodox Christianity.[68] In relation to reverse mission it is important to note that religious (and Christian) mobility in the Americas, Africa, and also in South Korea is much larger than in Europe. Changing religious affiliation and church membership in the course of a lifetime are fairly normal. In parts of Europe where the relation of territorial and religious identity is strong (national churches, *Volkskirche*), change of religious affiliation is deemed problematic. In areas where this relation is not strong, or even absent, the issue of proselytism is often not understood and placed in the framework of religious freedom. In ecumenically addressing the issue of proselytism, it is therefore important to carefully look at the local context and analyze the theological issues thoroughly.

Conversion and deconversion

The main focus of the preceding paragraphs was on conversion to the Christian faith. We would miss important issues, however, if we do not briefly consider deconversion. While leaving a church and joining another church or religion does take place, the trend of this "secular age" (Charles Taylor) in Europe is to leave one's own church while not joining any other religious institution. This ongoing process results in a growing number of religiously

---

66. David J. Bosch, "Evangelism, Evangelization," in Müller et al., ed., *Dictionary of Mission*, 153.
67. See the Evangelical–Roman Catholic dialogue on mission (1986), discussed in Rienk Lannooy, *Ecumenism and Salvation: A Critical Appraisal of the Concept of Salvation in Bilateral Ecumenical Dialogues (1970–2000)* (Amsterdam: Vrije Universiteit, 2013), 101–111.
68. On the ecumenical dialogue with Pentecostals, see Jelle Creemers, *Theological Dialogue with Classical Pentecostals: Challenges and Opportunities* (London: Bloomsbury T&T Clark, 2015).

unaffiliated or religiously indifferent people.[69] New research on deconversion tries to find reasons for the related processes.[70] It has shown that deconversion goes hand in hand with a loss of religious experience, intellectual doubts, and moral critique of one's own religious group. If the feeling of belonging to (or the feeling of security in) a religious group dwindles substantially, it may result in withdrawal and, finally, in leaving the community. While around one third rejoin the community eventually, the other two thirds remain agnostic or practice a (privatized) way of faith without any affiliation to a religious institution. The latter is not just a phenomenon that is visible in the membership of the traditional majority churches. Philip Harrold specifically writes about the somewhat surprising phenomenon of deconversion in the emerging-church movement, which is primarily related to its postmodern emphasis on deconstruction and to its anti-institutional attitude. Deconstructing traditional Christian faith and anti-institutionalism then become just one stage in an ongoing process of deconversion.[71]

8.1.4 Conversion in the case studies

When we now turn to the case studies in this book, the preceding sections may imply that we have to rephrase the initial question concerning the absence of the term *conversion*. If we build upon the idea that there are different types of conversion and that the *concept* of conversion (not the *term* as such) is still present in many evangelistic ministries, we can look at the case studies again.

At the beginning of this article we referred to Francis Brienen's case study on the Street Pastors in London (United Kingdom) and wondered why the ministry supposedly is not intentionally evangelistic even though its founder

---

69. Among others, see Grace Davie, *Religion in Britain since 1945: Believing without Belonging* (Oxford: Blackwell, 1994); Grace Davie, "Vicarious Religion: A Methodological Challenge," in Nancy T. Ammerman, ed., *Everyday Religion: Observing Modern Religious Lives* (New York: Oxford University Press, 2007); Detlef Pollack, "Religion und Moderne. Zur Gegenwart der Säkularisierung in Europa," in Friedrich Wilhelm Graf and Klaus Große Kracht, eds., *Religion und Gesellschaft: Europa im 20. Jahrhundert* (Köln: Böhlau Verlag, 2007), 73–103; Gert Pickel and Kornelia Sammet, eds., *Religion und Religiosität im vereinigten Deutschland: Zwanzig Jahre nach dem Umbruch* (Wiesbaden: VS Verlag für Sozialwissenschaften, 2011); Danièle Hervieu-Léger, "Secularization, Tradition and New Forms of Religiosity: Some Theoretical Proposals," in Eileen Barker and Margit Warburg, eds., *New Religions and New Religiosity* (Aarhus: Aarhus University Press, 1998), 28–44. For understanding the whole process of secularization, see Taylor, *A Secular Age*.
70. Heinz Streib, et al., *Deconversion: Qualitative and Quantitative Results from Cross-Cultural Research in Germany and the United States of America* (Göttingen: Vandenhoeck & Ruprecht, 2009).
71. Alan Jamieson, *A Churchless Faith: Faith Journeys beyond the Churches* (London: SPCK, 2002); Philip Harrold, "Deconversion in the Emerging Church," *International Journal for the Study of the Christian Church* 6, no. 1 (2006): 79–90.

had embraced Christian faith as the result of a conversion process (see ch. 7.1.1, above). It is probable, given the sensitive nature of the words *evangelism* and *conversion*, that the Street Pastors shy away from these words as such. Reading the case study in detail makes clear that the Street Pastors engage in animated conversations with Muslims about Jesus, the Bible, and the Qur'an (7.1.1), while in general emphasizing that they don't specifically preach the gospel. Although stating that they are "not out to evangelize, but to make streets safer and better," and assuming that the "right to share the gospel has to be earned" (7.1.1), the ministry is said to have an evangelistic dimension. This is based on the theological inspiration for the ministry: the evangelistic dimension flows directly from the calling to be light and salt in the world and thereby to show the love of Christ. The role of prayer in the ministry of the Street Pastors is remarkable. They pray for the people they encounter, the ministry is "supported" by prayer, and they promise to people on the street that they will pray for them (7.1.1). The case study doesn't make clear if "doing good" on the streets has also led people to embrace the Christian faith, but the style of evangelism in the ministry of the Street Pastors may be more intentional than is articulated. We hear about people who want to respond spiritually (one of the main lessons learned), and we read that the pastors do not have to push the faith element of their ministry. As a matter of fact, it is stated that "if we give people proper attention they are ready to engage" (see 7.1.7, above).

This invites the idea that avoiding the words *evangelism* and, no doubt, *conversion*, is rooted in the intention to voice the gospel message in a polite way, as a "guest" in a secularized society. In terms of the above-mentioned typology of conversion, the ministry of the Street Pastors, who predominantly minister to the dechurched (but also to unchurched people), mainly falls into the category of "conversion as discovery."

The case study on the International Christian Fellowship in Rotterdam (the Netherlands) shows quite a different picture, as it makes clear that some 80 adults were baptized since the start of the ministry (cf. 7.7.2, above). These baptisms were primarily administered to unchurched people, who were often adherents of other faith traditions. The community is explicitly evangelistic in its ministry and, in terms of the typology of conversion, focusses on "conversion as a life-turn" (*Lebenswende*). It wants to be an "attractive faith community" that "envisions to shape yet other missional multicultural faith communities" (see 7.7.5, above). It also explicitly invites people to participate in Alpha courses and catechism classes. As the congregation focusses on shaping a new Christian faith community, it is called a "mission congregation" (see 7.7.2, above) by the Christian Reformed denomination, and its first pastor was officially called an "evangelist" (7.7.2).

In the case study on MyChurch, the online church in the Netherlands (see 7.2, above), the focus is not conversional. It is, in their own words, "contextual." Yet, the evangelistic intention is very explicit. The intention is to shape a new Christian community that connects people with one another and with God. While using an open and postmodern style, the content is about God's love for everybody. The method is "mostly about listening and looking," and in doing that, intentional guidance is offered by giving meaning to life events. The invitation to embrace the gospel is certainly not made explicit in classic evangelistic terms. Offered spiritual guidance is not stated in a dogmatic way, but is offered as an opinion: "Could it be that . . . ?" This approach can be understood in light of the particular dechurched context. Many therefore resist a normative and dogmatic approach. In the terms of the above-mentioned typology of conversion: MyChurch, focussing on dechurched people, emphasizes "conversion as discovery."

The two case studies of evangelism in an Orthodox context (see chs. 7.5 and 7.6, above) seem to fall partly into the category of "conversion as assurance" and partly into "conversion as discovery." Both case studies make it clear that religious education in schools is considered as the primary means to (re) connect people to the Christian faith tradition. Especially the contribution on religious education in the Serbian Orthodox Church (cf. 7.6.1, above) makes clear that religious education, as such, played an important role in providing the assurance of faith in times of war. Learning prayers was a way to assure the children that the world was ultimately in God's hands. For the older, "deconverted" generation (the result of previous communist pressure on the Orthodox churches), the religious education of the children implied that they were sometimes evangelized by the younger generation. The word *conversion* as such isn't used in the two Orthodox case studies, yet it is obvious that reconnecting people with the Christian faith is at the heart of Orthodox religious education. Remarkably, especially in the case study on the Russian Orthodox Church (7.5), we can observe that conversion is effected by Christian vestiges in Russian culture. It was through "reading the culture" that some people found faith and aspired to become a servant of the church.

The case studies of Taizé and Sant'Egidio (see chs. 7.3 and 7.4, above) primarily exemplify the models "conversion as discovery" and "conversion as assurance." In the chapter on Taizé we read that through participating in the simplicity of life and in the worship of Christ, young people may, and often do, experience a change in their lives. It is not "aggressive evangelism" or a "hard-sell strategy." No one who comes to Taizé will be pressured to make a choice. Yet, it is through its ministry of worship and community that the hearts of young people are often touched and they discover the significance of the word of God. The mission of Sant'Egidio, however, doesn't shy away from calling its ministry explicitly missional: evangelization is the first goal of their ministry. The gospel is understood as both a gift and a responsibility. It needs to be shared and others are to be invited. It "revitalizes" the faith of church members, yet it also attracts newcomers. The word *conversion*, as such, is not used, yet the elements of discovery and assurance in its ministry are clear.

It is in the articles of Kwabena J. Asamoah-Gyadu and Dawit Olika Ter-fassa, both on reverse mission (see chs. 5.4 and 7.8, above), that we find many references to conversion. Remarkably, the emphasis on conversion in the migrant churches is juxtaposed to a reference to a so-called pre-Enlightenment theology of migrant Christians. They still have, according to "post-Enlighten-ment" Christians, "conservative views of homosexuality, emphasis on conver-sion, and problems related to their focus on spiritual experiences of healing, exorcisms and prophecies" (see 7.8.3, above). Pre- or post-Enlightenment is not the issue here, but conversion is. Indeed, migrant churches have a strong emphasis on conversion. We may wonder if, in practice, this amounts to "con-version as assurance" (a focus on Christian migrants) or to "conversion as turn of life" (a focus on non-Christian migrants). Both have their place in evan-gelistic ministries of migrant churches. The case study on the International Christian Fellowship in Rotterdam shows that the latter ("conversion as turn of life") is their primary model. In other cases, however, the primary type of conversion is actually the assurance model, just as this is the case for ministries of many indigenous old churches.

The Dutch missiologist Jan A. B. Jongeneel refers to this assurance model as "internal mission."[72] He upholds that this model deserves to be recognized as intentional mission that, though primarily focussing on people who share the same religious background, who speak the same language, and who belong to the same ethnic group, invites people to follow Christ and take their place in

---

72. Jan A. B. Jongeneel, "The Mission of Migrant Churches in Europe," *Missiology: An International Review* 31, no. 1 (2003): 29–33; see also Gerrit Noort, "Emerging Migrant Churches in the Neth-erlands: Missiological Challenges and Mission Frontiers," *International Review of Mission* 100, no. 1 (April 2011), 11–12.

the faith community. In our ministries of evangelism we have underestimated the significance of this internal mission. Guiding people toward the rediscovery of faith or toward finding assurance of faith is as much part of the ministry of evangelism as guiding people toward a turn of life.

8.1.5 Conclusion

We started out by asking why there are few references to conversion, even in the case studies. In discussing this we found that the question as such needed rephrasing. Though the term *conversion* has become highly suspect in post-Enlightenment and post-colonial Europe, and though many who are involved in church and mission have strong reservations about using the term, it is clear that religious change (the result of the invitation to turn to God and the related commitment to Christ) is still very much at the heart of Christian mission and evangelism. It is for this reason that in *Mission and Evangelism in Unity Today*, the main preparatory study document of WCC's World Mission Conference in Athens (2000), we read an unequivocal affirmation of conversion as an integral part of mission: "Evangelism, while not excluding the different dimensions of mission, focusses on explicit and intentional voicing of the gospel, including the invitation to personal conversion to a new life in Christ and to discipleship."[73] That the invitation to personal conversion is essential to this document is also shown in paragraphs 14 and 17. Paragraph 14 underscores that "Christians are called through metanoia to have the mind of Christ." This emphasis on *metanoia* implies that conversion is a prerequisite for living a Christlike life. And though we acknowledge that converting people is not something an evangelist can do, as it is the work of the Spirit, we do realize that a prerequisite for conversion is that we "take faith to the streets." That is the calling and privilege of the church: "To tell the story [of Jesus Christ] is the specific privilege of the churches within God's overall mission." *Mission and Evangelism in Unity Today* then continues with an explanation of what the invitation to believe in the triune God entails:

Evangelism includes explication of the gospel . . . as well as an invitation to believe in the triune God, become a disciple of Christ and join the

---

73. World Council of Churches, *Mission and Evangelism in Unity Today* (Geneva: WCC Publications, 2000), 2 (par. 7b). This document is not an official WCC statement on mission and evangelism, but it was adopted by WCC's Commission on World Mission and Evangelism as a study document. See https://www.oikoumene.org/en/resources/documents/other-meetings/mission-and-evangelism/preparatory-paper-01-mission-and-evangelism-in-unity-today.

community of an existing local church. Proclamation of Jesus Christ requires a personal response. The Living Word of God is never external, unrelational, disconnected, but always calling for personal conversion and relational communion. Such a conversion is more than appropriation of a message: it is a commitment to Jesus Christ, imitating his death and resurrection in a very visible and tangible way.[74]

Given this emphasis in ecumenical documents on conversion as commitment to Christ, in its three dimensions of assurance, discovery, and turn of life, one wonders about the observed reservations in some of our case studies to label the ministry as intentional evangelism. Although it is understandable in the context of post-Christianity, we call for a liberation of "evangelism" and to reclaim the central notions of its underlying theology. In a free market and a democracy of ideas, everybody has the right to exercise the right to promote products, views, and convictions. That includes freedom for Christians to invite people to believe in the triune God and share life, as much as it includes the obligation to maintain the highest ethical principles in doing this. People are free to proclaim their views as much as they are free to decline the offer.

When discussing conversion, Andrew Walls uses the metaphor of the "human auditorium."[75] On the theatrical stage we can see the enactment of the drama of life. This drama contains a plot, which Walls calls the "Jesus Act." The act doesn't signify a voice from heaven that stands apart from reality as we know it. It is part of human life, of the human auditorium. This "Jesus Act" is about incarnation and God's salvific will for this world. It has to be responded to. We intend to keep this in mind when we conclude this section on conversion. The gospel invites us to turn to the living God. It is a free offer. But the freedom to accept or decline is not just a matter of religious freedom and individual rights in democratic societies. The evangelistic call to conversion is about God's ultimate word to creation. Being a witness is about compassion and loving solidarity with the "other," but is also about the claim that the gospel reveals divine truth and direction. Ultimately, the call to the nations to choose life in its fullness doesn't reflect human aspirations to improve one's standard of living, but it flows from God's salvific will that all may have life abundantly (John 10:10). It is in the communal life of the sacramental and covenantal community that the promise of the messianic banquet (Is. 25:6)

74. Ibid., par. 17. This paragraph contains a direct quote from *Called to One Hope*, the report of the World Mission Conference in San Salvador (1996).
75. Walls, *Missionary Movement*, 43–44.

is celebrated. This liturgy directly leads to witness of what we have heard and received. The invitation to the nations to turn to Christ and to become disciples is therefore not just another offer in the marketplace of convictions. The Lukan mandate, "Compel people to come in," though certainly not a *carte blanche* to infringe on people's freedom, is a strong reminder that we may reason with people about the truth and ultimacy of God's good news for his creation. As Paul respectfully reasoned with the Athenians in the public square and tried to convince them of the truth of the gospel (Acts 17), so in evangelism we may testify by providing experiential and logical arguments how God's will is good news to Europeans.

8.2 Evangelism and Methods

Stefan Paas

8.2.1 *What is a method?*

According to the online *Merriam-Webster Dictionary*, a method is "a way, technique, or process of or for doing something." It refers to "a body of skills or techniques" that may or may not be applied in "a systematic procedure" or a "systematic plan." So, when we talk about evangelism and methods, we talk about the "how" of evangelism as distinct from its "what" and its "why." If we ask how evangelism can be done, the typical answer would point to certain skills, practices, or techniques that help us to achieve this task. The word *method* is often used as an equivalent for *strategy*, but for more than one reason it is important to differentiate methods and strategies. First, strategies tend to operate on a higher and more abstract level than methods. A strategy usually involves more reflection and long-term planning, and often several methods (techniques, skills) are required to make a strategy work. Second, some concern is justified whether "strategy" would be the right word to use in the context of evangelism, while "methods" simply are inevitable. After all, in any practice the question of *how* we do it cannot be avoided. Evangelism without methods is inconceivable, but it is perfectly possible to think of evangelism as an unstrategic activity.[1]

Although the "how" of evangelism is different from its "what" and "why," they must not be separated. Methods of evangelism are rooted in our ideas of what evangelism is, why we do it, and which purposes should be achieved. Take, for example, the apostle Paul in his first letter to the Corinthians. There he writes:

---

1. Being more long term and purposeful, strategies may (and sometimes do) lead to the instrumentalizing of evangelism. If, for example, it is our strategy to grow the church, we may be less interested in reaching out to the one unique individual around the corner (despite Luke 15:6). Or, if it is our strategy to influence culture (to change the world), we may be too focussed on doing evangelism in places that "matter" (as, for example, cities) and in reaching out to "influential" people. All this tends to corrupt the spirit of true evangelism. There is a place for wise administration and use of resources, and this will include some strategic planning, but altogether it is difficult to reconcile strategic thinking with Spirit-led, authentic, cruciform evangelism.

When I came to you, brothers and sisters, I did not come proclaiming the mystery of God to you in lofty words or wisdom. For I decided to know nothing among you except Jesus Christ, and him crucified. And I came to you in weakness and in fear and in much trembling. My speech and my proclamation were not with plausible words of wisdom, but with a demonstration of the Spirit and of power, so that your faith might rest not on human wisdom but on the power of God. (1 Cor. 2:1-5)

Clearly, the apostle sees a relationship between the "what" of his gospel (the crucified Christ) and the method by which he proclaims this gospel. He takes his distance from popular expectations about public speaking, refusing to impress people by a brilliant display of rhetoric, and choosing a humble, "cruciform" style instead. Thus, he does not just *talk* about the message of salvation through the cross, but he *models* it through his presence. This is merely one example out of many showing that the "how" of evangelism must reflect the "what" (salvation through Christ). Of course, the same is true for the "why." If evangelism is motivated by the deep love of God for God's creation, made visible and tangible in the life of Jesus, then evangelism should represent this loving and humble service in its methods. Certainly, in evangelism the end does not justify the means!

In this chapter we concentrate on methods, techniques, and skills used in the practice of evangelism. The case studies presented in the previous chapter offer a wealth of examples. Here, we place these methods in their biblical and theological context, we discuss some ways to categorize them, and we conclude with a number of ethical reflections on the use of methods in evangelism.

8.2.2 Evangelistic methods in the New Testament

Essentially, evangelism is an act of communication. If people communicate the gospel to other human beings, they are evangelizing. This simple observation should make us somewhat careful to apply the word *method* too soon. After all, communication is one of the most natural things people do. It is usually spontaneous; it happens without much reflection or planning. We are social beings; we love to talk about what concerns us or what makes us happy. Therefore, it sounds like overtheorizing too talk about a "methodology" when people share their faith with others in acts of ordinary conversation.[2] Most

2. Reversely, "overtheorizing" also happens when we call certain New Testament practices a "methodology" without taking into account that these practices simply were part of the culture, or not optional, anyway. A well-known example is the so-called house church. Modern house-church

people, as long as they do not leave their cultural comfort zone, are deeply steeped in all kinds of communicative behaviour which they use without much thinking. We talk with our relatives, we teach our children, we bond with our friends, we eat together, play together, work together, and so on. If something surprising happens to us—a "tiding of great joy"—we will normally try to involve others in this experience, especially our loved ones. Talk about "methods" starts if such spontaneous sharing becomes difficult somehow. This may happen when we enter other (sub)cultures with different conversational habits, or when our message is likely to meet resistance (as, for example, with people from other religions or deeply secularized people). In that case we need to reflect more carefully on how we bring the message across, and that is where "methods" begin to play a role. Thus, the question of evangelistic methods comes up where evangelism is part of a boundary-crossing mission or outreach to those who are religiously or culturally different from us. Nevertheless, we should be aware of the fact that by far the most common form of evangelism happens between people who know and like each other, and share each other's lives through all sorts of natural relationships.

The first Christians were Jews, and their evangelism was directed mostly to fellow Jews. Most of their evangelism was spontaneous and made use of generally shared conversational habits, or contexts for discussion (cf. Acts 5:42). The synagogue was such a context. In the book of Acts we read that Paul and Barnabas went to the synagogues whenever they had a chance and shared the gospel. When a male stranger arrived at a synagogue meeting, he would normally be invited to read from the scriptures and share his insights with the audience. Apparently, Paul and his companions used this invitation to evangelize among the Jews (Acts 13:13-43, etc.). Often, such preaching would result in follow-up activities in smaller groups where the participants discussed what they had heard. For example, in Corinth Paul "would argue in the synagogue, every Sabbath, and would try to convince Jews and Greeks" (Acts 18:4; cf. 19:8). The Greek word that is used for "argue" is *dialegomai*, from which the English word *dialogue* is derived. So, what we find here and in related texts is a context where people who share essentially the same cultural and religious values discuss the new reality of God as it has been revealed in God's Messiah, Jesus. In

---

movements often assert that their "method" of planting small-scale, informal churches in people's homes is supported by the New Testament, as if the early Christians had the option of building larger, formal churches, and as if households in Hellenistic culture were anything similar to modern Western private homes. See Eckhard J. Schnabel, *Urchristliche Mission* (Wuppertal: R. Brockhaus Verlag, 2002), 1243–47.

Ephesus Paul did the same for a period of three months (Acts 19:8), but when resistance grew among his fellow Jews, he separated from the synagogue and took residence in "the lecture hall of Tyrannus" (obviously a public space for education), where he "argued [*dialegomenos*] daily" for a period of two years (Acts 19:9-10).

This combination of public preaching and small-group discussion and instruction seems to have been Paul's favoured approach of evangelism, at least among the Jews. Apparently, if this process was not interrupted by persecution the period of instruction and dialogue could extend for some months or even years. Another example of evangelism through these natural relationships is Paul's contact in Corinth with the Jewish couple Aquila and Priscilla. We read in Acts 18:1-3 that they had been expelled from Rome by the anti-Jewish measures of the emperor Claudius. There is no indication that they were Christians already (or that they weren't, for that matter), but it is tempting to think that Paul evangelized them. Surely, they were of the same profession as Paul (tentmakers), and they lived and worked together for some time (Acts 18:3). It is quite inconceivable that conversations about the Lord would not have been part of their daily relationship. Be that as it may, they were certainly Christians somewhat later when the new convert Apollos came to the city. He was a well-educated man from Alexandria who "had been instructed [*katechemenos*] in the Way of the Lord; and he spoke with burning enthusiasm and taught accurately the things concerning Jesus, though he knew only the baptism of John" (Acts 18:25). Aquila and Priscilla take up the task of instructing Apollos "more accurately" (Acts 18:26). If we can speak about "methods" here, it is clear that teaching (instruction, catechesis) was part of the first Christians' evangelistic approach. As early as the 2nd century this resulted in an extended period of initiation into the Christian faith, in the practice of the catechumenate. Today's "Rite for the Christian Initiation of Adults" in the Roman Catholic Church continues the memory of this early-church practice, while late-modern seeker courses such as Alpha or Emmaus return to the catechumenate for their inspiration.

We may safely assume, therefore, that public speaking, small-group discussion, daily conversation at home and in the workplace, and one-to-one (or small-group) catechesis all belonged to the evangelistic practice of the early Christians in ordinary circumstances. Obviously, evangelism was normally done through existing relationships, and by Christians who worked together. We find the same practice in the ministry of Jesus. He proclaimed the kingdom of God by public preaching and miracles, instructed his disciples in private, and had one-on-one conversations with all kinds of people—such as, for example, the Samaritan woman at Jacob's Well (John 4). In the famous passage in Luke 10:1-12 Jesus sends out 70 disciples in pairs (underlining, again, the relational character of evangelism). He tells them to accept invitations and to become guests at peoples' homes. By travelling light and by being good guests (who wish peace, who eat what is given to them, who minister to the sick, and who do not overextend their host's hospitality) they will receive room to share the gospel of the kingdom. Again, we may assume that this simple practice characterized many of the (largely anonymous) early Christian evangelists who travelled around the Roman Empire.

Of course, much more can and should be said about early Christian evangelistic practice than can be done in this brief section.[3] We find examples where the activity is more instantaneous, seemingly provoked by circumstances. In Acts 14:8-18 Paul and Barnabas heal a paralytic in Lystra, upon which the crowd starts to bring sacrifices to the apostles. Immediately, Paul and Barnabas "rushed out into the crowd," shouting (*krazontes*) a brief evangelistic message. In Acts 17:15-34 Paul brings an unplanned visit to Athens. He walks around in the city, gets "deeply distressed" by the view of so many statues of idols, and soon runs into a somewhat heated debate (*sumballein*: disputing) with "Epicurean and Stoic philosophers." This encounter results in an invitation to address the gathered crowd of curious "Athenians and foreigners" at the Areopagus in a more formal speech. Paul's speech differs from his other speeches in the book of Acts, especially those delivered in the synagogue in Pisidian Antioch. He does not concentrate on the scriptures of the First Testament, nor on Jewish history, and when he quotes he does so from Greek poets. In terms of methodology, Paul seems to have been aware of his quite different audience, and to have thought through what would be the best way to approach them.[4] This reflects his comments in 1 Corinthians 9:19-23, where he states that he "has become all things to all people, that I may by all means save some." More or less the same sensitivity can be observed in Acts 16:3, where Paul circumcised his fellow worker Timothy, "because of the Jews."

The epistles in the New Testament also throw light on early Christian evangelistic practice. We may think, for example, of 1 Corinthians 9:19, where

---

3. For an extensive overview of early Christian missionary "vision, strategy and methods," cf. ibid., 424–539.

4. Cf. Dean E. Flemming, *Contextualization in the New Testament: Patterns for Theology and Mission* (Downers Grove, IL: InterVarsity, 2005).

Paul states that he has made himself "a slave" (*edoulosa*) in the service of evangelism. This is a clear reference to Jesus Christ becoming a slave (*doulos*) for us (e.g., Phil. 2:7). Again, this emphasizes his deep commitment that the manner of the evangelist should reflect their message. In Colossians 4:2-4 we read about the importance of prayer and intercession in evangelism. The first letter of Peter offers some profound insights into early Christian evangelism. What about situations, for example, when it is not possible to give any verbal witness? Such was the case for Christian slaves of pagan masters, or for Christian wives of pagan husbands, who often did not get the room to talk about their faith in Jesus. Peter admonishes them "to accept the authority of your husbands, so that, even if some of them do not obey the word, they may be won over without a word by their wives' conduct, when they see the purity and reverence of your lives" (1 Pet. 3:1-2). In a context of suffering, when "normal" ways of evangelism are hampered, it is important to "always be ready to make your defense to anyone who demands from you an accounting for the hope that is in you; yet do it with gentleness and reverence" (1 Pet. 3:15-16).

Finally, it is crucial to see how evangelism for the first Christians was a thoroughly *charismatic* activity. The apostle Paul, for example, summarizes his own missionary work in Asia as follows: "For I will not venture to speak of anything except what Christ has accomplished through me to win obedience from the Gentiles, by word and deed, by the power of signs and wonders, by the power of the Spirit of God, so that from Jerusalem and as far around as Illyricum I have fully proclaimed the good news [*euangellion*] of Christ" (Rom. 15:18-19). Apparently, for Paul to "*fully* proclaim" the gospel (*euangellion*) meant to combine verbal witness with "the power of signs and wonders." This points us back, again, to the earthly ministry of Jesus who was deeply conscious of the Holy Spirit, who challenged the demonic powers, and healed the sick. In the book of Acts, the healing of the sick and the casting out of demons is a normal ingredient in the practice of evangelism. We also find a constant awareness of the Holy Spirit guiding the work of evangelism, both in terms of geographical outreach and in terms of conquering resistance among audiences, and giving boldness and joy to the evangelists themselves. Chapters 2–5 in the book of Acts are a continuing witness to this particular work of the Spirit. Apart from all the miracles and signs which are done through the apostles and other Christians, there are three "hinge passages" describing the Spirit guiding the work of evangelism. One of them we find in Acts 8:26-40, where the evangelist Philip is led by the Spirit to meet an important man from

Ethiopia who is interested in the Jewish religion. This event foreshadows the breakthrough of the gospel to non-Jews, something which is articulated with even more clarity in Acts 10, where the apostle Peter is convinced by the Spirit that he should call nobody "profane or unclean." Another crucial moment of the Spirit's guidance we encounter in Acts 16:6-10. Here, the Spirit prevents the apostles from further travelling through Asia, and calls them through a dream to cross over to Europe. Another bridge is crossed, now from the East to the West. Finally, when Paul and his guards (who were to take him to Rome to stand trial for the emperor) shipwreck on the coast of Malta, Paul receives a dream. An angel appears to him and says: "Do not be afraid, Paul; you must stand before the emperor; and indeed, God has granted safety to all those who are sailing with you" (Acts 27:24). Here, the Spirit assures Paul that he will be able to evangelize in the very heart of the empire, the centre of the world.

Summarizing all this, we can say that early Christian evangelism as it appears in the New Testament reflects Jesus' ministry of sharing the good news of the kingdom. It is rooted in commonly accepted habits of public speaking, conversation, dialogue, and teaching. It is deeply charismatic, in the sense that the evangelists felt themselves dependent on the guiding and equipping work of the Spirit, while they expected signs and wonders to accompany the preaching of the gospel. Also, we find in the New Testament reflections of more difficult and challenging situations, in which persecution is real and sometimes speaking is not possible. In situations like these even more emphasis is laid on the importance of "walking the talk," and on persistent prayer for "open doors" (Col. 4:1-3).

8.2.3 Evangelistic methods in Europe
Relationship as core practice

The New Testament practice of spontaneous gospel sharing, rooted in generally accepted habits of conviviality (*convivencia, Konvivenz*), conversation, and dialogue, can be found in many places today, especially in the non-Western world. In Europe, however, the story seems somewhat different. The case studies presented in this book, though witnessing to vibrant evangelism, all reflect on the difficult cultural situation in Europe. Part of the problems experienced with evangelism lie in the past, when European Christianity had become implicated in all sorts of power plays. This creates a certain wariness around Christianity, which is a serious impediment for evangelism—both on the side of the evangelists and the evangelized. Another part may lie in a lack of conviction and spontaneous joy (*Entdeckersfreude*) that so often characterizes individuals and communities who experience the liberating truth of the gospel for the first time. To some extent Christianity is old news in Europe; people think they know what it amounts to; they think they know what the Bible says; and so on. Even for many Christians their faith just does not seem important enough to share it with others, sometimes at the cost of social ostracism or worse. And finally, a cause of this lack of spontaneous evangelistic zeal may be found in the fact that many European Christians have been raised in Christian families, churched communities, and Christianized local cultures. Often, they live in predominantly Christian environments, and most if not all of their friends are Christians. In other words, they lack the kind of natural connections through relatives, friendships, work, and leisure activities that helped the first Christians (and many Christians today) to share their faith in natural, unforced ways. Therefore, they need "programmes" and "methods" to do this. Sometimes, they may expect too much of new skills and techniques when what is required is a simple commitment to hospitality and friendships outside their immediate comfort zone.

An excellent example of this can be found in Dawit Olika's chapter on reverse mission (see ch. 7.8, above), which contains many examples of evangelistic methods. Taking his point of departure in a description of classical "street preaching" (which apparently no longer "works" in his Sweden), he advocates evangelism through "storytelling" (see ch. 7.8.4, above). Family life and church life are places of welcome and invitation, where the faith can be shared in all kinds of purposeful or unplanned conversations. People enter these communities because of friendship, all sorts of diaconal and service activities, or simply as guests at the table. Children invite their friends to play in their homes and to join the family for dinner. If the family has a devotional life, especially around the meals, these friends will one way or another get something out of it. The same is true for church life, which in migrant churches often is much more than what Europeans see as "church" life. The church is an anchor point for all kinds of meetings, where people from all beliefs and convictions can feel welcome, such as "student fellowships, international coffee hours, and celebrations of some important days like AIDS Day, Women's Day, and United Nations Day" (see ch. 7.8.2, above). Clearly, if conversions happen, they almost always happen through such contacts of friendship, in which the mercy of God can take shape in loving embraces, the sharing of time and food, honest attention to the needs of others, and having fun together.

It is important to underline, once again, that all this can hardly be called a "method." Essentially, it is nothing more than the fostering of natural human relationships, while being unembarrassed about the Christian faith. Or, in other words, it amounts to opening up our private lives for others, and talking about our deepest thoughts and feelings when the opportunity presents itself. Of course, this may very well be connected with more formal approaches of evangelism, such as the Alpha Course or catechesis around baptisms and church weddings. The bottom line, however, is a rich vision of human togetherness in which we are not shy about what ultimately concerns us. This is the core practice of evangelism, and nothing much will happen without it.

Discussion of methods

There is a wealth of skills and approaches used in the practice of evangelism. They may be categorized in different ways. A traditional categorization differentiates between "centripetal" and "centrifugal" approaches of evangelism. "Centripetal" (a combination of "centre" and the Greek word for "searching") means "going toward the centre," and it refers to practices that emphasize invitation and welcome within the circle of Christians. "Centrifugal" approaches, on the other hand, are about "going from the centre" (a combination of "centre" and the Latin word for "fleeing from"). They refer to practices that emphasize going out into the world and looking for a welcome among those who are not Christians. Often, these two directions are summed up as "come to us" vs. "go to them" (see Francis Brienen in ch. 6.2.1, above). Sometimes, this also implies an assessment ("go to them" being the better, more "missional" approach), but it is important to stress that both approaches are rooted in the Bible and in Christian tradition, and that both are needed in order to meet the challenges of a secularizing continent.

In the case studies we find both directions exemplified. We already mentioned Dawit Olika's contribution, which shows a richness of welcoming and inviting approaches. Francis Brienen mentions a number of centripetal practices in chapter 6, such as "Back to Church Sunday" in the United Kingdom (invite one friend to join you for this special Sunday in September, see ch. 6.2.1, above), inquiry and nurture courses (such as Alpha, see ch. 6.2.3, above), and the New Evangelization of the Roman Catholic Church, which in Europe essentially adopts a model of attraction rather than considering Europe as a classical "mission field" where missionaries must be "sent out" (see ch. 6.2.1 and Donna Orsuto's contribution on new evangelization in ch. 5.2, above).

In her chapter on this New Evangelization, Donna Orsuto points out that the Catholic approach requires an emphasis on the quality of Christian individual and community life, if this invitation to outsiders (particularly "those who have fallen away," ch. 5.2.2) is to be effective. The crucial word, used by several popes, is "witness," something which must happen in words and in lives. Although this takes shape primarily in practices of hospitality, it is important to add Pope Francis's emphasis on going forth from our own comfort zone in order to reach out to the poor, "who are privileged recipients of the gospel." Being a witness to Christ thus includes striving for justice and looking after the needs of the poor. Finally, Pope Francis emphasizes the urgent need for Christian unity as the most crucial witness to the world. These accents on the quality of Christian community life, outreach to the underprivileged, and working toward Christian unity, are also found in other traditions, as Francis Brienen's reflection on "engaging approaches" makes especially clear (cf. ch. 6.3, above).

While welcoming methods stress the importance of being good hosts, centrifugal approaches invite Christians on a journey of learning to become guests themselves. An example might be the International Christian Fellowship in Rotterdam (the Netherlands). This church has grown out of the "outgoing" initiative of an evangelist who simply could not find ways to bring his Muslim friends to church, even if they were interested in Christianity. Rather than being an academic hospital like many older churches, the International Christian Fellowship wanted to be a "field hospital," a Christian community presence amidst (often illegal) immigrants (cf. ch. 7.2.2, above). After the church more or less got "settled," a new initiative was set up in the form of a diaconal programme, House of Hope. In this way the church tries to keep its original movement toward the world "in flow," rather than falling back on good old habits of being as welcoming as possible. Reflection on who is *not* there on Sundays or who is *not* in contact with the community of the church drives such innovation. An older and much more famous example of this practice is the community of Taizé (ch. 7.4, above). Being as welcoming and inviting as one can imagine, the Taizé community originated from the personal quest of Brother Roger, who as a Protestant wanted to tap into the ancient monastic traditions. His plan, however, was never to withdraw from the world but, rather, to build a place from which Christians could be sent out into the world. Since the 1960s the community thus developed its best-known ministry, toward the secularized youth of Europe, building Christian presence within the emerging youth culture.

Two other initiatives stand out as even more experimentative and "outgoing," namely the work of Street Pastors in Dalston/London (United Kingdom), presented by Francis Brienen in chapter 7.1, and the online community "MyChurch," discussed by Gerrit Noort in chapter 7.2 (both above). Both initiatives do not aim so much at the formation of a (flesh-and-blood) Christian community, but they focus on sending out creative Christians in order to serve the needs of people in the "nighttime economy" of the city or those on the worldwide web, surfing for a sense of belonging and meaning. They go where people are rather than inviting them to come where Christians like to be, and they try to serve them there. At the same time, these outgoing initiatives illustrate the challenges Christianity faces in a secularizing, post-Christian culture, especially when they become guests rather than hosts. The Street Pastors' initiative in London explicitly states that it is "not out to evangelize," although prayer is offered on request. This makes sense, considering that these Christians are on someone else's turf, looking for acceptance, being dependent on the goodwill of their hosts. So, they are simply there to serve in the name of Jesus, without hidden agendas, and to see what comes out of it. They do not recruit for any particular church, but they represent "THE church," working together as Christians from different traditions. The more explicit message of the gospel is translated in five core values that guide the Street Pastors in their work, and that can be communicated more easily toward a secularized public—including local authorities. The point that they are making is that Christians, in order to be seen and heard at all, must leave their Christian subculture and find out all over again what it is that makes people tick, what concerns them, and how they communicate. This entails vulnerability and a certain theological (if not physical) risk taking (cf. ch. 7.1.4, above).

Finally, there are evangelistic methods that are not so much about inviting people into the Christian family or going out to find them where they are. They may be termed with an early Christian term as "preparational methods" (*praeparatio evangelica*), and they focus on building and sustaining a culture of Christian literacy among the wider public. In biblical terms one might call these methods "sowing" rather than "harvesting." Jesus' Parable of the Sower shows that most of the seed that is sown will not result in any harvest (conversions, belonging to the church), but, nevertheless, it must be sown if only to keep a background culture intact for the preaching of the gospel. After all, if people lose the language and cultural repertoire by which talking about God makes sense in the first place, evangelism will become very difficult. An example of this type of "pre-evangelism" is "the Passion Project" in the Netherlands (cf. ch. 6.3.1, above). More or less in this category we might also locate the approach of evangelism as education in the Orthodox areas of Europe (cf. chs. 7.5 and 7.6, above). Assuming an ancient link between "enlightenment" (or "civilization") and evangelism there is a strong emphasis on what we might call the teaching of a Christian worldview, in connection to broad areas of life, including the arts and literature. All this happens against the background of "Byzantine culture and heritage, which was shaped by Christian faith." This deep link between "being cultured" and "being Christian" has evangelized many members of the intelligentsia, which in turn helped foster a climate that is favourable toward Christianity, especially after the decline of communism. In an environment that is increasingly secularizing, this opportunity to educate a wider audience into Christian beliefs and values may be an advantage. It is a privilege that must be carefully exercised, though, as it depends, at least to some extent, on good relationships with the secular powers, rendering the church vulnerable to criticisms of being the religious department of worldly power. Also, additional methods of evangelism will be needed, as education alone cannot replace hospitality, witness, and the sharing of faith in personal relationships.

As a concluding comment, we may note the absence of "charismatic" dimensions in the case studies presented in the previous chapters. This is not to say that these practices do not include any "signs and wonders," but the writers do not elaborate on them or even mention them. This is remarkable, given the definite emphasis on these elements in the New Testament and their importance in evangelistic practices in the non-Western world. It may be true that many Christians in the West (irrespective of their own cultural background) have become a bit embarrassed about the counterfeit experiences and miracles that so often accompany the more charismatic streams in worldwide Christianity. This may betray a modern empiricist bias, however, because why should we be more embarrassed about faked miracles than about untruthful words? Unfortunately, human life is full of fraud and wishful thinking, and religions are no exception to this rule. Yet, this is no reason to become shy about the Holy Spirit, as long as the Spirit's work does not become part of a "method" or a "strategy." The Spirit goes like the wind, wherever he wills (John 3:8); he cannot be forced into a methodology. The Spirit's gifts are truly *gifts*; they are not rights. Also, it is important to stress that the Spirit works in human inventions, in medical science, and other kinds of wisdom. In a context where there is excellent medical care, it would amount to magical thinking to ask the Spirit to do by miracle what she has provided for by giving wisdom to generations of doctors. If evangelism addresses complete human beings, however—body, soul, and relationships—there is no doubt that it should be accompanied by expectations of the Holy Spirit working in healing and restoration. Often, this will happen through means that we can explain by science, and sometimes it will happen through means that we cannot (yet?) explain. Either way, it is a reason to praise God.

8.2.4 Concluding theological and ethical reflections
New Testament guidelines
In the New Testament we find little explicit reflection on the ethics of evangelism. There are a few remarks here and there, though, that can help us to develop a framework for the assessment of contemporary evangelistic practices. Without going into too much detail, it is important to remember once again the crucial notion that the style and manner of evangelism and the attitude of the evangelist should reflect the message of the crucified king Jesus. It should be done "with gentleness and reverence" (1 Pet. 3:16). In the same vein, the epistle to the Colossians says, "Conduct yourselves wisely toward outsiders, making the most of the time. Let your speech always be gracious, seasoned with salt, so that you may know how you ought to answer everyone" (Col. 4:5-6). One could summarize such texts as: be modest, honest, and authentic; try to avoid being dull, yet do not try to impress others with grand rhetoric (or, in our times perhaps, with flashy video clips); and, above all, remain focussed on what Christianity is all about. In short, do not "spin" the gospel; the good news can work for itself. Jesus' long conversation with the Samaritan woman at Jacob's Well (John 4) may be a splendid example of this evangelistic style. Although these texts do not give us much information as to which methods are allowed, they certainly indicate which methods are suspicious. Evangelism is there to serve and liberate people, not to manipulate and overpower them.

The New Testament also highlights the decisive role of prayer in the work of witness (cf. Col. 4:2). This role has been spelled out in so many texts that it is impossible and unnecessary to repeat them here. Time and again the apostles in the book of Acts bow their knees to give thanks to God, or to ask God for directions. Time and again the apostles urge their churches to remain persistent in prayer. Evangelism is an extremely vulnerable work; it puts us out in the open, it draws us out of our comfort zone. It confronts us with the extreme insufficiency of our efforts in the work of witness; like no other work it points us toward the Spirit, who is the true Persuader (John 16:6-11). There may be no other work that helps us to see more our day-to-day dependence on God's grace, and there may be no work that helps us more to see the abundance of God's love. Evangelism is a work of constant prayer and praise. No evangelistic method, regardless of how clever it has been designed, can replace prayer.

Finally, the New Testament gives some interesting insights in the problem of competition in the work of evangelism. Today, this competition is known under the label of "proselytism." This term is explained in different ways, but here we mean the kind of evangelism that has members of (other) churches as its target (cf. ch. 8.1.3, above). Of course, the New Testament is written in an age of Christian pioneering, so we cannot apply it directly to the European context of today. It is important, however, to stress that the apostle Paul did not want to evangelize where other evangelists had worked before him, "so that I do not build on someone else's foundation" (Rom. 15:20). This is a good warning against a sectarian type of evangelism that depends on a negative judgment of other Christians and churches for its own justification. On the other hand, Paul himself was quite relaxed about other evangelists coming to places where he had worked, such as Apollos in Corinth (1 Cor. 3:1-9). He might have remembered Jesus' word: "Whoever is not against you is for you" (Luke 9:50). When he hears that, during his own imprisonment, others have preached where he worked, even criticizing Paul, he shrugs his shoulders: "What does it matter? Just this, that Christ is proclaimed in every way, whether out of false motives or true; and in that I rejoice" (Phil. 1:18). This may be a good advice for churches that may guard "their" turf too zealously, to the extent of appealing to their governments for juridical measures against their "competitors."

Words, words, words?

There is no doubt that evangelism implies verbal witness. Nowhere in the New Testament nor in the lives of the great missionaries do we get the impression that it is possible to proclaim the gospel without "naming the Name." Among Christians there has often been dispute, however, how words and deeds relate. In terms of methods, should we always look for verbal witness and see anything else as "instrumental" at best? Two insights from the New Testament may help us to find more agreement here.

First, the strong charismatic element in biblical evangelism should make us consider to what extent the apostles had a holistic approach of mission. We do not find any "competition" between words and deeds, between verbal proclamation, on the one hand, and "signs and wonders," on the other. Paul writes about "fully proclaiming the gospel," and he clearly means that words and deeds of healing and exorcism are all part of this full gospel. Thus, a more charismatic approach of evangelism might restore this ancient and natural connection between words and deeds. Verbal methods and other methods should go together.

Second, it seems that there is some difference in the New Testament between those who are explicitly sent out on a mission (apostles, evangelists), and other Christians. When the apostles address their churches, they expect from them a life of integrity and discipleship, and they connect this with a challenge to give verbal account of their faith to everyone who asks about it (cf. 1 Pet. 3:15, etc.). This reminds us of the Sermon on the Mount, where Jesus tells his disciples to be a city on a hill, that is, to live exemplary lives. He adds: "Let your light shine before others, so that they may see your good works and give glory to your Father in heaven" (Matt. 5:16). Of course, this does not mean that Christians who are not apostles or evangelists should never take the initiative to talk about their faith, but it seems that they are expected first and foremost to *live* their faith, and then be ready when this provokes questions. In terms of verbal evangelistic methods, this means that they will only be effective if they are "secondary," that is, if they follow up on the good works of Christian communities.

8.2.5 Conclusions

Thinking about methods in evangelism begins with the core insight that it is all about sharing our lives with others, either by receiving others or by going to them. Evangelism begins and ends with true human relationships. Evangelistic methodology should be doxological, in that it praises God and respects God's sovereignty. Therefore, it cannot be manipulative, as this would betray a spirit of fear (righteousness by works). Evangelism should be done in the mindset of Jesus, who became a servant. It should reflect his life, his ministry, and the cross on which he died. Evangelism will be bold, because it testifies to a risen Lord. Finally, it is intrinsically connected to good deeds, to such an extent that "fully evangelizing" cannot mean anything else than addressing the fullness of human life: body, spirit, soul, and relationships.

8.3 Evangelism and Ecclesiology

Knud Jørgensen

8.3.1 Introduction: Paradigm shift

The church in the landscape of my youth was a yellow building where on Sunday morning we listened to a sermon and occasionally celebrated holy communion. In addition, my parents were active in the Inner Mission movement in Denmark, and they prayed for and donated funds to foreign mission. They modelled a life where faith found expression in lifestyle and care for others. But I cannot recall having heard about "evangelism" as such. If so, it must have been in relation to the InterVarsity movement. At the university where I studied theology there was never any mention of evangelism—or of mission, for that matter.

When I was sent to Ethiopia in the 1970s my world was turned upside down. I became part of a church with few buildings, but where Christ-centred preaching called for conversion and faith, where the vitality of the congregation attracted outsiders, where the church was open to the work of the Holy Spirit within a broad charismatic understanding, and where conversion, rebirth, surrender, and empowerment were interwoven in equipping the people of God for service.[1]

The church was far from flawless; there was power struggle, ethnic strife, control from above, male dominance, and fear from below. In the midst of this brokenness was an evangelizing church where evangelists and lay leaders modelled the way. I experienced a paradigm shift, from a church with mission as an added activity and with evangelism as a "foreign word," to a view of church as God's people on the move, trusting the word of God and enlivened by God's Spirit.

In the following section I will unfold this paradigm shift. First, I will show the interconnectedness between evangelism, mission, and church and briefly

---

1. Agne Norlander, *Väckelse och växtvärk i Etiopien* (Stockholm: EFS-Förlaget, 1997); Knud Jørgensen, "Trenger kirken omvendelse? På vei mot en misjonal ekklesiologi," in Tormod Engelsviken and Kjell Olav Sannes, eds., *Hva vil det si å være kirke? Kirkens vesen og oppdrag* (Trondheim: Tapir Academic Press, 2004), 51–68.

review some main ecclesial traditions in relation to evangelism. Second, I will look at mission as a foundational ecclesial category and describe forms of missionary engagement in relation to the local congregation. And, finally, I shall draw a picture of what I view as "attractive" churches.

8.3.2 Evangelism, mission, church

> Jesus calls all his disciples to be one family among the nations, a reconciled fellowship in which all sinful barriers are broken down through his reconciling grace. . . . the Church is the community of the reconciled who no longer live for themselves, but for the Saviour who loved them and gave himself for them.[2]

> Through Christ in the Holy Spirit, God indwells the church, empowering and energizing its members. Thus mission becomes for Christians an urgent inner compulsion (1 Cor. 9:16) and even a test and criterion for authentic life in Christ, rooted in the profound demands of Christ's love, to invite others to share in the fullness of life Jesus came to bring.[3]

These two quotes, taken from *The Cape Town Commitment* and *Together towards Life*, serve to underline that participating in God's mission should be natural for all Christians and all churches, not only for particular individuals or specialized groups. Evangelism is an essential dimension of the total activity of the church. We may view it as the core of the church's mission, a mission which, however, is wider than evangelism. The important thing in this connection is not the actual definition of evangelism, but to stress that evangelism cannot be isolated from the rest of the ministry of the church. Evangelism, mission, and church belong together in the same basic tapestry.[4]

To use a phrase coined by Marshall McLuhan, "the medium is the message": the church, the community that evangelizes, is in itself a manifestation of the good news it proclaims through witness (*martyria*), word (*kerygma*), deed (*diakonia*), fellowship (*koinonia*), and worship (*leitourgia*).[5] The very

2. The Lausanne Movement, *The Cape Town Commitment* (Peabody, MA: Hendrickson Publishers, 2011), 27.
3. World Council of Churches, *Together towards Life: Mission and Evangelism in Changing Landscapes* (Geneva: WCC Publications, 2013), 25.
4. David J. Bosch, *Transforming Mission: Paradigm Shifts in Theology of Mission* (Maryknoll, NY: Orbis, 1991), 412.
5. The International Missionary Council (IMC) used *kerygma* and *koinonia* in 1947; Prof. Dr J. C.

being of the church has evangelistic significance, to the extent that we may talk about "the evangelizing church" in the same manner that we talk about "the missional church." One of several implications is that the call to conversion (cf. ch. 8.1, above), as an essential component in evangelism, must begin with the repentance of those who issue this invitation.

To this should be added another foundational component: receiving Christ as Saviour and Lord means to become a living member of his community, the church. "Evangelism is the proclamation of the historical, biblical Christ as Saviour and Lord, with a view to persuading people to come to him personally and so be reconciled to God. . . . The results of evangelism include obedience to Christ, incorporation into his church and responsible service in the world."[6] The point is not to advocate church extension as such, but to emphasize that "discipling," as the key focus of the Great Commission, implies to become part of the community of two or more where Christ is present. Church planting, the multiplication of local congregations and incorporation are at the heart of mission and evangelism.[7] Without the church there can be no evangelism or mission. I am not sure which comes first—church or evangelism—but I am convinced that one must lead to the other. The church as a local community of believers witnesses to what God has done, is doing, and will do; and those who hear, respond to, and obey the witness to join the community of disciples, whatever form or (mission-) shape this community may take:[8] "Evangelism is sharing one's faith and conviction with other people and inviting them to discipleship, whether or not they adhere to other religious traditions . . . we can

Hoekendijk added *diakonia* in 1950; the CWME consultation in Willingen, 1952, accepted the threefold formula and added *martyria* as overarching concept (cf. J. C. Hoekendijk, "The Church in Missionary Thinking," *International Review of Missions* 41 (1952): 324ff.) See Bosch, *Transforming Mission*, 512, for *martyria* as (unfolding in) *kerygma*, *koinonia*, and *diakonia*. See also Willingen reports on *missio Dei* and *missio ecclesiae; leitourgia* was added later. WCC, *Together*, uses the five words in juxtaposition; see par. 85 and 86.

6. The Lausanne Movement, *The Lausanne Covenant* (Lausanne, 1974), par. 4.

7. See World Council of Churches, *Mission and Evangelism: An Ecumenical Affirmation* (Geneva: WCC Publications, 1982), par. 25: "It is at the heart of Christian mission to foster the multiplication of local congregations in every human community. The planting of the seed of the gospel will bring forward a people gathered around the Word and sacraments and called to announce God's revealed purpose."

8. Cf. WCC, *Mission*, second part of par. 25: "Thanks to the faithful witness of disciples through the ages, churches have sprung up in practically every country. This task of sowing the seed needs to be continued until there is, in every human community, a cell of the kingdom, a church confessing Jesus Christ and in his name serving his people. The building up of the church in every place is essential to the gospel. The vicarious work of Christ demands the presence of a vicarious people. A vital instrument for the fulfillment of the missionary vocation of the church is the local congregation."

still affirm that the Spirit calls us all towards an understanding of evangelism which is grounded in the life of the local church where worship (*leiturgia*) is inextricably linked to witness (*martyria*), service (*diakonia*), and fellowship (*koinonia*)."[9]

8.3.3 Ecclesial traditions and evangelism

Ecclesial traditions may share a common, or at least converging, heritage in such issues as apostolicity and catholicity; their interpretation of the heritage may differ, but they all claim to stand on the foundation of the apostles. The older traditions (Eastern Orthodox, Roman Catholic, Reformation churches) are more open in terms of confession and membership, while the free-church tradition emphasizes the idea of "the believers' church." Older churches emphasize community and the communal dimension, while newer churches pay more attention to the individual's responsibility. This may also be seen in their concept of ministry and evangelism. For the older churches, structures, preaching, and sacraments are foundational. Younger churches place more emphasis on the call to conversion and the response of faith. Reformation churches are placed in the middle.[10]

In traditions with a eucharistic ecclesiology and where the heart of church and mission lies in the sacramental life, God's people are those gathered for the eucharist, and *theosis* (deification) becomes central. Here, evangelism is centripetal: people are to be drawn to the centre of worship and eucharist, and mission becomes "liturgy after the Liturgy."[11] The faithful go out in peace / in mission after they have experienced a glimpse of the kingdom in their eucharistic gathering. Mission is therefore the outcome, rather than the origin, of the church.

Roman Catholics refer to "evangelization" as *missio ad gentes* ("mission to the peoples"), directed to those who do not know Christ. In addition, the concept "new evangelization" stands for pastoral outreach to those who no longer practice the Christian faith (cf. ch. 5.2 by Donna Orsuto, above).[12]

---

9. WCC, *Together*, par. 83 (31).

10. Veli-Matti Kärkkäinen, *An Introduction to Ecclesiology: Ecumenical, Historical, and Global Perspectives* (Downers Grove, IL: InterVarsity, 2002), 90ff.

11. See Ion Bria, *The Liturgy after the Liturgy: Mission and Witness from an Orthodox Perspective* (Geneva: WCC Publications, 1996). The term was originally coined by Archbishop Anastasios Yannoulatos.

12. See WCC, *Together*, 31. See about the Roman Catholic understanding of evangelization: Paul Grogan and Kirsteen Kim, eds., *The New Evangelization: Faith, People, Context and Practice* (London: Bloomsbury/T&T Clark, 2015). See also Pope Francis, *Evangelii Gaudium—The Joy of the Gospel: Apostolic Exhortation on the Proclamation of the Gospel in Today's World* (London: Catholic Truth Society, 2013), 13 (par. 15).

Behind both concepts we find an ecclesiology of the church as sacrament, sign, and instrument of community. And we find a rediscovery of a missionary/missional ecclesiology of the local church. The ecclesiology of Vatican II is mission focussed: the church as the assembly of God, the people of God, and the community of the faithful.[13]

Protestants of Lutheran and Reformed persuasions view the word and sacraments as the necessary marks of the church (*notae ecclesiae*). This means that the church is "the gathering of all believers, in which the gospel is purely preached and the holy sacraments are administered in accord with the gospel."[14] Added to this we find the belief that sharing in Christ's priesthood gives both the right to come before God and the obligation to witness. The priesthood of all believers implies that every disciple is authorized to evangelize—to proclaim the forgiveness of sins. The task of the ordained in this ecclesiology becomes to help do what the rest of the church members are doing. Ephesians 4:11-12 therefore describes the role and function of leaders as preparing all God's people for the work of Christian service. To this may be added the strong admonition to the Christian to be Christ to the neighbour: the love poured out into the believer's heart sets in motion and motivates love for their neighbour. We can do nothing for our salvation; God does not need our good deeds, but the neighbour does. This calls the church to preach the gospel, feed the hungry, and clothe the naked in an integral manner.

In the free-church tradition we find much of the same, together with a stronger focus on missionary vitality, unreserved testimony, willingness to suffer for Christ, and the mobility of the pilgrim. The church exists for mission. This is further emphasized in a Pentecostal tradition where charismatic spirituality stands at the centre of church life, a spirituality which produces new evangelism methods marked by the power of the Spirit. Empowerment through the Spirit for witness and evangelism receives centre stage. The dominant ecclesiology is marked by the fivefold ministry of Ephesians 4:11-13.[15] The (office of) evangelist is part of the fivefold leadership. Out of this grows the release of the

---

13. Bosch, *Transforming Mission*, 371ff.
14. Philipp Melanchthon, *The Augsburg Confession* (1530), 7:1.
15. As part of this fivefold leadership we find the evangelist. The evangelist is not a church planter, but one who presents the gospel with clarity and relevance in such a way that nonbelievers cross the border between nonfaith and faith. At the same time, the role of the evangelist should be seen in relation to the fact that all Christians are called to witness. Thus, the evangelist has a special responsibility for helping Christians and congregations to become more effective in their witness to the world—inspiring by example and helping local congregations to identify people with the gift of evangelism. The role of the evangelist has often been marginalized (to sects, monastic orders, and voluntary organizations). See Knud Jørgensen, *Equipping for Service: Christian Leadership in Church and Society* (Oxford: Regnum Books International, 2012), 39.

laity for ministry in church and world and the importance of the local church for nurture, discipling, and mission to the ends of the world.

8.3.4 Mission as an ecclesial category

The starting point in Miroslav Volf's definition of the church is Matthew 18:20: "For where two or three are gathered in my name, I am there among them."[16] According to Volf, this verse has been key in ecclesiological thinking since the early church (Ignatius and Tertullian). In this verse the *concrete and empirical* (people gathered in the name of Jesus) is combined with the *divine* presence of the Lord: "I am there among them." What constitutes the church is the presence of the resurrected Jesus Christ. "Two or three" indicates that the fellowship of believers is important, but, as such, it does not constitute the church. "To believe in the church is to believe in the promise that Jesus is present among those who are gathered in his name."[17]

The continued presence through history takes the form of the apostolic witness about what "we have heard, what we have seen with our eyes, what we have looked at and touched with our hands" (1 John 1:1). This witness is made manifest by the Spirit of the Lord, as clearly explained in Jesus' farewell discourses. The task of the Spirit is to remind his disciples of what Jesus already has told them (John 14:26). A church without the presence of the Holy Spirit is therefore a church without the presence of Jesus.

This flows together in the understanding of the church as sent into the world in a trinitarian mission: "As the Father has sent me, so I send you. . . . Receive the Holy Spirit" (John 20:21-22). The disciples are called to be Jesus' witnesses locally and globally. They are sent out to evangelize and make more disciples. Jesus is present when the disciples gather in his name, and he promises to be with them as they go out to disciple (Matt. 28:20). So, the presence of Jesus is the ecclesiological key to both church and mission. The two may have been separated in the course of history, but theologically and missiologically they hang together. Mission is the church's mission. A church without mission (and evangelism) is a misnomer. Without mission there is no church. *Mission is therefore a fundamental ecclesiological category.* The very nature of the church is being sent—missionary, missional, mission-shaped.[18] This integral connection between church and mission became obscured in the long period

---

16. Miroslav Volf, *After Our Likeness: The Church as the Image of the Trinity* (Grand Rapids: Eerdmans, 1998), 135–37.

17. Harald Hegstad, *The Real Church: An Ecclesiology of the Visible* (Eugene, OR: Pickwick, 2013), 18.

18. See Archbishop's Council on Mission and Public Affairs, *Mission-shaped Church: Church Planting and Fresh Expressions of Church in a Changing Context* (London: Church House Publishing, 2004).

of the Constantine Christendom where "Christianization" (handing over the faith to new generations) replaced mission as crossing borders. And it remained obscured by the division between mission, evangelism, and church during the period of modern mission from William Carey until the second half of the 20th century. Since then, the rediscovery of *missio Dei* has helped all of us gain a larger perspective: the church is God's instrument in the world. The goal is not the church, but God's kingdom. This eschatological perspective takes mission and evangelism into a dimension of *already and not yet*. We shall engage in mission and evangelism today—we shall plant apple trees today—because we know that Christ returns tomorrow—and only therefore.

> As the church is sent into the entire world with the gospel this means mission does not cease even in established contexts, but should continue to break through into different social, cultural and geographical boundaries . . . the mission objective is until "the ends of the earth." The fact that the church in mission goes out to the whole world is itself a sign that the kingdom of God has come. Conversely, it is a betrayal of the gospel and a false witness of the kingdom of God if the church settles down in familiar contexts and fails to cross new frontiers.[19]

8.3.5 Forms of missionary engagement: The local church[20]

Edinburgh 1910 was a missionary conference with a focus on traditional mission, mission societies, missionaries, and the missionary encounter in foreign lands. The past century has radically changed this way of thinking. We have come to see the church as essentially missionary; it exists in being sent. Missionary activity is not the work of the church but the church at work. God is a missionary God (*missio Dei*),[21] wherefore God's people are a missionary people. Edinburgh 1910 talked about church *and* mission; today, we must talk about the mission *of* the church. In the words of David Bosch: "It is not the church which 'undertakes' mission; it is *the missio Dei* which constitutes the church."[22]

The church-in-mission is today primarily *the local church* everywhere in the world. This local church is part of the universal church (hence, the church is

---

19. Hegstad, *Real Church*, 85.
20. See the following: Knud Jørgensen, "Edinburgh 2010 in Global Perspective," in Tormod Engelsviken, Erling Lundeby, and Dagfinn Solheim, eds., *The Church Going Glocal: Mission and Globalisation* (Oxford: Regnum Books International, 2011), 12–15.
21. See John G. Flett, *The Witness of God: The Trinity, Missio Dei, Karl Barth, and the Nature of Christian Community* (Grand Rapids: Eerdmans, 2010).
22. Bosch, *Transforming Mission*, 519.

glocal).[23] From the very beginning the local churches were complete churches. Roland Allen (1868–1947) suggested that their success was due to the fact that they trusted both the Lord and the people to whom they had gone.[24] It took decades before foreign mission took Allen's views and advice to heart. Slowly, the Edinburgh 1910 concept of "older" and "younger" churches was replaced, and the church-*for*-others was turned into the church-*with*-others.[25]

In the past, the parish structure prevailed. In some places this may also be an appropriate structure today. The parish structure grew up together with the notion of *Corpus Christianum*, where the church was married to the holders of power. This turned the church into a pastoral institution that adopted the shape of society's structure with parochial churches and a division between *clerici* (priests) and *idiotes* (laypeople). Even with the parish structure as the dominant structure, however, there have always been alternate models with more focus on the small community (*ekklesiola* within the *ekklesia*), for instance, the monastic community, the fellowship of believers, and the missionary bands.

Today, we see experiments with new forms and structures. One such model is *the house church*, which, for instance, in the Chinese context, exemplifies the characteristics of the early church: no church building, often no professional form of leadership, and sometimes considered an illegal religion. Home groups or house churches also play a central role in multiethnic congregations like the International Christian Fellowship in Rotterdam (see ch. 7.7.5, above). Using the images of *clan, synagogue, and temple*,[26] the house church is the clan living together in a small "hamlet"; the synagogue is a community where the smaller groups gather regularly; and the temple is the place for the bigger celebration, where the many come together.

Other models are called *emerging churches*[27]—new forms that try to bind together the original apostolic core with new, imaginative, relatively disorga-

23. See WCC, *Together*, 27: "Like the early church in the book of Acts, local congregations have the privilege of forming a community marked by the presence of the risen Christ. For many people, acceptance or refusal to become members of the church is linked to their positive or negative experience with a local congregation, which can be either a stumbling block or an agent of transformation. Therefore it is vital that local congregations are constantly renewed and inspired by the Spirit of mission. *Local congregations are frontiers and primary agents of mission*" (my emphasis).

24. Roland Allen, *Missionary Methods: St. Paul's or Ours?*, 4th ed. (London: World Dominion Press, 1956), 183–90.

25. Bosch, *Transforming Mission*, 379.

26. Lausanne Committee for World Evangelization, *The Local Church in Mission: Becoming a Missional Congregation in the Twenty-First Century Global Context* (Pattaya: Lausanne Committee for World Evangelization, 2004).

27. Eddie Gibbs and Ryan K. Bolger, *Emerging Churches: Creating Christian Community in Postmodern Cultures* (Grand Rapids: Baker Academic, 2005).

nized forms, and gathering in cafés, dance clubs, on riverbanks, in theatres, and the like. These emerging churches live as communities that transform secular space and live in a spirituality similar to that of the desert fathers.

Or we may go to what have been called *independent* churches (or African indigenous or initiated churches), which encompass a total of 400 million people worldwide—churches that reject historical denominationalism and seek a more effective missionary lifestyle.

All these new forms signal more *fluid* communities,[28] providing multiple options depending on the context and target group. At the same time, there is a growing dissatisfaction with traditional forms of church, and more and more Christians, primarily in the West, live without a local church, alienated from current expressions of church.

8.3.6 Attractive churches

It is through God's people that God means to communicate with those God longs to reach. Evangelism is the responsibility of the church. The reality of what God offers is best seen in the lives of those who have been changed by this offer. Conviction is best communicated by those who have themselves been convinced. We are God's fellow workers (2 Cor. 4:1). We are under obligation both to Greeks and to barbarians, both to the wise and the foolish (Rom. 1:14). Evangelism means incorporation into the body of Christ. It is deeply ecclesial. And evangelism draws people to God through "attractive" churches.

Michael Green, in his treatment of *Evangelism in the Early Church*,[29] has painted a picture of the early evangelists, of their lives and example, their fellowship, their transformed character, and their joy and power. He quotes the church father Athenagoras and his description of the moral lives of early Christians:

> Among us you will find uneducated persons and artisans, and old women who, if they are unable in words to prove the benefit of our doctrine, yet by their deeds exhibit the benefit arising from their persuasion of its truth. They do not practice speeches, but exhibit good works; when struck they do not strike again; when robbed they do not go to law; they give to those who ask of them, and they love their neighbours as themselves.[30]

---

28. Pete Ward, *Liquid Church* (Peabody, MA: Hendrickson, 2002).
29. Michael Green, *Evangelism in the Early Church* (London: Hodder and Stoughton, 1970).
30. Ibid., 180.

In his book *Evangelism through the Local Church*,[31] Green uses the stories in Acts 11:19-30 and Acts 13:1-3 to show what makes churches attractive:

- *They were open to change.* The Hellenists of the church in Antioch believed in a God who is always on the move and who makes all things new. And therefore they turned the world upside down. The only thing that does not change is a cemetery.

- *They were open to lay initiatives.* The church in Antioch was founded by laypeople while the apostles were in Jerusalem. The division of clergy and laity seldom makes for growth. We need the fivefold ministry of Ephesians 4, primarily to equip God's people for service. When in my youth I was sent to serve the Ethiopian Evangelical Church Mekane Yesus, it was believed that the education of pastors was the key to growth, but we never managed to train enough. In 1970 the church had 157,000 members. Today it has seven million members, largely evangelized by laypeople.[32] A European illustration of developing the gifts of people and structuring the church as a priesthood of all believers is found in the case study from the International Christian Fellowship in Rotterdam (cf. 7.7.3 and 7.7.5, above).

- *They were open to faith.* The church in Antioch expected great things of God. In a similar way, churches in China, Korea, and Africa have shown that faith often spells risk.

- *They spoke about Jesus.* The church of Antioch spoke "to the Greeks also" and a great number of them became believers (Acts 11:20). Witnessing to Jesus was then, and still is, the best way of evangelism. We in the West do not talk about Jesus even though Jesus is the supremely attractive one. My old friend, Bishop Festo Kivengere from Uganda (1919–1988), loved to talk about Jesus as *the magnet* that draws people to himself. Gossiping about the Lord made the early church grow.

- *They were open to training.* We hear that Barnabas and Paul met with the church for a whole year, "and taught a great many people" (Acts 11:26). Training in scriptures is foundational then and now. In addition we need

---

31. Michael Green, *Evangelism through the Local Church* (London: Hodder and Stoughton, 1993), 79–103.
32. See Temesgen Shibru Galla, *The Mission Thinking of the Ethiopian Evangelical Church Mekane Yesus (EECMY)* (Master's thesis, MF Norwegian School of Theology, 2011), 11.

training in specific matters, like personal evangelism, Sunday school, the multireligious context, and so forth, depending on the context. We also need training on the job: let John Mark join Paul and Barnabas on their travel to learn the trade. Until the 18th century most pastors in Scandinavia were trained on the job, and not in seminaries and universities. Today, in some of our Lutheran seminaries in the North, we handle theology as if we were still walking the streets of Wittenberg in Germany in the 15th century. Unfortunately, the same applies to those seminaries in the South where the curriculum and the education of teachers are based on Western models.

- *They were open to love.* Love is the most attractive quality in the world. It lies at the heart of the gospel. Without love and the demonstration of love, a church is an empty shell. The fellowship of love between the Christians at Antioch was their major attraction. Love is a climate and a culture which allow gifts to bloom. It begins at the door to the church and continues at coffee or potluck and grows in the small group. Home groups, Bible-study groups, and house churches are the key to love in many churches all over the world. The phenomenal growth among Christians in China is primarily a result of love demonstrated in house churches.

- *They were open to need.* They took up a substantial offering for the famine-struck congregation in Jerusalem and sent Barnabas and Paul to deliver the gift. Churches which live for themselves die for themselves. *Diakonia* is one of the signs of the church, both in terms of meeting surrounding needs and in terms of being a voice for the voiceless. Both mission and *diakonia* belong to the essence of the church. The evangelizing church is a diaconal church; evangelism and *diakonia* are integrated in the nature of being church. Different models of diaconal thinking and caring for the whole person are described in the two case studies in this volume on Street Pastors in the United Kingdom and the International Christian Fellowship in Rotterdam (cf. chs. 7.1.4 and 7.7.2, above). Particularly in multiethnic contexts the diaconal responsibility is central for the evangelizing church.

- *They practiced shared leadership.* There were five leaders at Antioch (Acts 13:1), and the impression is that this diverse leadership, consisting of people from different countries, worked as a team. It would seem that they embodied the unity and togetherness which they wanted for the congregation at large. The Antioch leadership was international and cross-cultural; some seem to have been prophets and some teachers. I believe that such modelling is essential for an evangelizing church.

• *They practiced a dynamic worship.* The pictures in Acts 11 and 13 show order, sincerity, a focus on prayer and openness for intervention: they waited for the Lord to show them the way. In addition to that, they were obedient to what God had shown: they let Barnabas and Saul go as their missionaries, chosen by the Holy Spirit and representing the congregation. Here is the first instance of *the missionary band structure*, a go-structure growing out of the localized come-structure. The attractiveness of worship as central to evangelism relates to word, sacrament, and community; the clear exposition of the good news goes together with the eucharist as the partaking in Christ and baptism as incorporation in his death and resurrection. Here is the gateway through which Jesus comes to his church:

> If we want to hear his call to discipleship, we need to hear it where Christ himself is present. It is within the church that Jesus Christ calls through his word and sacrament. . . . To hear Jesus' call to discipleship, one needs no personal revelation. Listen to the preaching and receive the sacrament! Listen to the gospel of the crucified and risen Lord! Here he is, the whole Christ, the very same who encountered the disciples. Indeed, here he is already present as the glorified, the victorious, the living Christ. No one but Christ himself can call us to discipleship. . . . That was true in the same way for the first disciples as it is for us.[33]

The coming of Jesus in word, sacrament, and *communio sanctorum* (communion of saints) is the centre of—and constitutes—worship, church, and evangelism.

• *They were open to outreach.* It would seem that the Antioch church was founded by conversational evangelism. At the same time, the church was associated with overseas missionary work. Teams of evangelists went away from there for a shorter or longer period. Antioch in this

---

33. Dietrich Bonhoeffer, *Discipleship*, trans. Barbara Green and Reinhard Krauss, Dietrich Bonhoeffer Works, vol. 4, ed. Geffrey B. Kelly and John D. Godsey (Minneapolis: Fortress Press, 2003), 202.

way became a centre where Christians criss-crossed from all parts of the Roman Empire and beyond. My dream is to see the same happen in today's church: personal evangelism, missionary involvement in Judea, Samaria, and to the ends of the earth, and the sending out or support of missionary bands. If the church has two structures—come and go—they should be implemented also by smaller, local congregations. Emerging churches in our urban centres and in contemporary society worldwide (including the case studies in this book from the Netherlands and the United Kingdom) exemplify the importance of structures for walking the streets (Street Pastors) and communicating with people in multicultural contexts.

As I read the New Testament, I meet an early church which made evangelism its number-one priority; a church with a deep compassion for people without Christ; a flexible church in terms of methods and structures. I meet a church which was not overly minister-conscious. In this church every member was expected to be a witness—*martyria* may be used to depict what mission is all about. Buildings were certainly not important to this church; instead of efforts for upkeep and maintenance, I see a spontaneous chattering of the good news: go where people are, and make disciples. "Inviting people to church" is not evangelism. The maximum impact was made by the attractiveness of changed lives and the quality of the community. Says Michael Green:

> I am convinced that there is no evangelistic force so powerful as a really loving, outward-looking local church. It is the key to evangelism in this age which is suspicious of the high-powered sales-technique and at the same time well aware of the emptiness of materialism, the breakdown of relationships, and the shortness of life. There is plenty of spiritual hunger out there. We do not have to make people hungry; we do have to persuade them that we have bread. And the only way that will be done will be by individuals and churches so full of the love of God that it is palpable. People will see it in the worship. They will see it in the caring. They will see it in as the good news is explained against such a background.[34]

---

34. Green, *Evangelism through the Local Church*, 408.

In Luke's ecclesiology we find the bipolar orientation of "inward" and "outward."[35] The community of believers devotes itself to "the apostles' teaching and fellowship, the breaking of bread and the prayers" (Acts 2:42). At one and the same time it is actively engaged in a mission to those still outside. The picture is that the inner life is connected to the outer life. Going inward becomes a source and motivation for going outward. The centripetal and the centrifugal dimensions are two sides of the same ecclesiology.

8.3.7 Conclusion

The shift of paradigm in mission, evangelism, and church has marked my life since my early years in Ethiopia. The subsequent encounters with the East African revival, the house churches in China and elsewhere, and the influence from both the ecumenical and the Lausanne movement have served to affirm the new paradigm and widen my horizon. *Ekklesia* means "to be called out"—to be called out for the purpose of taking part in God's mission—a mission which has its focus in telling the story of God's gift in Jesus Christ. This is not another programme or an additional activity to be involved in when other ecclesial chores have been done. Evangelizing is what we do because of whose we are. We meet the living Lord when two or three gather as *communio*, and we are sent from this gathering to evangelize locally and globally.[36]

The evangelizing church has its base in local congregations, but structurally it includes both the come-structure (*modality*) of the gathered community and the go-structure (*sodality*) of the missionary band. Therefore, evangelistic teams and all sorts of mission societies are also part of the ecclesial dimension of evangelism.

---

35. Bosch, *Transforming Mission*, 119ff.
36. Richard H. Bliese and Craig Van Gelder, eds., *The Evangelizing Church: A Lutheran Contribution* (Minneapolis: Augsburg Fortress, 2005), 71ff.

8.4 Evangelism and Spirituality: Our Words and Life with God

Rebecca A. Giselbrecht

8.4.1 Introduction

Say the words *evangelism* and *spirituality* together, envision them, imagine them, and see how they make you feel. For the average European, the word *evangelism* likely wakens a memory of collective Christian colonialism, power, control, and an unjust accumulation of wealth;[1] while the word *spirituality* often elicits individual notions of a higher power, maybe God. Many people in contemporary Western societies attribute a meaning to evangelism and spirituality that is coloured and influenced by history and their individual religious socialization process. Yet, the words themselves are not guilty of what our senses perceive and our emotions tell us. The words are inevitably associated with Christians in the context of mission and with Christendom. Since the words feel old and religious, they have been increasingly rejected and damned to the peripheries of our European culture because of how some people feel about them (cf. ch. 8.1.2, above). Even in a number of Christian denominations, the words *evangelism* and *spirituality* fall on deaf ears or enrage well-educated minds.

Even so, this should not be all that worrisome to Christians in Europe today because outside is a good place for reclaiming and redefining both the horizontal and vertical values—a good location for reassessing the relationship between evangelism and spirituality. In contemporary Europe the religious liminal condition of Christendom, what Elaine Heath refers to as "the church in the dark night of the soul," does not necessarily mean doom.[2] Liminality can

---

1. See Bryan P. Stone, *Evangelism after Christendom: The Theology and Practice of Christian Witness* (Grand Rapids: Brazos, 2007), 201 n.21; 246: "Because salvation here is less about the subordination of one's will and more about a lived participation, what it means to follow Jesus as Lord implies a distinctive sort of obedience—one that cannot be co-opted by another form of obedience because it is entirely unlike any other. This obedience requires an end to the entire scheme of domination and subordination that, since Adam and Eve, is the curse of sin. In other words, what is subordinated in our surrender to the lordship of Jesus (and thereby nailed to the cross) is every form of worldly domination whereby one person's freedom, dignity, or regard is achieved at the expense of another."
2. Elaine A. Heath, *The Mystic Way of Evangelism: A Contemplative Vision for Christian Outreach* (Grand Rapids: Baker Academic, 2008), 25ff.

also serve as a location to determine whether to revive the old words *evangelism* and *spirituality* by infusing them with new vitality and meaning or to make up new words to uphold the meaning, the truth, the principles, and reality of our Christian identity and the Great Commission.

In the following, I will share what I have learned about evangelism and spirituality in higher education in middle Europe, and then begin to develop a somewhat practical spirituality of evangelism as I interpret 1 John 4:8 in conjunction with Romans 10:8-10. First, in 1 John 4:8, we read, "Whoever does not love does not know God, for God is love." Second, in Romans 10:8-10, we read, "But what does it say? 'The word is near you, on your lips and in your heart' (that is, the word of faith that we proclaim); because if you confess with your lips that Jesus is Lord and believe in your heart that God raised him from the dead, you will be saved. For one believes with the heart and so is justified, and one confesses with the mouth and so is saved." A plain exegesis of these texts tells us that the sound of a voice confessing Christ, that is evangelism, leads to salvation—not only for the one heralding the good news, but maybe also for those who listen.

Whereas evangelism is, of course, to proclaim the gospel of the living Christ, spirituality is a contemporary buzzword that for the average secular citizen usually means seeking to reach beyond the self to something or, in the Christian sense, someone who transcends the self. Christian spirituality is, simply said, life with God. With these rudimentary definitions in mind, our common task is to understand what it might mean to proclaim the good news of the living Christ in our European world as we live our lives with the living God. I imagine a picture—a world—in which evangelism and spirituality function together. The two are the movement of a person—a soul—toward knowing God and participating in God's plan for salvation of all people everywhere. Then, in my mind, with the knowledge of God, that person who has been blessed to know God cannot help but take the love of God and move toward another person or people to share the good news of God's love in Christ. Christian evangelism and spirituality are per definition christocentric; Christ is at the center of the message, which is precisely what makes Christian evangelistic spirituality particular.[3] In addition to placing our faith in and worshipping

---

3. Veli-Matti Kärkkäinen, *An Introduction to the Theology of Religions: Biblical, Historical, and Contemporary Perspectives* (Downers Grove, IL: InterVarsity, 2003), 25: "Christocentrism. This is the inclusive approach, according to which Christ is the Saviour but the benefits of his saving work may be found outside of the Christian church and Christian religion. However, whoever is saved is only saved through the work of Christ." Also see "Christocentric Positions," in ibid., 345–50.

the most high, triune God, the good news for the world is that God became flesh in Jesus Christ and atoned for our sins. Therefore, Christians are zealous advocates of the reality of the Messiah sent by God, whose work makes it possible for all people to be reconciled with the triune God. Hebrews 8:6 underscores the continuity of Christ's mediation: "But Jesus has now obtained a more excellent ministry, and to that degree he is the mediator of a better covenant, which has been enacted through better promises." Christ the mediator, Godself, rejoices in multiplying godly people, which has been God's hope for people and creation since the beginning.[4]

8.4.2 Evangelism

Preaching and evangelism are closely related. Actually, after the resurrection, Peter preached at the first public evangelistic event, which was initiated by the Holy Spirit and held for international guests. As the disciples of Christ sat together in a place, "Suddenly from heaven there came a sound like the rush of a violent wind, and it filled the entire house where they were sitting. Divided tongues, as of fire, appeared among them, and a tongue rested on each of them. All of them were filled with the Holy Spirit and began to speak in other languages, as the Spirit gave them ability" (Acts 2:2-4). The basic message and good news of Christ's birth, death, resurrection, and exultation, the *kerygma*, is always an apologetic initiated by the Holy Spirit. The Spirit of God coaxes us to accept the task of convincing the nations of the truth of the gospel message. Thereby, the gospel is an apologetic message that recalls the actual truth of Christ's resurrection. As Scott Sunquist puts it, "Evangelism is about Jesus Christ," and "Christianity is about truth in personal relationship."[5] Evangelistic spirituality is proclaiming Christ through the power of the Holy Spirit.

Sunquist has, in fact, done some of the best defining and differentiating of evangelism and witness. In the chapter "Witnessing Community: Evangelism and Christian Mission," in his book *Understanding Christian Mission*, Sunquist rightly claims, "for evangelism is, at heart, introducing Jesus to others and inviting them to become partakers in his kingdom."[6] Sunquist extends his definition of evangelism, adding that, "Evangelistic witness is the good news demonstrated and described."[7] Then, he points to Romans 10:17, which

---

4. Consider, for instance, the creation narratives in Genesis 1–3, but also the Tower of Babel, Noah's flood, and God's continuing efforts to reach out to people, culminating in the advent of Christ.

5. Scott W. Sunquist, *Understanding Christian Mission: Participating in Suffering and Glory* (Grand Rapids: Baker Academic, 2013), 318–19.

6. Ibid., 312.

7. Ibid., 321.

undergirds this, because "Faith comes from what is heard, and what is heard comes through the word of Christ." Even when the question of evangelism is established as the good news of Jesus Christ, the larger question of spirituality and evangelism in Europe is still an elephant in the room. Particularly in my context of practical theology at the theological faculty of a secular university, teaching students to eventually pastor in a state church, evangelism and spirituality are difficult to address.

8.4.3 Evangelism and spirituality in higher education

A few semesters ago, I taught a course at the university titled "*Kerygma* in the Postmodern." The class was subordinate to the curriculum of practical theology and spirituality and served as a bridge between discourse on evangelism and spirituality in my academic context. The notions of telling others about Jesus Christ, and the student's personal experiences in relationship to Christ were fragmented. My students were skeptical and treated evangelism and spirituality as a phenomenon irrelevant to academic expectations. Coming from progressive liberal church homes, for the most part, there was a certain stigma on and prohibition against proselytizing (cf. ch. 8.1.3, above). A taboo regarding the subject of evangelism in a public university, however, does not forbid a discussion of mission or evangelism as long as the material has historical value for reflection and stimulates critical inquiry. The serious divide between the intellectual and the physical was remarkable. As I probed deeper into the subject, the idea of embodied faith was consistently rejected, intellectualized, and the students consistently argued for Cartesian mind-and-body dualism in higher education. The cleft was deeply engraved in the students' understanding of academic theology so that even if the topics of evangelism and spirituality were broached, they remained fractured in most students' personal faith categories. Luckily, my class fit neatly into the category of practice in practical theology.

At the start of the semester, in order to begin our discussion of the subject of the kerygmatic content of a sermon, we examined the debate concerning *kerygma* by Jürgen Moltmann (b. 1926) and Gerhard Ebeling (1912–2001).[8] In order to define proclamation inside and outside of the church, that is, preaching and evangelism, we examined Ebeling and his explanation that "the meaning of the noun '*kerygma*' oscillates between the content and the act of

---

8. Jürgen Moltmann, "Das Kerygma und die Existenz," in Jürgen Moltmann, *Kirche in der Kraft des Geistes: Ein Beitrag zur messianischen Ekklesiologie* (Gütersloh: Gütersloher Verlagshaus, 1975), 236–39; Gerhard Ebeling, "Kerygma," in Hans Jürgen Schultz, ed., *Theologie für Nichttheologen: ABC protestantischen Denkens* (Stuttgart: Kreuz-Verlag, 1963), 93–99.

proclamation."[9] As Moltmann would have it, we discussed whether "theology is a Christian and spiritual undertaking. . . ."[10] With Ebeling we asked, "But what purpose does a book actually serve? Is it not actually a testimony of life that generates life? The Bible serves this in immanent measure."[11] Spirituality in relation to *kerygma* was inevitably at the centre of our discourse on proclamation.

Given the decline of church membership in our postmodern Christian state-church culture, with approximately 60,000 Swiss people resigning their membership in the church in Switzerland last year alone, the students were stimulated to understand the role of the biblical message in preaching. The ecclesial demise in our context is an ever-present partner in the theological academy in Europe. Our study led us to conclude that if *kerygma* is a "word event," as Ebeling contends, or "effective word," as Luther would have it, then the biblical mandate of Christian spirituality is sharing the good news.[12] Our discussion of *kerygma* thereby took on a personal and practical dimension for the students. Nonetheless, the historical problems of mission, colonization, and the taboo to convert people of other religions were also our companion.

Since our class was about the practice of spirituality in relation to *kerygma*, we began each class by reading Acts 2 from various hermeneutical perspectives. The apostle Peter's sermon to the nations provides a superb example for the kerygmatic, that is, the first sermon about the good news of Jesus Christ in the Bible. One female student rolled her eyes when I announced in week one that we would work with the same text at the start of each weekly meeting. We spent between 15 and 20 minutes on the Bible text in each of our two-hour classes. Our weekly "practice" with Acts 2 eventually served to discern the power of the word, and as it is when a person reads the word of God, the students began to personally experience "the word event." Through a critical examination of the layers of the biblical text, it opened the church in culture and added systematic and philosophical arguments to the mix. In other words, reading behind the text, in the text, and in front of the Bible text, the meaning of the text allowed my students to enter into the meaning of the words.[13]

9. Gerhard Ebeling, "Kerygma [1964]," in Gerhard Ebeling, *Wort und Glaube, Dritter Band; Beiträge zur Fundamentaltheologie, Soteriologie und Ekklesiologie* (Tübingen: J.C.B. Mohr, 1975), 517.

10. Moltmann, *Kirche*, 20–21.

11. Gerhard Ebeling, "Theologie in den Gegensätzen des Lebens," in Gerhard Ebeling, *Wort und Glaube, band 4; Theologie in den Gegensätzen des Lebens* (Tübingen: J.C.B. Mohr [Paul Siebeck], 1995), 18.

12. Gerhard Ebeling, *Theology and Proclamation: A Discussion with Rudolf Bultmann* (London: Collins, 1996), 43; Martin Luther, *Werke: Kritische Gesamtausgabe Bd. 1* (Weimar: Böhlau, 1883), 54.

13. Joel B. Green, *Seized by Truth: Reading the Bible as Scripture* (Nashville: Abingdon, 2007), 103.

In the middle of our semester, the students began to understand the central tenet of Peter's sermon to the nations in Acts 2. The good news gained a new centrality in our discussions for all of the theology students in my class, and Jesus Christ was perceived to be at the heart of the text. At the end of the semester, the young lady who had rolled her eyes gave a testimony of how surprised she was to meet new dimensions of Acts 2 each week, and that our work with the text had inspired her to share with others the good news and her experience reading and rereading Acts 2.

8.4.4 Evangelism and spirituality in Europe

The reformer Heinrich Bullinger (1504–1575) and Lutheran theologian Dietrich Bonhoeffer (1906–1945) agree with the apostle Peter, Sunquist, Ebeling, Martin Luther, and my students: "'The word is near you, on your lips and in your heart' (that is, the word of faith that we proclaim); because if you confess with your lips that Jesus is Lord and believe in your heart that God raised him from the dead, you will be saved." In his commentary on Romans, Bullinger emphatically presents Matthew 10:7 as an imperative—"proclaim the Good News"—and John 1:4 as absolutely true—"God abides in those who confess that Jesus is the Son of God, and they abide in God."[14] No doubt, one who knows God certainly has the desire to talk to others about God. As John claims in his gospel, "Out of the believer's heart shall flow rivers of living water" (John 7:38).

Evangelism pours forth toward others as a result of personal Christian spirituality—the life with God mentioned above. Daily prayer with our God fills us to overflowing. The others in our lives and communities need us to share our spiritual capital and help them envision, imagine, see, and feel the living water of Christ (cf. the references to the relationship of prayer and evangelism in chs. 7.3.1; 7.3.7; 7.4.4; and 7.8.2, above). Near the end of his little book *Life Together*, at the start of his excursus on community, Dietrich Bonhoeffer has a lovely section on testimony that extends to a more robust and demanding proclamation of the word, that is, evangelism.[15] In his chapter titled "The Ministry of Proclamation," Bonhoeffer explains the natural outcome of life with God and life together with other Christians.[16] Bonhoeffer boldly speaks

---

14. Heinrich Bullinger, *Kommentare zu den neutestamentlichen Briefen: Röm.—1Kor.—2 Kor.* (Zürich: Theologischer Verlag, 2013), 166.
15. Dietrich Bonhoeffer, *Life Together: The Classic Exploration of Faith and Community* (New York: Harper & Row, 1954).
16. Ibid., 22–23, 108.

about absolute truth and the theological imperative of a spirituality of evangelism. He contends, "When one is struck by the Word, he speaks it to others."[17] Clearly, this pertains to evangelism, testimony, witnessing to the risen Christ. Bonhoeffer emphasizes the responsibility of a believer, who is dependent on the grace of God, for transporting the words of the truth of Jesus Christ to others. Bonhoeffer connects this thought to community itself and maintains the necessity for sisters and brothers to speak God's word to each other. "The Christ in his own heart is weaker than the Christ in the word of his brother; his own heart is uncertain, his brother's is sure."[18] A spirituality of evangelism requires vigilance even in the church. The church must continue in a spirituality of evangelism—speaking the good news of Christ to each other. In Bonhoeffer's work on ministry and proclamation, the nature of shame and the difficulty of speaking Jesus into the world are in no way ignored. He makes it clear, however, that the word spoken in community is what gives us the confidence to speak the name of Christ when we are alone in public.[19]

Where the horizontal meets the vertical, where heaven kisses earth, is where the Holy Spirit and Christ meet us. Lest we become arrogant or overly confident, Ephesians points away from our achievements to Christ, "The gifts he gave were that some would be apostles, some prophets, some evangelists, some pastors and teachers, to equip the saints for the work of ministry, for building up the body of Christ, until all of us come to the unity of the faith and of the knowledge of the Son of God, to maturity, to the measure of the full stature of Christ" (Eph. 4:11-13). Luckily, both evangelism and spirituality are gifts of the Spirit of God. Neither being spiritual, nor being able to talk about spiritual things, can be earned, although both require learning and practice.

8.4.5 Evangelism and spirituality: The work of the Holy Spirit

Entering the discourse of evangelism and spirituality, a series of ontological questions arise. First, the nature of how an individual perceives reality is the key to one's spirituality. If, after reading and discussing Acts 2 for 14 weeks, the word of God itself convinces a student that the good news of Jesus Christ is the truth and telling that truth is essential to the student and the salvation of others, the student has appropriated the reality of the horizontal and vertical. A transfer of ownership has taken place. Contemplating God, being amazed by the reality of the Holy Spirit and what Christ has accomplished for us, are

17. Ibid., 22.
18. Ibid., 23.
19. Ibid., 103–108.

only part of being a Christian. Second, from an ontological perspective, we are faced with the question of the individual reality of the others around us. For a Christian, God sent Jesus Christ to lead the world to be reconciled with God, to coexist in God's reality. Our reality has physical/metaphysical meaning in eternity. As evangelists led by the Holy Spirit, however, we must know that everyone's reality is absolute for them.

Let me break this down. David J. Bosch wrote about this in his little book titled *A Spirituality of the Road* (Wipf & Stock, 2001).. As a missionary scholar, already in 1979 he realized that spirituality was most often referred to in relation to an individual's own relationship with something—anything that transcended the self. Moreover, now 35 years later, the most common response to the word *spirituality* in my culture is that spirituality is a deeply personal aspect of the self. Focussing on the biblical principle of 1 John 4:8, that "[w]hoever does not love does not know God, for God is love," in my context love means to tolerate the other. In relation to evangelism, however, we have established that love is something that goes beyond the self and is proven in caring relationships with other people. In fact, as Christians, salvation is at stake in relation to where we locate our God reality. Is my God relationship, my spirituality, located at the centre of my being and available for sharing? The question is important because evangelism and spirituality are quintessential to the question of all reality, which for Christians includes Jesus Christ. No doubt, the most contested and rejected aspect of Christian spirituality for those outside of the Christian faith is the reality of Jesus Christ in the world and in the lives of individuals, who claim to be Christians.

Evangelism and spirituality are the work of the Holy Spirit of God (cf. ch. 7.8.2, above, which addresses prayer and Spirit-filled evangelism). The Holy Spirit is the glue that holds these realities together, whereby the word of God is necessarily the baseline for both. The Word of God is Jesus Christ. The word of God is in the biblical narrative of the people of God. It is the word that reaches and resonates, its message connects people to meaning and understanding God and each other. "In the beginning was the Word and the Word was with God, and the Word was God" (John 1:1). Even in a practical sense, within the secular higher educational system, we work with words and they shape our reality.

8.4.6 Conclusion

The Word of God became flesh (John 1:14). Exactly this Word is what we are commissioned to communicate to others—the evangelistic word. The *kerygma* and the mystery of God became flesh, and that is what we share with others. After the resurrection, Jesus told Mary, "Do not be afraid; go and tell . . ." (Matt. 28:10). The word leads to reconciliation with God and each other. In the WCC pamphlet *Common Witness*, God the Father, Jesus Christ the Son, and the Holy Spirit are noted to be the source of Christian common witness.[20] No doubt, our spirituality depends on the Spirit of God, and the Spirit guides us in how to be the people of God, alone and together. Without the Holy Spirit, we cannot know or discern that God is God. Through the work of the Holy Spirit, a person meets the word of God, in the shape of Christ. Now, this can occur as it did with my students or through the words of another person, in a dream as we see it happening all over the word, or through the Bible as it did for me as a child.

The word, however, must be envisioned, imagined, seen, and felt. The Bible, the living words of God, captures us, thrills us, and makes us curious about meaning, spirituality in context, life beyond the self, and life with God. Wherever and however we meet the living word, the Holy Spirit is leading and unfolding the mystery before us. Here is where it gets mysterious and strange: when a person meets the word, the word becomes part of our flesh. We embody the word of God and the horizontal intersects with the vertical.

And when that moment is here, and the word is flesh, it spills out of our mouths and our actions. The spiritual dimension of the knowledge of—and our relationship with—the living God becomes flesh and pours from us as living souls. Our flesh cannot keep the truth within, and it comes out as a "word event." God's Holy Spirit holds all of this together. The miracle of the Holy Spirit is, while the Spirit is doing all of this, that the Spirit points away from the Spirit to the word of God. Understanding this means that we have understood our identity as spiritual living beings. Evangelistic spirituality is the word, the word become flesh, and when we meet the word, the word becomes part of our flesh, our cup overflows, and our words become spirit, that is, the Spirit of God is transferred to another person in order to become flesh and the living word of God once more. That's what evangelism and spirituality are about.

---

20. Commission on World Mission and Evangelism, *Common Witness: A Study Document of the Joint Working Group of the Roman Catholic Church and the World Council of Churches* (Geneva: WCC Publications, 1982).

PART FOUR

Evangelism as Church
in Transformation

CHAPTER 9

Gerrit Noort and Stefan Paas

Toward a Missional Identity of Ministers and Church Workers

9.1 Introduction

In this chapter we will discuss the role of theological education in shaping a missional identity of ministers and church workers. We will argue that preparing theological students for the ministry in European churches requires preparing them for the post-Christian and therefore missional context in which they will minister.

It goes without saying that in the past two centuries the context in which churches and mission agencies educated their workers for missional ministry has changed radically. In the 19th century Christian ministry in Europe took place in a Christendom context. There was a clear distinction between mission far away amongst the "blind heathens" and pastoral ministry to the "baptized heathens" of the Christianized European continent. In that century, preparing for mission, according to common understanding, equalled preparing for ministry overseas. But now that the heyday of colonialism and Western responsibility for "young" mission churches is long past and Europe itself is a post-Christian continent, preparing for mission and evangelism requires "dramatic adjustments" and a "directional shift in any given context, including the secularized European context."[1]

The fact that in theological education the training for mission and evangelism needs to be an integral part of preparing for the ministry seems to be of little urgency to many. Varying reasons, including theological convictions, may contribute to this lack of urgency. Some, honouring King Frederick the Great's "Everyone shall be saved in his own way" (*Jeder soll nach seiner Façon selig werden*), may hold that in a pluralistic world training for missional work is no longer necessary at all. Others may say that mission was part and parcel of a superior Western attitude that also produced colonialism and slave trade. Good riddance, therefore, if missiology is replaced by intercultural theology. Then there are those, however, who state that theological education for mission and evangelism is urgent. In the Western post-Christian context, they say, those who prepare for the ministry need to reflect anew on the implications of the invitation in the gospel to follow Christ as well as on the "adaptive challenge"[2] for the church and its mission. Furthermore, as churches in Europe increasingly appoint workers for missional ministry in the local context, these evangelists need training just as much as the "classic" missionaries who prepared for ministry in a "foreign" context. The issue, then, is not *if* we need theological education for mission and evangelism, but *how* we can shape the curriculum accordingly.

In what follows we will briefly look at training for evangelism in the past and the present. Foremost will be the question, *What* is needed for theological students in Europe, who by definition prepare for the ministry in a missional context? We will start by looking in retrospect at the discussion about theological education for mission in the ecumenical mission movement. In the second part we will address preparing for evangelism in today's context of theological education. Finally, we will suggest five programmatic fields for the theological education of ministers of the word in post-Christian Europe and will make a few remarks on the structure of theological education.

---

1. J. Nelson Jennings, "Divine Superintendence," in Stephen Bevans et al., eds., *Reflecting on and Equipping for Christian Mission* (Oxford: Regnum Books International, 2015), 376.
2. Robert Doornenbal, *Crossroads: An Exploration of the Emerging-Missional Conversation with a Special Focus on "Missional Leadership" and Its Challenges for Theological Education* (Delft: Eburon, 2012), 366–67.

9.2 Preparing for Evangelism in Retrospect

The WCC's mission affirmation *Together towards Life* (2013) states that churches "mainly and foremost need to be missionary churches," and it acknowledges that evangelism is part of the mission of the church.[3] The ecumenical mission movement often discussed the training of professionals and laypeople in order to effectively shape mission and evangelism. This discussion on the content of education initially took place in the context of "foreign mission," but in the 1960s this changed due to the ecumenical affirmation that mission takes place in six continents. The *locus* of mission was also Europe and North America, and therefore the discussion on training for mission widened to theological and missionary institutions in the West.

Starting with the 1910 world missions conference in Edinburgh, we can observe that its commissions III and V dealt with "missionary education." The discussions in commission V focussed specifically on the "preparation of missionaries."[4] The background of this discussion was that mission societies discerned that many missionaries were educated at theological seminaries that provided little education on foreign cultures and cross-cultural missionary skills. The commission stated that it was urgent to drastically improve knowledge of non-Western sociology and "general principles of missionary work." In their attempt to determine the requirements of missionary training, the commission first sought to identify the functions of a missionary. They established three basic functions: the presentation of the Christian message, the manifestation of the Christian life, and the organization of a Christian church and nation.[5] In their aspirations to achieve necessary improvements in missionary training, these functions were foremost. Missionary formation should emphasize efficient preaching of the gospel, professional ability to manifest the Christian life through, for instance, teachers and doctors, and training missionaries with leadership skills. For all types of missionaries an integration of spiritual, moral, and intellectual dimensions was foundational. As improving the quality of missionary training was not to be taken lightly, the commission therefore prioritized ecumenical cooperation in training for mission in order to facilitate

---

3. World Council of Churches, *Together towards Life: Mission and Evangelism in Changing Landscapes* (Geneva: WCC Publications, 2013), par. 58.
4. See Jooseop Keum, "Theological Education in Mission," *International Review of Mission* 98, no. 388 (April 2009): 2–3; Kenneth Ross, "Perspectives on Education and Formation from the World Mission Conference, Edinburgh 1910," in Bevans et al., eds., *Reflecting*, 29–32.
5. World Missionary Conference 1910, *Report of Commission V: The Preparation of Missionaries* (Edinburgh: Oliphant, Anderson & Ferrier, 1910), 97–98.

a process of learning from each other's experiences. The commission's ideal was to set up missionary colleges, where mission societies could cooperate in developing a curriculum that would include history and methods of mission, social sciences, comparative religion, pedagogy, and linguistics. Next to that, the commission recommended the creation of a Board of Missionary Studies, which should supply guidance and render assistance to missionary societies in the preparation of missionaries for their work.[6]

In the 1930s the preparation of missionaries was increasingly discussed in the framework of the changing relationship of church and mission. The *Laymen's Report on Foreign Mission*, published in 1932, was very critical about the expansionist model of mission.[7] Following the discussion on this report, the International Missionary Council requested the Dutch missiologist Hendrik Kraemer to write a study on the Christian message in a non-Christian world, which was published in 1938. He stated in his book that the missionary movement and its "young mission churches" should be anchored in the international network of churches and no longer in the network of mission societies. The changing relationships of "young receiving churches" and "old sending churches" in the West, of course, also had implications for the preparation of missionaries. They needed to be prepared for a shift from pioneer ministries to working in the ecclesial structures of the young churches. Missionaries had to report to local church leadership. Related to this development the International Missionary Council's conference in Tambaram (1938) observed with great concern that the "weakest element in the entire enterprise of Christian mission" was theological education.[8]

This observation in Tambaram eventually led to the start of the Theological Education Fund (1958), which aimed for improving the quality of theological education. Especially in the 1970s the Theological Education Fund called for the "renewal of theological education and ministry." Its staff regarded contextualization as the "focal concern" that could help to realize "reform and renewal."[9] In these years the Theological Education Fund prioritized *theological education by extension*, which radically opted for the social and professional

---

6. Ross, "Perspectives," 32; World Missionary Conference 1910, *Report*, 189.

7. Cf. Kenneth Scott Latourette, "The Laymen's Foreign Missions Inquiry: the Report of its Commission of Appraisal," *International Review of Mission* 22, no. 2 (April 1933): 153–73.

8. International Missionary Council, *The World Mission of the Church: Findings and Recommendations of the Meeting of the International Missionary Council, Tambaram, Madras, India, Dec. 12–29, 1938* (London, 1939), 85; Nyambura J. Njoroge, "An Ecumenical Commitment: Transforming Theological Education in Mission," *International Review of Mission* 94, no. 373 (2005): 248, 251.

9. Njoroge, "Ecumenical Commitment," 252.

context of the theological student. When in 1977 the WCC integrated the Theological Education Fund into its programmes, it based its decision on the firm conviction that contextual theological education is vital for the mission of the church.

In the 1980s and 1990s the *International Review of Mission,* published by WCC's Commission on World Mission and Evangelism, devoted several issues to mission and theological education.[10] The common denominator in all these issues is the call for a radical shift in shaping theological education for mission. It affirms with urgency that missiology is not just another theological subject that needs to be awarded its proper place in the curriculum, but that the mission of the church should be the constituting dimension of all theological education. This conviction is strongly voiced in the words of Christopher Duraisingh: "My increasing conviction is that we can simply no longer avoid to 'tinker around' with theological curricula and teaching methods with a view to adding mission as one more subject, but what is called for is a radical revolution in doing and teaching theology and in ministerial formation."[11] He aimed for "recovering the 'sentness' of the church" as the main concern in ecclesiology.

In Duraisingh's approach the influence of missiologist Johannes C. Hoekendijk is obvious, especially in the way he refers to the WCC's position in the 1960s, that the church is a function of mission and not vice versa. Mark Laing also addresses the relationship of church and mission in his article "Recovering Missional Ecclesiology in Theological Education" (2009). He argues that church and mission societies have long exported a "defective" and "missionless" ecclesiology, which has resulted in a strict separation of church and mission.[12] This unhealthy separation has led to "the production of clergy who have an inadequate ecclesiology and largely neglect the apostolic nature of the church." He stresses that, in theological education, students need to learn that mission is the *raison d'etre* of the church and that students do not graduate in order to conserve the existing church in its current condition. He makes a plea for a

---

10. F. Ross Kinsler, "Equipping God's People for Mission," *International Review of Mission* 71, no. 282 (April 1982): 133–44; Bonnie L. Jensen, "Processes in Education for Mission," *International Review of Mission* 81, no. 321 (January 1992): 91–96; Desmond P. van der Water, "Transforming Theological Education and Ministerial Formation," *International Review of Mission* 94, no. 373 (April 2005): 203–211; Jooseop Keum, "Theological Education in Mission," *International Review of Mission* 98, no. 388 (April 2009): 1.
11. Christopher Duraisingh, "Ministerial Formation for Mission: Implications for Theological Education," *International Review of Mission* 81, no. 321 (January 1992): 33.
12. Mark Laing, "Recovering Missional Ecclesiology in Theological Education," *International Review of Mission* 98, no. 388 (April 2009): 11–12.

"radical reappraisal" of an ecclesiology that takes the missionary nature of the church seriously.[13]

Mark Laing may call for a reappraisal of the missionary nature of the church, but it is necessary to observe that in the postcolonial era earlier theological "reappraisals" had led to just the opposite, namely, a *marginalization* of mission and evangelism in theological institutions. The normative side of missiology was increasingly criticized and therefore replaced by intercultural theology, intercultural hermeneutics, or world Christianity.[14] Often, the descriptive aspects were stressed at the cost of the normative aspects. The effects of this development were not "uniformly beneficial," as the local churches were at risk of losing their perspective on mission and the worldwide church.[15] In this context Alan Neely mentioned two reasons why we should prioritize mission in theological education, namely, first, "the need to awaken as well as to inform the church of ways to continue Christ's mission in the world," and, second, "the need to prepare and support those whom the Spirit sets apart for a ministry and mission to the world."[16] Neely observes that the *locus* of education for mission is not so much the theological institution but, rather, the local church. He rightly observes that a lot of preparation for missional ministry is done in those local churches: they involve their members and they provide training for mission on the spot (cf. chs. 7.7.5 and 7.8.2, above). Local initiatives for missional training should be highly valued, yet Neely states that there is a downside as well: especially bigger churches run the risk of isolating their training for evangelism from the experience and expertise of other churches. Good preparation for evangelism should be radically ecumenical. Inviting others to follow Christ is not about the church as an institute.[17] Learning and training together prevents "confessional evangelism" and ensures that those who embrace the Christian faith won't become "denominational proselytes," but followers of Christ.

Foremost in education for mission, according to Neely, should be Lesslie Newbigin's well-known question, "What must we be?"[18] That brings us to the next section, on preparing for evangelism in our days and time.

13. Ibid., 24.
14. Cf. Frans Wijsen, "Intercultural Theology and the Mission of the Church," *Exchange* 30, no. 3 (2001): 218–28.
15. Alan Neely, "The Teaching of Mission," in James M. Philips and Robert T. Coote, eds., *Toward the 21st Century in Christian Mission* (Grand Rapids: Eerdmans, 1993), 269.
16. Ibid., 276.
17. Ibid., 277.
18. Ibid. See Lesslie Newbigin, *Foolishness to the Greeks: The Gospel and Western Culture* (Grands Rapids: Eerdmans, 1986), 124–50.

9.3 Preparing for Evangelism Now[19]

9.3.1 Why is evangelism largely ignored in theological education?

Does formal theological education in Europe prepare students for the ministry of evangelism?[20] Missiologist Wilbert Shenk recalls that he conducted a survey in 1990 and 1991 in several Western countries to determine (1) if there were programmes whose object was the training of missionaries to the peoples of modern Western culture; and, if so, (2) what comprised the curriculum. His conclusion: "I never advanced beyond the first question."[21] There were occasional courses on missiology or evangelism, to be sure, but there was nowhere any sign of a complete rethinking of the theological curriculum in terms of the missionary identity of the church.

In our country, the Netherlands, there have been some improvements since then. In most theological faculties, especially those connected to denominations, missionary competencies have been included in the profile of future ministers. It is recognized that a minister of the word today is inevitably a kind of missionary in his or her own culture. This insight has been translated to some extent into the curricula of universities. The Protestant Theological University in the Netherlands, for example, has included two or three missionary modules in the training of future pastors of the largest Protestant church in the Netherlands. And the Theological University in Kampen (Free Reformed) offers a full year (60 European credits) of missiological training, which may be included as a year of specialization in the three-year master's study of future ministers of the word.

But overall, it is still possible in the Netherlands to become a pastor in one of the Protestant denominations without much missiological training of any substance. We have no evidence that this is different for future priests in the

---

19. What follows is based on Stefan Paas, "Prepared for a Missionary Ministry in 21st Century Europe," *European Journal of Theology* 20, no. 2 (2011): 119–30.

20. In the Netherlands there are two types of universities: professional and academic. Theologians who have been trained in a professional university (university for applied sciences) receive four years (240 ECTS; Bachelor of Theology) of education, of which one year consists of specialization in, for example, pastoral work or evangelism. However, Protestant churches in the Netherlands do not accept this type of training for their pastors. They hire these theologians as church workers—pastoral assistants, co-pastors, evangelists, youth workers, and the like—but not as their ministers of the word. To become a pastor you need an academic theology education of six years (360 European Credits; Master of Theology).

21. Wilbert R. Shenk, "The Training of Missiologists for Western Culture," in John Dudley Woodberry, Charles van Engen, and Edgar J. Elliston, eds., *Missiological Education for the Twenty-First Century: The Book, the Circle, and the Sandals—Essays in Honor of Paul E. Pierson* (Maryknoll, NY: Orbis, 1997), 120.

Roman Catholic Church in the Netherlands. Even now, the curriculum reflects that mission is for those who are interested in it, for special people, "practical" people—but not for "real" theologians. Why is this still the case? Let us consider some causes:

1. *Old habits die hard.* A theological curriculum that has been developed in centuries of Christendom is not likely to change overnight. To quote Newbigin once again: ". . . it seems clear that ministerial training as currently conceived is still . . . far too little oriented toward the missionary calling to claim the whole of public life for Christ and his kingdom."[22] In other words, theology is something that is done within the church, as far away from the world as possible. We may therefore even wonder how many students take theology as their route, just to be in a safe, predictable environment. And how many professors do they meet who seem just to reflect this position? Wonderful, faithful, and learned people, but "hospitalized" to such an extent that they lack the competence to communicate with anyone outside the walls of their seminary, let alone with unbelievers.

2. *A gap between evangelism and theology.* Here is a serious difficulty in Western theology: it considers mission, and especially evangelism, as something that is indispensable in practice but not really interesting from a theological perspective.[23] Evangelistic practice, on the other hand, has increasingly been hijacked by marketers, sales managers, and church-growth gurus. There is a deep hidden covenant here between theologians and evangelists: they both know that theology and evangelism are not really interested in each other. We may confess that all good theology is born in mission, out of reflection on the gospel crossing new borderlines, but this insight has hardly been processed in our theology. Whoever has studied John Wesley or Jonathan Edwards knows that mission experiences can produce very strong theology. The same applies today in many non-Western contexts. But when our students are really interested in theology, they opt for systematics or biblical studies. Missiology or evangelism is for "practitioners"—for the less intelligent, perhaps?

---

22. Lesslie Newbigin, *The Gospel in a Pluralist Society* (Grand Rapids: Eerdmans, 1989), 231.
23. Cf. William J. Abraham, *The Logic of Evangelism* (Grand Rapids: Eerdmans, 1999).

3. *A lack of exercise.* This is partly due to the Christendom system. Most theology professors have been educated within this paradigm. This means that they have loads of experience in the field of preaching (for Christians, that is), pastoral work, and church politics, but very little in social-justice advocacy, leading Alpha courses, and creative evangelism. As a consequence, they speak with confidence about matters that concern the inner life of the church, and hesitantly, abstractly, and without much inspirational force about mission. But the same applies to the students. Even if they have personal experience with evangelism themselves, they lack the opportunity to reflect on these experiences in class. Their practice and their theology remain separated. The organization of the curriculum reinforces this problem, since our theological education is focussed on books and classroom work. Doing social research, being involved in (for example) leading a "Christianity Explored" course, or doing volunteer work in the red-light district of Amsterdam are not part of the curriculum. Thus, these practices will not become sources of theological reflection, or help students to develop a missionary spirituality. They remain enclosed in a predominantly middle-class, family-oriented, white, Christian environment, of which they have incorporated the cultural rules to such an extent that they easily identify it with "biblical" Christianity.

So, there is a double challenge here. First, we must overcome a very strong tradition of inward-looking theological education. And, second, we must find ways to understand and do mission and evangelism in a post-Christian, post-missionary context, full of uncertainties. This leads us to the following programme of theological education today.

9.3.2 Programme of Theological Education

In this section we mention five programmatic fields in the theological education of pastors:

1. *Ministers of the word in post-Christian Europe must be strangers again.* A missionary is a guest, not the owner of the house (cf. Luke 10:1-16). This is easier to accept when we are sent to foreign continents than in our own country. "We who are indigenous to this culture too easily

accept the dubious assumption that we know it in its depths."[24] Becoming a stranger has three different dimensions:

- *Accepting our marginalization without losing our love*: our post-Christian situation may teach us that Christians are never truly at home in the world. The fact that Christian pastors have lost their status and respectful position may teach us something about the wisdom of the cross. Learning to become a stranger again begins with joyfully accepting our marginal position as a minority in secular Europe, but without losing our love for God's world. We do not need to control our societies in order to love our neighbours and pray for our governments.

- *Developing a curiosity for the unknown and rejecting rash judgments*: both those who are thrilled by everything new and those who abhor the new tend to judge too quickly. If we learn to become strangers again in our own culture, we will be more impressed by its complexity. We will accept that the only way to know it is to be involved in it, and that it will take years before we can understand it somewhat.

- *Developing a critical sense and resistance against the dominance of modernity*: becoming a stranger again helps us not to be impressed too quickly by the modern attitude toward our religion. Western culture is powerful, all-pervasive, and it is saturated with irony. This can be very discouraging for every missionary. We must learn to see through this mask of self-confidence. How? First and foremost, through relationships with Christians from other parts of the world, especially those parts that suffer under Western power; and, second, by relationships with the marginal people of our own society. For example, in our own context, reflecting on the issue of trafficking and sex slavery can help us to see the dark underside of the city of Amsterdam (and many other cities as well). This is a city that is determined by consumption. Everything seems negotiable, there seems to be no room at all for firm convictions about anything. But at the same time, this city brings in a lot of money by advertising its red-light district. If we do not develop an outlook as committed strangers in our own culture, we will end up being absorbed by it, or being so revolted by it that we become sectarians. Mission consciousness entails that we realize that all cultures are human constructs, full of sin and

---

24. Shenk, "Training of Missiologists," 125.

grace. None, including the culture of Christendom, approximates the kingdom of God.[25]

2. *Ministers of the word must be deeply rooted in the scriptures.* Newbigin once said that every missionary must learn to speak two languages: their first language is the language of the Bible, and their second language is that of the culture where they are sent. Some time ago a group of Brazilian theology students met a Dutch theology professor. The latter asked them what would be their "theological" response to the health-and-wealth gospel that currently pervades their country. Every one of them immediately grasped a Bible (so much for trained instincts!). When they opened them it turned out that all these Bibles were full of underlining and colour. It was obvious that their Bibles were their tools, not just sources of data. After this, there was a half hour of discussion, which is to say that the students very gracefully exchanged Bible quotes (sometimes very unexpected ones, but virtually always to the point), compared scripture with scripture, and made some astonishing wise remarks. Everything showed that they were people highly trained in using the Bible, not just as a box full of texts that can be used in whatever way we like (usually to manipulate others), but as a way of communal reading aimed at shared challenges. We have to admit that our Dutch students rarely bring Bibles to their class. Somehow, we have learned that quoting the Bible directly in a theological university is too simple, bordering on naïveté. Of course, we believe the Bible and we do read it, individually, but we are so aware of hermeneutical difficulties, historical problems, and the dangers of biblicism that one of the things our students may learn is never to use the Bible to solve practical problems in ministry. We should try to change this. Whenever a theological issue is discussed in class (say, conversion or ecclesiology or secularization), we can ask students to prepare for this at home by looking up passages from the Bible that they feel to be relevant for this discussion. Then we can set apart the first 30 or 45 minutes of every course to discuss these passages together. It is important to be aware of hermeneutics and historical analysis, and we should sometimes insert remarks on this in our

---

25. Ibid.

discussions, but we must never forget that the Bible has been given us first to transform us and not to inform us.[26]

3. *Ministers of the word must be acquainted with practice.* As stated above, it is indispensable for theological education to immerse students in practices of mission and evangelism. They are sources for theological reflection, and invaluable opportunities to learn to become strangers again. They invite us to study the Bible together. They help us to be theologians of the church. They give us credibility when we address others, both Christians and non-Christians.

4. *Ministers of the word must be people of paradox.* Every good book on leadership will tell us that paradox is an important ingredient of effective leaders. They must be capable of being close to people, but without being swallowed up by them. This is called "self-differentiation": a minister should not be dependent on the approval of people for his own identity, but neither should he or she be cold and indifferent to them. Intimacy without fear is the gracious quality of a godly leader. This same quality, however, also applies to us as cultural beings. Post-Christian culture is paradoxical to its core. Modern trends and religious responses to them are not uniform; they point in a wide variety of directions, often contradicting each other. Liberalism and fundamentalism are both modern religious positions, and we often find them in our own immediate environments—or even in our own soul. To do mission and evangelism in this culture we must be so close to it that we feel the relativity and the pluralism in it, without losing our hope and desire for God's glory. We must be people of the paradox. We must accept that we will never completely understand our own culture and its effects on us. We must certainly accept that we will never control it. This is a hard lesson to learn. We like consistency and building logical systems. But people of the paradox know how to "muddle through": they like to think and work step by step. They seek consistency, but they accept that this is often a futile search. Post-Christian missionaries will always look for the high ground, but they know that we often have to wade through swamps to get there.

---

26. Cf. Brian Brock, *Singing the Ethos of God: On the Place of Christian Ethics in Scripture* (Grand Rapids: Eerdmans, 2007).

5. *Ministers of the word must be spiritual guides.* In a recent survey, Dutch people were asked what associations they had with "spirituality." These associations were generally positive; many modern people are looking for more spirituality, for a sense of meaning and purpose. But when asked which persons and institutions they would go to in their search for spirituality, hardly anyone mentioned the church. According to them, churches are not spiritual; they are moralistic, dull places teaching doctrine instead of experience. Much can be said about this. We do not want to suggest that this judgment is entirely correct. But it is not very helpful to become defensive about this. The first Christians were considered as very peculiar and sometimes dangerous people, but they were never seen as dull. If people look at the church as a place where your spirituality is extinguished, we do have a problem. In our culture of "seeker" spirituality, we need to be on the road where people are. It would be great if ministers of the divine word would be seen again as "those strange guys outside the camp, who seem to know how to knock on heaven's doors." Spiritual formation needs to be included in our theological curricula, both in theory and in practice. Our students need to know how to help people who ask questions such as "How can I pray?," "What will happen if I become a Christian?," "Why can't I control my temper?," "How can I find more balance between my work and my life?," or "What does your faith have to say about family feuds?" They need to become sensitive to the pathfinder spirituality of modern people and find ways to be along the road with them. "We do not want to lord over your faith," Paul writes, "but we are workers with you for your joy" (2 Cor. 1:24).

These five fields of attention are no doubt pivotal in the theological training of our ministers.

9.4 The Structure of Theological Education

We return to Newbigin's intriguing question, "What must we be?" The *International Review of Mission*'s issues on theological education for mission not only highlight a much-needed, sound theology of mission, but they also underscore that more diversity in theological education for mission is needed. In that context Fergus King observes that many of our theological institutions are excellent in doing research and teaching students scientific skills, but that there is a great need for theological education that focusses on "education or training of the whole person" and for differently structured education that fits the needs of those who want to pursue theological training while having a nonecclesial profession.[27] King and others therefore make a plea for different types of theological education that aim for "theological formation, ministerial formation, personal formation and skills development."[28] This means imagining theological education that values knowledge as well as skills, that provides space for various levels and with varying length of the educational programmes.

In order to realize a "re-envisioning" of education for mission and evangelism, Darren Cronshaw mentions seven guideposts: the structure of theological education shouldn't only be academic and individual, but if it is to be relevant for mission it should also encompass the notions *communal, conversational, contextual, cross-cultural, character forming, contemplative,* and *congregational.*[29] Whoever is familiar with the educational tradition of the "classic" training institutes for foreign mission will recognize that old concepts for missionary training resonate here. Education for mission is about the inextricable relationship of "reason and heart," of knowledge of Christian doctrine and Christian piety, of thorough knowledge of cultures and awareness of one's own culturally shaped character. In this respect, we need to be reminded of the words of J. Nelson Jennings, who wrote: "If God is not somehow involved in shaping mission servants, the most polished and carefully refined methods of preparation ultimately will prove inadequate."[30]

Practice, however, seems to suggest that the position of this integrated missional education of "reason and heart" is constantly under pressure in academic theological institutions, even though churches have claimed for a long time that mission is the lifeblood of the church. Often, setting up mission-training centres that are affiliated with "regular" academic theological institutions may be the best way. That will enable the shaping of contextually adaptive training for mission and evangelism and it will empower churches and agencies for mission and evangelism to have a voice in shaping the educational approach.

27. Fergus King, "Theological Education and Mission," *Mission Studies* 19, no. 1 (2002): 79.
28. Andrew Wingate, "Overview of the History of the Debate about Theological Education," *International Review of Mission* 94, no. 373 (April 2005): 247.
29. Cf. Darren Cronshaw, "Reenvisioning Theological Education, Mission and the Local Church," *Mission Studies* 28, no. 1 (2011): 95–112.
30. J. Nelson Jennings, "The Broader Implications of the Missio Dei," in Bevans et al., eds., *Reflecting,* 34.

Education for mission and evangelism requires that all courses and professors are working from a mission perspective.[31]

If we take the previously mentioned five fields of attention as well as Cronshaw's seven guideposts seriously, they can help to reform our theological education for mission and contribute to the formation of the next generation of servants of the divine word.

---

31. See Walter Sawatsky, "Centers for Historical Research and Mission Studies in the Anabaptist World," *Mission Focus: Annual Review—Mirror on Globalization of Mennonite Witness* 19 (2011): 217.

CHAPTER 10

Gerrit Noort

Toward a Common Understanding of Evangelism

10.1 Introduction

In the preceding chapters we have discussed theological and practical aspects of evangelism. We have seen differences in the understanding of evangelism, but we have also observed that there is common ground as well. In discussing the ecumenical prospects for common witness, the British missiologist Kirsteen Kim even refers to "striking convergences" and "confluence" in *Together towards Life* and *Evangelii Gaudium*.[1] The German theologian Claudia Währisch-Oblau observes that, though *Together towards Life*, *Evangelii Gaudium*, and *The Cape Town Commitment* show differences in terminology, "all three documents share basic theological outlines."[2] In light of these two observations by Kim and Währisch-Oblau it may not come as a surprise that in the foreword to *Together towards Life*, "the world church and mission bodies of the WCC have

---

1. Kirsteen Kim, "*Evangelii Gaudium* and the Prospects for Ecumenical Mission," *International Review of Mission* 104, no. 2 (November 2015): 344.
2. Claudia Währisch-Oblau, "Evangelism in *Evangelii Gaudium*, *The Cape Town Commitment*, and *Together towards Life*," *International Review of Mission* 104, no. 2 (November 2015): 264.

been able to reach a common understanding of and commitment to God's mission today."[3] Reaching a common understanding in the ecumenical fellowship is, however, a remarkable achievement and we should acknowledge its great significance. This final chapter will briefly reflect on the reached ecumenical consensus and will then address the need for an ongoing dialogue on the theology and practice of evangelism.

10.2 Understanding of Evangelism

The previous chapters have shown that the diversity of confessional expressions in churches on the European continent caused a range of understandings of mission and evangelism. Some churches tend to emphasize Christian witness in terms of living in solidarity with the poor, while others prioritize the proclamation of the saving gospel in teaching and preaching (see also ch. 2, above, on historic models of evangelism). A sizable segment of the missionary movement continues to put emphasis on the call to conversion and church planting (cf. chs. 5.4 and 7.7, above), others unremittingly stress evangelism as religious education of its church members (see chs. 7.5 and 7.6, above) and as the missional dimension of the Christian community (cf. chs. 5.1, 7.3, and 7.4, above).

This diversity of confessional expressions and ways of doing evangelism, however, has not precluded a growing ecumenical consensus on important issues in Christian witness. Währisch-Oblau points out five areas of theological convergence in the understanding of evangelism in the three mission documents.[4] First of all, she says, *Together towards Life*, *Evangelii Gaudium*, and *The Cape Town Commitment* all place evangelism within the framework of a theology of *missio Dei*, "a movement of God's love which aims to transform the world."[5] Second, these documents all point to the calling of the church, both universal and local, to be a witness of this divine love. Third, all three documents share the basic theological outline that churches and Christians have fallen short of their calling and that, fourth, they see the need "for a renewal of evangelistic practices" that contradict the powers and idols of this world.[6]

---

3. World Council of Churches, *Together towards Life: Mission and Evangelism in Changing Landscapes* (Geneva: WCC Publications, 2013), vii.
4. Währisch-Oblau, "Evangelism," 264–65.
5. Ibid., 264.
6. Ibid.

Finally, she points out that the mission statements all understand evangelism as the communication of the gospel story and as an "invitation to a life following Christ in the power of the Holy Spirit."[7] Währisch-Oblau even goes as far as to say that the differences in the documents can be explained by looking at the different contexts, differing processes of production, and diverging interests of their authors.[8] Remarkably, she refers to only one fundamental difference in the mission documents, namely that *Evangelii Gaudium* puts emphasis on evangelism as *affective* transformation—"The joy of the gospel fills the hearts and lives of all who encounter Jesus"[9]—whereas *Together towards Life* and *The Cape Town Commitment* emphasize evangelism as an *ethical* transformation. Evangelism is about divine love, but also about the command to love and the call to a change of attitude.

There is one more difference, though. *Evangelii Gaudium* and *The Cape Town Commitment* represent documents from well-defined confessional traditions. The first document was written by Pope Francis and draws on the Roman Catholic understanding of evangelism. The last document is the fruit of Evangelical reflections about evangelism. Although the Evangelical tradition is not limited to one church or denomination, its spirituality is distinct. *Together towards Life*, on the other hand, is the fruit of the ecumenical dialogue of many churches and confessional families in the framework of the World Council of Churches. Because of this context of theological and ecclesial diversity, *Together towards Life* itself, especially its section "Spirit of Pentecost: Good News for All," can therefore be characterized as a significant result of the search for a common understanding on evangelism.[10] The converging text of this section reminds us both of the consensus that already has been reached and of the desire to contribute toward overcoming remaining differences in the theology and practice of evangelism. The emphasis on (the search for) a common understanding in this section of *Together towards Life* is unmistakable in its references to important ecumenical documents on mission and evangelism, such as the WCC's earlier official statement *Mission and Evangelism: An Ecumenical Affirmation* (1982), the Evangelical *Cape Town Commitment* (2010), and *Christian Witness in a Multi-Religious World* (2011), which was issued as a joint statement of the World Evangelical Alliance, the Roman Catholic Pontifical Council for

---

7. Ibid.

8. Ibid.

9. Pope Francis, *Evangelii Gaudium—The Joy of the Gospel: Apostolic Exhortation on the Proclamation of the Gospel in Today's World* (London: Catholic Truth Society, 2013), 7 (par. 1).

10. WCC, *Together*, 29–36 (par. 80–100).

Interreligious Dialogue, and the WCC. These references serve as a reminder that the document was not drafted in a theological and ecclesial vacuum, but is the fruit of ongoing ecumenical dialogue.

So, how then does *Together towards Life*'s text actually show a common understanding and convergence in the perspectives on evangelism? Without going into detail we will point out several concepts that show convergence. First of all, the text takes as its starting point the unequivocal commitment to communicate the whole gospel "to the whole of humanity in the whole world."[11] As self-evident as this may seem, this certainly was not always the case. Maybe especially in churches in the postcolonial and rapidly secularizing societies in Europe, many have had (and still have) doubts about the call to evangelize and to intentionally articulate the gospel "for those who do not yet know him."[12] The text in this section, however, clearly affirms that evangelism is not about the choice of individuals to articulate their personal Christian convictions, but that evangelism is about the salvation of the world and the glory of God.[13] The mission statement therefore unmistakably upholds and affirms that "the gospel of Jesus Christ is good news *in all ages* and *all places*."[14] It is a powerful reaffirmation of the ecumenical conviction that the context of a secular age and a multireligious world does not alter the commitment of the church to evangelism.

Second, the mission statement recognizes evangelism as a mission activity that "makes explicit and unambiguous the centrality of the incarnation, suffering, and the resurrection of Jesus Christ. . . ."[15] As such it upholds that evangelism is about God's love for this world, manifested in Christ and his ministry. The affirmation of the centrality of Christ's ministry is an important common understanding. Evangelicals especially expressed concerns in the 1970s and 1980s that churches and mission bodies, affiliated with the ecumenical movement, had lost their perspective on the unique character of Christ and his redemptive work (cf. chs 4.2.5 and 8.1.2, above). It shouldn't go unnoticed, however, that the mission statement also affirms that we cannot set limits to the saving grace of God. In other words, we know that it is God who saves but we do not know the extent of salvation. God works "in mysterious ways and we do not fully understand the workings of the Spirit in other faith traditions."[16]

---

11. Ibid., 29 (par. 80).
12. Ibid., 29 (par. 81).
13. Ibid., 29 (par. 80-81).
14. Ibid., 39 (par. 109).
15. Ibid., 29 (par. 80).
16. Ibid., 34 (par. 93).

Although the relationship of evangelism and interfaith dialogue may easily turn into a theological bone of contention, the affirmation of the centrality of Christ's work, the shared conviction that we cannot fully understand the workings of the Spirit, and the firm belief that we need to listen to others and be enriched by them[17] are important stepping stones for reaching a common understanding.

Third, *Together towards Life* shows convergence on the issue of conversion. As observed above (ch. 8.1.2), the call to conversion—and the gathering of converts in planted churches—had a central place in mission and missiology through the centuries, but after the Second World War this goal in mission seemed to recede in parts of the ecumenical mission movement. As we have seen in Kwabena J. Asamoah-Gyadu's contribution on reverse mission (see ch. 5.4, above), the call to conversion is a central notion in Pentecostal mission. For developing a common understanding of evangelism, it is important that *Together towards Life* fully recognizes the call to conversion as an integral part of evangelism. In evangelistic ministries we do not "only" share the gospel with other people, but we also invite them to "an experience of life in Christ."[18] This includes "personal conversion to a new life in Christ."[19] Evangelism even "provokes conversion," as hearing the truth in the face of sin and evil demands a response.[20] This provoked response (conversion) results in "salvation of the lost, healing of the sick, and the liberation of the oppressed and the whole creation."[21] As such, conversion is, in the words of *Evangelii Gaudium*, "a constant reorientation toward the kingdom of God."[22]

We can observe a fourth area of convergence in the relationship of evangelism and solidarity. In its section "Evangelism in Christ's way," *Together towards Life* affirms that evangelism is sharing the good news both in word and deed.[23] While recognizing that it is profoundly biblical to evangelize through verbal proclamation or preaching, the mission statement affirms that our evangelism is inauthentic if our words are not consistent with our actions (cf. chs. 4.2.4 and 8.2.3, above). The text quotes here from WCC's 1982 mission statement and upholds the double criterion for mission and evangelism: "There is no evangelism without solidarity; there is no Christian solidarity that does not

---

17. Ibid., 35 (par. 95).
18. Ibid., 29 (par. 80).
19. Ibid., 31 (par. 85).
20. Ibid., 30 (par. 84).
21. Ibid., 30 (par. 84).
22. Pope Francis, *Evangelii Gaudium*, 58 (par. 111).
23. WCC, *Together*, 31 (par. 86).

involve sharing the message of God's coming reign."[24] This double criterion is mirrored in evangelical publications on integral mission that were published since the late 1970s. These writings, especially so in contributions from Latin America, were intended to overcome unfruitful dichotomies that overemphasized the distinction of word and deed in evangelical mission practices, partly due to the polarized debate in the 1960s and 1970s.[25]

As a last and fifth topic of convergence, we point out the relationship of evangelism and church. The mission statement acknowledges that there are different articulations and understandings of evangelism,[26] such as leading people to personal conversion through Christ or being in solidarity with oppressed peoples. These understandings, however, are subsumed under the ecclesiological affirmation that evangelism is "grounded in the life of the local church" where worship (*leitourgia*) is inextricably linked to witness (*martyria*), service (*diakonia*), and fellowship (*koinonia*). In his contribution on evangelism and ecclesiology, Knud Jørgensen specifically addresses the paradigm shift in the understanding of missionary engagement in its mutual relationship to the local church. Evangelism can no longer be considered as "an additional activity to be involved in when other ecclesial chores have been done" (see ch. 8.3.7, above). The understanding that evangelism is rooted in the local church has gained wide recognition. Affirmations to this effect can be found not only in *Together towards Life*, but also in *Evangelii Gaudium*[27] as well as in *The Cape Town Commitment*.[28] One of its remarkable results is that none of these documents devotes attention to cross-cultural missionaries. The focus is decidedly on the witness of the local fellowship of believers, who locally share the good news.

It is important to note that the WCC's ecclesiological document *The Church: Towards a Common Vision* (2013) also emphasizes that church and evangelism cannot be separated. It prominently affirms the ecumenical conviction that the ministry of the church is based on the calling to proclaim the kingdom:

---

24. World Council of Churches, *Mission and Evangelism: An Ecumenical Affirmation* (Geneva: WCC Publications, 1982), par. 34.

25. Cf. Orlando E. Costas, *Christ Outside the Gate: Mission beyond Christendom* (Maryknoll, NY: Orbis, 1982); C. René Padilla, *Mission between the Times: Essays on the Kingdom* (Grand Rapids: Eerdmans, 1985); Christopher J. H. Wright, *The Mission of God: Unlocking the Bible's Grand Narrative* (Downers Grove, IL: InterVarsity, 2006).

26. WCC, *Together*, 31 (par. 85).

27. Pope Francis, *Evangelii Gaudium*, see ch. 1, "The Church's Missionary Transformation," 16–30.

28. Cf. the preamble of *The Cape Town Commitment*, which refers to missional engagement as "the participation of the church in God's mission."

At the heart of the church's vocation in the world is the proclamation of the kingdom of God inaugurated in Jesus the Lord, crucified and risen. Through its internal life of eucharistic worship, thanksgiving, intercessory prayer, through planning for mission and evangelism, through a daily life-style of solidarity with the poor, through advocacy even to confrontation with the powers that oppress human beings, the churches are trying to fulfil this evangelistic vocation.[29]

The church, according to the ecumenical document, is to be "a community of witness," "inviting all human beings from all nations to saving faith."[30] The *locus* of mission and evangelism is the congregation of believers. The emphasis is not on the calling of mission societies or on the ministry of individual evangelists. The ecumenical conviction has grown that the church is, by its nature and mission, called to evangelism. This common understanding is without doubt one of the most significant developments in the understanding of evangelism in the 20th century.

Finally, when the landmark document *Christian Witness in a Multi-Religious World* (2011) was issued, this signified yet another important example of reached ecumenical consensus on mission and evangelism. This brief document, not intended as a theological statement on mission but as a set of recommendations for conduct on Christian witness, acknowledges right away that there are varied interpretations of Christian witness. That is the reality of diversity in world Christianity with its many confessional and denominational expressions. Nevertheless, the preamble starts with the shared conviction that mission belongs to the very being of the church and that witnessing to the world is essential for every Christian. In the sections on the basis and principles of witness, the document articulates the common understanding—of Roman Catholics, Evangelicals, and churches affiliated with the WCC—about the authentic way of evangelism. Remarkably, this common understanding includes principles on potentially divisive issues, such as the dialogue with people of different religions and the call to conversion. It can be argued, of course, that the brevity of the document is both its strength and its weakness. The principles are indeed very concise in their wording, and for the actual practice of evangelism they may not suffice to overcome differences in understanding. Yet, to quote the World Evangelical Alliance's representative Thomas

---

29. World Council of Churches, *The Church: Towards a Common Vision* (Geneva: WCC Publications, 2013), 6 (par. A4).

30. Ibid., 5–6 (par. A2–3).

Schirrmacher, "a serious process of appropriation and application of the text and its principles should be hoped for, as they are designed to address a very complex set of problems and needs in missionary practice."[31]

10.3 Understanding Unity

The growth of the worldwide community of Christians, and its rich theological and cultural diversity, has also raised the issue of the unity of the church. This unity is a key issue in mission as well. The WCC's Commission on World Mission and Evangelism provides an important framework where Roman Catholics, Orthodox, Protestants, Anglicans, Evangelicals, and Pentecostals reflect and work together closely on relevant issues in mission, including the unity of Christian churches in mission. Unity was already on the agenda of Commission VIII of the world mission conference in Edinburgh (1910), which addressed "cooperation and promotion of unity." The organizers were concerned about the lack of unity in church and mission, which resulted in a waste of available missionary resources. Competitiveness, parallelisms, conflicts, and divisions "gravely undermined the credibility of the witness of love of Christ."[32] This realization, and the desire to cooperate in mission, eventually led to the formation of the International Missionary Council (1921), followed by national councils.[33] The ecumenical movement also came into being "out of the conviction of the churches that the division of Christians is a scandal and an impediment to the witness of the church."[34] This conviction was once again affirmed in the WCC's 1982 *Mission and Evangelism*, which states, "There is a growing awareness among the churches today of the inextricable relationship between Christian unity and missionary calling, between ecumenism and evangelization."[35]

---

31. Thomas Schirrmacher, "In Context: Christian Witness in a Multi-Religious World. Recommendations for Conduct," http://www.worldevangelicals.org/resources/rfiles/res3_299_link_1310653627.pdf.

32. Commission on World Mission and Evangelism, "Towards *Common* Witness to Christ Today: Mission and Visible Unity of the Church. *Study Paper on Theme 8 of the Edinburgh 2010 Study Process, Submitted by the Commission on World Mission and Evangelism, World Council of Churches,*" *International Review of Mission* 99, no. 390 (April 2010): 87.

33. Ibid., 86; see also Brian Stanley, "Edinburgh 1910: Evangelization and Unity," in John Gibaut and Knud Jørgensen, eds., *Called to Unity: For the Sake of Mission* (Oxford: Regnum Books International, 2014), 3ff.

34. WCC, *Mission*, par. 1.

35. Ibid.

But what, then, is the nature of this relationship? The ecumenical movement has embraced that being "ecumenical" not only entails the quest for unity, but also the pursuit of common witness in the worldwide task of mission and evangelism, as well as a joined commitment to *diakonia* and the promotion of justice and peace.[36] Witness is thus regarded as an integral part of the ecumenical endeavour and vice versa. In a 1951 definition of the term *ecumenical*, it is said to describe "everything that relates to the whole task of the whole church to bring the gospel to the whole world." This definition sought to fruitfully integrate the concern for both unity of the church and cooperation in mission and evangelism.[37] It resulted in the understanding that participation in the ecumenical movement also implied accepting the mission of the church "as a joint responsibility shared with others, rather than engaging in missionary of evangelistic activities in isolation from each other."[38] These elements of the common calling to unity and witness are foundational to the ecumenical movement and are therefore summarized in the WCC's constitution (article 3). It stipulates that the function and purpose of the ecumenical council is to call the churches to unity, to facilitate common witness, and to support the churches in their worldwide missionary and evangelistic task.[39]

10.4 The Need for an Ongoing Dialogue

Clearly, the preceding sections point to the growth of a common understanding about evangelism and about the unity of the church in mission.[40] That does not mean, however, that all those who are involved in evangelism are in agreement. On the contrary, there is a world to win. While diversity is celebrated as a gift, at times the different ways in which we do evangelism are also experienced as a painful reality. The document *Towards Common Witness* (1997) addresses this very issue. It makes abundantly clear that the issue around the unity of

36. World Council of Churches, "Common Understanding and Vision of the WCC (CUV)," 14 February 2006, https://www.oikoumene.org/en/resources/documents/assembly/2006-porto-alegre/3-preparatory-and-background-documents/common-understanding-and-vision-of-the-wcc-cuv, par. 2.2.
37. Ibid., par. 2.3.
38. Ibid., par. 3.7.7.
39. Ibid., par. 3.10.
40. See also "*Evangelii Gaudium* and Ecumenism," *International Review of Mission* 104, no. 2 (November 2015): 193–301, which offers a range of articles that compare key concepts in mission and evangelism (such as the Spirit, evangelism, dialogue, the church, the poor, justice) in *Together towards Life, The Cape Town Commitment,* and *Evangelii Gaudium.*

the church in mission is persistent and problematic. Ecumenical statements have "repeatedly" expressed the need for both a clearer *practice* of ecumenical relationships in mission and a sharper *commitment* to witness in unity.[41] This in itself shows that a true consensus with all involved churches and mission bodies, inside and outside WCC's constituency, has not yet been reached.

The WCC has repeatedly started a dialogue on this issue, bringing together representatives of both its member churches and representatives of Evangelical, Pentecostal, and charismatic constituencies.[42] The text of *Towards Common Witness* is based on these dialogues, which took place in a series of consultations in the 1990s, and on a related broad consultative study process with mission agencies, churches, local congregations, and monastic orders. The document clearly upholds the right to change one's religion and religious affiliation,[43] but also calls for authentic witness that renounces "[u]nfair criticism or caricaturing of the doctrines, beliefs and practices of another church without attempting to understand or enter into dialogue on those issues," or tendencies to present one's own church or confession as "the true church."[44] The document states that shaping common witness will require further dialogue, reflection, and study. It therefore calls for further reflection on different and contradictory understandings of issues such as the content of Christian faith, the nature of individuals church membership and Christian commitment, the aim of mission and related ethos and style of the missionary work, and the universality of mission in relation to the principle of "canonical territory."[45] In the light of these different understandings it is not surprising that the text observes that "the way to evangelizing in ecumenical fellowship and partnership is still long."[46]

Not without reason the prayer "may they all be one . . . so that the world may believe" (John 17:21-23) has been described as a double wrestling between evangelism and unity.[47] The quality of ecumenical relations, of being one body, has a direct impact on our witness. Giving witness while openly showing dissent in the ecclesial ranks is not credible. And vice versa, the way we shape

---

41. World Council of Churches, "Towards *Common* Witness: A Call to Adopt Responsible Relationships in Mission and to Renounce Proselytism," 19 September 1997, https://www.oikoumene.org/en/resources/documents/commissions/mission-and-evangelism/towards-common-witness, preface.
42. Ibid.
43. Ibid., section I.3.
44. Ibid., section II.
45. Ibid., section IIIA.
46. Ibid., section IIIA2.
47. Commission on World Mission and Evangelism, "Towards Common Witness," 98.

evangelism has a direct impact on the unity of the church. The study paper *Towards Common Witness to Christ Today* (2010), written as part of the study process that marked the centenary of Edinburgh 1910, submits that ecumenical evangelism is not conquering or winning against the others, but that it is the humble invitation to the "feast of the kingdom of God" (Luke 14:15).[48] We fully recognize that authentic evangelism is about this invitation to the feast of the kingdom, yet one may wonder what is meant by "winning against the others." The statement may not be very helpful to overcome diverging practices in evangelism, as this "winning against the others" seems to overlook how Christian identity is defined. Pentecostals and Evangelicals tend to articulate spiritual unity, whereas other confessional traditions emphasize institutional unity. This leads to different practices in evangelism as well, as Christian identity is defined differently. That implies that the way forward to a common understanding of evangelism and unity has to address these different understandings of Christian identity.

Reports on bilateral ecumenical dialogues, such as the Roman Catholic–Evangelical dialogue on the understanding of mission (1986), have shown that some of the rough edges in the debate have worn off and that churches in mutual recognition and acknowledgment increasingly accept a "polyphonic way of thinking about salvation."[49] Nevertheless, *Towards Common Witness* makes clear that remaining differences on the meaning of salvation and differing articulations of Christian identity in the practice of evangelism constitute "problems still to be overcome."[50] It is an unfinished agenda that requires further dialogue for the sake of the kingdom. Its aim is not conformity in the understanding of evangelism, but unity of Christian witness that reflects both a recognition of the catholicity of all churches and a firm commitment to share the gospel contextually with neighbours who haven't heard the gospel story, as well as to strengthen faith formation of church members. Without doubt, new forms of evangelism in Europe, such as Pentecostal reverse mission, new monastic movements, missional communities, Alpha courses, and emerging house churches, challenge traditional understandings of being church and doing evangelism. The same, however, is true the other way around, as

---

48. Ibid.
49. Rienk Lannooy, *Ecumenism and Salvation: A Critical Appraisal of the Concept of Salvation in Bilateral Ecumenical Dialogues* (1970–2000) (Amsterdam: Vrije Universiteit, 2013), 188. On the ecumenical dialogue with Pentecostals, see Jelle Creemers, *Theological Dialogue with Classical Pentecostals: Challenges and Opportunities* (London: Bloomsbury, 2015).
50. WCC, "Towards *Common* Witness," preface and section IIIA2.

traditional understandings of church and evangelism also challenge new expressions of evangelism and its underlying theological concepts. A shared commitment to authentic evangelism requires mutual recognition of the way confessional traditions shape Christian identity and it presupposes a willingness to seek cooperation in evangelism that transcends ecclesial boundaries for the sake of the salvation of the world and the glory of God. Only then can the church truly share the experience of life in Christ with those who are in need of God's redeeming grace and presence.